Partnering with Microsoft

Partnering
with Microsoft

How to Make Money in Trusted Partnership with the Global Software Powerhouse

Ted Dinsmore and Edward O'Connor

Contributing Editor, Paula Rooney

CRC Press
Taylor & Francis Group
Boca Raton London New York

CRC Press is an imprint of the
Taylor & Francis Group, an informa business

Published by CMP Books
An imprint of CMP Media LLC
Main office: CMP Books, 600 Harrison St., San Francisco, CA 94107 USA
Phone: 415-947-6615; Fax: 415-947-6015
www.cmpbooks.com
Email: books@cmp.com

ISBN: 1-57820-317-1

For individual orders, and for information on special discounts for quantity orders,
please contact:
CMP Books Distribution Center, 6600 Silacci Way, Gilroy, CA 95020
Tel: 1-800-500-6875 or 408-848-3854; Fax: 408-848-5784
Email: bookorders@cmp.com; Web: www.cmpbooks.com

Distributed to the book trade in the U.S. by:
Publishers Group West, 1700 Fourth Street, Berkeley, California 94710

Distributed in Canada by:
Jaguar Book Group, 100 Armstrong Avenue,
Georgetown, Ontario M6K 3E7 Canada

Cover design by Cuvee Design Associates
Cover Photo: Comstock Images
Text design by Brad Greene
Text composition by Greene Design

"You all have to make money today . . .
I don't think we need to change,
but get the pedal to the metal and keep accelerating."

———■———

—Steve Ballmer, Microsoft CEO, addressing Microsoft's partners
at the Worldwide Partner Conference,
Toronto, Ontario Canada, July 2004

Contents

Contents

Chapter 5: SP Tactics for Successful Partnership with Microsoft   183

Chapter 6: Reseller Tactics for Successful Partnership with Microsoft 247

Chapter 7: Extend the Opportunity Focus: Partnering with Other Microsoft Partners 293

Contents

Contents

Foreword

There may no better example of a love-hate relationship than that of a high-tech vendor and the solution providers that take that vendor's products, add a host of services and other technologies, and deliver a problem-solving solution to the end user.

When the two are in sync, it makes the sound of a beautiful opera. When they are at odds, it sounds more like a bad tryout for "American Idol."

The love comes when there is lots of communication and the solution provider understands how to get the most out of the relationship. The hate part comes when the vendor doesn't communicate to its partners and deploys policies that cause channel conflict and margin degradation.

Successful vendors and solution providers understand the importance of the relationship. The trouble is, understanding its importance isn't enough. You have to be able to truly work it to your advantage. That requires a focused effort that spans beyond a single deal.

A business partnership is a lot like a modern-day marriage. One-third of them will end in divorce; one-third will limp along but not amount to a whole lot, and the remaining one-third will be a partnership in which both parties really work at it, producing a wonderful experience that never stops growing.

Unfortunately, most solution providers fall into the under-$10-million-in-sales range and don't have the resources to dedicate even a single individual to maneuver the partner programs of the vendors they work with.

And while there are some books out there that talk about the theory of partnerships and building "win-win relationships," none focus on a single vendor in high-tech and how a solution provider can work with it.

In addition, theory is a whole lot different than selling a solution that comprises on average four different technologies and more than 40 different products that tie into a legacy system.

As we all know, the devil is in the details and those theoretical business trend hard-covers don't get into the details.

That's why I was so excited when I first heard about this book and, more importantly, that it would be written based on real practical experience of running a solution provider business and dealing with a host of vendors and customers worldwide.

Working with Microsoft as a reseller, service provider, or ISV brings with it all sorts of challenges and rewards. Let's face it, being a $5 million or $10 million solution provider and trying to work with a $40 billion company can sometimes feel like trying to make the ocean rise by throwing a cup of water into it.

Thankfully, Microsoft is a company that has always focused on selling its products through the indirect channel. While Microsoft certainly wants to do more business through partners, it doesn't mean the hundreds of thousands of solution providers out there don't need some help in understanding how to work with the vendor.

The information in *Partnering with Microsoft* is something you should look at as a set of tools you can use to build business and revenue. Like any tool-set it's up to you to decide if you want to use it to construct a completely focused Microsoft practice that drives your entire business or to merely tinker around with it for some incremental revenue.

In either case Ted and Edward have unlocked the toolbox, now you need to decide how to use the contents.

—Robert Faletra
President, CMP Media Channel Group

Introduction

The present book began with a need. The need itself was peculiar to one firm that intended to partner with Microsoft, but it is common to all engaged in the same initiative. In the early 1990s, Ted launched a firm whose success depended on partnering with Microsoft. He sought a book on the subject but there was none. Until now, no such book existed. Ted's need for guidance in partnering with Microsoft—and with other Microsoft partners—was met through hard experience in learning the ropes for himself and especially with the help of others, particularly Mike Altendorf and Richard Thwaite (Conchango Limited), and Gary Bond (Versicon, a New York firm). Today, Ted serves on a Microsoft partner advisory council (PAC) and has an enviable network of Microsoft colleagues and friends, in addition to an extensive network of connections in myriad other Microsoft-partner firms.

The need for this book became an opportunity. Ted decided to write the book that he sought long ago. In discussions with other Microsoft partners, who expressed the same need, and with Edward, the opportunity to share what they had learned in the absence of such a book for the benefit of all Microsoft partners became apparent. Edward had orchestrated the growth and success of dozens of firms during his tenure at Chase Capital Partners and JPMorgan Partners, premier venture-capital investors, and has continued this work at Exertus Partners, a management-consulting firm he founded that is focused on early and mid-stage software, hardware and technical services firms. Ted and Edward partnered to write this book.

The flow of this book's argument is roughly as follows. Microsoft has ascended to the pinnacle of the information-technology industry, within 20 years becoming the richest, most powerful company therein. It has done so by virtue of its commitment to partnering with other firms in a manner and to an extent unparalleled by other large companies in the industry. Microsoft has created a partner ecosystem that is unrivaled, and designed partner-program structures in which partner-firms engage with the company.

Yet, for all its structures, communications, materials and initiatives, Microsoft has neither precisely nor completely advised its partners how to engage the company as such. Not that partners are entirely in the dark about how and when to engage Microsoft, but they often only know certain principles and employ *ad hoc* tactics in partnering with the company.

The ordinary Microsoft partner's experience is a lot like the blind fellows in the elephant story—feeling its trunk, one thinks it is a snake; walking into its side, another thinks it is a wall; grabbing its tusks, yet another thinks it is a pair of swords; and so on—so that each partner knows only part of the approach to Microsoft and altogether they do not know the entire approach.

Many partners are mindful that they operate within Microsoft's expansive partner ecosystem, but few seem to know the depth and breadth of its outgrowth from Microsoft's culture. Nor do they uniformly appreciate the dynamism of that culture, and the corresponding vitality of Microsoft's strategy and organization, both of which, too, reflect the company's culture. Without a full appreciation of Microsoft's culture, strategy and organization, a thorough understanding of the partner ecosystem—and the best ways to work within it—is elusive.

So Microsoft's partners need to refine their knowledge of the company's inner workings—culturally, strategically, organizationally—to understand how best to engage Microsoft. The principles of engaging the company as a partner are derived from such knowledge, and the best practices for doing so emanate from the principles.

Microsoft's partners engage the company in different ways depending on what type of partner they are—independent software vendors (ISVs), service providers (SPs) or resellers—and the best practices for each are exhaustively enumerated in this book.

In addition, partners' engagement of other Microsoft partners—as leverage on Microsoft and in their respective markets—is another essential element of partnering with the company that we explore.

Through a nearly scientific analysis of Microsoft as a company and the experiences of case-studied partners, we demonstrate that the manner in which successful high-technology firms partner with Microsoft is more of an art than may seem readily apparent.

Successful partners of Microsoft understand and act on abiding verities rooted in the company's culture—Microsoft is product-centric, customer-focused, partner-driven, relationship-motivated and results-oriented—and align their firms artfully with Microsoft on this basis. So, while there is a good bit of theory in this book, its aim is highly practical.

This book will help your firm engage Microsoft—and other Microsoft partners—in order to help you gain more market traction and make more money as a result. It will do so by emphasizing that most of the burden of practicing what is preached falls to Microsoft partners, who must know themselves, and work their way to potentially rich rewards in the partnering experience.

We are grateful to our friends and colleagues at Microsoft and to the many Microsoft partner-firms that we have interviewed in writing this book.

We also thank our contributing editor—Paula Rooney, a senior writer at CRN since 1997, formerly a senior writer at *PC Week* (now *eWeek*) and a graduate of Columbia University's Graduate School of Journalism—for her keen insight on Microsoft, which she has covered for 15 years, and her facilitation of this book's completion. We are also very grateful to our publisher—Matt Kelsey and his team at CMP Books, particularly production editor Gail Saari—for their guidance and expertise, and for all the help they have provided us in bringing this project to completion.

Finally, we are thankful to our families—especially our wives (Ted's Kristen and Edward's Molly)—and our friends for putting up with us throughout the process of bringing this book to market.

To Microsoft's partner community of 841,000 firms—and growing—we dedicate this book, and hope that it meets your needs and opens many doors of opportunity in your successful partnership with Microsoft.

—Ted Dinsmore
Killingworth, Connecticut USA

—Edward O'Connor
New Haven, Connecticut USA

Chapter 1

Why Partner with Microsoft?

The question of *why* a software, services or reseller firm would partner with Microsoft is relevant because *every* firm in the information-technology (IT) industry must come to terms with Microsoft. Whether as friend or foe—or somewhere in between—high-technology firms' coming to terms with Microsoft is rarely characterized by ambivalence. For those firms that elect to engage Microsoft as partners, the guiding question addressed in this book is *how* to partner with Microsoft. Yet, for the sake of a clear, compelling and comprehensive answer to the latter question—and to address counter-arguments as to why one would partner with the company at all—we must consider Microsoft's position in the IT industry, as well as the risks and rewards that high-technology firms have in partnering with Microsoft and, indeed, with its competitors.

Microsoft: the Money Machine

Microsoft is a software empire, with a current market capitalization of US$272 billion, and it dominates the information technology (IT) industry. The company was incorporated nearly 30 years ago by chairman and chief software architect, William H Gates III—Bill, as he is called—a Harvard dropout who has become the richest man in the world as a result of co-founding and leading Microsoft since its inception.

Microsoft's Windows desktop operating system, which first debuted in 1985, runs on more than 95% of PCs worldwide, a colossal market share that continues to expand in spite of antitrust prosecutions and mounting competitive pressures worldwide. As of this writing, Windows' market share of server operating–system revenues fell just under all UNIX servers combined while its market share of new servers shipped surpassed the 50% breakpoint several years ago.

Microsoft's partners should consider some basic facts attesting to the company's global market power. In terms of overall raw market value, Microsoft is the most powerful software company in the world. Microsoft's current market capitalization of US$272 billion is buoyed by gross annual revenues that exceeded US$30 billion in 2003, climbed to US$36.8 billion in 2004, and are projected to reach US$40 billion in 2005—despite a major slump in IT spending since 2000. Of that, Microsoft earned US$10 billion in profit in 2003, and posted a lesser but nonetheless respectable gain of US$8.2 billion in 2004, making it a company that verges on *US$1 billion per month* in net income.

Microsoft ranks in the top 25% of the Fortune Global 500 and the top 10% of the Fortune 500. There are only two other high-technology companies ranked ahead of Microsoft, and their fortunes are tied to selling more expensive hardware:

- International Business Machines (IBM), which posted US$7.6 billion in its fiscal year 2003 (FY03) but whose current market capitalization of US$146 billion is about half of Microsoft's, and whose number of employees (319,273) exceeds Microsoft's headcount by nearly six times; and

- Hewlett Packard (HP), whose 2003 net income was US$2.5 billion, with a current market capitalization (US$58.2 billion) about one-fourth of Microsoft's, and whose number of employees (142,000) exceeds Microsoft's headcount by almost three times.

Ranked well below Microsoft on the Fortune 500 list is Oracle, whose 2004 net income was US$2.7 billion, with a current market capitalization (US$65.5 billion) about one-fourth of Microsoft's, and whose number of employees (41,658) is about 75% of Microsoft's.

Viewing Microsoft's earning power in perspective is instructive: in its fourth fiscal quarter of 2003, Microsoft realized more operating income (US$3.1 billion) than HP reported for its full fiscal year 2003 and more than Oracle in its fiscal year 2004. Microsoft's net profit in FY03 and FY04 exceeded that of IBM by a substantial amount, as well. Unlike its two closest rivals on the Fortune list, Microsoft has grown year-over-year for 20 consecutive years and the company projects double-digit growth in its fiscal year 2005.

Microsoft's consistent growth accounts for its ability to amass nearly US$60 billion in cash and short-term investments since its founding. Of the nine companies with the greatest cash holdings at the end of the first quarter of 2004 on the Standard & Poors (S&P) 500 List, Microsoft ranked at the top. Its cash holdings were nearly four times greater than the second-richest company, Aetna, and greater than the top three combined (Aetna, Exxon Mobil and HP).

In mid-2004, the company announced an increase in its regular dividend as well as a payment of an unprecedented one-time US$3-per-share "special dividend" to its investors—a US$32 billion payout—to dispose of a significant portion of its cash war chest. The special dividend payout rewarded founder Bill Gates with an additional

US$3.4 billion, and Microsoft CEO Steve Ballmer with US$1.2 billion; Mr Ballmer will benefit to the tune of US$132 million from the increased regular dividend alone. Put its wealth in perspective: after that US$32 billion payout, Microsoft continues to retain more cash than Aetna. Microsoft's cash holdings, in fact, were more than one-and-one-half times greater than the three other high-technology companies on this same S&P 500 list: HP, for example, had US$15 billion, Intel banked US$13 billion and Cisco had US$8.9 billion.

There has been much public debate about the future of Microsoft in light of its legal challenges and competitive threats. Following a guilty verdict on antitrust charges issued by a US District Court in 2001, Microsoft faced—but evaded—two potentially devastating penalties: a possible breakup of the company and a court order forcing the company to remove Internet Explorer from Windows. Microsoft was ultimately forced to make changes to its business practices and to release more technical information to competitors but it essentially side-stepped remedies that would have adversely impacted the company. As a result, Microsoft is free to extend its massive desktop and server operating-system business, and to take bigger steps into the business-applications market.

In the midst of a massive legal crisis that might have toppled any other company, Microsoft's senior management displayed remarkable resolve. After a grueling four-year court battle that cost millions to defend, Messrs Gates and Ballmer shifted strategy, as well as positions, with Stanford-trained Mr Ballmer assuming the reins as new CEO and Mr Gates going back to his developer roots to serve as chief software architect. Together, the two businessmen charted a future course that would move them out of the litigation spotlight and focus public attention on Microsoft's next-generation .NET technology. By the end of 2004, Microsoft had resolved the vast majority of antitrust litigation filed against it by a bevy of entities, including US federal and state governments, and rivals AOL, Sun and Novell. Between 2004 and 2005, Microsoft was found guilty of anti-competitive practices in the European market and paid a one-time fine of US$613 million to the European Commission. It was also forced to release a version of Windows XP without Media Player.

In total, Microsoft spent more than US$3 billion settling antitrust litigation and acknowledged that the final tab could exceed US$4.5 billion—half of its revenues in FY2004. Yet its decision to settle most of the outstanding litigation has enabled the company to set aside legal distractions and focus on new growth. Increasingly less subject to regulatory and judicial penalties, for which it has held cash in reserve, Microsoft announced in mid-2004 that it would buy back US$75 billion of its own shares over the next four years in order to boost its stock price and renew investor confidence in the company's future.

In the midst of its legal battles and a serious downturn in the global economy and IT spending, Microsoft moved ahead with its vision for growth. As many CEOs cut operating costs and stockpiled cash to allay the fears of jittery investors, Microsoft sailed briskly forward, investing heavily in its research and development (R&D) efforts, headcount and partner channel in order to advance its empire. At a CEO Summit in mid-2004, Mr Gates committed to spending more than US$40 billion on R&D through 2010, in order to drive a new era of business productivity and IT spending. Microsoft increased its R&D budget again in its fiscal year 2005 to approximately US$5 billion (up four percent from FY04), approaching the net income of HP and Oracle combined. Much of that investment is tapped for emerging ventures: Microsoft Business Solutions group, for instance, received nearly US$1 billion of that R&D budget in order to accelerate its growth into a projected US$10 billion business by 2011.

Microsoft's revenue growth has slowed in recent years but partners have little reason to question the company's health or longevity. Its sustained growth over the past two decades, its cash-backed push for innovation and its enviable cash war chest taken altogether with its confidence in accelerating results defy market analysts' perceptions that Microsoft is a mature company incapable of growth. In fact, Microsoft intends to accelerate its growth into new markets worldwide with innovative products.

Microsoft's per-share earnings are consistently favorable as a consequence. In 2003, amidst a sustained downturn in IT spending, Microsoft's growth rate was 17% (US$32 billion). A year later, it had grown by 14% to US$37 billion, far better than the results of many of its competitors. For its FY05, Microsoft projects its annual revenues will grow still more toward its US$40 billion milestone.

Microsoft on the World Stage

Microsoft's enormous wealth and productivity are unparalleled in modern business industry. In fact, it rivals the gross domestic product (GDP)—the gross earnings per employee—and the per-capita income of most nations.

That is, if Microsoft were a nation rather than a global corporation, its annual gross revenues would rank it 80th on the list of 227 nations—ahead of Uruguay, Costa Rica, Greenland, Iceland, Lithuania, Estonia, Croatia, Yugoslavia, Kuwait, Qatar, Bahrain, Mauritania, Turkmenistan, Mongolia, North Korea and 132 other nations. In fact, Microsoft's gross annual revenues exceed the combined GDPs of the lower 56 nations on this list whose populations taken altogether exceed 10 million.

Then, too, if Microsoft were a nation, there would be no rival for its per-capita share of its GDP: each of Microsoft's 55,000 employees generates on average US$654,000 in revenues annually. By comparison, the 442,000 citizens of the world's most productive nation—Luxembourg—generate on average US$35,894 per year, only five percent of their Microsoft counterparts' productivity. Luxembourg is ranked 112th on the list of national productivity.

Microsoft's global earnings power is indisputable regardless of the fact that only four of its seven profit-and-loss (P&L) product centers—Windows Client, Server and Tools, Information Worker, and Home and Entertainment—are profitable. In 2004, each of its business units grew by at least 11%, comparing favorably to the US annual rate of growth of six percent. Imagine if Microsoft were hitting on all cylinders—if all of its P&L centers were profitable—how successful the company would be!

Although only more than half of its business units are profitable, Microsoft's per-employee ratio of net income wildly exceeds that of its competitors. In its FY04 results, on average, IBM employees generated US$23,804, HP employees generated US$17,606 and Oracle employees generated US$64,813 in net income. By contrast, each Microsoft employee generated on average US$149,091 in net income, more than 626% greater than IBM, 847% greater than HP and 230% greater than Oracle.

Consider, too, Microsoft's continued financial strength in spite of inroads made by Linux. The threat is indeed of global proportions as developers and distributors worldwide refine and disseminate the Linux kernel and commercial distributions of the platform, the first major competitor to Windows on the Intel platform since Microsoft's founding. The competitive pressure on Microsoft from open-source technologies—especially Linux—has chipped away at Microsoft's historical competitive advantage of being the software price leader of the world. Even so, low-cost or free Linux distributions—pushed by the likes of long-standing rivals IBM and Novell, among many others—have not substantially dented Microsoft's share of revenues in consumer and enterprise markets. According to market researchers, Linux is the fastest-growing operating system, yet Windows Server shipments and revenues continued to outpace Linux by significant margins through 2004. While Linux server shipments grew 29% during the fourth quarter of 2004, their total shipment value was US$1.3 billion, or nine percent of total server revenues for the period. By contrast, OEM partners generated US$4.6 billion of Windows Server-related revenues for the same period.

Open-source technologies have an immeasurable gap to close to overcome Microsoft's product integration strategy, whose success is measured by strong growth of its desktop and server software. Windows Client software sales grew 23% to US$2.9 billion in 2004, while Server and Tools sales grew 20% to US$2.3 billion in the same fiscal year. Moreover, Microsoft's growth in multiyear licensing-agreement revenues increased to US$8.2 billion in FY04. While Linux is conventional-wisdom's pick as the strongest competitor to Windows, its admittedly significant gains in server-units sold—eg, up 50% in the third quarter of 2003, year over year—have yet to match Microsoft's revenue. In the US, for example, Linux sales reached US$743 million while Microsoft earned US$3.4 billion for Windows sales; nor has Linux approached Windows Server's market share, which various analysts estimate to be between 60% and 75%.

The introduction of several enterprise-ready Linux desktops from Linux distribution leaders Red Hat and Novell as well as Sun's Linux desktop made headlines in

2004, as German and Chinese government agencies signed on as customers. But there is little doubt about Microsoft's continued ownership of the desktop; it is estimated that between 95% and 98% of all personal computers worldwide run some flavor of Windows. Linux's share of the desktop market remained in the low single digits through 2004, and is expected to rise only slightly by the end of the decade.

There are several reasons to expect Windows' continued dominance. The first is user reluctance to change. Unlike IT administrators, who are more open to experimenting with new technologies, users of PCs that have grown comfortable with the Windows operating system and user interface are far more reluctant to switch to a new operating system. Additionally, Microsoft's desktop-to-data center integration strategy—which provides for tight integration between Windows and Office, on the front end, and server application data stored on servers, on the back end—will remain a strategic advantage for Microsoft. Additionally, the company's push for multi-year licensing and software maintenance revenues all support Microsoft's continued dominance for many years to come. Moreover, with a vigorous marketing campaign behind Office Professional 2003 and Windows Server 2003, and advance marketing for the next upgrade of the Windows client and server platforms, code-named "Longhorn" and due in 2006-2007, Microsoft is sure to continue dominating the operating system market for the foreseeable future. Linux is a threat—and one that Microsoft has to come to complete competitive terms with—but Microsoft remains in the ascendant position in the market, relatively unassailed by open-source alternatives to its products. Open-source technologies introduce new pricing pressures and alternative business models that could threaten Microsoft's wealth engine longer term, but there is no imminent threat to its power.

Governmental regulatory threats and competitive pressures notwithstanding, Microsoft remains the premier, most powerful software company in the world with earnings that rival those of many nations. And it remains unchallenged by less costly, globally distributed alternatives. In brief, Microsoft is successful and rich, a global market power.

What Does Microsoft's Power Mean to Partners?

Yes, without a doubt, Microsoft is powerful. But what does that power mean to its services, software and reseller partners, actual and prospective? Is Microsoft's market power any incentive for your firm to partner with Microsoft? Are there better high-technology companies with whom to partner?

These questions must be answered in order to understand what partnering with Microsoft—or any major software vendor—can do for its different and wide-ranging partner constituencies.

More than any other company in the computer industry, Microsoft has proved the value of partnering and the efficiencies of the channel model. In fact, many attribute Microsoft's monumental success to its early recognition that it would need a strong channel of service, reseller, developer and manufacturing partners in order to seed the PC industry. Some observers suggest that Apple squandered the same potential to grow its Macintosh OS platform by retaining most of the Mac-related hardware, software and services business for itself with only a small number of partners relative to Microsoft's channel.

While it is difficult to pinpoint the precise value of Microsoft's partner ecosystem, Mr Gates provided an estimate at a partner briefing in the company's Manhattan office in 2003. At that time, he claimed that for every dollar that Microsoft earns in sales, eight dollars go to partners in services revenue. Based on Microsoft's FY04 results, this ratio translates into more than US$300 billion in revenues for Microsoft's partner channel.

Why Partner at All?

At the same time, though, one might reasonably ask: why partner with anyone? Some say that partners are for dances, not for business. Yet corporate partnering has been steadily increasing for the past decade and for some good reasons.

Companies partner with one another to supply a defect: a company is not particularly capable in a certain area so it partners with one that is, or a company does not have access to a potentially lucrative market, so it partners with one that does.

Additionally, companies partner with one another to extend their respective opportunities: a company's product or service is complemented by that of another company, so they partner for leveraged marketing and improved market traction. One example of this is the partnering by Sun and IBM to advance market adoption of Java and to keep Microsoft, their common enemy, at bay.

There are other instances in which one company may have a strong offering for one vertical, and enters a partnership with another firm to leverage its capabilities in another vertical market.

Finally, companies partner with one another to extend themselves or their products and services: a company may have a product or service that has greater growth potential than the company can achieve in a certain amount of time and therefore partners with another company to extend its capabilities and improve its market success for its products and services. The pairing of Wal-Mart and Procter & Gamble on just-in-time inventory management is a classic example of the virtue of partnering to improve competitiveness and efficiencies.

Corporate partnerships have an analogue in international relations, of course. Governments have always pursued alliances for the same reasons that companies build partnerships. And, like governments, no company ever reasonably seeks to ally or partner with another firm that it thinks could reduce its chances of achieving its objectives. If your firm aims at improvement, it partners with a company with the same goals, and a company that it thinks will win or at least help it win. Of course, companies—and countries—can make mistakes in judgment, or overestimate the importance of capabilities and the nature of the opportunities that they expect to derive from partnerships and alliances.

Apart from a partner's capabilities, however, and more to the point: companies are well advised to partner with others whose visions, missions, cultures, products and services are complementary. The same applies to international allies. Stalin's Soviet Union entered a non-aggression pact with Hitler's Germany in 1939, and was devastatingly betrayed by an ally it ought not to have trusted; it vindicated itself six years later by invading Germany in tandem with its allies but, within 45 years, it ceased to exist in large part by making enemies of these very allies. In an effort to extend French power, Louis XII of sixteenth-century France allied with and contributed to the growing power of Venice, and then deprived Venice of its state; doing so, in the end, contributed to France's being undermined in Italy and on the European continent. (Or so, at any rate, judged Niccolo Machiavelli, who, when told that "the Italians do not understand warfare" replied that "the French do not understand statecraft.") Additionally, in a desperate move to shore up his power at Rome, Marcus Antonius allied himself with the Egyptian queen Cleopatra, and was subsequently vanquished at the naval battle of Actium by Octavian and Rome's forces in 30 BCE, for betraying Rome itself. None of these political leaders prudently considered the lack of complementarity of their chosen allies with their own political causes, and they suffered the consequences. Instructive historical examples of imprudently planned and poorly executed alliances abound, to the peril of the governments that made them.

So, too, companies that imprudently partner with others—whose cultures, visions, missions, products and services are at odds with their own—risk similar fates. Consider the principle that Machiavelli distilled from Louis XII's example—"whoever causes another to become powerful is ruined"—and how it applies, for example, to IBM in 1981, when it licensed Microsoft's MS-DOS for a line of personal computers that IBM viewed as insignificant at the time. IBM's licensing MS-DOS was the opening salvo in an enduring battle for computers in the market that undermined IBM's mainframe dominance and jumpstarted Microsoft as a global market power.

One need not dwell on extreme cases. The risks and the rewards of partnering clearly admit of degrees. But before entering a partnership, one must be mindful of the cultural traits, long-term strategy, management structure, organizational model and the mechanics of a prospective partner, to say nothing of its driving intentions and how the partnership will balance perils and profits.

Obviously, partnerships among firms with differing viewpoints on core issues, including business models, management theories, work ethic, customer service, or those with vastly different cultures and styles, are often doomed. IBM and Apple, for example, announced two significant alliances in the mid-1990s—Kaleida Labs and Taligent—both founded to develop an object-oriented scripting language and an operating system, respectively, and to keep their common enemy—again, Microsoft—at bay. While those technologies found their way into IBM and Apple products subsequently, both partnerships failed. At the time, culture clash was cited as one of the key reasons for the failed partnerships between those two fundamentally different companies.

Likewise, many dot.com startups in the late 1990s clashed with established vendors in the computer industry due to their laissez-faire approach to management and their relaxed, youthful cultures. Indeed, the increasing tension between open-source foundations and commercial Linux vendors is often cited as a potential obstacle to the technology's deployment, though parties on both sides maintain that they are committed to partnering to defeat the "tyranny" of proprietary software.

However one views the prospect of partnering, IT services and software firms are developing their relationships and alliances with vendors on a more formal basis than in the past. Acquisitions and consolidation fueled growth in the IT industry throughout the 1990s and continues well into the 2000s, yet an increasing number of partnerships between hardware and software vendors, reseller and services firms has also characterized the industry during the same period.

In early 2001, Cisco CEO John Chambers aptly sized up two major trends that would shape the computer industry for the next decade: a downturn in IT spending and a new era in which technology vendors would have to partner with software and services firms in order to deliver cost-effective solutions for customers that increasingly demand a demonstrable return on investment (ROI). "Corporations may have grown through acquisitions during the 1990s, but it will be partnerships that will drive growth in this millennium," Mr Chambers said. "You will see large ecosystems begin to grow up."

Consider the partnerships that IBM, HP and Dell have formed with commercial Linux companies and open-source foundations. Likewise, Microsoft has strengthened and invested more heavily in its partnerships across the board—with OEMs and systems builders, services firms, ISVs and resellers—in recent years.

This structured approach to partnering invites significant opportunities for partners but it requires a deep understanding of your own company and a strategy for growth. It also entails that you know your prospective partner's strategies and growth roadmap, as well. In order to succeed in partnering, prudent companies seek out and work with complementary and capable partners, and win as a result. These are the essential elements of any successful partnership, whether it is with a country or a corporation.

Microsoft was early to the partnering game. And its long term financial strength, sizable R&D and channel investments give partners certain assurances about the three most significant assets when shopping for a partner: viability, stability and growth. Still, is Microsoft the right kind of partner for your firm? Can partnering with Microsoft help your firm achieve its objectives? Can it be a winning partnership? Should your firm elect to partner with Microsoft?

Your Choice: Coming to Terms with Microsoft

IT services, software and reseller firms have many software vendors with whom they can partner, including Microsoft, IBM, Oracle, Sun, Red Hat, Novell and Apple. But, by far, Microsoft has more partners than all of these companies.

Some partners have a love/hate relationship with Microsoft, but all high-technology firms have a choice: they can either compete or partner with Microsoft or, increasingly less likely, deliver products or services in a market untouched by Microsoft. A firm needs to decide which path to take relative to Microsoft—to saddle up with the software giant or pursue a strategy based on alternative and competing technologies such as Java and Linux, for example. But one must take some basic facts into account before deciding which path to take.

Compete with Microsoft?

Software firms that have competed with Microsoft have usually lost despite attempts by government regulators to rein in the company. There are exceptions, of course, notably in the personal-finance software and online-services markets where Intuit and AOL, respectively, continue to dominate over Microsoft. Still, no vendor has been able to pose significant threat to Microsoft's dominance of the desktop operating system and application software markets.

Apple's early success in consumer equipment with an easy-to-use desktop operating system was whittled away by Microsoft's release of progressively more powerful versions of Windows on less-costly commodity hardware. Apple today still makes well-engineered equipment that runs a BSD (UNIX)-based operating system. But its market share is nothing compared to what it used to be, thanks to Microsoft and its ecosystem of services, software and reseller partners.

Netscape, too, virtually owned the web browser market it invented until Microsoft focused on the segment. Microsoft's Internet Explorer—which is integrated with Windows—is now the most pervasive web browser, and owns more than 90% of the market despite SEC constraints against Microsoft. Netscape's share of the web browser market was pronounced negligible at roughly three percent in 2002, compared to only five years before when its Navigator browser dominated it. AOL purchased Netscape and tried to resurrect Navigator but failed. Today, an open-source spinoff of Netscape called the Mozilla Foundation has gained some traction with a re-engineered web browser dubbed FireFox. Meanwhile, Internet Explorer remains the leading browser. In fact, Microsoft announced plans to ship a stand-alone version of Internet Explorer 7 in 2005, even as it continues to enhance its browser's integration with the next-generation Windows operating system, code-named Longhorn.

Novell competed against Microsoft in several software categories: enterprise-scale network operating system, directory services and an email platform. Yet Microsoft—again the latecomer to market—demolished Novell NetWare's market-share lead with progressively more powerful versions of NT, Windows 2000 and 2003 Servers, Active Directory and Exchange. Like Netscape, Novell watched the software category it created get usurped by Microsoft. Novell has since re-invented itself twice, first in consulting services, then in Linux-based desktop and server oper-ating systems with the completed acquisition of SuSE in January 2004. Still, its total Linux revenues fell under US$50 million in FY04 and its attempt to migrate its remaining channel partners from NetWare software and services firms into Linux companies has proved challenging. Since Windows 2000 debuted, many NetWare partners have become Microsoft partners.

Oracle has long held the lead in enterprise-scale databases although Microsoft has been diminishing that lead with SQL 2000 on Windows 2000 Server Data Cen-ter Edition, a high-end offering which it grew in 2003, to an 11% share of the data-base market. SQL still lags well behind IBM's DB2, which has 33% of the market, and Microsoft has some catching up to do to unseat Oracle. But recent acquisitions in the business intelligence and related niches as well as its planned release of SQL Server 2005 (code-named "Yukon") and a "Longhorn" version of SQL indicate Microsoft's relentless drive to pursue more market share in this lucrative software category. Moreover, SQL Server's increasing role as the underlying foundation and data store for all of Microsoft's server applications makes it an increasingly com-pelling piece of Microsoft's desktop-to-data center integration strategy.

Sun Microsystems is another longtime Microsoft antagonist and UNIX giant that capitulated in its struggle to drive a global standard for Java and to crush Microsoft's .NET programming model and software development paradigm. In 2004, the ailing Sun accepted a US$1.6 billion settlement from Microsoft to end Sun's longstanding antitrust suit against it and agreed to work with Microsoft, ostensibly for the benefit of customers and partners alike. The firms agreed to cooperate on the interoperability of Sun's Solaris, middleware and Java stacks with Microsoft's .NET platform, and to pursue joint standards and supportability. This historic pact, ensuring that Sun's Solaris UNIX operating system and Windows technologies play better together, is not only a play to please customers. The two former archrivals and vendors of proprietary operating systems are now united in spirit against a common enemy—Linux and the open-source movement.

In terms of Microsoft's competitors, only IBM has stayed the course. But much of IBM's annual revenues are still derived from hardware and services sales that pivot on its selling licensed copies of the Windows operating system for servers as well as integration services for Microsoft's platforms. Still, IBM's decision to exit the PC business unit, and to increase its foray and investment into Linux for its enterprise and down-market servers and software, is a clear threat to Microsoft's proprietary product base, one which Microsoft will presumably fight with all the vigor that proved its success against earlier competitors. And its track record is much better than its rival's. IBM has unsuccessfully attempted to compete against Microsoft on the PC software front. IBM's Lotus Software Division invented the top two killer applications that rocked the Windows market—the spreadsheet and Notes email/groupware—but both were overpowered by Microsoft's late-entry Excel and Exchange offerings. Today, Lotus 1-2-3 and SmartSuite—Lotus' competitor to Office—continue to have small installed bases but those products are no longer enhanced. Lotus Notes, once the darling application of the industry, retains an installed base in the multi-millions but most new growth in the email space is for Microsoft Exchange. It is worth noting that the inventor of Lotus Notes, Ray Ozzie, founded another collaborative-software firm (after IBM purchased Lotus) called Groove Networks that formed a close partnership with its former rival, Microsoft, and was acquired by it in 2005. This seems to be the case for many other ISVs that once competed with—and were defeated by—Microsoft.

Among other giants in the global information technology (IT) industry, Cisco Systems—with products in the internetworking and network-security space—has prudently chosen to collaborate with Microsoft and sells products that run on Microsoft server platforms. Yet Cisco's record as a partner with Microsoft—and with other high-technology firms, such as HP and IBM—has been spotty due to Cisco's intended reach into storage and network-layer security and management. Its technology often treads on product offerings of its partners and competes with their strategic direction. Cisco, for example, launched in 2004 a Network Admission Control (NAC) platform designed to establish network security at the network layer. Microsoft soon thereafter launched its competing Network Access Protection (NAP) platform, maintaining that security is an essential service of the operating system and should be managed at the software, not the network, layer. The pair initially locked horns on the issue but hammered out an agreement that calls for the two companies to provide interoperability between the two security architectures and to collaborate on driving industry standards in the security software arena.

These examples suggest that Microsoft has exercised its power to dominate almost every sector or competitor on which it has focused. Competing with Microsoft—even for giants like Netscape, Novell and Sun—is not for the faint of heart. Nor is it recommended for other high-technology companies for the same reasons. The smart money is usually on Microsoft, whose desktop products—and increasingly, its server software products—remain *de facto* global standards.

Out-Niche Microsoft?

Microsoft has a staggering list of product offerings for end-consumers and corporations of all varieties. The list is growing, too, into other sectors previously unclaimed by Microsoft.

Consider Microsoft's growth from its two main product lines: the Windows operating system and its Office Suite, each of which comes in end-consumer, professional, developer and small business editions.

Microsoft's products now include a multitude of other consumer and professional products: from Encarta to MapPoint, Visio to Great Plains, Xbox to SmartPhone (Windows Mobile-based) mobile devices, as well as enterprise-scale products: Exchange for email services, Internet Information Server for Internet services, SharePoint Portal Server for intranet/Internet portals, SQL Server for databases and a host of Windows server-based management offerings for high availability, performance and enhanced security. In addition, Microsoft is investing more heavily in security software and has released a new edition of its product in the network-security space (Internet Security and Acceleration Server) to compete with other firewalls, including such industry-leading firewall appliances as Cisco's PIX and Nokia's CheckPoint. It also intends to launch new anti-virus and anti-spyware products and services in the 2005-2006 timeframe.

Microsoft is a global marketing machine that drives its products into all geographical areas and every market sector irrespective of size or industry. One of Microsoft's strongest attributes is its ability to respond adeptly and speedily to competitive threats, to catch up to and then surpass its rivals. Microsoft has also branched into Internet-delivered content, from MSN to HotMail, customer relationship management and enterprise applications, and has developed a search engine intended to rival Google—all on a similarly global scale.

Finding a niche unclaimed by Microsoft is a tough thing to do these days. Unless your firm manufactures hardware or unique software, or provides services around open-source or "big iron" technologies, it is safe to say that Microsoft has staked a claim in almost every known IT software sector.

History suggests that when Microsoft stakes a claim where it never had a presence, and then focuses on winning the space, it will. This fact may not be appealing to software firms that have nurtured a profitable niche, but it is valuable for the entire partner ecosystem that is aligned with Microsoft.

> Competing with Microsoft is a high-risk proposition. Out-niching Microsoft is increasingly impossible. The only available alternative is to partner with Microsoft. The question is, how and on what terms?

Partner with Microsoft

If competing against Microsoft is not an option and working in a niche unclaimed by the software giant is increasingly unfeasible, the only other option for high-technology firms is to partner with Microsoft.

But what are the overall benefits of partnering with Microsoft? Successful Microsoft partners agree that the following benefits are compelling.

Leveraged branding and co-marketing. With Microsoft's global name recognition and market power, its partners gain credibility and market traction by partnering with Microsoft on product- and service-branding and marketing initiatives. Microsoft has significantly increased its investments to allow partners to leverage the Microsoft brand to sell their products and services.

Referrals by Microsoft to new business opportunities. With sales tentacles into every industry and geographical area, Microsoft opens doors to potential business for its partners more capably than most other global partners. Microsoft has thousands of account managers worldwide that oversee and represent thousands of partners. In 2004, Microsoft began featuring with each product advertisement a plug advising customers to avail themselves of services partners and a link to the Windows Resource Directory where services partners can be searched and the Windows Marketplace where software firms can list their products and services.

Grants, industry recognition and awards. Microsoft routinely recognizes its best partners with grants—in cash or in kind—as well as collaborative projects that are the subject of industry articles and case studies, and widely publicized awards. Among Microsoft's global channel of solution providers, Marketing Development Funds (MDFs) and Business Investment Funds (BIFs) continue to drive pilot projects and early adoption of new technologies. More recently, Microsoft has steered more funding to its "Make It Right" Fund to address customers' security issues and pain points. All of these benefits serve as engines for technical and commercial opportunity development, with partners as key beneficiaries.

Technical support, software, technical training and certification. Microsoft actively works with its partners to ensure that they are provisioned with resources, supported and trained, and that their employee and product certifications evidence Microsoft's backing, which further helps in branding and co-marketing as well as in deployment of products and services. In recent years, Microsoft has begun sharing resources once reserved for its own field sales force, such as increased pre-sales technical support for its base of solution providers and extended support systems to partners who also need Microsoft resources when facing competitive proposals from Linux in the market.

In summary, partnering with Microsoft extends your business and technical development opportunities into new accounts and new markets, potentially worldwide, with the globally powerful backing of the company.

Microsoft has built a strategic operating model that is contingent on, and that materially benefits, its partners, whether they are service providers, ISVs or resellers. This model is consonant with Microsoft's culture, which is customer-focused, product-centric and partner-driven, among other traits.

How to Partner with Microsoft

What must a partner do to achieve these and other benefits? What are the characteristics of a successful partnership with Microsoft? How does your firm partner with Microsoft? How will your firm work with Microsoft? This book answers these questions in depth and with real-world detail.

Generally, though, it is clear from all available evidence that *by increasing and working your firm's connections to Microsoft—at various levels and with different groups in the organization, playing to the company's culture and strategy—you will expand the terrain of shared interests between your firm and Microsoft. Doing so will help you enhance market traction and make more money in a trusted partnership through effective co-marketing, efficient channel relationships, assured referrals—joint success in selling your complementary products or services in the United States and, indeed, around the world.*

This book demystifies Microsoft's culture, global organization and strategic trajectory, and orients you to the tactics required to increase and leverage your firm's connections to—and trusted partnership with—Microsoft. We intend to help you realize optimal success in your business by working with Microsoft.

Common Myths About Partnering with Microsoft

High-technology firms come in all shapes and sizes, but they are generally one of three types: *IT solution and service providers*—including systems-integration (SI) and custom application-development (AD) as well as technical education and training firms—*independent software vendors (ISVs), and resellers*—including original equipment manufacturers (OEMs) and software resellers focused on various market segments and with various degrees of service accompanying the software that they sell.

Firms of each type that have successfully partnered with Microsoft have defied the common myths about doing so. The myths of partnering with Microsoft are many and well known. They tend to boil down to the following, which are most often registered as complaints.

Myth #1: *"Microsoft is fickle—at first they adore you, then they ignore you—and there is no one on the Microsoft team to represent its partners."*

This complaint is most often heard from services firms that may have challenges sustaining a relationship with Microsoft. Often, these services firms are in highly competitive markets in which demand for Microsoft's attention is keen and coming from many quarters.

Some ISVs, however, have also been known to utter this complaint. There is no shortage of add-on products and complementary solutions to Microsoft's product line. Disparate, often untargeted requests for Microsoft's help and facilitation from these quarters can get lost in the shuffle.

This complaint often indicates an ineffective approach to partnering, but it is valid nonetheless because Microsoft only tells its top-tier partners how to partner most effectively with Microsoft. So, in the absence of this formal guidance, it is not astonishing that some Microsoft partners would characterize the company as aloof or, indeed, even fickle. The present book is intended to reverse this perception by offering practical, field-level advice about creating and sustaining successful partnerships with Microsoft in the context of a responsible understanding of the company itself. To foster strong ties to its partners in the field, Microsoft has increased its number of partner account managers, instituted its new Empower partner program for ISVs and hired more executives to oversee ISVs on a global basis.

Myth #2: *"Microsoft will neither give you preferential treatment nor steer business to your firm."*

One hears such a complaint from services firms and ISVs on occasion, but it is a corollary of the above myth and simply not true. Yet there are reasonable grounds for this concern based on available resources: Microsoft has a large and growing but finite number of partner account managers and an overwhelming number of partners to manage: more than 841,000 globally at last count. There are limited engagements or business opportunities that Microsoft can steer its partners to and yet a seemingly unlimited number of partners from which it can choose.

This complaint, too, obscures more fundamental realities. The question services firms and ISVs ought to ask is, "how can we partner with Microsoft to gain equitable treatment?" It should be obvious that Microsoft will not simply give away prospects or leads to an unknown entity when it has so many proven partners to choose from in steering opportunities, granting recognition and investing resources.

One's standing as a Microsoft partner must be earned, nurtured and carefully managed. It is common knowledge that Microsoft typically recommends about three different partners per engagement that have special skill sets sought after by customers. So this myth fails to take into account the many successful Microsoft partners that get apparently preferential treatment and earn business opportunities from Microsoft. Do these successful partners have any special attributes that distinguish them from the ISVs and services firms who tend to make this complaint? If so, what are those distinguishing attributes? Read on.

———■———

Myth #3: *"Microsoft will steal your intellectual property or co-opt your product's capabilities."*

This complaint is seemingly pervasive among ISVs. There are many instances of Microsoft's crafting its own solution to compete with and neutralize its erstwhile partners' products when customer demand is there. Netscape, Stac Electronics, Burst.com and Eolas Technologies are ISVs that have filed lawsuits against Microsoft on these grounds. When such products were manufactured and sold as unique or complementary solutions to a Microsoft solution, their latent functionality or market potential may not even have been on Microsoft's radar. In time, however, Microsoft may have crafted its own alternative solution to be sold as a separate product or integrated with Windows.

For example, Plumtree is an ISV–partner of Microsoft's with a successful web-portal product. Microsoft's subsequent release of SharePoint Portal Server included much of Plumtree's functionality and beat Plumtree on pricing. In order to survive, Plumtree had to cut its pricing to compete with SharePoint, which continues to thrive at the expense of Plumtree and other web portal products, thanks, in no small part, to Microsoft's other partners in the space. Plumtree's experience is an example of Microsoft's ability to seize on an idea of its partner and to benefit while its partner languishes. There are numerous other ISVs that have been eliminated or marginalized by Microsoft's integration of data-compression, Internet-browsing, video/audio streaming, multimedia and wireless features into the Windows desktop, as well as its inroads into new collaboration, commerce, content-management, corporate instant-messaging, security software and business–applications markets.

Services firms also face a sensitive issue when they develop intellectual property in sub-contracting assignments with Microsoft Consulting Services. Microsoft's standard contract requires its services partners to waive the rights to this intellectual property, and many of them have recognized their code in subsequent server application and solution accelerators from Microsoft. This book will guide both ISVs and services partners on how to share and protect their intellectual property in Microsoft engagements, and how to draw up contracts that protect the interests of both.

These are problems not unique to Microsoft, however, as there are many firms that have done the same thing. Software developers like Microsoft and Oracle continue to innovate and add new features and functions to their products in order to sell upgrades and stay in business. IBM, Sun, and Red Hat sell middleware applications that compete with middleware offerings from their ISV–partners and open-source foundations. At the same time, there are numerous examples of ISVs whose products have peacefully co-existed with Microsoft's products and platforms, and fuller versions that have made those ISVs handsome profits.

One need only cite Veritas, which develops Microsoft's Backup utility that has been bundled with every operating-system version since Windows NT 3.5; Veritas has successfully retained a premium edition of that software on the market.

One could also cite Executive Software, whose Defragmenter utility has also been bundled with Windows for years. The integration of that code into Windows to the present day has neither crushed nor curtailed its business; in fact, it served as a built-in hook for a fuller version retained and sold on the market by Executive Software. The functionality and potential of these products have not been seized by Microsoft, nor have these ISVs seen their success impaired at all by Microsoft. Quite the contrary.

The question, then, is what have ISVs such as Veritas and Executive Software done differently from other ISVs to partner so successfully with Microsoft? This question is one among many that this book answers.

———■———

Myth #4: *"Microsoft will buy you out, but only after it has taken steps to put you out of business."*

This is a more extreme variation of the complaint above, and it is heard only from ISVs. There are no known clear historical examples of this, however.

In fact, there are many counter-examples of ISV–partners that Microsoft essentially competed with and yet did not buy out, such as Citrix. Yet there are examples, too, of firms that have rejected Microsoft purchase offers as insufficient and many more that have gone out of business indirectly as a result of trying to compete with Microsoft. The direct cause of their demise may, however, be assigned to imprudent management or simply lack of sustainable market traction.

But this is a complaint that is surprisingly common.

Its opposite is an equally often heard aspiration—if we build a "killer" application, Microsoft will buy us out—but this is equally unfounded for the most part. Microsoft has acquired many ISVs including Visio, Great Plains, and Navision but these were strategic acquisitions of mature Microsoft partner companies intended to bolster an existing product line or extend Microsoft's market opportunities. They were not one-off acquisitions of novel, "killer" applications that would have cost Microsoft dearly to develop and bring to market.

So these complaints are highly problematic. They rest on a semblance of truth: Microsoft is opportunistic, it has acquired many companies. In fact, between May 1994 and May 2004, Microsoft acquired at least 60 companies or their technologies. But what successful growth company has not pursued and closed opportunistic acquisitions?

———■———

Myth #5: *"Microsoft is purely self-interested, and it will pit you against your competition to see who wins and then it will back the winner."*

This complaint is common among ISVs, services and reseller firms who overlook the fact that Microsoft and all of its partners operate in a market environment. Market players are naturally competitive because they are self-interested; this does not make them "purely" self-interested. Nor is self-interest or competitiveness inherently a bad thing because, without it, Microsoft would not be a leading software company, your firm would not be in business, you would not have the opportunity to partner with the company, and we would not be writing this book.

Face it: in any market economy—even in command-and-control economies—there is always competition for scarce resources and decisions that must be made in allocating them. To say that Microsoft is maliciously inclined and arranges dog fights between partners is not sensible. Microsoft is self-interested. But what has the company to gain from pitting one partner against another and watching the contest? Nothing.

Microsoft's interest is to win in the marketplace. So is yours. It knows that it needs partners to win. So do you. It wants partners that are self-interested to win, too, and that will work with Microsoft to win, together. Are there problems in partnering with Microsoft? Yes. But there are problems all around us, and we overcome the most pressing ones in order to achieve our objectives. We mitigate the risks to win the rewards. Microsoft is no different. Like every responsible company, Microsoft is driven to pursue the interests of its shareholders. The only difference between Microsoft and others is that is has almost always won.

———■———

Myth #6: *"Microsoft has neither a clue nor a care about partners who are in the field trying to get its products to work, and to work together. Why bother partnering with Microsoft? It only hurts us."*

This complaint is most often heard from services firms although occasionally one hears it from ISVs, as well. For example, services firms in the information-security space have reasonable concerns about the integrity—indeed, the vulnerability—of the Windows operating system as well as other Microsoft products. Microsoft's campaign to focus energy and resources on securing its platforms and applications has yielded some favorable results, but there are distinct complications. Monthly security patches alone constantly remind users, administrators, support personnel and systems integrators that the Microsoft platforms and applications they are meant to secure are far from it. Routine viruses, Internet worms and other inconveniences assault ordinary end-users of Microsoft products and plague their administrators and supporters to keep them up-to-date and secure.

There is a reasonable perception that Microsoft products are more vulnerable than others. And this perception is acute at services firms that are held accountable by customers for securing Microsoft products. Microsoft's recent stepped-up efforts to mitigate these issues with knowledge-base articles, advisories and warnings, security patches and incremental updates such as Windows XP Service Pack 2 are helping to improve its reputation in security. Like all manufacturers, Microsoft must balance first-to-market and best-in-market needs and cannot always achieve perfection on the first product revision. Incremental improvements, updates such as Windows XP Service Pack 2 and advisories are a responsible step in that direction. Services firms are also concerned about the lack of interoperability of Microsoft software with other systems. Some Microsoft desktop and server platforms do not work favorably with other platforms. In fact, Microsoft identifies this optimized integration between its desktop and server products, called integration innovation, as a competitive advantage and a major benefit to its customers. In recent years, Microsoft has demonstrated pronounced sensitivity to the needs of most enterprise customers that have heterogeneous environments and is committed to backing XML and web-services standards to enable interoperability in the future.

Most systems-integration partners know infinitely more than Microsoft Consulting Services (MCS) about pains experienced in the field with the company's products. But few are able to work capably with Microsoft to soothe them. MCS is often of little help because it does not work as intimately as the company's partners with its products, nor much at all with the product groups to refine them. While any end-user can, in theory, open a Microsoft product issue and have its resolution published as a Knowledge Base article, only the truly savvy services firm knows how to get involved with Microsoft's product groups for advance insight on and accelerated resolution of technical issues with their products. This ability is worth gold in the field. So, while Microsoft listens—as a partner should—and acts—as a good partner must—only the most successful Microsoft partners are able to navigate their way to the product groups to get problems resolved. The inability of many services firms to penetrate the company is a common complaint, but it pivots on their inability to leverage the right resources at the right time at Microsoft to ease the field-pains with the company's products.

This complaint is also heard from ISVs, especially in the connector or add-on product space for Microsoft's products. But it, too, is overstated. As in any partnership, one realizes the limitations of the alliance and makes due as best one can in order to achieve reasonable objectives.

These security and interoperability dilemmas are problems yet they also open up opportunities for services partners and ISVs. Services firms in the security space, for instance, can co-market their services with Microsoft as specialists in securing Microsoft platforms and work with their clients at a higher level to institute new security-related operating procedures that have higher value and, consequently, higher bill rates in addition to the requisite systems-integration work. Moreover, government mandates and, more importantly, customer demand are forcing Microsoft to improve interoperability with competing platforms. This, too, spells definite opportunity for Microsoft's partners, especially ISVs.

—■—

Myth #7: *"Microsoft will eventually acquire a large consulting firm or grow a large services arm to compete with IBM Global Services in the enterprise space, thus hurting the business of its services partners."*

Microsoft's channel and services partners have feared this possibility for years, more so in recent years following the company's expanding enterprise agenda. Fear turned to worry when, in 2001, Microsoft launched a joint-alliance systems-integration firm—Avanade—with Accenture. Would this be the death knell of the channel? Would Microsoft eventually absorb Avanade or organically build a large services arm to compete with systems-integration and smaller services partners?

Every year, Microsoft CEO Steve Ballmer is asked this question and every year the answer is the same: No. Microsoft is a software company and will remain a software company. In some cases, Microsoft's enterprise customers demand that Microsoft has "skin in the game" as the lead contractor on select projects for the sake of accountability. But, unless some major shift occurs in the marketplace, Microsoft is unlikely to acquire a large systems integrator or scale up a large services arm. There are two key financial reasons for this conclusion: Microsoft product/license sales carry bigger margins than services. And Microsoft's business model cannot scale efficiently to support thousands of consultants.

Microsoft does not guarantee that this will never happen but, for the foreseeable future, Microsoft is depending on its partners to provide the bulk of services for its software empire.

—■—

These are the most common myths about partnering with Microsoft. Their underlying perceptions are understandable and, although they often reflect flawed reasoning, there is some merit to these myths. After all, where there is smoke, there is fire. But, fortunately, this fire generates more heat than light. One needs to qualify or dispel the myths about partnering with Microsoft on the basis of reality. Overshadowing these common myths are, in fact, uncommon realities that are rooted in the experience of successful Microsoft partners. This book illuminates some of them.

Overshadowing the common myths about partnering with Microsoft are uncommon realities rooted in the experience of successful Microsoft partners, which this book illuminates.

Successes in All Categories
of Microsoft Partner

As indicated, Microsoft has more than 841,000 partners. They are organized and their interactions with the company are structured in the "Microsoft Partner Ecosystem," which is the focus of Chapter Two. Generally, though, Microsoft's partners fall into the categories outlined below. Discounting the myths above about partnering with Microsoft, partners in each of these three categories have succeeded in doing so.

Service Providers

According to Microsoft's tally at the end of FY04, there were roughly 330,000 services partners worldwide. Of these, 334 were Global Systems Integrators (GSIs), such as Capgemini, HP, EDS, Unisys, Wipro and Accenture. These are typically very large firms with global reach in the systems-integration business. Of less geographically sweeping scope, Regional Systems Integrators (RSIs) were roughly 200 in number. RSIs have a presence in one or more of Microsoft's global regions, but do not extend globally. By far the largest set of SPs is the Local Systems Integrators (LSIs), which amount to nearly 328,000 systems-integration firms spread around the world. These are generally smaller firms with presence in one or more distinct local markets, but not inter-regionally and certainly not globally.

Clearly, there are many successful systems-integration firms that are Microsoft partners. A few of the largest are named above, but there are far more of them in the RSI and LSI ranks—such as Intellinet, Interlink Group, BORN and Tectura—as highlighted in Chapter Five.

Rounding out the list of SPs are the Microsoft Certified Partners For Learning Solutions (MCPLSs)—Microsoft's channel of technical training partners, formerly known as Certified Technical Education Centers (CTECs)—that amount to approximately 1,250 around the world. New Horizons, a US-based publicly traded company, is the largest of the MCPLSs, with operations in 54 countries.

Resellers

Microsoft counted 449,000 software-reseller partners in FY04. These firms are of varying size and market focus. For example, there were 582 Large Account Resellers, or LARs, worldwide (only about 20 of them were in the US) that are authorized to sell Microsoft software to corporate accounts; these firms—such as ASAP Software—deal in large volumes of software sales. They are also authorized to sell Enterprise Agreement (EA) licensing in countries where EAs are not directly billed to customers. Direct Market Resellers (DMRs), such as CDW, focus on selling Microsoft software to specific market verticals not necessarily including those served by LARs. Additionally, there were more than 282,000 Value-Added Resellers (VARs) that provide integration and other services for Microsoft software that they sell to smaller businesses and organizations. Microsoft listed 370 distributors, which are firms that sell its software as intermediaries to smaller resellers. However, Microsoft has narrowed the number of global distributors significantly in recent years. Among the reseller ranks are retailers, such as CompUSA and BestBuy, which number 14,690 and sell Microsoft software to consumers and small businesses.

Original Equipment Manufacturers (OEMs) are the other major class of partners that resell Microsoft software, which comes bundled with their hardware solutions, and they develop integrated PC and server systems in collaboration with Microsoft. These number 482 in total and include such well-known firms as Intel, HP (and Compaq) and Dell. And there were nearly 150,000 Systems Builders—"white-box" manufacturers who bundle Microsoft software with their own manufactured hardware solutions—in Microsoft's list of FY04 partners.

Of these 449,000 firms, one can readily identify more than 50 companies that are widely known to be eminently successful as a result of their partnership with Microsoft.

ISVs

Microsoft listed 63,000 software development partners in FY04, referred to as Independent Software Vendors, or ISVs. Of these, 213 were classified as global ISVs with distinct product sets that are sold worldwide, such as Citrix, Veritas and Executive Software—while 58,802 were denominated as "breadth" ISV–partners. Breadth ISVs have software products that fall into and among various functional categories—such as office automation, server utility, and the like—but lack the global selling characteristics of the larger ISV partners, whose wares are more tightly packaged around a set of complementary functions of more universal appeal. Finally, Microsoft listed 4,364 "Account Managed" ISVs, software developers whose products—whether shrink-wrapped or custom-developed—are more integrated with Microsoft products and whose leveraged selling accentuates the sale of their complementary Microsoft products. Microsoft works most closely with this category of ISV in defining and delivering products, as well as in selling them with wrap-around services.

Successful ISV–partners include those mentioned above in addition to those that were acquired by Microsoft, such as Visio and Great Plains Software.

———■———

Again, there are countless success stories among all three categories of Microsoft partner that either refute or qualify the myths mentioned above about partnering with Microsoft. Their success has entailed staying close to Microsoft and collaborating with the company for their mutual benefit.

There is another list of companies that met their demise as a consequence of *not* partnering with Microsoft. One need only consider Banyan, Viant, WordPerfect. Such companies opted to distance themselves from Microsoft, inevitably to their own peril.

And there is a short list of companies that selectively partner with Microsoft while maintaining a competitive stance where appropriate. Consider Sun Microsystems, one of Microsoft's fiercest competitors, which is now a beneficiary of and *de facto* as well as *de jure* partner with Microsoft for Java development even as it continues selling Solaris servers and other Microsoft-competitive software, including Linux on Intel platforms. And IBM—the longest-standing Microsoft competitor—routinely partners with Microsoft to set global technical standards—for, *eg*, the web services stack, and networking protocols and services—while it sells Linux software, hardware and services that compete with Microsoft technologies. Even HP and Dell fall into this category by selling both Windows *and* Linux server offerings.

In brief, the biggest and most successful high-technology firms in the world have come to terms with Microsoft's worldwide stature in the IT industry, and all partner with Microsoft to some extent. Those that do not tend not to survive or at least to thrive as do Microsoft and its closest partners.

Other Than Microsoft, with Whom Can You Partner?

Many IT firms have also partnered with Microsoft's principal competitors, including IBM and Oracle. But they generally prefer the advantages and the mechanics of partnering with Microsoft. A few comments about the differing partnering models of IBM and Oracle are in order.

Despite IBM's vaunted investment in its partner programs, IBM limits the revenue opportunities of its partners to hardware and software sales. IBM sells its hardware through channel partners and its software through qualified resellers. Regarding services, IBM Global Services owns its client relationships and tends to commoditize the services that its services partners can provide, relegating them to subcontracting assignments that IBM itself cannot deliver profitably.

In addition, IBM has a cradle-to-grave approach for its enterprise clients. That is, IBM can serve a wide range of IT needs for any client from inception through its lifecycle and demise, with multiple solutions and services at any given time. IBM thinks globally in this respect.

Consider its name: International Business Machines. IBM makes machines and delivers services for them to businesses around the globe. IBM's business focus is not differentiated, as its name suggests; unlike Microsoft—which builds software for microcomputers, as opposed to mainframes and mid-range systems that IBM built its business on—IBM thinks in terms of *any* machine that can be used as a business computer anywhere in the world. This apparent lack of distinction extends to IBM's partners, too, which IBM tends to view as peripheral mechanisms for getting IBM hardware, software and services to market.

In any event, IBM is the driver and chief beneficiary of its partner relationships. Although IBM appears to have many business partners, in fact, it has only 11% of the total number of partners in Microsoft's channel. Most ISVs and services firms prefer to partner with Microsoft because their revenue opportunities are more expansive. In fact, many services partners worry about partnering with IBM because its services arm, IBM Global Services, accounts for roughly 50% of the company's revenues and employs a whopping 180,000 people. Microsoft Consulting Services, by contrast, continues to be run as a not-for-profit center and has a headcount of between 4,000 and 5,000, representing approximately 12% of its total headcount.

Oracle is even more restrictive than IBM. Again, its name—"Oracle"—suggests an all-knowing entity, such as the Oracle of Delphi. Oracle's product line, not surprisingly, is eponymously presumed to be unapproachable in terms of its capabilities (although not in its market share). In short, Oracle positions itself as the software supplier with complete end-to-end solutions, which is not to say that is has all of the answers, and the best capabilities for manufacturing and selling database software products as well as providing services for them. Accordingly, Oracle only sells software directly—not through a reseller channel—and mostly sells consulting services directly, only rarely working with and through its services partners. That is, Oracle vertically integrates all applicable software into its product set and controls its intellectual property to the point of excluding its partners. With Oracle, there is very little room for lucrative partnering.

These two Microsoft competitors also share a reputation for inconsistent partnering. In contrast to Microsoft's consistently partner-friendly policy, with rare exception, the partnering strategies of IBM and Oracle fluctuate with changing economic conditions and executive temperament. The message that IBM and Oracle thus send to their partners is unfavorable to them: IBM and Oracle own the opportunities and will dole them out as they deem fit, with little give and take, to whomever they please. This is not so with Microsoft, as many successful partners have found. While there can be tensions in partnering with Microsoft, especially in the enterprise and corporate accounts space, the company's culture itself is very favorable to the partner model. Microsoft's culture has given rise to the Microsoft Partner Ecosystem, which has no reliable or lucrative analogue at IBM or Oracle.

The Culture: Why Microsoft's "Right-Handedness" Is Better for Partners

A firm's position on the need for and structure of a channel often has its roots in its very business model. In terms of the corporate schema developed by noted IT industry analyst Geoffrey Moore (see www.tcg-advisors.com/Library/ip/Business%20 Model%20Migration.pdf), IBM and Oracle are "left-handed" organizations. That is, at their core, *process* drives the business model. In their case, process consists of "complex systems" that encompass and integrate products and services. Their products are developed in a vertically hierarchical model, as stacks of software, or platforms that yield solutions, which are conjoined with services that are meant to facilitate their usefulness in the market. The products and services are sold to target customers, an undifferentiated mass in Mr Moore's model, with a bottom-up exclusivity among internal groups from product and services development to solution sales and delivery. Partners and their third-party products are on the periphery of this bottom-up development-to-delivery cycle, subject to internal processes and only supporting those approved by IBM and Oracle themselves. Partners, by definition, are outsiders to these firms and so are largely disengaged from their vendors' corporate activities, and they rarely touch customers. This is an unfavorable partnering model.

By contrast, as detailed in the pages that follow, Microsoft inherently has a more partner-friendly business model that actively recruits and nurtures symbiotic relationships with its partners. In Mr Moore's schema, and in contrast to IBM and Oracle, Microsoft is a "right-handed" organization that works according to a "volume operations paradigm." At the core of a right-handed organization, technology drives the business model. Increasingly, Microsoft's technology is spun outward into products with integral and channel-provided services leveraged appropriately to focus on distinct customer segments, rather than an undifferentiated mass of sales targets. That is, Microsoft partners with other firms in order to drive its own and complementary technologies to market and, in so doing, extend its capabilities without owning all of them—or even customers. For 841,000 high-technology firms throughout the world that have registered with Microsoft as partners, this partnering model is preferable to the partnering models of IBM or Oracle.

According to Mr Moore's schema, the challenge for such vendors is to be effective in their "off-handed mode," to develop capabilities that complement their core strengths just as the ability to swing a baseball bat both right-handed and left-handed provides one far greater flexibility at bat than hitting left or right alone. Ambidexterity is exceedingly difficult to achieve, yet firms that complement their core strengths with other capabilities approximate it. In this respect, Microsoft has proved itself very successful in terms of leveraging partners and, in fact, involving them in pre-sales initiatives for their mutual benefit. That is, Microsoft sells software directly *only* to its largest corporate customers. But any firm, any individual can buy Microsoft software from any of its resellers, of which there are literally hundreds of thousands. Microsoft sells the majority of its software through its channel.

Moreover, Microsoft services are sold through its channel with the backing and support of MCS. This "right-handed organization," then, is more channel friendly than the left-handed organization, which bundles services and products together as the solution.

In general, Microsoft has built a strategic operating model that is contingent on, and that materially benefits, its partners, whether they are service providers, ISVs or resellers. This model is consonant with Microsoft's culture, which is *customer-focused, product-centric and partner-driven*, among other traits.

Longtime Microsoft partners reminisce about the early days of Microsoft when Bill Gates would fly coach class and the company's first partner executive—Sam Jadallah, at the time a vice president reporting to then-sales chief Steve Ballmer— ran Microsoft's entire channel business. Today, the appointment of many executives across Microsoft's business divisions, customer segments, subsidiaries and local districts demonstrates the breadth and depth of Microsoft's expanded partner focus in parallel with its expanded products and solutions. Consider this when choosing to partner with either Microsoft or IBM: at Microsoft, there are roughly 30 corporate positions whose title includes the word "partner" and who carry some partner-facing responsibilities. There are many more whose compensation is based, in part, on the overall customer-partner experience (CPE), a recently introduced metric that puts partners almost on par with customers for Microsoft. In IBM, there are only three corporate titles with the word "partner" in them. Microsoft announced that, in FY05, it plans to invest US$1.7 billion in its partner programs— up 13% from FY04's US$1.5 billion and consistent with Microsoft's annual growth rate of 17%. By contrast, IBM claims to invest more than US$1 billion in partners worldwide yet it is unclear what this investment buys them given IBM's peculiar mode of partnering.

Microsoft has more than 841,000 partners distributed among the three categories—again, service providers, ISVs and resellers—whereas IBM has 90,000 business partners around the world, which are almost exclusively ISVs (especially WebSphere-related development firms) and IBM Business Partners of various flavors. Some of these are Lotus Business Partners that IBM inherited after acquiring Lotus in 1995.

So from these realities one can, in part, discern the relative merits—the strengths and weaknesses—of partnering with Microsoft. One strength is the number of corporate executives with partner-facing duties; therein lies a weakness, or a challenge, because it implies that one needs to know how to leverage the organization, navigate the labyrinth of the "Microsoft Partner Ecosystem," in order to succeed, which is the subject of this book. Another strength is the sheer number and breadth of Microsoft partners, a number that is approaching one million. But this also implies an inherent weakness, or a challenge: Microsoft's investment in its partners can stretch only so far with so many partners. Partner-demand for Microsoft resources far outweighs the supply. One needs to know how to make the most of—how to get the most from—partnership with Microsoft in order to capitalize on the partnering opportunity. This requires significant investment from partners. Partnership with Microsoft is neither cheap nor easy, but it can be rewarding if you know how best to achieve it.

Microsoft is very cognizant that its sizable partner community is a key differentiator in the market. Mr Ballmer summarized the company's confidence in its partners, products and business model relative to that of IBM at Microsoft's annual worldwide partner conference in Toronto, in July 2004. During his keynote, he emphasized that partners are better off working with a right-handed organization whose business model is more channel-favorable. "Go to market with IBM? You will be competing against IBM services. How does IBM sustain its investment in Linux when the only money they make is on services? They make no money on software; they make no money on hardware. They make money only in services. You all have to make money today. There is nothing magic about Linux on the desktop and server. We have better TCO, more applications and more partners. I do not think we need to change, but [we have to] get the pedal to the metal and keep accelerating." (CRN Online, 13 July 2004)

Microsoft's stated intention, then, is not only to sustain but to accelerate its market traction with its partners. It appropriately views its massive partner ecosystem as a competitive advantage over IBM and Oracle. Such front-and-center focus on partnering in itself distinguishes Microsoft from IBM, which is appropriately more modest in its communications about business partners. IBM attempts to grow its base of partners but is largely content with its partnering model, which remains rather static; Microsoft's partnering program, by contrast, is dynamic, with new initiatives and aggressive campaigns unfolding at an accelerated pace. These are attributes of the Microsoft organization *per se*. One must understand Microsoft's culture, organization and strategy in order to make the most of partnership with Microsoft, as these are the well-laid foundations of the company's partner ecosystem.

One must understand Microsoft's culture, organization and strategy in order to make the most of partnership with Microsoft, as these are the well-laid foundations of the company's partner ecosystem.

What This Book Will Help You Do

Overall, most service providers, ISVs and resellers prefer to partner with Microsoft. As the following chapters detail, partners are at the core of Microsoft's operating culture and business model. Microsoft's organization—from the corporate level to field personnel—is given great incentives to work collaboratively with partners. That is, Microsoft's human and capital resources are placed at their partners' disposal. And Microsoft continually evolves toward generating more referrals and collaborative opportunities for its partners.

Microsoft needs good partners. It always has. It always will.

To be a successful Microsoft partner, your firm needs to understand Microsoft's culture and strategy and be able to navigate its organization. Your doing so will help Microsoft perceive your firm as a high-value partner. It is then that the rewards of partnership can best be realized.

But the question is, *how* does your firm help Microsoft perceive it as a good partner? And how do you manage the risks *and* the rewards of partnering with Microsoft? This book answers these and other questions in an easy-to-apply, manageable way. Our objective is to help you focus on the many material growth opportunities of partnering with Microsoft.

In anticipation, here is a topical overview of the chapters to follow:

———■———

Chapter 2: *Microsoft's Culture, Organization and Strategy—And Its Partner Ecosystem*

This chapter details the core attributes of Microsoft's culture, organization and strategy, and explains the position of Microsoft's partners in its ecosystem. This explanation includes a functional overview of Microsoft's partner program, as well as an analysis of what it takes to be a successful Microsoft partner.

———■———

Chapter 3: *Principles Of Successful Partnering with Microsoft*

This chapter builds on the responsible understanding of the ecosystem provided in Chapter Two by elucidating the principles of partnering with Microsoft. These strategic principles, rightly applied, inform the tactical chapters to follow, whose guidelines address the most successful modes and mechanisms for various categories of Microsoft partner.

———■———

Chapter 4: *ISV Tactics for Successful Partnership with Microsoft*

This chapter focuses on the partnering tactics that successful ISVs employ vis-à-vis Microsoft. Case studies of the modes and mechanisms of successful ISVs in partnering with Microsoft are offered in the strategic context established by Chapter Three.

———■———

Chapter 5: *SP Tactics for Successful Partnership with Microsoft*

This chapter focuses on the partnering tactics that successful services firms employ vis-à-vis Microsoft. Case studies of the modes and mechanisms of services firms in partnering with Microsoft are offered in the strategic context established by Chapter Three.

Chapter 6: *Reseller Tactics for Successful Partnership with Microsoft*

This chapter focuses on the partnering tactics that successful resellers employ vis-à-vis Microsoft. Case studies of the modes and mechanisms of resellers in partnering with Microsoft are offered in the strategic context established by Chapter Three.

Chapter 7: *Extend The Opportunty Focus: Partnering*
with Other Microsoft Partners

This chapter advances the tactics implicit in the foregoing chapters: how to leverage other Microsoft partners not only to improve your relationship with the company, but to accentuate your firm's success by working productively with other partners in Microsoft's Partner Ecosystem.

This book is meant to help your firm come to terms with Microsoft, to assess and mitigate the risks of partnering, and to pursue and realize the rewards of partnering with this globally successful company. Only by understanding what makes Microsoft "tick" and how the company thinks and behaves—culturally, strategically, organizationally and with respect to its partners—can your firm be a successful Microsoft partner. The next chapter lays the foundation.

Chapter 2

Microsoft's Culture, Organization and Strategy—and Its Partner Ecosystem

Microsoft's market dynamism and unparalleled success reflect its equally dynamic culture. The company views and embraces change as a constant, which often makes partnering with it a wild ride. But there are underlying consistencies in the Microsoft organization that guide its ability to shift strategic direction—its market, product and partner focus—on short notice. This high level of maneuverability is made possible by having a highly focused, energetic, vibrant and flexible corporate culture and an unusually fluid, decentralized organization, unique for a company of its size and market presence. Microsoft can move swiftly, and its culture is the engine of change and the rudder that steers its success in the market.

Picture a battleship cruising the high seas. We can call it the SS Microsoft, as Olivier Thierry—senior vice president of worldwide marketing and alliances at Microsoft ISV-partner NetIQ—considers it. The SS Microsoft cruises at top speed with all hands on deck. Smaller boats that sail unceremoniously in front of the ship—partners seeking Microsoft's attention—can get crushed by its bow. Similarly, boats that steer astern of the SS Microsoft, or those that follow too closely or have malicious intent, risk getting caught in its backdraft and sucked into the battleship's propellers. Obviously, then, the optimal place for partners to sail with the SS Microsoft is amidships, to starboard and port, riding the waves of its wake. For those ships oriented properly, sailing compatibly with the SS Microsoft, the opportunities are as vast as the horizon. Yet sailing—like partnering—is not for the inexperienced and there are many perils entailed in the journey, including the possibility of collision and capsizing. The more prudent and capable partners of Microsoft are tuned to proper positioning because they know the inner workings of the SS Microsoft: who is at the helm, how the crew works, the course and speed of the battleship, and the nature of any obstacles in its path.

In other words, the best Microsoft partners know the company intimately and make provisions for working with it in a complementary way. After all, if you do not know the nature of your partner, whether a business partner or a spouse, you cannot partner effectively. This chapter is intended to help you know Microsoft more intimately so that you can partner with the company as effectively as other seasoned partners in Microsoft's partner ecosystem.

Microsoft's Organization and Culture

Microsoft's corporate headquarters sprawl across Redmond, Washington, a suburb of Seattle, and into Seattle itself. Given Microsoft's expansion into the metropolitan area, it is more appropriate (as we do in this book) to refer to Seattle as the home of Microsoft corporate. The software company employs almost 60,000 people and operates 67 subsidiaries worldwide; 17 of these 'subs,' as they are known, are located in the United States.

Microsoft's culture has developed around the tension and complementarity of two internal forces: the corporate organization and field organizations. The field, of course, refers to all other Microsoft offices, outside of Seattle, worldwide.

These two internal forces are unified by a single goal: to sell as much Microsoft software as possible. This goal is pursued relentlessly at all levels of the organization, making it unique from competitors that have mixed products and services businesses. Thus, the common goal binds Microsoft corporate and field closely together, though not without complication. While Microsoft corporate has global purview over setting direction and specifying standards—from defining product specifications to launching go-to-market (GTM) campaigns—Microsoft field personnel exercise discretion in refining products and pursuing GTM initiatives. In short, corporate has responsibility for products and growth; field has accountability for delivering on those sales objectives.

But, to repeat, Microsoft corporate and field are united in realizing a common goal—to sell as much Microsoft software as possible—so any complications arising from their inter-relationship pertain to *how* to achieve the goal, not *what* the goal is.

Microsoft's major corporate functions include:

- executive management;
- finance and administration;
- legal and investor relations;
- human resources;
- corporate strategy;

- research-and-development teams, which include product development; and

- marketing and communications.

There are obviously executives across all tiers of the company but the majority of Microsoft personnel in Seattle work in non-executive positions. Seasoned Microsoft partners understand the general organizational structure at corporate and how their field representatives interface with those various corporate functions. The corporate functions are stratified by product-centric groupings, and often have analogous organizations in field offices. For example, in some field offices, there are sales and technical personnel that work for the company's Information Worker business unit. They report directly to the local subsidiary, but they interface continuously with Information Worker product managers in Seattle. These product-centric field organizations are the primary paths for partners into Microsoft corporate, depending on their product or service offerings.

As indicated in Chapter One, there are seven Microsoft segments, or business units, which are profit-and-loss (P&L) centers, headquartered at Seattle and encompassing all of the company's products. Microsoft's P&L segments are as follows:

- **Windows Client:** Windows XP desktop operating system, Windows 2000, and Windows Embedded operating system;

- **Information Worker:** Microsoft Office, Visio, Project, and other stand-alone desktop applications;

- **Microsoft Business Solutions:** Great Plains and Navision business-process applications, and bCentral business services;

- **Server and Tools:** Windows Server System and integrated server-platform software, software developer tools, and Microsoft Developers Network (MSDN) offerings;

- **Mobile and Embedded Devices:** Windows Mobile for mobile devices such as Pocket PC, Mobile Explorer microbrowser, and SmartPhone software platform;

- **MSN:** Microsoft Network (MSN), MSN Internet Access, MSNTV, MSN Hotmail and other Web-based services; and

- **Home and Entertainment:** Xbox, consumer hardware and software, online games, and Microsoft's TV platform.

Some Microsoft products are spread across more than one segment. For example, SharePoint Portal Server falls into the Information Worker and Server and Tools business units. Most products, however, have a home in only one P&L center, as listed above.

Responsibility for defining, developing and refining products, distributing them across P&L centers and crafting marketing campaigns to bring new products to market are corporate functions. Microsoft's field personnel around the world provide input and guidance to corporate about product refinements and marketing tactics, and hold accountability for realizing aggressive quotas for product sales within their regions and offices.

Corporate and Field: Shared Sovereignty

Microsoft field teams are distributed and organized, first, by geography among its three regions:

- the Americas Region: this Seattle-based headquarters covers the US, Canada and all of Latin America and the Caribbean;

- the Europe/Middle East and Africa (EMEA) Region: the Dublin, Ireland-based operations center covers Europe, while the Middle East and Africa are head-quartered at Dubai, UAE; and

- the Japan and Asia-Pacific (JAPAC) Region: the Singapore-based headquarters covers Asia and the Pacific, including Australia, while the Tokyo-based office covers Japan.

Within each region, almost every country has a Microsoft office (or "subsidiary") that is its own P&L center. Some countries—such as the US, for example—have multiple subsidiaries. Within each subsidiary, field personnel are organized into teams by industry vertical or geographical areas. The teams are accountable for driving product revenue that is split among many—in some cases all—of the Microsoft product segments. For example, the New York subsidiary, based at Manhattan (the largest Microsoft subsidiary in the world), may have revenue obligations for all Microsoft business units, from Windows Client through Home and Entertainment; the same applies to other large subsidiaries. Most subsidiaries have revenue obligations for only a few of those business units, depending on their size, and the market in which they operate. But each subsidiary P&L must meet aggressive sales quotas, which are set by corporate and often entail a doubling of the previous year's quota.

So Microsoft's subsidiary P&Ls feed into Microsoft corporate segments based on their quotas and results for product sales. For example, Microsoft's Mexico subsidiary has personnel assigned both to geographical districts and industry sectors, as do the Tokyo and Paris subsidiaries. Microsoft corporate sets sales quotas for each business segment, which cumulatively includes all Microsoft products sold worldwide. The Mexico subsidiary's profit (or loss) in its entirety is comprised by the sales results that it generates for each business unit or product relative to its quotas. Its sales in any particular segment—eg, Server and Tools—roll up to that segment's P&L as do all other subsidiaries' sales results for the same segment. Thus, the corporate segment's profit or loss is composed of revenue from all subsidiaries globally as well as the results from any other channel that sells applicable products.

This rollup of results from field to corporate is an important feature of Microsoft's organization that evinces a cultural norm. While Microsoft corporate is responsible for establishing product direction and sales objectives, Microsoft field teams are accountable for driving Microsoft products to market more or less in alignment with corporate-defined go-to-market campaigns. There is shared sovereignty—co-dependence and collaboration—among Microsoft corporate and field in realizing their goals. Yet, because of the field's accountability for results, Microsoft's field personnel exercise enormous discretion in how they will generate the specified results in their respective markets. That is, co-dependence and collaboration aside, the adage "all politics are local" governs the bottomline relationship because Microsoft's field personnel ultimately have the most power in deciding *how* they will hit revenue targets. The ensuing tensions that this causes between corporate and field personnel is mitigated by the fact that the two are united and provided incentives to achieve a common goal: again, to sell as much Microsoft software as possible. But there is no doubt that the field has the ultimate say in how this will be achieved. The cultural norm that "all politics are local" has significant implications for Microsoft's partners.

Dynamic Culture: Organizational Evolution, Product Revolution

Microsoft is a dynamic firm capable of moving swiftly and refocusing the attention of its large organization on major objectives—*eg*, conquering Netscape and eclipsing Novell—but the cultural imperative for organizational and other change is evolutionary, not revolutionary. That is, Microsoft's cultural dynamism guides the firm's evident ability to *evolve* its organization—both corporate purview and field accountability—in a manner that is tightly focused on its product segments. The products, then, are the focus of *revolutionary* change, while the *engine* that drives the product revolution—the organization and culture—is itself evolutionary. This is evidenced by the company's substantial investment in research and development, and its strategic decision to invest still more each year. So the *basis* of the company's success is revolutionary—constant improvement in its product segments—while the mechanism for achieving the success is evolutionary, that is, strategic refinements and organizational shifts to drive these products progressively to market in a manner that accords with Microsoft's culture.

The basis of Microsoft's success is *revolutionary*—constant improvement in its product segments—while the mechanism for achieving the success is

---

evolutionary: strategic refinements and organizational shifts to drive these products progressively to market in a manner that accords with Microsoft's culture.

As a case in point, consider Microsoft's push to verticalization. After 2000, Microsoft began focusing field personnel on discrete industry segments on a phased-in basis. This was a significant shift for a company whose business model was predominantly horizontal, and predicated on the notion of a mass-volume model, that is, selling undifferentiated Windows software across all customer segments. Microsoft undoubtedly faced increasing customer pressure to focus on industry verticals in order to drive its desktop and server solutions deeper into the application stack and the data center in order to meet emerging customer requirements, including business process re-engineering. Financial services companies, for instance, have distinct IT needs from manufacturing firms, just as financial services companies in Tokyo have similar needs yet different buying patterns from their counterparts in London.

Shifting customer requirements warrant changes to Microsoft's products and organization and its ecosystem. Corporate and field groups each evolve, responding dynamically, to meet changing requirements because at its core—culturally—Microsoft is a customer-focused, product-centric, partner-driven company. Focusing on industry verticals is, for Microsoft as for any reasonable firm, better left to field offices and subsidiaries, which are closer to customers than corporate.

As Microsoft's power–sharing arrangement dictates, Microsoft corporate has a significant role to play in meeting vertical needs. Corporate correspondingly launched several initiatives to refine products and create solutions for various verticals in revolutionary ways, at least by Microsoft's standards. These attempts included the short-lived Microsoft Solutions Offerings (MSOs) and then a series of Office solution accelerators, pre-packaged solutions of Microsoft products with integration code designed to solve specific needs of customers in the healthcare and financial services industries, such as complying with HIPAA and Sarbanes–Oxley regulations. The evolution of the company toward closeness to its customers, combined with revolutionary products from corporate, accentuates the power of the field to drive results in their respective markets.

The *shared sovereignty* between Microsoft's corporate and field enables the delivery of these solutions, yet the politics and hence the power of the deal is increasingly local. This shared sovereignty is how Microsoft structures and moves on its response, dynamically, to shifting winds in the market and among its customers.

So, to repeat, both Microsoft corporate and field are united by the goal of selling all the Microsoft software that they can, but discretion pertaining to tactics has evolved outward from the center to Microsoft's periphery. This is a critical principle that all partners must grasp in order to succeed in their go-to-market approach with

Microsoft. It is also an occasionally enormous challenge for Microsoft from an organizational perspective, as it is for any global organization.

Consider the Roman Empire, which expanded far beyond the borders of the city of Rome, across the Mediterranean into Asia and Africa, and up the Atlantic into uncivilized regions of northern Europe. The central authority—Rome—could not hold the empire together without the steadfast "Roman-ness" of its peripheral colonies, whose founders brought with them Roman law, Roman customs and Roman culture. These Roman colonists, imbued with their mission of extending Rome's reach, even as they integrated with indigenous populations, tended to be, at least in the most successful Roman colonies, more Roman than their counterparts back home. Yet they also understood that Rome's reach was limited to their own efforts and initiatives, and tailored to indigenous cultures where they sought to establish Rome's extended presence. That is, Rome's most successful colonies were more purely Roman, more patriotic, than Rome itself, even as the peripheral colonists molded what they brought of Rome to fit their remote Roman outpost. So, too, Microsoft's periphery—its subsidiaries scattered around the globe—are often more vigorously *Microsoft,* more intense in their zeal for Microsoft products yet more realistic about their market potential, than corporate personnel at Seattle. At Microsoft as in Rome, the center rules the world through its periphery's loyalty and commitment to the global cause. If all politics are local, as they are at Microsoft, Seattle defines the law, and the interplay between corporate and field establishes the culture of the company on the foundation of their joint commitment to selling its products.

The Organization

We have examined Microsoft's cultural dynamism as the interplay between corporate and field. What, then, are the contours of Microsoft's organization given that Microsoft employees are spread worldwide, serving in diverse functions within a layered organization? Of Microsoft's approximately 57,000 employees, 37,440 (66%) work in the US; 28,007 (41%) work in corporate functions at Seattle; 9,433 (25%) work in field offices in the US; and 18,500 (34%) work in other parts of the world. One-third of all Microsoft employees work in a field office outside of the US. Of the total employee base, 23,200 (42%) are dedicated to research and development, which includes product development; 25,100 (46%) are engaged in sales, marketing and support; 4,300 (eight percent) are assigned to finance and administration; and 2,400 (four percent) work in manufacturing and distribution.

As of the time of this writing, Microsoft's organizational model may be depicted as below, with business units at corporate branching outward with reciprocal influence to the field, which reaches the market and its customers through the partner ecosystem. While this depiction is non-traditional—organizational charts are avail-

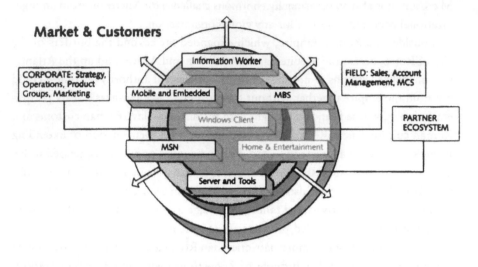

Figure 2.2: Microsoft, An Organizational Overview, 2005.

able elsewhere—it appropriately indicates the inter-connectedness, the meshed nature of Microsoft's organization.

To what extent does Microsoft's corporate organization reflect its culture, most notably the power-sharing structure of its corporate and field organizations?

Microsoft is purely interested in driving its products to market and this corporate directive is mirrored in the shared sovereignty of corporate and field, in which each business segment is managed by corporate but has personnel in the field to drive products into various markets, by geography and by industry vertical or market area. Microsoft's mission statement clearly reflects this core cultural driver:

"We are committed long term to the mission of helping our customers realize their full potential. Just as we constantly update and improve our products, we want to continually *evolve our company* to be in the best position to *accelerate new technologies* as they emerge and to better serve our customers" (emphasis added).

Take this message at face value. Microsoft's mission is to develop revolutionary new products while simultaneously evolving from an organizational standpoint in order to deliver them most effectively into the market, and to extend product sales. This dynamism is Microsoft corporate's direction and the overriding cultural driver of the company. Microsoft field teams execute on this mission to achieve the goal that binds them to Microsoft corporate: to sell as much Microsoft software as possible.

Healthy Cultural Tensions

At Microsoft, priorities are driven from the top down, from corporate to field, while results are driven from the bottom up, from field to corporate. As indicated, field teams have definite say, in aggregate, as to Microsoft's corporate priorities. That is, Microsoft's field force and partners provide feedback about market conditions and customer needs to corporate. And Microsoft corporate works actively with field teams to drive sales results. As outlined, this symbiotic operating relationship between Microsoft corporate and field is based on their shared sovereignty in advancing Microsoft's strategy.

What binds corporate and field teams together—the *what* and *why* of their symbiosis—is the progressive increase in sales of Microsoft products. *Microsoft is a product-centric company.* Microsoft corporate and field are complementary in that they both agree that selling Microsoft products is the most important goal for the company. Microsoft invests heavily in maintaining this culture and expends much capital and training to ensure due collaboration among the corporate center and its peripheral outposts, with perhaps mixed results depending on the subsidiary's country of origin. Therein lies a source of Microsoft's dynamism, the high-energy interplay between corporate and field centered on selling Microsoft products.

But there are also occasional tensions between Microsoft corporate and field pertaining to product sales. For example, each Microsoft subsidiary is accountable for its own results and responsible for its own profit and loss (P&L), in the same manner as Microsoft's seven product-centric segments or business divisions, are their own P&L centers. At the start of Microsoft's fiscal year, which runs from 1 July through 30 June, corporate executives announce a new set of sales and marketing initiatives for the coming fiscal year. Microsoft subsidiaries routinely pursue their own defined subsets of these initiatives, now known as corporate GTMs, based on their own discretion and the needs of the customers in their respective districts. At the beginning of FY04, for instance, Microsoft's corporate sales chief issued an edict to all worldwide field offices instructing the field to market and sell products according to an elaborate chart of 22 GTMs, granularly defined product-specific marketing campaigns, including marketing angles and prescribed channels, tactics and metrics of success. Subsequently, field offices concluded that many of these GTMs were either inapplicable to their markets or they had limited personnel and simply chose a few workable GTMs to execute in order to meet their sales quotas. In this case, the field's stringent selectivity in implementing only a few GTMs, and opting to use only selective tactics, caused some tensions with corporate. But rather than force field personnel to reverse course, corporate incorporated the feedback and adjusted the company's direction and speed to handle actual market conditions. At the beginning of FY05, Microsoft corporate issued a much more scaled-down set of GTMs— seven in all—that were far less onerous in their scope and specificity. These new GTMs give subsidiaries across the globe a more manageable and flexible way to reach their sales goals. Microsoft global subsidiaries and field teams similarly pick and choose what they will implement from Microsoft's worldwide directives, often elect-

GTM	TARGET AUDIENCE	KEY PRODUCTS
Global GTMs for Midmarket and Enterprise		
Business Applications	Business executives	Microsoft CRM, SQL Server
Connected Productivity Infrastructure	Executives, information workers	Exchange, Office, Outlook, Pocket PC, SharePoint, Windows Server
Connected Systems	Developers, IT professionals, executives	Windows Server, SQL Server, SharePoint, Visual Studio, BizTalk
Operational Efficiency and Productivity	IT professionals	Exchange, Microsoft Operations Manager, Office, Outlook, Pocket PC, SharePoint, Systems Management Server, Virtual Server, Windows Server
XP Reloaded	Executives, consumers	Windows Media Center Edition, Windows XP SP2, Tablet PC
Specialized GTMs for Midmarket and Enterprise		
Portals	Executives	SharePoint, Content Management Server
Enterprise Project Management	Executives	Project, Project Server, Outlook
Office Live	Executives	Live Meeting, Live Communications Server, Windows Messenger
Web Platform	Executives, hosters	Windows Server, SharePoint, Visual Studio
Small Business GTMs		
Servers for Small Business	Executives, IT professionals	Windows Small Business Server
Desktop Value	Executives	Office, Windows XP
Business Productivity	Executives	Office, OneNote, Windows Small Business Server
Business Operations Management	Executives, IT professionals	Windows Small Business Server, Group Policy Management Console, Windows Update Services

Figure 2.3: Microsoft's FY05 GTMs.

ing their own means to achieve the desired ends. In this way, marketing tensions between corporate and field are resolved in a manner that best advances their common goal, to repeat, to sell as much Microsoft software as possible.

Corporate vs. Field: Partnering Decisions

In addition, there can be corporate tensions within the Microsoft field regarding Microsoft partners. For example, field teams decide with whom they should partner. At Microsoft, there is no option: all corporate executives and select personnel in the field are compensated *in part* on customer and partner satisfaction, in that order, according to a corporate dictate issued in FY04 by Mr Ballmer. In this way, corporate measures field-level performance on the basis of two key metrics—"partner attach" and "partner assign"—and holds various field personnel accountable for them (see below for more on these key partner-related metrics). In the event that field teams do not know which partner to select for certain service opportunities, they are mandated to seek corporate advice. But this collaborative posture has on occasion raised tensions when the field's interests in potential candidates do not align with corporate counsel.

Corporate vs. Field: Limited Resources

There are also tensions between Microsoft corporate and field organizations with respect to employee headcount. A common complaint from the field is that there are too few personnel in the field to accomplish the sales quotas set by corporate. Compounding that complaint is the field's perception that Seattle engages apparently too many contractors for work that it does not value highly enough to invest in full-time employees. It is simple for field personnel to spot these contractors because their Microsoft email addresses begin with the letter "V"; some Microsoft partners and perhaps Microsoft field personnel have auto-delete rules for email messages received from Microsoft contractors. The rationale for the complaint is that, if Microsoft corporate does not think the work in question is worth the time of a full-time employee, and if the contractors do not have the authority to make decisions, then Microsoft's field force—employees and partners alike—do not consider it worth their time to receive and respond to email from contractors. The underlying tension is that corporate spends significant capital on contractors for work that is perceived to be meaningless and yet the field, which is engaged in the most important work, is strapped for human capital. This creates significant tension between corporate and field, especially when field teams and the partners with whom they work most closely often ignore requests for assistance and information coming from Seattle. It is a significant problem, a broken link in the chain that can impair getting deals done in the field and some collaboration with corporate.

Another factor that causes occasional tension between corporate and field is the perception that employees must be at corporate in order to be recognized, rewarded and promoted. It is no wonder that Microsoft field personnel are often eager to take positions at corporate. There has been such an influx to Microsoft corporate from UK field offices, for example, that one astute observer noted that there is a lot of 'English' spoken in Seattle, alluding to the preponderance of British accents heard at Microsoft headquarters. But this brain drain away from local offices is a sore spot in the field. From the field's perspective, Seattle represents a drain on scarce human resources and is a voracious personnel machine that absorbs talent better mobilized in the field where customer opportunities are. So tensions between Microsoft corporate and field run deep and broad, despite the singleness of purpose that unites them.

Field vs. Field

Finally, there can be tensions among field teams themselves. Consider the occasional conflicts between field groups and Microsoft Consulting Services (MCS). The consulting arm of Microsoft is charged with engaging in implementation projects of a technically significant nature for large customers and creating prototypes and architectural blueprints that can be replicated by partners and customers. MCS would not be asked to perform, for example, Active Directory migrations and other projects that are routine relative to its mandate. MCS is expected to heed the corporate rule that it assign such routine projects to Microsoft services partners, and not prime projects for itself; that is, MCS cannot hold the risk, own the agreements, control such projects and be accountable for the results. Occasionally, though, MCS takes on this role for its own reasons. Naturally, tensions arise between partners and MCS that impact the relationship between partners and their field personnel, which causes tensions in the field itself.

Microsoft partners recall a modest MCS buildup in 2001 that raised concerns and questions among services partners about the company's future plans for the IT services market. As a result of the conflicts, Microsoft responded, implementing new rules of engagement for how MCS ought to work with partners and new mechanisms to help mitigate these natural skirmishes. There have been instances in which a Microsoft Partner Account Manager (PAM) challenged MCS over a decision to "prime" a routine project, arguing that managed partners are more appropriately suited for particular engagements. The PAM can appeal directly to Seattle and cite another corporate rule: MCS must secure corporate approval for its role in projects based on their size and technical complexity. Often, the PAM's challenge results in a project win for a services partner—either a systems-integration or a custom application-development firm—that MCS preferred for itself.

Additionally, there are also tensions in the field among vertically aligned groups that are competing with geographically focused groups for customer accounts and market traction. There are numerous examples of this type of intra-field tension, which usually pivots on the shortage of human resources in the field. For instance, Microsoft's sales representatives in its Healthcare vertical may pursue the same customer being courted by a Microsoft field representative from its Waltham, Massachusetts office. Such tensions must be resolved in favor of the customer, but partners can get caught in the crossfire of such skirmishes. In general, Microsoft corporate is a relatively quiet party in resolving tensions between field teams. Its role is largely to issue rules governing their inter-relationship but it is up to field teams to agree on and apply the mandates and then to resolve conflicts in the field. In keeping with the corporate principle that all politics are local, the field is empowered to sort out its own issues and advance on the overriding goal of selling Microsoft products.

So there are occasional tensions both between corporate and field and within the field itself. Partners need not fear or back off from these situations. In fact, these tensions are often favorable for partners because it is to them—rather than Microsoft corporate—that field teams often turn in order to achieve their objectives. Likewise, Microsoft's frequent reorganizations can benefit partners in the consequent expansion of their connection points in the company. PAMs that oversee partners often get moved around. While this constant reassignment of personnel can be trying, partners often benefit from this revolving door since it allows them to sustain a relationship with their former PAM and build a new relationship with the PAM's replacement. Microsoft's headcount challenge often causes tensions and frustrations in the field but can be as beneficial to its partners as its frequent reorganizations. Both types of tension, together, can benefit partners who are alert to these dynamics at Microsoft and who exploit them for their own best interests.

Corporate and Field on Microsoft Partners

In spite of these tensions, the hull of the SS Microsoft—its culture and organization—is built to adapt and evolve. Returning to the original thesis of the chapter, the harmony of Microsoft corporate and field on the *what* and *why* of their symbiosis, while leaving the *how* up to the field, has shown itself to be an enviable and profitable business model. Despite its size and meshed organizational structure, Microsoft has demonstrated great agility to respond to market needs. For example, in early 2001, Microsoft corporate and field focused their combined strength on driving Exchange sales to neutralize Lotus Notes and Novell Groupware. By mid-year, having re-oriented its field personnel to focus on that goal, Microsoft achieved its objective. And it has sustained this dominance: Exchange was a newcomer when it entered the market in the early 1990s, but quickly usurped its rivals and now owns an overwhelming share of the groupware software market. From a technology standpoint, Microsoft's integration of the Outlook email client in Office with the Exchange server—its integration innovation—drove a great deal of customer adoption. So you can see that Microsoft's cultural dynamism is core to its success. The products are the focus of *revolutionary* change, while the *engine* that drives the product revolution—the culture and organization—evolves to achieve the common goal: sell as much Microsoft software as possible.

Microsoft's push in 1999 to drive Windows NT 4.0 sales in an offensive against Novell NetWare resulted in similar success. As well, Microsoft quickly reversed its slip-up in the Internet browser market by developing and integrating Internet Explorer with the Windows operating system. Within four years, Microsoft seized Netscape's near complete share of the web-browser market and relegated its competitor to a paltry three percent market share.

There is no doubt that Microsoft's ability to integrate its applications with its ubiquitous Windows operating system gives it unparalleled advantages over its competitors. Yet, the dynamic culture—the power-sharing business model of corporate and field, and organizational shifts—cannot be overlooked in assessing its success.

Corporate and field tensions notwithstanding, Microsoft wins big when it focuses its organization's efforts on the *what* and *why* of the matter and leaves the execution up to the two complementary forces within.

The *how, when* and *where* of their symbiotic inter-relationship is often a source of tension between Microsoft corporate and field but the field usually dominates despite any ambiguities in corporate and field spheres of responsibility.

Fortunately for partners, the *with whom* question is never in doubt. Microsoft corporate and field agree that partners are essential to the company's cultural dynamism, indeed, to its success. Microsoft uniformly views its partners as extensions of the company's product and sales forces, hence the oft-heard phrase in the Microsoft culture that "it is not a solution without a partner."

But a caveat applies here: Microsoft views its partners in terms of their commitment and ability to drive product sales. Corporate and field teams agree that partners exist to help Microsoft realize progressively higher revenues. Microsoft is willing to make whatever investment in its partners that it deems necessary and sufficient to that end.

Again, Microsoft corporate sets the strategic direction and field teams execute on it in tandem with Microsoft partners. Together, Microsoft corporate and field determine how much to invest—as well as when, where, how and why—in the partner program, and how to structure it, in order to expedite Microsoft's achievement of its mission. *Microsoft is a partner-driven company.*

Accordingly, Microsoft continues to boost its investment in partners. Between FY03 and FY05, Microsoft invested US$1.5 billion in partners. In FY05, Microsoft increased its investment another 13% to US$1.7 billion. And Microsoft has shifted its partner-program structure to facilitate the impact of the investment on its bottomline, which is bolstered by product sales. Microsoft uniformly views its partners as extensions of itself—tentacles into the market—to drive product sales, and it drives its partners toward customers in order to achieve this very objective. Microsoft corporate establishes the parameters and Microsoft field teams execute the partner-program objectives.

Similarly, Microsoft corporate manages the cost of doing business while sales management is distributed geographically, and by industry segment. Partners are part of the cost of doing business at Microsoft and its most important channel for selling Microsoft products. Thus, Microsoft corporate and field, united by their common goal, are completely in agreement on the importance of Microsoft partner relationships. Every region and each subsidiary has field teams with pools of local, regional and global partners assigned to them. Field teams have direct interface back to corporate for the definition of product specifications, resolution of customer issues, counsel on partner challenges, and marketing and communication needs.

Corporate and field work together to market the company to Microsoft's partners.

They host seminars for partners, for example, where local marketing personnel work with the Business Marketing Office (BMO) to determine event details including which partners to invite and, more importantly, which partners to engage more deeply within local, regional or vertical markets. In 2002, channel-development staffers in Microsoft's government vertical lobbied Microsoft corporate directly for funds to create a public-sector partner-management program aimed at recruiting new services partners outside of the traditional large systems integrators pool. As part of the partner-engagement campaign, Microsoft hosted events and webcasts for partners to educate them about public-sector business and paid for sales and solutions training, technical readiness and tele-support.

Field personnel help resolve cross-district problems for partners. For example, a partner who is active in one district may wish to expand operations into another one. The partner's PAM leverages corporate and field relationships on the partner's behalf to help the partner grow seamlessly into other districts. In this way, the PAM is an outstanding resource for managed partners to expand their connection points in Microsoft and their success as partners.

The symbiotic interplay between Microsoft corporate and field is centered on product sales, driven to mobilize its partners to that end and, equally as important, focused on its customers. Recall Microsoft's corporate mission, which emphasizes the company's heightened goal to serve its customers most effectively.

This has not always been the case. For many years, Microsoft—as well as many other software companies—designed software based on requested features and innovations driven by what their product-development teams thought customers needed. That is, many of the product requirements were driven internally rather than externally. As a result, the term "bells and whistles" was coined to describe compelling features of software that customers sometimes ignored. The animated paper clip in Word is one example of an innovative feature that inspired more irritation among customers than actual use. Based on changes to its charter, Microsoft has become in recent years far more externally focused in terms of setting product specifications and building products based on customers' actual business needs. The company hosts more customer focus groups and customer advisory groups to glean market needs and requirements and is pursuing a strategy based on delivering solutions that meet its customers' business needs.

One need not simply infer that Microsoft's focus begins and ends with its customers. Microsoft states it explicitly. *Microsoft is a customer-focused company.* And while this is true for other "right-handed" corporations, Microsoft's progressive investments in research and development and new products signifies a sincere effort on the company's part to meet customers' needs and changing requirements than it has in the past. This is a very positive shift for partners since Microsoft views its partners as its primary vehicle to enter and expand its product presence to customers.

In summary, then, Microsoft is a customer-focused, product-centric and partner-driven company. These three facets of its culture—which are reflected in its organization—account for consistency and predictability in Microsoft's operating model despite its constant evolution, dynamism and change. To partner effectively with Microsoft, one must be mindful of these cultural drivers, and view organizational and partner-program changes in this context.

Shared Sovereignty from the Top

A quick note about Microsoft's organization and culture: generally speaking, a business organization is an entity formed for the purpose of conducting commercial activities. It has a system of laws and contracts. In a sense, the organization is the hull, the mast, the mainsail of a ship. Corporate culture, on the other hand, is the defining spirit, personality and character of a corporation, encompassing the intangibles—its mission, values, guiding principles and ways of doing business. These intangible qualities differentiate one business culture from another. The organization, then, mirrors the culture; the culture reflects the organization.

In many ways, Microsoft's culture mirrors the personality of its leadership. In fact, the culture has remained consistent by virtue of the consistent, long-term tenure of its two top executives. Mr Gates co-founded the company and served as lead developer and chief executive officer, and then hired Mr Ballmer in 1980, as his first business manager. Mr Gates defined the product-centric nature of Microsoft, and his personality—confident and aggressive—continues to resonate throughout the culture today. One observer, who has followed Microsoft for many years, concurs. "Microsoft's culture is very, very product-focused, with development teams at the top of the corporate pyramid. Bill Gates is, by choice, the Chief Software Architect—the über-Programmer—and not the Chief Salesman, and that choice by Microsoft's top leader sets the tone for the company: software is what it is all about. Microsoft's singular goal is to sell more software. They do not measure how nice you are or how many years you have been a partner, but how much of their software you can sell in the next quarter," observes Paul DeGroot, senior analyst at *Directions on Microsoft* of Kirkland, Washington, which employs several former Microsoft employees.

Meanwhile, Mr Ballmer has influenced the business side of Microsoft and can be credited with developing and enhancing the two other pillars of Microsoft's culture: customer focus and partner-drivenness. During his two decades at Microsoft, Mr Ballmer has served several Microsoft divisions, including operations, operating systems development, and sales and support. In July 1998, he was promoted to president and ascended to the coveted role as Microsoft CEO in January 2000. Mr Ballmer's energetic, enthusiastic and aggressive approach to winning is reflected in the company's personnel worldwide, even as the company tries to become "kinder and gentler" in the post-antitrust phase of its corporate history.

It is striking how much the culture and orientation of Microsoft reflect a blend of the personalities of its two top executives. It is also striking how much Microsoft's culture and organization reflect the nature of their business partnership—the shared sovereignty—of Messrs Gates and Ballmer. Mr Gates, as chief software architect, delegates much of Microsoft's business execution to Mr Ballmer in the same way as Microsoft's product-centric corporate organization assigns business execution to the field, so the shared sovereignty between them is similar to that between corporate and field. Again, both executives are united by a common goal—to sell as much software as possible—and their power-sharing partnership enables a similar empowerment between corporate and field.

Cultural Shifts

Microsoft's culture has been profoundly influenced by its growth. Yet we see the culture evolving from one of mass volume to widespread, focused customization. Some have characterized the increasing focus on tailored solutions for vertical industries as the "IBMization of Microsoft," referring not only to IBM's size (more than 300,000 employees relative to Microsoft's 55,000) but also its enterprise customer focus and complexity. By the latter, critics mean IBM's multiple layers of management, bureaucratic burden and slowness to move to market. Others have cited the influx of ex-IBM personnel into executive positions at Microsoft and the company's resulting business-model changes.

While there is little reason to fear that Microsoft will grow six times its current size and add burdensome management layers and administrative red tape to its operations, the company has in fact grown substantially, both organically and as a result of multiple acquisitions. In part as a result of its growth, Microsoft reorganized itself. Three years ago, Mr Ballmer streamlined Microsoft's management layers and refocused—some say re-invented—the company around the current seven segments or business units.

Yet Microsoft has worked to preserve its cultural dynamism. Mr Ballmer's annual memo to employees in FY04, for instance, emphasized the need for financial constraints—tighter budgets, belt-tightening—to preserve Microsoft's substantial profit margins and annual growth prospects. He mentioned the need for Microsoft to "renew [its] culture and values" particularly around accountability. Nothing solves "big company ills quite like a strong focus on accountability for results with customers and shareholders," Mr Ballmer wrote.

This signals a maturing, appropriate shift for a company whose revenues continue to increase but whose market growth has slowed. In fact, Microsoft doubled its profit during its second fiscal quarter of 2005 even though its revenues grew modestly, at seven percent, due to the reduction in operating costs. The view from the top at Microsoft corporate indicates that the company is not yet ready to grow into a bureaucratic organization, but that its employees must return to its energetic small-company roots in moving aggressively forward through FY05 and beyond. This benefits all partners in the ecosystem—ISVs, services firms and resellers—the expanded Microsoft Partner Ecosystem that grows with the Microsoft empire.

As Mr Ballmer's 2004 memo to employees suggests, massive growth has challenged the company's culture. Microsoft's growth since its founding has been impressive: in its first fiscal year, 1985, Microsoft earned US$24 million on US$140 million in revenues. A decade later, profits skyrocketed to US$1.5 billion on revenues of US$6 billion. And by the end of fiscal year 2004, Microsoft reported more than US$8 billion in profit on US$37 billion in revenues. And, for FY05, which ends 30 June 2005, Microsoft expects to reap US$10 billion in net income based on revenues projected to approach, if not exceed, US$40 billion. It is worth exploring the different aspects of Microsoft's historical growth, which admits of three inter-related phases or at least concurrent themes, and its impact on the company and its partners.

Organic growth: Microsoft's growth for its first 20 years was essentially organic, despite some acquisitions, with headcount added to accommodate the development of new products and entry into new markets that were financed by existing product sales. During this time, Microsoft's culture was established, and its essential framework abides despite other cultural and organizational shifts in the firm.

Acquisitions: In the late 1990s and the first couple of years of this century, Microsoft aggressively pursued other large, established companies to entrench and extend its strategic positioning. For example, Visio, Great Plains, Navision and Axapta were acquired in order to round out, solidify and broaden Microsoft's product portfolio and its strategic presence in various existing and new markets. With these acquisitions, Microsoft brought into its fold many new employees, whose views and approaches—while consonant with those of Microsoft—also refined some facets of Microsoft's culture and accounted for organizational changes as well.

Organic change: Microsoft's native dynamism accounts for the historical frequency of its organizational change, as exemplified by the company's predictable re-organization at the end of each fiscal year. It is also reflected by more regular, consistent re-assignments, with employees assuming new positions every few months, as well as the entry of personnel into key management positions from outside the company and the promotion and rotation of existing employees to new management and executive positions. This continual organizational tweaking and employee reshuffling is key to Microsoft's success, one academic observed. "Microsoft defies the gravity of organizational inertia," said Michael Useem, professor of management at the University of Pennsylvania's Wharton School of Business. "Microsoft has an amazing fluidity on the inside, a lack of history of defined divisions, and that is the way they have always managed it."

Of course, Microsoft eventually defined seven segments or business divisions and faces growing pains as a result. With growth comes maturity, though maturity does not necessitate disruption in its dynamic culture. This is why Mr Ballmer's memo urges employees to return to the company's "roots" so that Microsoft can "renew [its] culture and values."

As it continues to grow, Microsoft faces challenges to its culture and organization. While it must slow the rate of change to accommodate its increasing berth, its approach to maturation must balance its need for a dynamic culture that has historically steered its success.

Mr Ballmer, in his memo to Microsoft employees, observed that "we need to reduce churn (eg, org[anizational] structure, people and strategy changes) and its impact on productivity, accountability and execution, and do a better job of executing well when change is necessary."

"Even positive change implies churn and customers do not like churn. Even positive change, unless it is dramatic enough, you probably should not make because the overhead is so high for our partners and everybody. In a sense, that is what I am learning, we should save all of our change-management energy for things that make a huge difference. Bunches of tiny changes can sometimes be distracting to the overall mission of satisfying the customer."

Microsoft's three growth phases or growth-related themes have been accentuated by or tempered with other organizational changes and cultural shifts at Microsoft. They have also been intended, at times, to strengthen two of Microsoft's core assets: its products and its partners. For example, the Visio acquisition was a corporate-driven move—a more product-centric strategy to complete the Office suite—whereas the Great Plains acquisition was a field-enhancing move—a more partner-driven strategy to establish Microsoft's channel into the middle market. But one must understand the cultural impact of Microsoft's growth in addition to grasping its impact on Microsoft products.

Specifically, the introduction of "outsiders"—executives brought in from outside of Microsoft—has caused a great deal of change in the company. For example, former Microsoft Worldwide Services Chief Mike Sinneck was brought in from IBM Global Services to bring order to Microsoft Consulting Services. He is alternately credited with the "IBMization of Microsoft" and with easing conflicts between MCS and Microsoft's services partners. Yet Mr Sinneck is no longer with the company. The conventional interpretation for his relatively short tenure is that he—like other high-profile hires from outside Microsoft—found himself at odds with Microsoft's culture. In fact, few such high-profile hires from outside of Microsoft have survived. In 2001, for example, Microsoft hired HP veteran and former Silicon Graphics Chief Executive Rick Belluzzo to serve as president and COO. Mr Belluzzo, who came to Microsoft in 1999, and was the first outsider to be named to a top executive post at Microsoft and to serve side by side with Messrs Gates and Ballmer, lasted little more than a year at Microsoft.

Such hires, which are still made in order to reinvigorate the company with new ideas, serve as cultural "blips" that disrupt and energize the firm. While some changes do little more than spark controversy and dissent, Microsoft tends to integrate the best of the changes and to normalize itself on the outside executive's departure. There are exceptions to this observation. Gerri Elliott—another ex-IBM Global Services executive who was hired by Microsoft to serve as corporate vice president of US Enterprise and Worldwide Industry Solutions—has made a promising impact on refining the company's ability to define and pursue vertical segments in the corporate sector. In her way, Ms Elliott is driving forth the new vertical product–and–solutions focus while not disrupting the partner-driven culture of Microsoft.

But achieving this delicate balance—delivering integrated solutions to vertical markets while relying on outside partners to execute—is challenging for a former executive of a left-handed organization with an in-house, integrated product-and-service delivery model. Naturally, this struggle has a direct bearing on many of Microsoft's partners, whom—Ms Elliott advises—must refine their customer focus and demonstrate that their products and services are appropriately positioned for optimal market traction. As Ms Elliott observes, "Together, we [read: Microsoft and its partners] need to understand the customers' business."

To achieve this balance, Microsoft made organizational changes that make the company more accountable to enterprise accounts yet preserve its partner-driven model. In 2001, Microsoft co-launched a systems-integration company with Accenture, called Avanade, and took its enterprise licensing direct. In this way, it has opted for a mixed indirect and direct model, with the emphasis on a largely indirect model for services delivery. At the time, Mr Sinneck, an ex-IBM Global Services executive, characterized the direct-indirect mix as a brilliant, unique solutions and services delivery model.

Mr Ballmer publicly acknowledged that Microsoft is disadvantaged by not having a large services organization like IBM Global Services but insisted that Microsoft's core culture—customer-focused, product-centric, partner-driven—cannot be fundamentally altered if the company wishes to succeed. Microsoft will not evolve into a left-handed company, he maintains. "I do not want to have 70K or 50K consultants as part of Microsoft. I do not want that. There is a downside to not having them, and there is an upside to being IBM. But [services] is a different business. As soon as you do that [gobble up a large systems integrator], you think of yourself more as a services company, and less of a product company, and we are a product company. And our profitability stems from our product business, and I do not want people around here confused about that." (CRN Online, 25 May 2001)

The constant promotion and rotation of existing Microsoft personnel into new executive roles has also accounted for cultural changes in the company. For example, Mr Sinneck was hired into Microsoft to replace Bob McDowell, who, having created MCS, was reassigned to another executive position. Mr McDowell had assumed an approach to Microsoft services that was more typical of Oracle than true to Microsoft: own the intellectual property and own the service opportunities. As this approach was prejudicial to partners, and thus contrary to Microsoft's culture, Mr McDowell did not last in that services-related position. But such an approach has become a stigma, "the Extreme Swing Effect," which connotes a situation in which a native Microsoft employee steers a course contrary to Microsoft's culture. Often an outsider is brought in to restore the proper direction. Mr Sinneck, in turn, was replaced a year later by another long-time Microsoft employee—the former chief information officer—Rick Devenuti, who has also steered MCS in a direction more in accordance with Microsoft's culture.

Another Microsoft sales executive—Orlando Ayala—has accounted for great change at Microsoft. Mr Ayala tends to shake up and accelerate promising change wherever he is positioned. He is responsible for dramatic growth as top sales executive in the Latin America Region, where he started with Microsoft in 1991, and then as chief of the Intercontinental Region, the South Pacific and Americas Region and, finally, as Group Vice President of Microsoft's Worldwide Sales, Marketing and Services Group from 2000 to 2003. Signaling Microsoft's intention to conquer the small and middle market, Mr Ayala is currently the senior vice president of Microsoft's Small and Midmarket Solutions and Partners (SMS&P) group. Like other Microsoft executives, Mr Ayala has accounted for dramatic revenue growth consistently in accord with—and advancing—Microsoft's culture.

Executive mobility and the hiring of new executives is not uncommon in such a dynamic firm. In some instances, these have disrupted cultural norms. In others, they have simply served as mechanisms for experimenting with new strategies and approaches. The appointment of Mr Belluzzo to serve as president and COO of Microsoft was unprecedented. And while his tenure was short, it is important to note that one of the most significant organizational changes to occur at Microsoft was announced on the same day as Mr Belluzzo's resignation: the creation of seven business units, each a P&L center. Microsoft acknowledged that Mr Belluzzo played a role in the reorganization of 2002. Microsoft does not get stuck—at least for too long. It has proved quite capable of welcoming and synthesizing the best of these cultural and organizational innovations, at times painfully, and moderating or reversing any perceived negative impact on the company.

Culture-Driven Growth

Microsoft's strategic development and, consequently, its growth and scope have taken their cue from its culture. Despite its substantial growth, then, Microsoft's organization has remained competitive, fiercely loyal and dynamic because its employees—at corporate and in the field—are imbued with its cultural values. Of course, Microsoft's reading of market realities and opportunities has fostered its strategic growth. But, like other companies, Microsoft's interpretation of the market does not occur in a cultural vacuum.

A company's culture forms its interpretive context and guides its decision making. And, while strategic market and organizational change molds a company and refines its culture over time, Microsoft's *modus operandi* has remained consistent with its cultural values.

Microsoft is a product-centric and an increasingly customer-focused, partner-driven company. The company sells software products, not implementation services or PCs or servers. Microsoft's culture has, by and large, remained constant and unchallenged because of its unprecedented success and growth, which both mirrors and reinforces Microsoft's culture itself. *A cultural value of Microsoft is to preserve its culture.*

This was highlighted by Mr Ballmer in his memo advising Microsoft employees to "renew our culture" and nothing is more deeply esteemed in Microsoft's culture than two things: its products and its customers. It is significant that for each mention of Microsoft's partners in Mr Ballmer's memo, he discusses them in the context of products or customers. Partners are integral to the company's culture as the third element of core importance to Microsoft, next to its products and its customers.

Because of that deeply-ingrained culture, there is little question that Microsoft will continue cruising swiftly over the high seas and maintain forward momentum. It is a reflection of the culture itself: always advancing while steering the course. Its crew is mobilized to ready the ship for sudden shifts in the current and competitive climate, and continues refining its expanding arsenal of products. Microsoft's partners sail along with it as allies. Some partners yaw astern of the battleship, obscuring their navigational view in the spray and risk potentially getting drawn into its screw. Others lose momentum or steer off course, drifting leeward or windward, and lose sight of Microsoft. Still others sail forward of the ship, risking their craft to its oncoming bow.

The SS Microsoft sails aggressively forward to seize customer opportunities and to protect its steered course from market dangers. One might think of Linux perhaps as a set of icebergs that could scuttle the ship, and governmental regulation as treacherous shoals that must be avoided or out-maneuvered. Large competitors, such as IBM and Oracle, generally steer clear of the SS Microsoft but occasionally engage it in skirmishes. All hands are on deck on the SS Microsoft, ready for trouble and prepared to launch new product offensives. The atmosphere is dynamic and charged: Microsoft's culture binds its crew around its product arsenal, heaving to and welcoming over the gangway their best partners, who are focused on their customers and ready to engage the enemy.

The metaphor is appropriate. Microsoft's senior management and employees take great pride in what the company has accomplished and view themselves as an elite crew. As a result, there is a marked arrogance exhibited in the interaction of Microsoft with outsiders, even with partners, and there is steadfast loyalty to the Microsoft way.

In order to partner effectively with Microsoft, one must appreciate this ethos: Microsoft's employees know their success, exercise healthy paranoia to sustain it and view themselves as elite sailors on the high seas who can navigate and grasp the sea of change better than anyone. Microsoft's culture is infused with elitism, a quality often associated with its chairman that has trickled down throughout the company. And it accounts in part for the company's ability to seize and retain industry leadership despite antitrust and competitive pressures.

Microsoft's Culture Impacts Its Partners

If a partner misses Microsoft's elitist attitude—or chooses to ignore it—the partner misses the boat, and likely many opportunities. Since partners work mainly with Microsoft field personnel, this is an important verity. Remember the Roman colonists' zeal for the Roman way? Partners ought to bear in mind that Microsoft field personnel are no different from their Roman-colonist counterparts who are often more Microsoft than their corporate counterparts. Consequently, prudent Microsoft partners take pains to communicate clearly and effectively that they are as purely Microsoft as a non-Microsoft entity can get. Doing so is an affirmation of the field personnel's pride in the company and an indication of the partner's loyalty to the global cause. It would not be in a partner's best interest, for instance, to discuss openly any potential benefits of Linux over Windows with Microsoft field personnel.

At the same time, partners must recognize that Microsoft is culturally realistic about not being the only ship on the high seas. And this is certainly true more in the field than at corporate, which is somewhat removed from the day-to-day battles that salespeople and partners face in selling to or pleasing customers with Microsoft products and platforms. Microsoft knows that its technology is not the only option available to end-consumers, small and mid-sized businesses and large enterprises. Microsoft, at the root of its culture, does not want to be all things to all technology buyers—it knows it cannot be—but it does intend to be the center of the universe for all things Microsoft that its customers might buy. In its ownership of the PC operating system and applications, the leading user interface between customers and the computer, Microsoft assumed this central role quite easily. In its dealings with partners, Microsoft will lay first claim to any product or add-on or service offering that accentuates its arsenal of products. This is not to suggest that Microsoft will necessarily, inevitably and invariably co-opt the partner's technology. Rather, Microsoft will seek to determine the right place for the partner's technology in the context of its core products, and it will work with its partner—at times arrogantly, always with a focus on how the technology accentuates its own products—to position the partner's technology for optimal leverage to drive Microsoft's product sales.

Regarding technologies that Microsoft acquires, it will rewrite them to make them full-fledged Windows offerings and take on the "look-and-feel" of Windows because, again, the company views its value in the context of how it can expand the Microsoft software empire. Any code that it welcomes aboard will simply be absorbed and subsumed within Microsoft's technology. This is true of nearly all of Microsoft's acquired products, including Visio, FrontPage, Content Management Server, and Virtual PC and Virtual Server.

There is an interesting caveat to Microsoft's realism: Microsoft uses product integration as a strategy to grow and extend the Windows franchise. In fact, its ability to integrate new services and functions into the core operating system—an approach at times characterized by the US Justice Department as "product tying" (linking one product to another in a sale) and by Microsoft as "integration innovation"—enables it to grow the value of Windows and its business in a way that competitors cannot match. And conversely, Microsoft will rarely if ever touch technologies that help it integrate with non-Microsoft technologies. Rather, Microsoft will relegate those integration tasks to its ISVs and services partners. Again, this reinforces Microsoft's core cultural goal—to sell as much Microsoft software as possible, while also expanding the Microsoft empire by leveraging partners. This preserves Microsoft's purview over its own technology and its influence over outside partners that complement it.

These are high-level considerations that adduce principles about how Microsoft thinks and works as a global organization. Microsoft's partners need to understand the internal workings of the company, the culture, strategy, direction and *modus operandi*. They also need to appreciate its externalities: Microsoft's size, scale, speed, complexity, threats and its commitment to success. Observers note that it is important for partners to embrace Microsoft's high level of confidence and expectation for success. "Microsoft creamed competitor after competitor in the 1990s against incredible odds, and in the 2000s against the US Justice Department. You have a culture that expects to win, really, deeply, always expects to always win," said Paul DeGroot of *Directions on Microsoft*.

By knowing the company in depth, and what makes Microsoft tick, Microsoft's partners will be in the best position to sail as aggressively with it and to win. Doing so entails understanding corporate and field contributions to partnering itself.

Microsoft's partnering approach, initiatives and programs are established at the corporate level but executed almost entirely in the field. Like its products, Microsoft's increasingly complex partner assets contribute to individual business units or, in some cases, multiple business units. For example, Microsoft's traditional certified services partners drive revenues for multiple business units—Windows Client, Information Worker, and Server and Tools—while other distinct partners such as those in Microsoft Business Solutions (MBS) contribute, in most cases, singularly to the MBS business unit. Meanwhile, ISVs and services partners in the Windows Mobile Solutions Program drive sales primarily for the Mobile and Embedded Devices business unit, although these partners are likely to contribute revenues to the Server and Tools division, as well.

Generally speaking, Microsoft's partner ecosystem is vast yet still expanding and evolving in step with corporate and field. At Microsoft, partners have historically been viewed as natural extensions of the company's field organization. That symbiosis is deepening as Microsoft faces new competitive challenges and returns to its roots to conquer them. This includes a heavy emphasis on strengthening relationships with two key constituencies, developers and partners. For instance, Microsoft redefined its corporate policy to include partners as a requirement for every transaction. That requirement, which made partnering effectively a law in Microsoft's empire in 2002, binds partners more integrally to the field organizations in an unprecedented way. Mr Ballmer is widely viewed as Microsoft's primary proponent for the channel but he is supported by the company's chairman. In 2001, Mr Gates reiterated the integral role that partners play as part of Microsoft's DNA: "The key to the .NET platform is the partner support we get for it—the ISVs and consultants," he said; "There is always going to be a fight over the hearts and minds of those people. It is in our genes to use that model." (CRN Online, 24 July 2002) Partners are integral to Microsoft because the company's partner ecosystem is ingrained in its culture.

The Microsoft Partner Ecosystem

What can we discern from Microsoft's culture, strategic-growth history and organizational dynamism that is instructive for Microsoft's partners? Several things, in general:

Stay close to Microsoft. Because of the rapid pace of change at Microsoft, partners need to remain informed about strategic initiatives, organizational changes and product- and customer-specific issues that are important to Microsoft. As importantly, partners need to understand the underlying culture and cultural shifts that account for much of this dynamism.

Work connection points. Due to Microsoft's meshed, global organizational structure and its own dynamism, partners need to sustain their relationships with key Microsoft personnel and expand their circle of relationships to other relevant areas in the company. In fact, many connection points are essential for partners to succeed as such, and understanding how to leverage them is essential.

Help Microsoft help you. As a result of the symbiosis between Microsoft's two cultural forces—corporate and field—partners need to understand that their local Microsoft representatives may not be the only ones with whom they should interact. But partners must first start in the field. That is, their needs can best be served through productive interaction with local and regional Microsoft personnel—and, through them, global personnel—who have an interest in a particular partner's area of expertise. That is, staying close to Microsoft field personnel and working connection points naturally extends to deepening ties with Microsoft globally to ensure that your concerns are heard and that your joint success is fostered. This theme, as you will see, is echoed in many partner case studies in this book.

These are core principles of what is known within the company as the "Microsoft Partner Ecosystem," or the ecosystem for short. Partners are by definition central to it; the ecosystem exists for and is made up of Microsoft's partners. To Microsoft, the ecosystem is essential since the majority of its revenues are generated by its partners, the company maintains.

At the risk of repetition, let us break this down for the sake of absolute clarity: Microsoft makes money by selling its products, which are near and dear to its heart. Microsoft sells its products to its customers, which we know from Microsoft's mission are also near and dear to its heart. Therefore, also near and dear to Microsoft's heart are its partners, through whom essentially all of its product revenues earned from its customers are made.

The crowning principle of Microsoft's culture and, by extension, of the ecosystem is plainly this: *Microsoft is a customer-focused, product-centric and partner-driven company.* The ecosystem is a reflection and an offshoot of Microsoft's culture, so understanding the culture is a prerequisite to understanding the role and purpose of partners within it.

The crowning principle of Microsoft's culture and, by extension, of the ecosystem is plainly this: Microsoft is a customer-focused, product-centric and partner-driven company . . . understanding the culture is a prerequisite to understanding the partner ecosystem.

The ecosystem is the cultural and organizational context in which Microsoft's partnering program is defined, refined and executed. It is the nexus between Microsoft and its more than 841,000 partners. Within that nexus, the nature of Microsoft's interaction with its partners evolves.

The same attributes apply to the ecosystem that govern Microsoft's culture, organization and growth strategy—it is dynamic, it abides, it improves, it is aggressive. The ecosystem is the face of Microsoft to its partner community, an image of Microsoft's culture, strategy and organization altogether.

As indicated, partners help drive the firm's development and growth culturally, strategically and organizationally around the world. But all roads lead to and from Seattle by way of the field. Corporate headquarters defines the structure of the company's partner program, as well as its standards and benefits based on various factors, including the formal input of partners and guidance from the field.

PACs and PABs

Microsoft has a formal structure and process by which it gathers feedback from partners on a routine basis. At its core are two sets of partner advisory management bodies whose members Microsoft alone nominates. These are Partner Advisory Councils (PACs), whose members are nominated for one-year renewable terms, and Partner Advisory Boards (PABs), whose nominated members serve at Microsoft's pleasure on a permanent basis. These entities are generally composed of Microsoft personnel and representatives from Microsoft's top partners in various types of firms. That is, there are PACs and PABs for services firms, ISVs and resellers. The purview of the PACs and PABs is governed by Microsoft; the councils function as sounding boards for Microsoft's product and solutions groups as well as sales and marketing teams. PAC and PAB members provide feedback and critique ideas to improve Microsoft products and processes prior to their deployment to the field. Nominated members benefit from knowing what Microsoft is considering in advance of the rest of the company and the world, but they serve at Microsoft's request and are obligated to focus on Microsoft's interest, not their own, in PAC or PAB membership. For most partners, it is sufficient to know that Microsoft works with its PACs and PABs to assess and refine its partner program, and to communicate to partners the contours of the Microsoft Partner Ecosystem.

Microsoft field personnel have a fundamental role to play in the ecosystem. The PAC and PAB governance structure enables Microsoft corporate to stay abreast of its partners' needs and aspirations but it is the field that has ultimate control and purview over how the partner ecosystem operates in the field. Because nothing happens in Microsoft customer accounts without Microsoft's field approval in some fashion, field executives are responsible for implementing partner-specific initiatives including "partner attach" and "partner assign."

While the programmatic governance of the partner ecosystem comes from corporate, *how* things get done is quite local. It is worth noting that Microsoft revised its corporate charter in 2002, increasing accountability to customers and partners, and thus changing *how* the company operates. Microsoft's field personnel's performance, for example, is measured in large part on the Customer Partner Experience (CPE), a metric that reflects Microsoft corporate's stated view of partners as mechanisms for Microsoft's servicing its customers. Microsoft field personnel obviously see partners in the same way because it is in their professional interest to do so.

More importantly and in keeping with the adage that "all politics are local," Microsoft field personnel have the ultimate say in *attaching* and *assigning* partners to opportunities. They invariably do so on the basis of what is in the best interest of customers and, secondarily, on the relationships they have with partners in their respective districts. Field personnel exercise great discretion. But, first, they must answer to corporate standards according to a two-level internal process, as indicated: partner attach and partner assign.

Partner Attach and Partner Assign

There are a number of programs that come and go from corporate to compel field personnel to improve their relationship with Microsoft partners. These programs have enjoyed varying degrees of effectiveness. However, Microsoft implemented a fundamental change in the field organization's structure in FY05 designed to enable the revised mission of pleasing customers through partners. In any organization, the most reliable way to impact personnel, that is, to change their behavior, is through financial incentives. Microsoft corporate decided to establish a phased-in modification of field pay structures in which the overall performance of subsidiaries is measured on the relationship between projects and partners.

This is commonly referred to as "Partner Attach," the first level of the internal performance-measurement process. Per corporate rules, each project opportunity in Microsoft's Siebel-based customer relationship management (CRM) system should have a partner attached to a project within the structured sales process. Microsoft field managers review their pipeline of projects on a weekly, semi-monthly or monthly basis, depending on the district's practices. Hypothetically, if there are 100 opportunities in a market and only 10 have partners attached to them, then the attach rate for that market is 10%. Microsoft corporate stipulates that field partner attach rates must be between 10% and 20%. Partner-attach rates vary immensely but typically range between 10% and 40% in most markets. The salaries and bonuses of the general manager (GM) and all Microsoft account representatives in each district are affected by the partner attach–rate percentage; their compensation is reduced if the partner-attach rate is low, and increased if it meets or exceeds corporate's standard. It stands to reason, then, that partner-attach rates will increase, unless there is a dramatic turnaround in its partner policy.

Partners should know that being attached to an opportunity does not necessarily mean that the partner will be engaged in it. Partners that are attached to a project may never even know they are attached. For example, Microsoft's partner account manager might select three partners suitable for a given project but only the selected partner will be notified.

The second level of the internal performance-measurement process is called "Partner Assign." When a partner is assigned to a project opportunity, whether or not the partner was first attached to the opportunity, a follow-on process is automatically initiated and its name enters the CRM system. The partner is referred to "Partner Central," a virtual CRM clearinghouse of project-and-partner opportunity management. At the very least, a partner receives an email message indicating that it is attached to a project opportunity. Most often, this is simply a formal notification confirming prior discussions between Microsoft field personnel and the partner in question. In some cases, it is the partner's first notice about the opportunity. (In fact, the overwhelming majority of communications between Microsoft and its partners—indeed, among Microsoft personnel themselves—is through casual email, not the CRM system or the Partner Central management channel).

From the perspective of the Microsoft sales team, there is some cause for concern about the two-level partner-attach and partner-assign performance measurement. Once a project opportunity is in the CRM system and a partner is attached, for example, pipeline managers are under immediate pressure to close the deal since they are being measured on it. Microsoft corporate is serious about measuring its field personnel on their partner-related progress and the CRM system is monitored closely. However, the vast majority of project opportunities—that is, 80% to 90% of them—are not required to be in the CRM system for the partner-attach metric. Consequently, it is business as usual for field personnel and Microsoft partners who continue to collaborate informally on the basis of established and growing relationships for their perceived mutual benefit.

Partners can favorably influence their attach and assign rates by leveraging appropriate field and corporate organizations. One can discern the field-level and corporate relationships to build in order to optimize partner-attach and partner-assign opportunities by considering the structure of the ecosystem itself. The following graphic depicts the ecosystem's partner categories and types, with Microsoft's estimates as to their numbers, as well as partner connection points within the ecosystem.

At its core, the ecosystem is built on the foundation of collaboration between Microsoft and its partners to influence and achieve sales of Microsoft products as well as the software, services and hardware of its partners. The mission of the ecosystem is to achieve sustainable, repeatable and increasing growth at progressively lower costs of goods sold. Accordingly, the partner program—the hallmark of the ecosystem—is structured to provide partners of all types appropriate incentives to work capably and effectively so they can together achieve such efficiencies with Microsoft.

Partners ought to know that the partner program is the entry point for partnering with Microsoft. Satisfying its requirements is only the first step in partnering with the company. The partner program is a hurdle that must be overcome in order

PARTNER CATEGORIES Quantity	PARTNER TYPES BY %AGE OF CATEGORY AND SCOPE OF OPERATIONS			CONNECTION POINTS
	LOCAL	REGIONAL/NATIONAL	GLOBAL	
RESELLERS 449,000	VARs (62.9%) Systems Builders (33.4%)	Retailers (3.3%) DMRs (0.1%) Distributors (0.1%)	OEMs (0.1%)	Field Sales, Corporate Marketing, Product Groups, MBS, MCS
SERVICES 329,000	LSIs (99.6%)	RSIs (0.1%) MCLSPs (0.4%)	GSIs (0.1%)	Field Sales, Field Management, Corporate Marketing, Product Groups, MCS
ISVs 63,000	Breadth (93.3%)		Account-Managed (6.9%) Global (0.3%)	Field Sales, Field Management, Corporate Marketing, Product Groups

Figure 2.5: The Microsoft Partner Ecosystem, 2005: Partner Categories, Partner Types and Connection Points.

to realize the real rewards—and to manage the real risks—of working with Microsoft. It is not the end-game; in fact, it is only the starting gate to the race.

The partner program is the public face of Microsoft corporate to its world of partners. But there is another and more private view from the field, which is where, by definition, partners work day-to-day with Microsoft. So, while you need to understand Microsoft's partner program—as an exemplar of its culture, a reflection of the ecosystem—you also, more importantly, need to understand the principles and the mechanics of achieving successful partnership with Microsoft in the field. These are native to the partner program.

At its core is the imperative to build and to work relationships within Microsoft in the field, where the partner program is viewed quite differently from corporate. Such is the essence of this book—to analyze in a scientific manner the Microsoft Partner Ecosystem but to demonstrate that the practical experience of partnering with Microsoft is more of an art than a science. The partner program is only a structured context within which Microsoft works with complementary firms; it is not the essence of the partnering experience. The partner program gets you into the game. Whether you win is up to you.

History and Features of the Partner Program

Microsoft announced its first partner program in 1992, then called the Microsoft Solution Provider Program. By 1996, when Windows NT 4.0 first shipped, Microsoft had 11,000 partners registered in this program and held its first annual Fusion partner conference. In 2000, Microsoft changed the name of that program to the

Microsoft Certified Partner Program and pledged to expand it to include more partner types aside from solution providers. OEMs and independent hardware vendors (IHVs) were folded into the program in 2003. ISVs and systems builders joined in 2004.

In keeping with its dynamic culture and organization, Microsoft changes programs annually or even more frequently to drive partner activity. Yet Microsoft revamped the partner program in a more substantial manner in October 2003, in order to correct certain deficiencies in its previous program. The company's partner program had survived with few modifications for roughly a decade but had become increasingly criticized for a number of reasons and market realities. The revamped partner program—which took effect in January 2004—intended to correct the following deficiencies of the previous program:

- *Outdated:* the previous partner program did not keep pace with Microsoft's product offerings and was inappropriate for the reorganization of Microsoft's lines of business;

- *Top-heavy:* the previous program was under-represented by tens of thousands of smaller yet qualified potential partners that lacked Microsoft certifications and were disinclined to pay the fee;

- *Inconsistent:* some partners exaggerated their credentials, which diluted the field of more qualified partners;

- *Inequitable:* all partners paid the same fee but more qualified partners often received fewer rewards than they deserved due to the indiscriminate distribution of perks across the whole partner ecosystem;

- *Unclear:* there were homegrown, competitive partner organizations within Microsoft that were undocumented and had less rigorous requirements, which opened the door for less-qualified partners to earn perks; and

- *Ineffective:* the partner programs were fragmented and did not provide adequate guidance on how to partner effectively with Microsoft, frustrating many legitimate partners.

In 2004, Microsoft took significant steps to address these weaknesses. It consolidated nearly all partner programs into one worldwide partner organization and eliminated the more informal groupings. It documented objective criteria for achieving partnership and put into place a structured system for advancing up the ranks of partnership. Microsoft invested its partner funding directly into the partner program and began advising partners on the mechanisms for successful partnering and earning rewards.

Another effort was made to bring previously unqualified partners into the ecosystem for the purposes of expanding Microsoft's channel and improving collaboration among various partner types. Specifically, Microsoft folded ISVs into the formal partner program and gave developers incentives to partner with Microsoft product groups while also encouraging its services partners to partner with the Microsoft Business Solutions (MBS) group. In addition, systems builders and certified training firms were tapped as partner types that would benefit from the program and its refined criteria and were thus indoctrinated into the program.

The revised partner program is geared to achieve better efficiencies given Microsoft's small direct sales force and high ratio of sales achieved through partners.

Moreover, the establishment of a more systematic approach to partnering was required following Microsoft's acquisition of Great Plains Software and its integration of that firm's middle-market partner channel into Microsoft own channel of partners. Microsoft's down-market sales thrust needed a substantial partner boost in order to drive greater sales into the small and mid-sized business (SMB) market.

The new partner program achieved those objectives, with the following advantages for partners:

- one program for all Microsoft partners;

- clear guidelines for partner entry to the program;

- objective criteria for partners' competence with various Microsoft solutions;

- more explicit rules about how to engage with Microsoft as a partner;

- coherent stratification to distinguish various partner types;

- actionable guidelines for advancing in the partner program; and

- established criteria for gaining rewards for advanced work with Microsoft.

It is worth considering the core attributes of Microsoft's new partner program. Its results to date have been impressive and it appears that Microsoft is intent on using the model for years. Microsoft did not issue any material changes to the program at its 2004 worldwide partner conference at Toronto. The new program levels the playing field for all partners since it consolidates most other partner programs and extends the program to previously unqualified potential partners such as ISVs and systems builders. As a result, Microsoft now counts roughly 841,000 services firms, ISVs, OEMs and certified training firms in its overall partner base. The original Certified Partner program, by contrast, favored services firms—especially systems integrators—and had a membership of approximately 35,000.

In addition, the program more appropriately organizes partners by category and into stratified tiers. The numbers in each tier are equally impressive, as indicated in Figure 2.5 (above). The core attributes of the revamped partner program are detailed below.

Stratifying Partners

Microsoft announced a set of functional IT domains called "competencies" or skill sets according to which partners are categorized and assessed for entry to the program and for advancing in it. These are general IT competencies that are not tied specifically to Microsoft products, though partners must be competent in Microsoft technologies to achieve certification. This is the group of FY05 partner competencies, which are subject to change:

MICROSOFT COMPETENCY	SOLUTIONS COVERED
Advanced Infrastructure Solutions	Proven competency in crafting high-availability infrastructure solutions that include one or more of the following: Exchange, Identity Integration Server, Active Directory; data migration, storage solutions, systems management, hosting solutions.
Business Intelligence Solutions	Proven competency in implementing solutions that feature: data warehousing, business intelligence, OLAP, data mining, decision support.
Information Worker Solutions	Proven competency at building collaboration and group productivity solutions, including: collaboration and mesaging, portals and content management, project and process management, business productivity tools.
Integrated E-Business Solutions	Proven competency in the deployment of Internet-based business solutions and infrastructure (eg, Internet business, extranets and web hosting, web applications and portal development, web workflow and orchestration solutions).
ISV/Software Solutions	Proven competency in developing and marketing packaged software solutions based on Microsoft technologies.
Learning Solutions	Proven competency in providing individuals and organizations with the high-level technical knowledge and skills required to maximize their investments in Microsoft-based solutions (eg, skills assessment, mediated training, certification exam preparation, specific training solutions for IT pros, .NET, solutions, career).
Licensing Solutions (available for enrollment later in 2005)	Proven competency in providing customers with Microsoft software licensing and asset management solutions. These partners have experience in licensing and distributing Microsoft software technology and solutions and software asset management.
Microsoft Business Solutions	Proven competency in deploying Microsoft Business Solutions focused on financial management and ERP (Axapta, C5, Great Plains, Solomon, Navision), customer relationship management (CRM), supply chain management, and analytics applications.
Networking Infrastructure Solutions	Proven competency in implementing technology solutions based on Microsoft Windows Server and Windows Small Business Server operating system technology.
OEM Hardware Solutions (available for enrollment later in 2005)	Proven competency in: PC and server builds with Microsoft products preinstalled per customer business requirements, as well as OEMing and/or hardware development.
Security Solutions	Proven competency in building the most advanced Microsoft security solutions to protect the customer's information assets (eg, security solutions, management and operations; identity and access management; platform and application-layer security).

Figure 2.6: Microsoft Partner Competencies, 2005.

The competencies approach is a general but coherent mechanism for stratifying partners according to their breadth and depth of IT skills for the purposes of assessing their fitness for entry to the partner program and promotion—or demotion—within it. But there are specific requirements in most of these competencies for Microsoft partners to be able to claim them, and these requirements have a Microsoft-specific reference.

For services firms, as an example, these include:

- a minimum number of Microsoft certifications—*eg*, Microsoft Certified Systems Engineer (MCSE), Microsoft Certified Professional (MCP), Microsoft Certified Database Administrator (MCDBA), Microsoft Certified System Administrators (MCSA) and Microsoft Certified Application Developer (MCAD)—that a services firm must hold in order to achieve partner status; and

- annual submission of three client references, whom Microsoft will contact to confirm the partner's successful deployment of applicable Microsoft solutions.

For ISVs, there is at least a similar requirement: the ISV's software must have met at least a minimum number of Microsoft certification requirements.

For systems builders, there is an OEM hardware competency that must be earned in order to participate in the program.

For large account resellers, there is a licensing solutions competency that must be earned in order to participate in the program

So, too, for technical-training firms, the requirement that each training facility must meet certain criteria is equally Microsoft-specific.

Partners can have multiple competencies—in systems integration, application development and/or technical training, for example—but they must meet the minimal requirements for any or all of these in order to be formally recognized. The requirements focus places the burden of proof on solicitous prospective partners and forces a natural stratification of all partners in the program based on partner skills and merits as determined by Microsoft.

The strata—or "tiers"—of the Microsoft partnership program admit of a distinct hierarchy of firms whose qualifications—and Microsoft benefits—are granted in descending order of rank:

Gold Partners likely have large staffs, several competencies and more customer relationships than most. They must pay an annual partnership fee (US$1,500 per year in the US, although the fee varies by country), and are fewer in number than those strata that follow. In exchange, Gold Partners are listed in a global partner database according to their competencies and have access to a Microsoft technical services coordinator (TSC) as well as faster access than others to Microsoft executives and management. They also get an annual subscription to the Microsoft Developer Network (MSDN) service for internal use and training, and a number of free and discounted software licenses. Finally, they receive discounted technical training and marketing services from Microsoft, as well as free customer-satisfaction measurement services. There are approximately 5,000 Gold Partners.

Certified Partners pay an annual partnership fee (US$1,500 per year in the US, although the fee varies by country). They must have at least one competency, a Microsoft-certified hardware or software product and two or more Microsoft-certified staff members. Certified Partners are listed (per a search function) in the global partner database according to their competency, and they have telephone access to a partner account manager (PAM) as well as to a TechNet concierge for accelerated access to Knowledge Base articles. They can also customize a page on Microsoft's partner web portal. They are granted five free support incidents, discounted technical training and marketing services, and 10 free software licenses for internal use. Finally, Certified Partners receive a TechNet subscription, five MSDN subscriptions and additional discounted software. There are approximately 30,000 Certified Partners.

Registered Partners—by far the most populous partner group—generally have no formal competencies, no Microsoft-certified personnel and no requirement to pay an annual partnership fee. Registered Partners are not privy to additional support or services from Microsoft.

The higher a firm's ranking in these tiers, the more support the firm receives from Microsoft. With each earned competency, partners also gain access to additional technical support and marketing resources appropriate to the earned competency. There are some regional and country-specific variations on the theme. But the overall guidelines are reasonably standard and represent a marked improvement on the previous program's lack of coherence, marching orders and impact. So, too, are the guidelines for promotion in the partner program, according to the number of points a partner receives.

Partner Points

Partners can earn points in a variety of ways in order to advance upward in the program, from at least 50 points for admission as a Certified Partner to a minimum of 120 points in order to qualify as a Gold Partner.

Unlike the former Certified Partner program, the partner point system is not based on the number of Microsoft-certified personnel but on actual solutions-deployment in the field and customer satisfaction with those experiences. That is, partners must demonstrate revenues, earnings and satisfied customers in order to advance in the pool. The point system is designed to provide a higher degree of quality and equitability than in the previous program.

Some point-earning methods include:
- achieving US$1 million in license revenue in any given fiscal year on qualifying

Microsoft products (this is worth 60 points in most regions and countries, although the point value varies among some of them);

- maintaining a Microsoft-certified application hosting facility (70 points);

- submitting 10 additional customer references (20 points);

- earning selected Microsoft Certified Professional certifications (maximum of 40 points);

- demonstrating customer satisfaction (40 points);

- gaining an initial competency or a Microsoft-certified application for Windows 2003 Server (50 points); and

- gaining a second competency (25 points), after which no more points are granted.

Additional competencies bring additional rewards, as suggested above (technical and marketing benefits, especially), and increased recognition in the global partner database.

There are smaller point allotments for referring new customers to Microsoft (2 points), for example, and sending up to three staff members to Microsoft's worldwide partner conference (3 points). Firms with multiple sites in one country can generally pool competencies and earn points through personnel and with activities at the various sites in order to qualify as one firm for higher points. Local systems integrators can apply this rule to become regional systems integrators, which enables them to work across districts.

Microsoft tracks each partner's earned points on its partner website. It also counsels Certified and Registered Partners on ways that they can earn points in order to advance to the higher tier(s).

In general, the new partner program and the point system are dramatic improvements over the previous program, not only for the objectivity of the guidelines and the merit-based stratification of partners, but also for the coherent perks, including Microsoft guidance and facilitation.

Yet the partner points system also carries with it a risk of point-mongering and the potential of a cold distance between Microsoft and its partners with point calculations that could potentially separate rather than bind them closer together. Of necessity, and with 841,000 partners in its ranks, Microsoft structured the program on an objective, measurable basis.

This point system gives partners a framework for best tailoring their engagement in the program in a manner that works for them and for Microsoft. Microsoft is encouraging specialization. Such an approach might be viewed as an attempt to replace working engagements with Microsoft with objective-driven metrics that could actually impair collaboration between vendor and partner. Or so it would seem if one took the points program at face value as the be-all, end-all of partnering with Microsoft.

But this is not the case. Firms that aim to partner effectively with Microsoft should not construe the partner program and the points system as such. Rather, they should think of the points system and the partner program *per se* as this: a simple mechanism or gatekeeper, if you will, to get partners in the door and active with Microsoft. Partner points and Gold-Certified-Registered ratings can be thought of in the same manner as a driver's license: you have to earn points in order to partner with Microsoft just as you have to pass the driver's tests to be licensed to drive. It is only the first step. Earning competencies and partner points does not make you a successful Microsoft partner just as getting a driver's license does not mean you will inevitably, invariably and exclusively drive 200 kilometers per hour on the Autobahn. You need both credentials, but what you do with them—what you achieve once you have them—is, again, up to you.

The promotion of partners within the program is a subject of concern because the point-earning and Microsoft-consultation mechanisms remain somewhat vague and inconsistent. For example, the quality of Microsoft partner-account management is variable, and that can be disadvantageous to some partners and prove inordinately advantageous to others.

Additionally, the program itself may give partners the impression that they are working for—rather than with—Microsoft. This is not the message Microsoft wishes to impart. Some aspects of the new program, especially checking customer satisfaction, convey encroaching control, as if Microsoft were acting like "Big Brother" by checking up on its partners and their accounts, watching for mistakes. This is an element of the partner program Microsoft implemented in order to raise the bar on customer satisfaction, but it is not intended to generate intimidation or fear among its ranks of partners. The intent is to reward, not to punish; to hand out resources based on objectively measured results. It is, fundamentally, a Pavlovian approach to business-behavior modification: positive conditioning for positive behavior. Even so, these incentives do not convey what partnering with Microsoft is all about.

This consideration suggests a problem: the partner program tells you *how to qualify* as a partner but it does not tell you *how to partner* effectively with Microsoft. This book is intended to overcome this problem. In overcoming some of the pitfalls and problems that others have faced, and shedding light on best partnering practices with this book's guidance, one can safely overlook the flaws in the partner program to succeed in partnering with Microsoft.

At its root, one troubling reality with the partner program is that there is no clear guidance on how to build the best relationship with Microsoft. Microsoft has implemented an objective point system for partners to know how to earn ranking in Microsoft's program. But Microsoft has not been as instructive as it could be on how to engage with Microsoft as a partner, and that is because partnering is more of an art than a science. Microsoft cannot give partners a paint-by-numbers partnering strategy any more than a parent can teach a child precisely how to form friendships and romantic relationships.

Again, that is the subject of this book—to fill that void from the perspective of experienced partners who have navigated and leveraged what abides in Microsoft's culture rather than from partner programs and other elements that are bound to change in a dynamic company. There are some shortcomings in the new program but, fortunately, Microsoft bought some time in phasing out the previous partner program to give it time to transition completely and to refine it.

Partner Program Transitions

Effective in January 2004, Gold and Certified Partners from the previous program were inducted to the new partner program at their prior levels. Since that time, those partners have been assessing whether their competencies and customer references will qualify them for placement in the new partner program, which officially launches in 2005. Some may need additional competencies, qualified personnel or customer references in order to retain their grandfathered status.

Competency requirements were first issued by Microsoft in April 2004. The mechanisms for validating credentials of existing Gold and Certified partners' credentials have been published and the results are available online to applicable partners.

There are other changes being phased in over a two-year period. In July 2004, for example, Microsoft phased existing MBS partners into its worldwide partner program, thus integrating the previously separate MBS and Certified Partner programs. Yet MBS partners that are new to Microsoft's partner program must certify their partnership credentials by mid-2005 since the fiscal year of the former MBS partner program ends on 30 June 2005.

This represents a particularly complex transition because former MBS partners included ISVs, services firms and product resellers of Microsoft products and of legacy products acquired by Microsoft, including Great Plains, Axapta and Navision. These MBS partners are, by definition, channel partners who serve the mid-market and in large part have been integrated into the ecosystem in order to advance Microsoft's penetration of the SMB market.

Microsoft grandfathered existing MBS partners into the new partner program on a commensurate basis in July 2004, as indicated above. Those partners must demonstrate their credentials again in July 2005, according to the new partner program's requirements.

There are approximately 10,000 MBS partners who fear that their interests may not be best served in Microsoft's global partner program, which is fast approaching the one million-partner mark. These partners are particularly concerned about being cast as mass-market players when in fact their consulting and services focus is more tailored to specific mid-market industries and technical functions associated with them. They fear, consequently, the dilution of the status and quality of the MBS designation due to new involvement by a glut of lesser-qualified consultancies.

To address these concerns, Microsoft restricted the selling of its enterprise resource planning (ERP) products—Axapta, Great Plains and Navision—to these qualified resellers to avoid the feared dilution of their market stature. Microsoft also instituted an MBS Solution Provider Agreement (SPA) that resellers must qualify for in order to sell authorized MBS products, but they are not required to meet MBS competency requirements of services partners that deploy, configure and support MBS products. This distinction between authorized resellers and authorized service providers in the MBS space creates a distinctly tiered, hierarchical channel that preserves the respective statures of MBS consultants in the SMB market.

Additionally, under the new partner program, Microsoft will streamline into a global standard the MBS partner rules that often tended to vary by region and subsidiary. Finally, Microsoft cut program fees for MBS partners and made some selections such as software support optional.

There are other complexities inherent in the transition for candidates to the revised partner program. For example, Certified Training and Education Centers (CTECs)—which were renamed Microsoft Certified Partners for Learning Solutions (MCPLSs) in early 2004—are required to earn a Learning Solutions competency. The rationale for the change is to reflect the evolution of learning technologies such as web-based training with on-site classroom instruction. Unlike other partners, whose competencies carry across districts, each Learning Solution facility must earn its own competency and be certified on a per–site basis. For instance, if a learning solutions partner has more than one training facility, all of those facilities must meet new network and hardware requirements in order for the learning partner to qualify for partnership. New Horizons, for example, operates more than 250 training centers in more than 50 countries, so the certification investment is substantial. These partners are required to pay a US$2,500 fee per qualified training facility (this applies to US-based MCPLSs, the amount varies by country). But they are required to provide only one client reference per qualified training facility.

By contrast, ISVs are subject to more general guidelines than applied in the previous partner program. Specifically, they are not subject to personnel certifications, such as Microsoft Certified Software Developer (MCSD). Nevertheless, they must either qualify at least one of their products for tested compatibility with Microsoft platforms or meet a platform requirement for their application's depth of use of a tested Windows platform's features. ISVs must also demonstrate their expertise in integrating their qualified application on various Windows platforms (*eg*, Windows Server or SQL) or applicable components (*eg*, .NET).

No transition, of course, applies to the overwhelming majority of Microsoft Registered Partners, which had no prior relationship with Microsoft and no criteria for partnership with the company.

Partner Program Flaws

Again, Microsoft's objective to standardize and bring all of the various partner programs under one umbrella is laudable, as is the stratification of the partner program in a manner in which partners can define their own specialty and preferred levels. Moreover, the new program is more coherent and comprehensive and hopefully will contribute to its relative success over the previous partner programs.

This new partner program, however, is relatively untested. Not all of its details have been worked out by Microsoft, and this has delayed its intended plenary refined launch in early 2005, to later in the year. Its ramifications in the field are unknown, and unintended impacts—some good, some likely not so good—are to follow.

Some of Microsoft's historical partner-program weaknesses have not been sufficiently addressed. Among the perennial complaints is the application of paper certifications (eg, MCSE, MCP) to measure a partner's qualification. Partners believe that this is a false conveyance of competence and they bemoan the lack of a systematic tie-in of existing certifications to the new competencies and the partnering scheme.

The competency scheme, for instance, constrains Microsoft partners to specialize in their relevant areas of skill rather than to generalize. In a program that ostensibly welcomes a massive number of registered partners and encourages them to advance to the next tier, the stratification model is inapplicable because many of these partners are IT generalists who serve all the needs of small and medium-sized businesses. In spite of the fact that customers demand generalist partners in the SMB space, the long-term prospects for upward mobility for this group of partners, according to the current terms, are not favorable.

Additionally, partners bemoan the lack of an established mechanism to earn points for customer purchases of software that partners influence. The point scale ought to account for how partners indirectly and directly influence product purchases and earn program credit as well as compensation. Finally, partners are subject to Microsoft's own certification test before gaining approved status in the program. This causes a two-fold problem: first, it adds an administrative burden on Microsoft, and that overhead can dig into the intended efficiencies of this streamlined partner model; second, it places partners at the mercy of account managers, who make the final decision. This is often a highly subjective process.

These are viewed as negatives because they re-introduce some of the historical bureaucratic (not to say capricious) tendencies partners hoped would be eradicated in the new program. The program also conveys the feeling that partners are working for Microsoft rather than with Microsoft.

While many believe that the benefits of the new program outweigh the liabilities of the previous program, there are bound to be problems in any new system. Microsoft's stated commitment, however, is to continuous refinement of the program for the mutual benefit of itself and all of its partners.

In the meantime, what do you do about all of these shortcomings in the partner program?

Crafty and clever partners will seek, find and exploit benefits available to them and work on other facets of partnership with Microsoft. The program is not the bible of partnering with Microsoft.

Second, one should wait and provide feedback to one's appropriate Microsoft contact. The new program is an improvement over predecessor programs and will be updated and changed every year.

Most importantly, partners should focus their efforts on alliance- and relationship-building within Microsoft and within the ecosystem. Rather than build the foundation of your partnership with Microsoft on the shifting sands of a partner program, which will invariably change, build your partnership on the solid foundation of Microsoft's culture and with other like-minded partners in the ecosystem. This book is intended to guide you on how to do this.

Managed partners earn the most rewards from Microsoft by taking fullest advantage of what is core to the company's culture—relationship–building—as fundamental to partnering with Microsoft.

Above all, bear in mind that the partner program is a gatekeeper and the first portal for you to pass through in order to qualify and be credentialed as a Microsoft partner. If you are serious about partnering with Microsoft, the goal is to differentiate your firm from Microsoft's 841,000-partner ecosystem rather than to strive for a cookie-cutter profile. One key to such differentiation and elevation of one's status is to become a managed partner. Microsoft has thousands of faceless partners; it is important to become a known player. There are many thousands of Microsoft ISVs but only 30 or so have been named globally managed ISVs that get premier benefits and support from Microsoft. How did they become managed partners?

Principally they did so through working with Microsoft on the basis of something that is core to its culture—relationship building. Partners need to understand that *Microsoft is a relationship-motivated company* and that it expects partners to become deeply involved in Microsoft's success. Otherwise, the majority of partners are faceless, card-carrying members of the partner program who merely get admitted to the party.

This is not to suggest that they are not important to Microsoft. In fact, the new partner program was introduced precisely to expand immensely the number of partners, and most of them will remain unmanaged partners. They will do what they must do to earn points and advance as far as they wish as Microsoft partners. To Microsoft, these are the foot soldiers, allies in the field helping Microsoft sell products and in some cases selling Microsoft products. There are many financially rewarding opportunities for those who play the game. But the fact is, managed partners earn the most rewards. So how does your firm become a managed partner?

Managed Partners

Managed partners are the elite among Microsoft partners. All partners—Registered, Certified and Gold—are eligible to become managed partners. While most managed partners have Gold certifications, what truly distinguishes an unmanaged partner from a managed partner is the scope and quality of that partner's relationships with Microsoft. Managed partners generally have the deepest relationships with the company, and are invariably strongest at the local level. Microsoft, for example, assigns at least one Partner Account Manager (PAM) to each managed partner.

The PAM is the most significant internal advocate for a Microsoft partner. PAMs coordinate their managed partners' work with Microsoft in the field and serve as partner advocates within the applicable segment. A partner may have a PAM in the corporate-accounts segment of a particular geography and yet another PAM in the SMS&P segment in the same geography. Each PAM is responsible for promoting the partner in its respective business unit and in the field organization. Not every managed partner has multiple PAMs but many do because they work in various product segments and their projects and revenue streams cut across various business units. The PAM is not part of the opportunity cycle but gets involved by many different Microsoft sales processes and is charged with determining which partner is best to work with in a particular product segment or geography. Traditionally, PAMs also have the role of recruiting partners if there are unmet needs and gaps in specific segments or geographic areas. And PAMs spread the word within Microsoft about their managed partners, referring them to other field and corporate teams. So the PAM is a functional clearinghouse of information on partners and the best internal advocate a Microsoft partner can have. Prudent partners leverage their PAM relationships to secure introductions to other Microsoft teams depending on their professional focus. As discussed in Chapters Four, Five and Six, a managed partner's positioning vis-à-vis its PAM depends on the objectives of that partner. But securing a PAM—which is equivalent to becoming a managed partner—is achieved essentially for one reason only: advancing Microsoft's business goals.

Managed partners achieve that status by differentiating themselves from the majority of other Microsoft partners. They do so by building relationships with the right Microsoft personnel and by collaborating with them to advance their mutual objectives. This means that the managed partner leverages its relationships in the Microsoft field, and increasingly at Microsoft corporate, with foresight: the managed partner must understand how the field personnel are measured and compensated, what their challenges and limitations are and what they need to succeed at Microsoft. Some partners make it a point to find out the priorities of their district's General Manager's Scorecard, or what kind of deals a field salesperson needs to achieve their management by objective (MBO) status.

Since *Microsoft is a relationship-motivated company*, the managed partner works to build relationships with the right Microsoft personnel. In the manner of the most loyal Microsoft personnel, managed partners must work hard to demonstrate their loyalty, dedication and undivided attention to Microsoft. Loyalty is rewarded. The managed partner views the world as Microsoft does, concentrating on being *customer-focused* and *product-centric* and driving results that matter to Microsoft. In this way, managed partners should build their firms' culture to mirror that of Microsoft. It is the managed partners, after all, that sail closest amidship to Microsoft, that ride the biggest waves of revenue-generation opportunity in its wake. Your firm can, too. Microsoft works with both managed and unmanaged partners, but prefers to work with managed partners because that is where the rewards are greatest and the risks are fewest for both Microsoft and its partners.

What Microsoft Wants from Partners

Clearly, Microsoft expects a certain level of performance from its partners. Its new partner program stratifies the partners into three tiers, each with its own set of acronyms, expectations and rewards. The stated paybacks for each tier of partnership are minimal relative to their potential, just as there are minimal requirements for being and remaining in the partner program.

Microsoft expects three qualities of its partners—loyalty, perseverance and results—that cannot be measured by the partner point system. But they are essential to Microsoft's culture and, therefore, to success in partnering with the company.

Generally speaking, though, what does Microsoft really expect of its partners? The answer boils down to three important qualities: loyalty, perseverance and results. Those qualities cannot be effectively measured by the partner point system, yet they are essential in Microsoft's culture and to partnering success with the company.

From ISVs, Microsoft seeks certifiable add-ons and complementary solutions for Microsoft's products and platforms. It favors ISV products that enhance and extend the Windows platform in compelling ways. It also expects quality of implementation in the form of Windows certifications and customer support for those certified products. It is important, for instance, for ISVs to have updated drivers and applications ready at the time of launch of a Windows update or upgrade. And Microsoft will not look favorably on equivocations or inexplicable delays in fulfilling those obligations of partnership. Microsoft was not too pleased with ISVs that failed to produce compatible drivers to ensure product compatibility with Windows XP Service Pack 2, which delayed corporate deployment for several months because of application crashes and incompatibilities. Nor will Microsoft exercise much patience for ISVs that also craft technical solutions for Linux and other competitive platforms such as IBM's WebSphere in derogation of Microsoft timelines and priorities.

Similarly, from services firms, the company expects a Microsoft-centric operating model. Microsoft will not work favorably with its services-firm partners who actively support its competitors. Systems-integration and custom application-development firms that provide Linux, Oracle, Novell or IBM solutions in addition to those based on Microsoft platforms and products will likely not thrive in the new partner program regardless of the number of points they earn. Microsoft is investing heavily to convert services partners from competitive platforms such as NetWare and UNIX into dedicated partners loyal to "the Microsoft Way." Additionally, many services partners maintain that the cross-platform services business model is inappropriate since many customers have already made their decision about which platform to embrace. This is a baseline at Avanade, the premier Microsoft systems integration partner co-founded by Microsoft and Accenture, which is dedicated purely to Microsoft technologies.

Among OEM resellers, Microsoft has a dwindling number of Microsoft-only partners. HP and Dell, for example, have been constrained by market demand for Linux and competitive pressure, most notably the need to keep up with big Linux supporter IBM. Among resellers and training firms, Microsoft cannot reasonably expect a Microsoft-only model but it is motivated to compete for the hearts and minds of partners who are evaluating open source technologies. The company's legal problems in the US, EU and Japan frustrate Microsoft's efforts to push reseller partners to sell only Microsoft platforms and applications. Some systems integrators and developers have opted to support Linux, after all. But Microsoft has proven that it can and will leverage reseller relationships to gain more market share in non-traditional Microsoft spaces, including server products, mobile devices, Smartphones and the like. Microsoft is increasingly moving into such Microsoft-offered hardware alternatives powered by its software technologies, which requires partnerships with hardware and appliance vendors. Generally speaking, Microsoft is encouraging its resellers, OEMs and distributors down a similar program path as well as its ISVs and services firms, including a greater push for specialization and meeting the distinct needs of vertical markets.

The Rewards of Partnering with Microsoft

Microsoft has specified a base level of minimum rewards for partners in exchange for their participation and investment in the partner program. But the real and most substantial rewards, of course, are not made public; they are quietly reserved for managed partners. They include, of course, collaborative marketing, funding, early access to new technologies and product roadmaps, referrals and collaborative execution with Microsoft field personnel in a trusted, enduring relationship. Therein lies the opportunity for partners to sail—with Microsoft's backing and credibility—into new markets, geographical and vertical, on a global basis. Responsible firms must answer whether these potentially substantial rewards are worth the risks of partnering with Microsoft. The risks are in fact pervasive and unmitigated by the new partner program. But managed partners, no doubt, enjoy the greatest rewards and the fewest risks when partnering with Microsoft vis-à-vis its competitors.

The Risks of Partnering with Microsoft

For partners, the risks are implicit in the myths outlined in Chapter One. ISVs have reasonable cause for concern that Microsoft will co-opt their products or integrate their functionality into its own products or platforms. For instance, Microsoft's decision to integrate Windows Media Player into Windows hurt ISVs such as Real Networks, and its decision to sell anti-virus solutions and services is similarly concerning for Symantec and McAfee among others. Microsoft will arguably integrate into Windows almost any services that can extend its empire. The intent is not to crush third-party ISVs but, rather, to sell as much software as possible to satisfied customers. ISVs also worry that Microsoft's product certification tests will measure the quality of their products incompletely or inappropriately.

Services firms have reasonable cause for concern that Microsoft will change its services partnering model again or that, in seeking to administer the partner program, Microsoft's product support and development groups may suffer.

Reseller risks are limited to Microsoft's unclear program requirements, or that Microsoft will take all of its software licensing direct to the market. They also express concern about Microsoft's pulling back on its as-yet untested scope of hardware/software combination products.

All partners have reasonable cause for concern that Microsoft will be unable or unwilling to implement its new partner program effectively. Microsoft may fail in its down-market thrust—where IBM and various Linux distributions have already experienced setbacks—and a retrenching of the strategy may ensue to the detriment of promising advances in tighter collaboration with its partners.

For Microsoft, there are pronounced risks, as well. These include concerns that the channel will push Microsoft-competitive products, thus diluting the impact of its partner program and harming Microsoft's market image; that partners will remain static in their respective tiers, not pursuing the upward mobility that Microsoft intends; and that the channel will not be able to deliver solutions as Microsoft expects and Microsoft will have to staff up and incur higher-than-desired overhead, especially in the US, to supply the defect. In general, and to repeat, Microsoft's perceived risks are the undoing of what the company expect of its partners: loyalty, perseverance and results.

The Bottomline on Partnering with Microsoft

As in any joint venture, it is imperative to look deeply into the soul of your partner to understand its nature before engaging it. It is also wise to stay alert while on board, especially on a dynamic ship such as the SS Microsoft, which often shifts without warning. Partners need to know with whom they are partnering in order to partner effectively. And it is better to partner according to the established culture and known strategic trajectory of a company than to rely on its potentially transient partner programs.

As in any partnership with a far bigger player, one must recognize not only the playing field but also master and heed the rules of the game. Partnering with Microsoft is a game and Microsoft defines the rules. One must know the rules and play by them in order to win. There are certain principles of the Microsoft-partnering game, which is the subject of the next chapter.

Chapter 3

Principles of Successful Partnering with Microsoft

Football—or soccer, as it is called in the US—is the most commonly played team sport in the world. The essential principle of this team sport is to keep the ball moving and away from your goal, and help your team get the ball into the opposing team's goal. It is a fast-paced sport with a focus on teamwork and clear objectives for each team subject to distinct rules of play.

Successful partnership with Microsoft corresponds to many of the principles of football. These include:

- constant, fluid action to achieve goals;

- definite positioning of players on the field, some forward and some rearward;

- variability of player quality, but all players are very committed to victory;

- established rules and regulations for playing and winning the game;

- intense, chaotic interplay proximate to each goal, with players scrambling for control over the ball; and

- potential for all team members to claim glory, whether they are on the field or on the sidelines.

Because partnering is a game whose rules are set by Microsoft, Microsoft defines the playbook, determines the strategies, drives the action, and keeps score. In order to play and win, then, partners must know Microsoft intimately, and understand and heed the rules of the game. As in football, there is opportunity for all partners to play.

The rules of the game can and do change. But the principles of successful partnering with Microsoft do not change since they emanate from Microsoft's culture and organization, which you must understand in order to engage in business with the company. Chapter Two explains the core facets of Microsoft's culture. The present chapter explains the general and practical principles of successful partnering with Microsoft.

Like Microsoft, You Must Be Product-Centric

We have explained Microsoft's strategic and organizational dynamism in depth. Historically there has been and continues to be constant reassignment of field representatives who move from one job to another. This, we have seen, is both a challenge and an opportunity for Microsoft partners. It is a challenge because it is a very relationship-driven company and partners thus need to maintain continuity of relationships with Microsoft field personnel. On the other hand, it is also an opportunity since outgoing personnel with whom partners have relationships move on to other positions that can lead to other business opportunities, and also form new relationships with personnel that move into those positions. Given the constant personnel changes, an abiding and critical challenge for partners is to keep Microsoft field personnel informed and educated about their competencies and value to Microsoft.

Compounding that challenge is the fluctuation of customer accounts that accompany these personnel changes. Partners often find, for example, their new field representatives assigned to different accounts than their predecessors. And Microsoft's partners must go along for the ride. Fortunately, such personnel changes have generally been seasonal, occurring in July of any given year—the start of Microsoft's fiscal-year cycle—so the randomness of the changes in personnel and customer accounts is mitigated by their regular timing. The imperative for partners, then, is to develop appropriate messaging for Microsoft and to communicate it consistently to the company's representatives, new and old, with whom partners deal.

Of equal importance is the need to develop and sustain multiple connection points within the company based on appropriate messaging, consistently delivered, in order to build a network within Microsoft of sympathetic representatives who clearly grasp your firm's value in the partner ecosystem. This is particularly important due to the potential change in accounts that accompanies the personnel changes. Partners often find themselves too cozy with one set of Microsoft field representatives and in various customer accounts - only to have both changed at a moment's notice. Then they must re-establish that comfort level by rebuilding their relationships and their perceived value with their new Microsoft representatives. It is important for partners to view this as a predictable imperative in partnering with Microsoft.

Given the extent of organizational change at Microsoft, one might think that the core elements change too much to be predictable. One is reminded of the early Greek philosopher Heraclitus' description of cosmic flux: "one cannot step twice in the same river" because new water is constantly moving down river and it changes the composition, the very identity of the river itself. "All things are flowing," all is in flux, there is no predictability.

While Microsoft's dynamism invokes the same dilemma, there is predictability in the organization since it is rooted in the company's culture. In spite of annual organizational changes, the culture, the core aspects and elements of the company, rarely change. Microsoft's restructuring of its organization into the seven business units was indeed a major change, but the last significant change since 2002. And it was a decision grounded in market and corporate realities, and Microsoft's own cultural drivers. Even broad change such as this can be understood in terms of Microsoft's evolving culture. And it is focused on driving Microsoft's products to market. This is the essence of Microsoft's strategic intent and, while Microsoft's strategy may change, its strategic intent never changes because it is also rooted in Microsoft's culture. Microsoft is a product-centric company and all changes and reorganizations, particularly its most recent one in 2001, are based on its product-centric strategies. The Information Worker business unit, for instance, was established to pave the way for the creation of an Office system or family of products working in concert with the company's overarching desktop-to-data center integration strategy.

The point is that one must understand Microsoft's culture, strategy and organization in order to partner most effectively, rather than in a disorganized or *ad hoc* fashion. You must know what is strategically important to Microsoft in any given fiscal year or period thereof. You must also know the organization's major components— the leadership and groupings of personnel—and their functions as well as their interrelationships—from corporate out to the field level.

You must also master Microsoft's "alphabet soup," that is, its widely used acronyms and terms that relate specifically to the Microsoft business. These change more often than the organizational functions, but they usually refer to the same categories albeit in different terms. For instance, today's GTMs are yesterday's market initiatives. Keeping up with Microsoft's organizational and semantic changes enables your organization to speak Microsoft's language to the right Microsoft personnel. This is exceedingly important! For it conveys to your Microsoft representative the depth of your understanding about how the company operates, its culture, and the depth of your commitment to the firm as an extension of its sales force. For example, some Microsoft partners will speak with their field representatives about "knowledge workers"—a commonly used IT industry term—when they should be referring to the Microsoft-coined "information worker" designation. The distinction may appear on its face innocuous but it is revealing: the former, for instance, refers in the minds of Microsoft employees to front-end desktop user productivity (Office product functions), while the latter refers to back-end architecture (search and content management as in SharePoint functions), which are more urgent in Microsoft's current strategy. Driving sales of information-worker products is more important to Microsoft than selling licensed instances of Office. And information worker is indeed a partner competency. Any Microsoft partner that confuses the terminology will either be misunderstood or, worse, characterized by Microsoft personnel as not invested enough to partner successfully with the company. In either case, such a partner runs the risk of having its relationship with Microsoft marginalized because of a simple communication issue that reflects ignorance.

Knowing Microsoft's business language is another metric that relays a partner's alignment—or lack thereof—with Microsoft. The importance of this is noted by several successful partners whose firms are the subject of case studies in this book. When engaging with Microsoft as a subcontractor on a project, for example, your personnel ought to be able to answer Microsoft precisely when asked to rate the opportunity. If your sales person roughly sizes up one customer prospect at 60%, when in Microsoft's parlance the status ought to be conveyed at 80%, there is obviously a language gap that can translate into business problems. Microsoft assigns very specific ratings to customer opportunities in the field and they expect partners to speak the same language.

There are ways that partners can learn Microsoft's business language. Gaining access to the Microsoft 101 indoctrination course for new employees is a good start. Another way to become fluent in Microsoft sales terminology is to attend the Solutions Selling course specifically for Microsoft sales and field personnel. Take one of your close Microsoft contacts out to dinner and tactfully extricate some of the finer points of substance that may not be readily available to most partners. Consider such networking for resources a key, or cultural norm, that benefits you and informs Microsoft of your efforts to partner successfully with the company.

Microsoft's organization and its nomenclature revolve around what is near and dear to its cultural heart: its products. The major product groupings are well-defined, intact, and the organization is built around developing and driving them to market with partners. Who plays what role and what they are called changes, but the company—in keeping with its core culture—is centered on its products. Naturally, knowing Microsoft's products—how they work, how they interoperate, how to develop and sell them—from the perspective of your expertise, or Microsoft competencies, will be of enormous help to you in navigating such a fluid organization despite its occasional strategic shifts and shifting terminology. Like Microsoft, successful partners center their messaging and activities on the products and platforms in accord with their expertise, and speak the same language as Microsoft to help the company drive sales. And the successful partner does so with a focused view on Microsoft's customers, the second pillar of its cultural heart. Remember, Microsoft is product-centric and customer-focused. You must be, too.

Like Microsoft, You Must Be Customer-Focused

Underlying Microsoft's historically routine reassignment of employees is an important principle: Microsoft wants to own the relationship with its customers. And Microsoft's organizational changes are intended to position the company increasingly closer to its customers with the motive of driving ever-more product sales. This requires that partners master a difficult skill set captured in the phrase "back-seat driving," In the movie, *Driving Miss Daisy,* Miss Daisy's relationship with her chauffeur becomes more complicated as they grow older and the back-seat driving consequently fosters tensions that draw the two closer together. Their experience echoes the tensions and complementarities in new Microsoft field representatives' getting acclimated to their positions with their assigned partners' help. Microsoft obviously wants to do the best it can for its customers and its partners, but its personnel must retain ownership of their accounts.

There are various techniques that can be used to overcome the back-seat driving challenge: one can bark out directions, gently guide or coax, or simply go along for the ride and caution the navigator to obvious pitfalls and dangers. Ideally, Microsoft partners will position themselves to be thought leaders in any given technical or market area, and as the go-to firm in specific instances, should supply answers on how best to navigate a situation. Partners that employ such graceful tactics properly foster the Microsoft account teams' view of them as trusted advisors and extensions of the company itself. Trusted advisors display a strong ability to work with Microsoft personnel, speak Microsoft's product and sales language, and are committed to achieving the best customer relationships.

Establishing and maintaining that trust is of paramount importance. This does not mean that partners must accede to the Microsoft field team's leadership and remain in the back seat in all cases. There have been instances in which the most practical and effective course for partners is to go directly to the customer, leading Microsoft from the rear, so to speak. Internosis, a Microsoft Gold Partner heavily entrenched in Microsoft's government accounts, has taken this approach at times due to the trust it has established with government customers, including agencies such as the US Department of Defense that are increasingly using Linux and open–source solutions. If the Microsoft field team recognizes that the partner is doing what is best for the customer, for Microsoft and for itself, any tensions that arise will be overcome. Such a delicate situation warrants extensive communications with Microsoft and an emphasis on building trust in the relationship around shared goals and concerted action.

One thing to be wary of is the confusion and concern a customer experiences when it hires Microsoft, which then brings in a services partner and backs off of the account. It is often unclear to enterprise clients whether Microsoft fully sanctions the partner and whether the partner speaks and acts on Microsoft's behalf or on its own. Microsoft field personnel are cautious to avoid this, and partners must be, as well. In almost all instances, corporate customers want straightforward solutions to problems. They must be comfortable that these solutions are designed by Microsoft and delivered by partners in coordinated, cooperative execution. That is, they must view Microsoft and its partners as one team, two sides of the same coin.

Successful partners help Microsoft field personnel steer customers to this realization, and help the customer understand the supporting role of the partner vis-à-vis the Microsoft field team in addressing the customer need. This is back-seat driving *par excellence* because, while the Microsoft field team is accountable for the relationship with the customer, the partner can play a key role in communicating how Microsoft and its partners go to market together to deliver integrated products and services. It need not get muddled. It behooves the partner to help both the Microsoft field team and the corporate customer make the connection and see the value that is intended, designed and delivered by Microsoft in conjunction with its partner.

But whom do you approach at Microsoft? You know that Microsoft is a worldwide giant. It extends globally and aligns locally. So your partnership with Microsoft must usually align first at the field level — and you must work to extend your reach within Microsoft from the field to the corporate product and marketing teams. This means that you must master relationships with your Microsoft field personnel and align your messaging with the corporate go-to-market (GTM) initiatives that they adopt. That is, if Microsoft corporate mandates a push, for example, of Office products but your local Microsoft organization does not, then your marketing Office—true to corporate—will avail you next to nothing in the field.

Aligning your messaging and activity with your field organization is essential to your success in partnering with Microsoft. Still, it is also essential that you understand Microsoft corporate GTM strategy, and drill down with your field representatives on what they deem important to their success so that you can work with them to help them succeed. The best mechanism for this is to spend time with Microsoft corporate personnel in the July timeframe—at the worldwide partner conference—to understand the overall strategy for the fiscal year, and to work with your field organization shortly thereafter to determine the GTMs that they plan to pursue. This also enables you to learn about any organizational changes that will help you develop your messaging and co-marketing strategy with field personnel.

Your success in partnering with Microsoft depends on your relationships in the field. And field personnel are your best conduit to establish corporate relationships in product groups and the marketing organization. Most importantly, field personnel own customer relationships. You want Microsoft customers to become yours, as well.

Echoing another principle explained in Chapter Two, Microsoft believes that customer satisfaction comes first, before partner satisfaction. Microsoft personnel are measured on CPE, not PCE. So Microsoft partners must align their interests and their messaging with Microsoft along the same lines. That is, partners must consistently and clearly communicate as well as demonstrate that their objective is to achieve the highest possible customer satisfaction with Microsoft. The occasional argument heard from partners is that that they should be of primary concern to Microsoft—not the customer. This is both unrealistic and prejudicial to the partners' own interests. Like Microsoft, its partners must be focused on achieving the highest customer satisfaction possible. And they must be able to communicate this focus, or commitment, to Microsoft itself.

Sometimes things go wrong—the software does not work, the solution is unstable or a server crash forfeits data. Partners should know what resources are available to them. There are well-defined and often complex escalation paths and funds available to partners to help Microsoft's customers achieve satisfaction. For example, Microsoft established a "Make It Right" Fund from which customers can be reimbursed for discontinued software that they purchased or to settle customer disputes without the red tape of upstream managerial approvals. The Make It Right Fund is managed by an independent group within Microsoft, and corporate management keeps constant tabs on customer complaints and expenditures from the fund.

Microsoft also has a formal customer complaint system, which is managed by another independent group in the company. This system provides for rapid escalation within Microsoft of customer problems that warrant rapid and decisive resolution. From these structures you can infer that customer satisfaction comes first at Microsoft because there are no similar mechanisms for reporting and resolving partner disputes. Always remember: you are playing Microsoft's game and the company sets the rules of engagement. These rules provide a structure for partners just as Microsoft structures itself to drive products to customers and to achieve high customer satisfaction with its products and services. This structured approach to customers and partners points to the third broad principle of partnering with Microsoft.

Drive! Or You Will Be Driven by Microsoft

Microsoft views customer satisfaction with a sense of urgency and of primary importance. This is not to suggest that Microsoft views its partners as secondarily important. Rather, partners are viewed as an extension of the Microsoft organization and assessed in terms of their fitness with Microsoft products and the satisfaction of customers with the partners' products and/or services.

There are programmatic, occasionally painful mechanisms for partners to demonstrate the success of their services and solutions by listing customer references. Just as Microsoft holds itself accountable for customer satisfaction, it also puts partners on the hook to prove their value to customers. And if partners cannot satisfactorily and consistently offer favorable customer references, Microsoft has in place follow-on mechanisms to help partners overcome their problems or to take remedial action in the relationship.

Successful partners understand that their work with Microsoft—in the field, at the corporate level—is structured around enhancing and selling Microsoft products and Microsoft-driven solutions to satisfied customers. This is a cultural norm that helps one find the proper course when navigating Microsoft amidst its dynamic evolution. In other words, if you know that Microsoft's product-centrism and customer focus are constant, and indicative of cultural norms, you can make sense of and anticipate how organizational and nomenclature changes might impact your partnership, indeed, your business.

Another approach that will help you get ahead of the curve is to help Microsoft field personnel enhance their product pitches and customer relations. Doing so helps them succeed—which is essential in your role as a Microsoft partner—and may well earn you a grateful advocate in the organization who will move into other roles in the organization, higher up the corporate ladder.

It is better to drive than to be driven. Successful partners understand and engage Microsoft on this principle. Partners that master Microsoft's culture and its paramount mission—to sell progressively higher value-added products and deliver them effectively and efficiently—are embraced by Microsoft. This partnering approach fosters symbiosis—literally, living and breathing together—singularly focused on a common goal and real results. Talk is cheap. Since Microsoft is an organization that highly prizes results, partners must consistently deliver results that serve as a predictor and a measure of partnering success.

Proactive and consistent contribution to Microsoft's bottomline is what typically differentiates a mediocre partner from a successful one. To contribute effectively, you should:

- consistently help Microsoft sell product (eye on the ball, ball into the goal);

- play where the market action is most intense (field-level strategy);

- navigate the field (organization) and work dynamically within it (teamwork); and

- focus on efficiency (lower cost of sales) and efficacy (build co-branding, satisfy customers).

As intimated, these characteristics of successful partnering with Microsoft are not dissimilar from the principles of football. Partners must realize that successful partnerships with Microsoft are achieved by knowing the rules and nurturing a "spirit" and passion to win the game in conjunction with Microsoft.

Partners that master these principles find themselves in the driver's seat in their partnership with the company because they have earned Microsoft's respect as trusted advisors in the field and market. These are practical principles that have been tested and approved by many successful ISVs, services firms and resellers. The following firms have found themselves in a driving capacity, rather than a back-seat role, as a result of mastering these principles. Consider the following:

- Citrix, a global ISV–partner, which leveraged the highly valued brands of Microsoft and IBM to develop a market niche for multi-user functionality common in UNIX that Microsoft included, for a fee, in subsequent operating systems (see the Citrix case study in Chapter Four);

- Accenture, a global systems integrator and Microsoft partner, which leveraged Microsoft's brand to expand its project-based service offerings to deliver far more services and created a profitable joint services venture with Microsoft called Avanade; or

- Intel, a global OEM partner, whose aggressive co-development and joint-marketing with Microsoft as the other half of the WIntel alliance is perhaps the epitome of partnering symbiosis between a hardware manufacturer and a software company.

You need not be an iconic global firm to master these partnering principles and succeed in working with Microsoft. Each of the referenced subsequent chapters highlights the tactics of various smaller, local and regional ISVs, services and reseller partners that have succeeded in building and expanding their relationships with Microsoft in order to become trusted advisors and to make more money with Microsoft.

It is essential that you understand what is core to Microsoft's success in order to drive—rather than be driven—as partners. It is a principle that is central to this book. The remainder of this chapter essentially parses our thesis to elucidate practical principles that you, too, can apply as other firms highlighted in this book have done. Our thesis—which we repeat from Chapter One—is simple and practical:

By increasing and working your firm's connections to Microsoft—at various levels and with different groups in the organization, playing to the company's culture and strategy—you will expand the terrain of shared interests between your firm and Microsoft. Doing so will help you enhance market traction and make more money in a trusted partnership through effective co-marketing, efficient channel relationships, assured referrals—joint success in selling your complementary products or services in the United States and, indeed, around the world.

Practical Principles of Partnering with Microsoft

Work and Grow Your Microsoft Connections

In order to partner with Microsoft, you must know Microsoft. Specifically, you must know Microsoft's organization—understand how the organization reflects the company's culture and how its changes mirror Microsoft's strategy; know how the company is structured, and why it is structured as it is; what financial incentives drive each group in the organization, especially the groups your firm will work with at Microsoft—and you must be able to speak Microsoft's language.

The best measure of your understanding of Microsoft's language is your ability to communicate your firm's value to Microsoft employees in a manner that they can grasp immediately, that is, in numbers. You must thus also learn Microsoft's precise language for identifying the status of potential deals. Think of your relationship as a dynamic organism that needs to be fed and nurtured. Strive to build your relationships with your Microsoft colleagues at multiple levels of the organization to gain utmost visibility and respect, and to be perceived as of progressively higher business value to Microsoft. To the extent that all of your Microsoft-facing personnel are communicating this value to Microsoft in a manner that its representatives can understand and appreciate, your firm is on track to be successful. But only if your firm is working with the right Microsoft personnel, within the appropriate corporate-and-field structures and with the proper *modi operandi*.

Know The Microsoft Organization

Successful Microsoft partners invest time regularly to stay up-to-speed with changes in Microsoft's organization. As you will see in the next several chapters, all partners devote significant resources and personnel to ensure that they are constantly apprised of happenings in the company. This, of course, assumes that the partner has a familiarity with the organization and how its massive historical growth is an expression of the company's culture. We explored this cultural and organizational affinity in Chapter Two. In order to appreciate how the organization changes—the shifting of personnel among positions, the mobilizing of various groups in tandem to achieve specific corporate objectives, the upward mobility of rising stars at Microsoft—partners keep their hands on the pulse of Microsoft's strategy. Corporate change at Microsoft—neither random nor centrally planned—is not an elaborate orchestration of people in roles but, in fact, an expression of a systematic response to market conditions and fast-paced technical innovation and development. These are core attributes of Microsoft's culture—market-responsiveness and talent—that account for ongoing organizational changes as well as the overall implementation of Microsoft's strategy.

Microsoft personnel are imbued with these cultural attributes and trained to embrace change—strategic, organizational, tactical—as a requirement of their jobs and recognize its value in realizing the company's mission. New employees are indoctrinated to the corporate culture during Microsoft 101 training at Seattle in their early weeks of employment. Microsoft's people "soak up" the culture, cultivate and nurture it, sustain it and pass it on. This is how the central organization ensures that the culture abides at each of the subsidiaries, in similar respects to how Rome molded the Roman-ness of its colonial outposts. Spend fifteen minutes with three Microsoft employees and you will discern a common and intense personal commitment to maintaining Microsoft's world-class profile and leading market position. There is a distinct energy among its personnel that accounts for the single-mindedness of Microsoft employees, individually and collectively, to drive the company's culture and success. Not all are equally talented, intelligent or capable—but each belongs to an elitist "society," whose aspirations and mores are distinct from all others and that subscribes to a peculiar corporate allegiance that binds the Microsoft assembly close together. This trait is noticeable in partners, too. Although you are technically an "outsider" as a Microsoft partner—a non-employee—you know from Chapter Two that one of the three pillars of Microsoft's culture is its partners (along with its products and its customers). Yet out of a pack of 841,000 other partners in the ecosystem, you need to find a way to stand out. You do that by what you know, whom you know, what you say and how you contribute to the partnership.

Begin developing your inroads into Microsoft in the field. The "field," of course, can mean local, regional or global personnel—anywhere except corporate—but in most circumstances field personnel are in the same locale, the same city or area as your firm. You will know you are an extension of your field office when you are able to talk about Microsoft's field-office structure and the inter-relationships of its personnel using relied-upon company acronyms, which we discuss below. It is important to know Microsoft's acronyms and understand how each group fits in and works together with or separately from others in the field and at corporate. This will, indeed, set you apart from other partners with whom your Microsoft field representatives work. It will also help you to navigate among groups within Microsoft, extending your network and building requisite connection points to be successful at partnering with Microsoft. Note that Microsoft's terminology—its organizational titles, product and initiative nomenclature, its acronyms and market references—change constantly. This is an expression, of course, of the company's dynamism, a restless drive to stay on top of things and an embracing of change as a cultural norm.

In addition, Microsoft's terminology can differ from country to country, from district to district, so—while it is helpful to have as global a perspective as possible on the names and significance of the most important things to Microsoft writ large—you must have a nuanced understanding of what terminology is appropriate to your field organization relative to what will work elsewhere within Microsoft.

Finally, Microsoft's field organizations differ in terms of partner-specific structures and roles. Some, for example, may have only one partner account manager (PAM) servicing all local partners while others may have five PAMs focused, respectively, on account teams. Since "all politics are local," there is no comprehensive corporate guidance or requirement for field organizations. Each Microsoft district or subsidiary can assign its people as it sees fit to achieve its core objectives within the context of all corporate GTMs. For this reason, there is a saying in Microsoft: "if you know one Microsoft district, you know one Microsoft district." No two are alike; each has autonomy and must be approached and understood somewhat uniquely. There has been significant corporate effort expended over the past few years to give the subsidiaries, or "subs," a uniform structure but at this time nothing like that is in place. It is, therefore, essential for partners to grasp the unchanging aspects of Microsoft that account for and guide change itself, and these constancies are of a cultural nature.

A core principle of partnering with Microsoft, therefore, is to know the cultural source from which the company's strategy and organization emanate, and then operationally embrace and extend it. If you do not do this, you may not be as strong a Microsoft partner as you could be and will likely see less business as a result.

Know Their Drivers, Speak Their Language

Successful partners are aware of the performance metrics of Microsoft personnel, especially those who are evaluated on partner pull-through. That is, it is in the interest—professionally and financially—of such Microsoft employees to work with and to advance the cause of Microsoft partners. All field personnel that work with partners are measured—and compensated—on "partner attach," and PAMs are measured on, and rewarded for, "partner assign." The metrics for each of these partner-related activities are the subject of constant refinement within Microsoft, and have recently been expanded to include resellers (ISVs and services firms have historically been the subject of these metrics).

As the Microsoft partner program has developed and matured, so has the internal partner matrix, which has become progressively more specific about how Microsoft field employees are compensated for specific activities relative to partners (eg, subcontracting). What every Microsoft partner should bear in mind is that each Microsoft subsidiary, district, region and country has full discretion in choosing which partners to pull-through, attach and assign. That is why local alignment is so important. Therefore, the key to success for Microsoft partners is to determine what priorities drive Microsoft's local field office or a district office, for example, relative to the company's GTMs and, consequently, their needs of local partners. Once those drivers are understood, partner messaging to each Microsoft office of interest must be developed and communicated so as to align the partner's capabilities with Microsoft's interests.

There are as many drivers as there are corporate groups, subsidiaries, and district offices. Again, it is often said that "if you know one Microsoft district, you know one Microsoft district." This is an important reality to grasp. In spite of the common culture of the outposts, each office is run differently. Nevertheless, there are sets of drivers that can be distilled down to a variety of Microsoft groups and their interests. Consider the following examples.

ISVs and services partners may find fertile partnering contacts within corporate product (and solutions) groups if their timing and approach are appropriate. That is, they must determine these groups' product cycles and gauge their wish lists for applicable add-on products and services. On the latter point, if these groups have a need for a set of services that a services partner has provided in the past or a product add-on that an ISV has finished, a fit is likely if timed appropriately to the product cycle. Once this preliminary investigation is complete and, if it suggests a correspondence of interests between the product/solutions group and the partner, the appropriate person from your firm should make an attempt to set up a meeting with this group's product manager. Note, however, that the people in this role change positions with some regularity so it is advisable to keep tabs on who is in the position by leveraging field (or select corporate) personnel for reconnaissance. If and when you meet with the group's product manager, focus the discussion on your firm's ability to provide the essential service (in the case of SPs) or add-on product (in the case of ISVs) to drive success of the new Microsoft product or solution. Highlight a compelling customer design or implementation or support service most likely as an add-on value extender for the product. Product groups will not release product roadmaps or list features and functionality unless they are assured that the partner is committed to providing support for the lifecycle of the product; in other words, a commitment of five-to-seven years worth of add-on services and support. For ISVs, value-added extensions to Microsoft's products and platforms are almost always welcome, particularly if the ISV has a successful track record of providing similar functionality and features for other Microsoft products. In recent years, Microsoft has been particularly aggressive in recruiting ISVs for its new initiatives such as the ISV .NET Program and Empower, a program that helps startup-ISVs develop their first commercial product. Like Microsoft, ISVs must adopt provisions in order to guard its intellectual property (see Chapter Four for more about this).

Services partners—and ISVs—can and should tap into Microsoft's corporate marketing groups, the central source of funding for all Microsoft-marketing initiatives. Microsoft, after all, is considered among the best marketing machines in the world and is touted for its creativity and openness to new ideas. One Microsoft partner in Atlanta, for example, once convinced Microsoft's central marketing group to launch

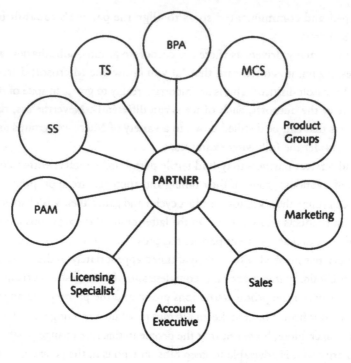

Figure 3.1: Microsoft Connection Points For Various Partners.

a television-advertising campaign in order to boost the company's results. While this convincing required great effort in research and chasing the marketing team, it worked to the benefit of Microsoft and the partner. This is a good example of how to leverage Microsoft marketing's core driver and deliver solid results for both parties by getting the most bang for the buck in advertising.

Services partners—and ISVs—should attend and send all of their Microsoft-facing employees to a Solutions Selling course developed by Microsoft, which defines how Microsoft qualifies and quantifies opportunities in the field, status of negotiations, and all facets of the initiative. Microsoft subsidizes between 60% and 70% of the cost of solutions-selling training for its partners. These courses are important insofar as partners need to use the same sales terminology and practices of the Microsoft field force.

"You learn Microsoft's partner-progress tracking lingo in the Solutions Selling course. For example, if you tell Microsoft you are in zero mode, in Microsoft lingo it means you have no prospects. At 60%, you have a solution that is proposed to a customer. If you have 80%, Microsoft may think you will close the deal but, in Microsoft lingo, it just means that you have a solution that

---

has been validated. Microsoft tracks its partners' sales progress and, at 80%, they call you to see if they can help you close the deal. This helps a lot because customers are skeptical. If you can get Microsoft out to visit them it is a big deal." —Rich Figer, IT Advisor Group (Cincinnati, Ohio)

Field-level drivers vary depending on the particular office and its GTMs. Get the scorecard for the General Manager (see Chapter Five for more about this) that you are aiming to approach and sway. Obviously, account executives and managers are measured on and compensated for Microsoft product sales. There are some key field personnel, however, who are more heavily customer-facing and thus should be informed about any partner's solutions or services. These include:

- Technical Sales (TS) personnel: often called the "show up and throw up" role, technical sales professionals attend customer meetings to demonstrate just about any Microsoft technology the customer might be interested in seeing. These are quick and diverse demonstrations, generally, and the TS makes a quick departure when the demonstration is completed. In larger markets, the TS roles might be filled with specialists—for Exchange and SQL, as an example, or Office and SharePoint—but all TS personnel are knowledgeable and highly respected within Microsoft and by customers, and they are thus capable of swaying sales in the direction desired by the Microsoft account team.

- Solution Sales (SS) experts: this is a more specialized role in Microsoft field offices and it is focused on server-side solutions expertise. Not all markets have solution sales specialists but nearly all have server-side specialists who perform this function. In addition to providing technical demonstrations of solutions, the SS experts are grafted onto account teams in a specialized technical pre-sales capacity, and are essential contacts for ISVs and some services partners whose products or services are based on or implement Microsoft server technologies.

- Account Manager (AM): this is the point person for the account team, who manages from one to 100 customer accounts depending on their size and the broadness and complexity of the market. Ideally partners want to have deep penetration in accounts so that they know them more intimately than the Account Manager. The services partner, for example, that has such account intimacy can play a trusted advisor role to the account manager. But, to be successful, the partner must understand core realities about this position: the AM is subject to a sales quota for each account and must remain intensely focused on software sales. So, for example, if you intend to help the account manager move an Enterprise Agreement forward with an account you will have a very receptive partner but if you are looking for the account manager to expend more cycles for you apart from closing a sale, you may be disappointed.

- Microsoft Consulting Services (MCS) or Microsoft Business Consulting Services (MBCS) personnel: these are, of course, overlay services organizations in Microsoft subsidiary offices that assist account teams to close sales and to provide requisite higher-end services. Yet MCS and MBCS personnel can also serve as evangelists for partner firms within field account teams, so it is important for ISVs and services partners, for example, to have friends in these organizations, too.

Knowing what drives people in these roles—how they are compensated, what their goals are—is essential for Microsoft partners in order to work with Microsoft in the field. Remember, Microsoft's culture is diverse and many people are brought together to form account teams. All of these people, therefore, need to be informed about a partner's product or service in order to make a successful connection. This, of course, depends on the partner's ability to express itself in terms that these Microsoft personnel can understand. The best partners complete Solutions Selling training, master Microsoft's terminology and keep abreast of their acronyms in order to speak their language.

Make Your Messaging Effective

Assuming you understand Microsoft's language and can express your firm's capabilities in a manner that is readily understood by the company's representatives in the field and, as applicable, at corporate, you must develop and implement a marketing plan to convey your firm's message to Microsoft. Your marketing campaign must reflect essential elements of any marketing initiative, including

- *precision, clarity and differentiation:* it must express who you are and what you can do in as accurate and succinct a manner as possible and with crystal clarity, while indicating what makes your firm unique and valuable relative to all of the other firms in the Microsoft ecosystem that work in your space;

- *propriety for your target audience:* it must make sense—be delivered in terms that are understood by and in a context that is important—to your Microsoft counterparts, especially in sales (your TS, SS, AM and MCS colleagues in Microsoft field organizations, for example), and so it must be timely and expressed in terms of what is most important to them (sales and accounts, historical delivery of results, etc.); and;

- *refined:* you will get solicited and unsolicited feedback on your messaging from Microsoft, and you should take it to heart in tweaking your message to Microsoft as warranted in order to keep it targeted and up-to-date relative to current success and work in progress with Microsoft.

A classic example of such a marketing campaign is a services partner that decides to sell Microsoft CRM-related services in any given district (assuming that the district is pushing CRM-related products and services). The firm will assess Microsoft's CRM marketing and develop its own messaging in a complementary manner. In order to deliver its message, the firm will identify the relevant personnel in the field sales as well as the field and corporate marketing groups that work with the CRM solution group. It will then go to the relevant Microsoft field personnel, deliver its message and persuade them why they should steer CRM services business its way. Stressing the message that CRM-related solutions drive SQL and Exchange sales, the firm works with both these product groups and with account teams to analyze their customer base and determine which Microsoft customers in the district would be likely targets. This enables the services partner to work alongside Microsoft account teams to help open doors for the company at specific customers. In so doing, the CRM services partner engages Microsoft in the market and, together, they engage customers. Once the marketing campaign is underway—first to Microsoft, then with Microsoft in the market—the services partner will refine its messaging on a quarterly basis at minimum. It will also use seminars, webinars, and other sales events to deliver its message to market with Microsoft, incorporating feedback from both its internal and Microsoft's sales teams and from the market. Microsoft subsidizes some of the core costs of these seminars for many partners.

Aristotle said "a good beginning is half the whole." First impressions are important. Before engaging Microsoft on any level, the Microsoft partner must first master its core competency and gain necessary certifications to convince Microsoft that it can deliver what it promises. The right messaging to reflect what it can deliver follows next. As part of its preparatory work, a partner must also understand its target market, the needs of this market and the relative presence of Microsoft technologies vis-à-vis competitors (this pertains to knowing the customer universe, generally and particularly). It must also develop a corporate strategy and position itself to achieve it through stratified and measurable goals and objectives. And it must orchestrate its personnel and their work to pursue and accomplish the firm's partnering objectives. In other words, the first step in corporate success—and in partnership with Microsoft—is rudimentary business analysis and focused execution. The successful Microsoft partner understands that these are essential first steps. For partnership with Microsoft is a means to an end—corporate success—and not an end in itself, which is a vital principle for Microsoft partners to understand. While a successful Microsoft partner positions itself to be perceived as of utmost service to Microsoft, the firm recognizes that its own interests are paramount and that its Microsoft relationships and collaboration with the company will help the firm advance its own cause. We have worked with many firms, whether Microsoft partners or not, in order to help them realize their own strategy and how best to position themselves in the market and for successful partnership with Microsoft. Failure to heed these fundamental principles of business is surprisingly pervasive and often destructive. In order to drive the partnership forward, the partnering firm must be strong, and its strength is best expressed in the soundness of its own corporate strategy.

Put more plainly: you must know your firm and you must know Microsoft in order to realize a vibrant partnership, and mutual prosperity. Essential to that partnership is the complementarity of your firm's products and services with Microsoft and its products. Of course, the opposite of complementarity in this context is competitiveness, and you must avoid the perception by Microsoft of your products' or services' competitiveness with Microsoft's products or initiatives. But complementarity is more than mere non-competitiveness. It is also the ground for alignment between your firm and Microsoft, organizationally and strategically. If there is a poor fit between your firm's culture or people and Microsoft's, the partnership will be difficult to establish and sustain. If your firm's strategy is contrary to or obstructive of Microsoft's strategy, it is better not to attempt partnership with Microsoft because you will run the risk of being perceived as competitive and thus your aspirations may be foiled by your would-be partner. If your firm sells a product that either competes with a Microsoft product or is tightly aligned with a Microsoft competitor's product, it is best, of course, not to dwell on this product or to minimize its importance to your firm when conducting any discussions with Microsoft about partnership; it may even be best not to partner with Microsoft in this circumstance as it will see through any attempt on your part to minimize the potential downside of Microsoft's partnering with you when you do essentially compete with the company. In short, your firm's messaging reflects your firm itself. And your firm may be distilled to your organization, your culture, your products and/or services and your strategy—just as you understand Microsoft in terms of these core elements. You need to attend to these fundamental realities in order to discern if partnering with Microsoft will help your firm advance its cause or, in fact, obstruct the partnership and even detract from your corporate success.

If partnering with Microsoft will help your firm succeed in its strategy, you need to be able to express how Microsoft will benefit from the partnership. And, to repeat, this must be in terms that your Microsoft counterparts will understand. Specifically, heed the following principles of messaging to Microsoft:

- *keep your messaging simple:* state who you are and what you do (eg, "we are a New York Metro-focused certified partner with competencies in information-worker and business-intelligence solutions"), what you have done for Microsoft lately (eg, "we have driven US$10 million in Exchange and SQL sales in the past year, and have brought Microsoft into three major accounts in the past five months and we have the highest customer satisfaction ratings in our sector within the district") and what you seek from Microsoft (eg, "we are the best fit around for Microsoft accounts that need SharePoint, Exchange and SQL services, as well as

Office and "back-office" integrated solutions, and want to work with you to boost your sales and our services in those accounts");

- *align your messaging with your field office's priorities:* if Microsoft corporate is pushing what you deliver but your field office is not, do not waste your time unless you can spin your competencies and results in a manner that makes sense to and is important for your field–office counterparts;

- *disseminate your message among as many Microsoft personnel as possible:* communicate with technical and solutions sales personnel and account managers in the field, as well as their MCS colleagues where applicable, and extend your messaging to corporate groups, as well, in product and solutions groups and marketing teams; and

- *do not sway from your message:* remember, Microsoft personnel are short on time and high on focus so do not muddy the waters of their understanding of your firm with shifted messages—*do not* change your message to fit any occasion and *do not try* to be all things to all people—and avail yourself of every opportunity to get your consistent message across to Microsoft—*do* repeat your message as often as you can so that all Microsoft employees in the field office know what you do as soon as they see you.

There is a great deal of corporate discipline that goes into crafting and delivering a compelling message to Microsoft. And this discipline is first applied to defining the fundamentals of your firm in order that your partnership with Microsoft is for the right reasons and has the right objectives, which you define and achieve.

If your firm is strong in your field office as a partner, you have two opportunities to go either deep or wide with and within Microsoft. That is, you have two possible strategies for leveraging your Microsoft field office for your firm's benefit: first, you can expand geographically through corporate's sponsorship of your expertise in a competency into other Microsoft field offices, potentially worldwide; second, you can deepen your expertise in the competency to such an extent that Microsoft corporate sponsors you as its best-in-class partner in specific accounts in various field offices.

Give Your Firm One Voice To Microsoft

In addition to defining your corporate strategy and orchestrating your resources— human and capital—to realize that goal, and along with reflecting what you can do with and for Microsoft to help your firm and the company succeed, you must ensure that your firm's personnel speak as if with one voice to Microsoft in delivering your partnering message. This entails educating your firm's personnel on your corporate mission and your particular purpose in partnering with Microsoft.

Train your people—at all levels—on your Microsoft messaging just as you would on the intricacies of your products' or services' capabilities and your target market's need for them. You never know whom your people will meet or talk with and you need to ensure that, if they encounter Microsoft personnel at work or during off hours they will know what to say, univocally, so that your message is consistently delivered to Microsoft at all available opportunities.

Just as the quality of your firm's products or services and your firm's ability to market and sell them are a means to your firm's end—success—so, too, is the vibrancy of your relationship with Microsoft. And your messaging to Microsoft is a core component of your partnership with the company. Ensuring that your people—no matter what their job function or their interaction with Microsoft—can express to any Microsoft employee that they happen to meet what your firm is all about and what it can do for Microsoft is a top priority for successful Microsoft partners. So educate, educate and educate again your firm's employees on your Microsoft messaging and, underlying it, your firm's overall corporate strategy and its success measures.

Work Within Microsoft's Structure

The stakes in partnering with Microsoft are higher today than ever before given the size and complexity of the Microsoft ecosystem. At 841,000 Microsoft partners, the ecosystem is likely to increase rather than decrease in size. Its complexity is a function of Microsoft's geographical expansion and vertical penetration, and of its continuing evolution of products. Set aside the ecosystem's complexity, though, and consider the competition-for-mindshare aspect of partnership with Microsoft from a quantitative basis in order to appreciate the difficulty of getting Microsoft's attention. Microsoft's 841,000 partners must get the attention of an important subset of the company's 55,000 employees—that is, 15 partners for every employee—where the relevant subset is employees who have market- or customer-facing responsibilities, of whom there are, for the sake of argument, 25,000—that is, 34 partners for every employee. In any given field office, the ratio could be higher or slightly lower—it is almost always higher for relevant employees in corporate product, solutions or marketing groups—and the difficulty of getting their attention is compounded by the fact that their customers come before partners. Field employees can focus on either a handful of large accounts, which has its own complexity, or many accounts, which is complex in other ways. And their work in servicing customers and leveraging partners to gain traction in accounts means that their available time is *now*, and the intensity of their focus is high. In such situations, good relationships with partners—where there is comic relief and constructive advances to help Microsoft's field employees advance on their objectives—are at a premium for Microsoft field employees.

This is especially the case today when, despite the explosion in the number of field-based partners, the organizational emphasis at Microsoft is to be "thin on the ground." So not only is there limited timing opportunities to deliver your message to Microsoft employees and to work with them, but there are also fewer of these employees to get in front of and their work demands are such that partnering, while important, is a means to their end, software sales to satisfied customers.

So how does the successful Microsoft partner succeed in its focused messaging and collaborative work with Microsoft given the limited and constrained counterparts in the company? The answer is simply to work primarily within the structure—work the ecosystem at all possible moments—and secondarily to develop solid relationships with Microsoft employees.

The former initiative is facilitated by Microsoft's partner-focused model as expressed in the three partner-relevant "effects" of the model itself:

- *Direct MCS Effect:* it was often the case historically that MCS was not available when a services partner wanted MCS assistance on a client project or that MCS would or at least could compete for client engagements with Microsoft services partners; the effect of the current ecosystem is that MCS has an incentive to cooperate with services partners in that its measured success is tied to its partners' success, and MCS cannot enter a client engagement without jumping over some serious internal hurdles without partners.

- *Account Team Effect:* partners are today engaged in every aspect of an account team's work with customers—from licensing through deployment—by virtue of the account teams' measured success in partner assign and partner attach; that is, "without a partner" assigned or attached to a customer account, the Microsoft mantra is that "it is not a solution." This is so despite the arduous work and collaborative complexity of a partner's engaging Microsoft account teams on joint selling and delivery of solutions.

- *Product Team Effect:* product teams can no longer rely on MCS to create and implement solutions for markets, geographical or vertical, so they mitigate their exposure in needed solutions by working with and through Microsoft partners, on a measured-success basis, which is a departure from historical norms for their operation.

These three effects, which provide incentives for prominent groupings within Microsoft to engage and collaborate with partners, point to these groups' needs (they need partners to do their work and to get compensated) and partners' opportunities (partners that work within this structure will be in a position to succeed as partners). Viewed cynically, the current ecosystem entails Microsoft's partners assuming a great deal of the work that was traditionally done by Microsoft and Microsoft's still reaping many of the rewards of the work. But it is inappropriate to view it thus because the ecosystem provides ample rewards for Microsoft partners that work within the structure. In addition, the ecosystem affords partners the opportunity to reduce their cost of sales by disseminating information about their products and services throughout Microsoft, which can drive Microsoft's marketing of their firms and foster collaborative selling. The alternative is that each partner would assume the burden of its own marketing and sales, and not be able to leverage the Microsoft marketing machine.

Still, we caution partners not to view their work with Microsoft so structurally, in terms unwieldingly rigid and subject to rules and regulations. Rather, consider that partnering with Microsoft is less a thing that must be done in a particular manner and more a thing that should be done as a general business principle. In other words, your firm must observe the requirements of the newly implemented and constantly refined partner points system. Its structure and mechanics shed light on Microsoft's need for partners and rewards for them, as well as their stratification and more or less objective measurements of their success as partners. But, as indicated before, the partner points system—the ecosystem's structure—is a gate-keeping mechanism in that it qualifies partners for entry to the ecosystem and advancement within it. This is the structure within which partners become and advance as partners. Its rules and regulations must be respected in order to enter the partnering game, whose rules Microsoft sets and whose score Microsoft keeps. Once a partner is admitted to the game, the rules for play are much more general and less restrictive, and there is a definite focus on winning it. The way to play and win the Microsoft partnering game—once you are admitted with good standing subject to the partner points system—is far less structural and is subject to common business principles. Manage your relationships. Satisfy your customers. Collaborate with your partners. Work to win, together.

These principles—things that should be done—apply especially in partnering with Microsoft. The most difficult element of succeeding in this partnership is to secure customers with Microsoft's blessing and to win Microsoft medallions certifying these wins and the company's help to move forward in the game. What matters are the partner's relationships with Microsoft. A good relationship with many connection points in the company enables a successful partnership in which Microsoft helps its partner extend relationships in the company, the ecosystem and the market; land and satisfy customers; collaborate for joint success; and work together to win one account at a time. This is, of course, a rosy scenario. *The point that matters is that the partner points system-structure is the gate through which a partner qualifies to become a partner and the ecosystem is a product-centric, customer-focused, relationship-motivated and results-oriented milieu in which a partner succeeds*. At the end of the day, then, the structure for partnering with Microsoft is far more unstructured than what Microsoft conveys in its messaging about partnership, and this book is, of course, intended to help Microsoft partners know how to succeed in the ecosystem.

Expand the Terrain of Shared Interests with Microsoft

The Microsoft Partner Ecosystem is the context within which partners engage Microsoft, the market and other Microsoft partners. It is, in other words, the forum that defines the shared interests between Microsoft and its growing number of partners. It has a distinct terrain—heights and valleys, forests and plains, waterways and deserts—all its own, within each segment of which the shared interests between Microsoft and its partners are expanded. Expanding your firm's shared interests with Microsoft depends on the nature of your particular terrain—what you do to stay alive within it—and your collaboration—whom you work with to thrive. Note the necessity and the opportunity implied in the imagery: your firm must master its own products and services, its strategy and organization; and engage Microsoft as well as its other partners on equitable terms for collaborative success. Doing so successfully results in your firm's expanding its shared interests with Microsoft and staking a larger terrain for your free movement, subsistence and flourishing. What are the elements of this expansion in the terrain of shared interests with Microsoft?

Deepen and Increase Your Competencies

Microsoft's point system stipulates that its partners have certain competencies that matter to the company. Partners are encouraged to deepen their competencies and to expand them. Analogously, successful Microsoft partners follow the example of Brazil, which is known worldwide for one product in particular: coffee. The nation of Brazil has, over centuries, mastered the art of coffee production: from its terrain, seeds and method of cultivation to its processing and shipping. Growing, selling and shipping coffee is core to Brazil's culture—and the country and its people constantly refine, or deepen, this mastery for consistently high results. The worldwide market rewards Brazil for its coffee production, and the partners of the country's coffee growers and dealers benefit in turn.

Successful Microsoft partners similarly deepen their Microsoft-sanctioned competencies and gain the recognition of Microsoft and the market, in turn. A services partner with an information-worker competency will round out and deepen its expertise in the area to achieve the highest customer-satisfaction ratings within Microsoft for the competency.

Along with deepening its competencies, the successful partner also extends them. That is, the successful partner identifies complementary Microsoft-sanctioned competencies and develops and deepens those, as well, so that it can provide expert services in as many Microsoft competencies as possible. In so doing, Microsoft escalates the partner's standing in the ecosystem pursuant to the rules of the partner points system. Yet, just as Brazil does not grow coffee for coffee's sake but for profit's sake, the partner must be practical in cultivating its expertise in competencies to ensure their marketability at a premium price. And it must market its expertise, as Brazil markets its coffee to the world, within Microsoft and, with Microsoft, to the market. So the cultivation of Microsoft competencies occurs in the context of the partner ecosystem and the market, and leverages messaging and marketing success to advance the cause.

In addition, this expansion of competencies helps the Microsoft partner, which can now provide expert services in new competencies rather than farming opportunities in them out to partner firms.

And, of course, it expands the particular terrain of shared interest with Microsoft in ways that matter for other benefits, such as marketing and collaborative sales as well as solutions development and delivery—all of which increase the partner's clout within Microsoft.

Finally, the cultivation of competencies enables the partner to express its capabilities in a manner that is quickly and accurately understood by Microsoft personnel: "our competencies are XYZ" is immediately understood by Microsoft personnel and expressed in the blink of an eye whereas "we do work with Exchange and SQL" is nebulous and warrants a follow-up question for clarification by the Microsoft employee who hears a partner utter these vague qualifications. Competencies are handles for Microsoft to grab and carry your firm by. So make it easy for the company's personnel to do so by expressing all you can do as quickly and fully as possible to get on in your collaborative work with Microsoft. And get certified in as many competencies as you can in order to advance more quickly in the partner ecosystem, which also indicates your respect for and ability to work within their structure.

Help Field Teams Succeed

So your firm's Microsoft-sanctioned competencies enable Microsoft field personnel to grasp in an instant what your firm can do with and through Microsoft. Microsoft personnel will appreciate the succinctness with which you express your competencies since they may have dozens of other partners who are not so considerate. Your opportunity is to capitalize on and compound their appreciation. The best way to do this is to position your firm to help them succeed, individually and as a field team. In addition to enabling them to grasp what you do, you must understand their priorities, particular GTMs, and market constraints and opportunities. And you must position yourself and your firm to work intensively with them.

Each Microsoft subsidiary—country, district, regional or municipal office—will have its own market and operational priorities as well as its own focus on a subset of corporate-mandated GTMs. Because the focus from corporate is entirely on its subsidiaries' fulfilling their annual quotas and only marginally on their heeding corporate GTMs, each subsidiary can pick and choose which GTMs are right for it to pursue given its personnel and market conditions. The subsidiary's choice of GTM is a sort of measuring stick for its partners—if they do not measure up in terms of the fitness for their competencies with the subsidiary's GTM, the partners will get little traction—and partners need first and foremost to understand not only how they are being measured by field personnel but, more importantly, the rationale for that measurement. In a nutshell, partners need to engage their Microsoft field counterparts on their own terms, in terms of what is important to them.

The most reliable way to do this is to establish and develop relationships with relevant personnel in Microsoft field offices. Learn from Microsoft personnel directly what their constraints, GTMs and success measures are, and position your firm to help them succeed. If you determine that their market energies are being expended in a particular area—product or vertical—in which you do not have a competency, you can either develop this competency or find another field office to work, which is often less likely. The good news is that GTMs change annually, so if your firm is out of luck in one field office in one year, your fortunes may change next year.

The need for alignment of strategy and operations—your competencies and the field office's GTMs—is essential for you to help your Microsoft counterparts and to benefit from the partnership. In terms of particular help that you can render them, the nuts and bolts vary depending on their needs, which are derived from the market and their elected GTMs, but the thrust of your help is to drive sales of Microsoft products, which is the nature of their quota, by providing value-added products and services to their customers. This entails collaborative marketing and selling, which is their principal function, so any help that you can provide in these areas is not only essential to their success but also rewarded in enhanced opportunity referral from Microsoft to your firm.

Leverage the Field to Influence Corporate

Assuming that your field relationships are strong, the opportunity to work the field to expand your connection points at corporate is great. For field offices have tremendous upstream influence on which partners get perceived by corporate as experts in any given area, and field organizations can open doors to product and marketing groups for select partners that help the field most.

Consider your firm's breadth and depth—it is deep in one competency and expands to another—as an apt metaphor. If your firm is strong in your field office as a partner, you have two opportunities: to go either deep or wide with and within Microsoft. That is, you have two possible strategies for leveraging your Microsoft field office for your firm's benefit: first, you can expand geographically through corporate's sponsorship of your expertise in a competency into other Microsoft field offices, potentially worldwide; second, you can deepen your expertise in the competency to such an extent that Microsoft corporate sponsors you as its best-in-class partner in specific accounts in various field offices. In either case, your field office serves as your firm's bridge to corporate, which can help you extend your opportunities with Microsoft based on your relationships and whatever leverage you can gain from them in Microsoft's organization.

Align Your Firm's Strategy to Mirror Microsoft's

Of course, none of the above opportunities are possible if your firm is not aligned or if it is misaligned with Microsoft as a partner. Yet alignment of your firm's strategy is not fully possible if your firm's competency has lapsed, if your field-level relationships are weak or your visibility into Microsoft corporate strategy is negligible. These are the basics, the foundational pieces that must be in place in order to be successful. To get the most from your partnership with Microsoft, your firm's corporate strategy—for marketing, operations and growth—should be mapped out to be in alignment with Microsoft's strategy. And it should be re-assessed annually, in July, to be renovated in light of Microsoft's issuance of its strategic roadmap for the fiscal year, especially its GTMs. This is a best practice simply, and the surest way to avoid collisions with Microsoft or in the market.

Although alignment can take many forms, the most fundamental alignment is in the field where "the rubber meets the road." This is especially the case in the ecosystem as it stands today, where Microsoft expects its partners to play a front-and-center role in crafting solutions and delivering services that help sell Microsoft products. Solutions and services in current high-value areas are of utmost importance to Microsoft, and partners that step into these areas step, as well, into the limelight insofar as their respective field organizations are also pushing them to market. The current high-value areas are depicted at right.

It is important to note that alignment does not mean subordinating your goals to Microsoft's wishes, nor defining your goals strictly in light of their GTMs. Rather, alignment as we mean it involves your firm's development of a strategy that provides value, and is complementary to Microsoft's corporate strategy. We have noted before that Microsoft knows that it is not the center of the information-technology universe and that it relies on its partners to fill gaps for it. Occasionally, though, there are collisions as Microsoft, too, tries to fill some gaps. It is important to note that whenever there is a collision, the key to resolution is to have a strategy already in place to resolve it. Collisions in strategically aligned partnerships are normal, to be expected, and what matters is that both parties work together to resolve the issues and get back on track together. It is the ability to remain strategically aligned and productive together when tensions from collisions arise that mark—and make—a strong partnership. And strong partnerships grow with trust between partners.

OPPORTUNITY AREA	RATIONALE
Business Intelligence (BI)	BI drives SQL, which is a critical component to beat Oracle. Microsoft loves to beat Oracle. The profit margin on SQL sales is substantial, so partners that can sell BI and, therefore, SQL will earn the attention of Microsoft field teams.
Information Worker	Especially in industry verticals, this is a hot opportunity area for partners. It is all about SharePoint and Office. As a bread-and-butter money maker for Microsoft, Office sales drive Enterprise Agreements, too. Microsoft is trying to establish Office as a platform. Break into a couple of big accounts helping to sell the value of the latest and greatest version of Office—and SharePoint—and Microsoft will want to work with your firm more.
Security	Security is NOT a money maker for Microsoft (yet), but Microsoft corporate is investing a lot of money in this area to shore up and preserve the value of its crown jewels: Windows and Office. There is plenty of unused funding available for partners in the security area, especially if they have complementary products or expert services that will bolster customers' view of Microsoft as security-conscious.
Mobility	The battle for the user interface in mobile platforms is evolving. Currently, Microsoft is behind market leaders but it is mobilizing, so to speak, to unseat them. As a global play, this is shaping up to be a major initiative as more and more resources are being applied to mobile solutions that will become predominant companions to Information Worker platforms and products.

Figure 3.4: High-Value Microsoft-Opportunity Areas That Warrant Partners' Attention.

Achieve Trusted Partnership with Microsoft

The ideal position for an ISV, solution provider, reseller or manufacturer is to be in a trusted relationship with Microsoft. Getting to this place is a function of heeding the principles discussed above. Yet remaining a trusted partner admits of its own principles, as discussed below.

Don't Use Cruise Control

For most partners detailed in case studies in this book, two key elements of trusted relationship with Microsoft emerge cleatly:

First, *be constant:* stay on message and do not change your messaging or your partnering approach too often. This is not to suggest that you should be entirely predictable nor that you should establish a routine. Rather, your firm should position itself for consistency with Microsoft. Consistent messaging. Consistent performance. Consistent results. Many firms aim to be superstars all the time and their performance suffers. No one can hit a home run on every turn at bat; the best teams consistently hit singles and drive in runs. Other firms change their messaging as new market situations or hot trends come to light, but this can be disorienting in that

Microsoft can know the players but never know what their play will be. Constancy is important in partnering with Microsoft. At the very least, a partner's constancy can be a respite from Microsoft's dynamism! A partner's constant performance and consistent results will enable it to build a track record of trust and help Microsoft personnel appreciate its true value.

Second, *do not let up:* find a pace and stick with it; never, ever slow down in working with Microsoft. Attune your firm's interaction with Microsoft to its pace, which is almost always fast, and do not rest—for a break or on your laurels—from selling. In fact, heed Microsoft's mantra: sell, sell, sell! Because Microsoft has a culture that values getting things done and nothing gets done until someone sells something, your activity as a Microsoft partner must be directed at two objectives: sell and deliver. Fast pace. Constant motion. Keep the ball moving. It is advisable always to attend Microsoft events, and there are always events—one after the other—selectively but always with a view to maintaining a strong presence vis-à-vis Microsoft personnel. Many of the firms we interviewed dedicate multiple personnel to coordinate their interface with Microsoft and to ensure their attendance at Microsoft events. A key to their success is to leverage one set of relationships in Microsoft to extend their relationships with other Microsoft personnel. Such an extension of your network within Microsoft is never sufficient but it is essential to position your firm as a trusted partner.

Find and Grow Your Niche on The "Iron Quadrant"

A function of your approach to Microsoft and of your messaging is to find and grow your niche on the so-called "iron quadrant," whose sectors are, on the Y-axis (alignment), product and market, and, on the X-axis (differentiation), undifferentiated and differentiated.

Some definitions are in order: "product" refers to your alignment with at least one of Microsoft's products whereas "market" pertains to your firm's alignment with a specific vertical or a set of them into which Microsoft's products can be sold albeit with requisite industry-specific customizations; "undifferentiated" indicates that your product or service, whether aligned with a Microsoft product or a vertical market, is not unique and is subject to competition, while "differentiated" indicates that your product or service is unique and is not subject to competition.

Your position on this quadrant must be plotted according to *how Microsoft perceives your firm,* not how you perceive it, which means that you must put yourself in the position of your Microsoft counterparts to assess your firm's strengths and weaknesses from their perspective, since that is what ultimately matters in your partnership with Microsoft. How your firm sees itself is less important than how Microsoft sees your firm for the purposes of this exercise and, indeed, for the sake of partnership. Most often, there is a gap between a firm's self-perception and Microsoft's per-

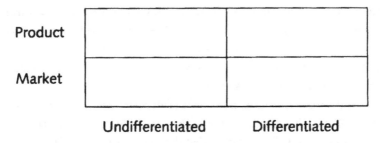

	Undifferentiated	Differentiated

Figure 3.5: The Iron Quadrant: Partners Must Assess How Microsoft Perceives Them.

ception of the firm, and this gap must be closed and can only be closed through a synergistic relationship with the company, which is the ultimate aim.

Now, your position on this quadrant—based on your alignment with Microsoft, whether particularly (product-focused) or generally (market-focused), and the extent of your differentiation relative to other players in your product or service space— is important for your partnership with Microsoft. Ideally, you are in the upper right quadrant, product-aligned (Microsoft is a product company) and differentiated (not much competition for Microsoft mindshare). From your differentiated product alignment, your firm should be able to push directly downward into market align- ment with Microsoft as the need warrants; for Microsoft is a product company that is engaged in verticalization, focusing its products' customized applicability on spe- cific industries. If you find yourself, on the other hand, market-aligned—with an expertise for a particular industry vertical and a general proficiency with Microsoft products—and undifferentiated at that, subject to competition in that sector, then you may survive as a firm but you will likely not thrive as a Microsoft partner. This is one reason that Microsoft's partner competencies are so important, in that they focus partners on specific products or rich functionalities that transcend products. Yet your ability to make your firm perceived by Microsoft as having unique value to the company is equally important, and is a lever for you to gain partnering mindshare in the mass of players in the Microsoft ecosystem.

Your firm's differentiation from Microsoft is incredibly important, then, in the ecosystem especially as a result of Microsoft itself. Its acquisition of Great Plains, Navision and Axapta essentially created the Microsoft Business Solutions (MBS) market, currently known as the Small and Mid-market Solutions and Partners (SMS&P) division. This division enveloped these three acquired companies' exist- ing partners, which swelled the ranks of Microsoft services partners worldwide by many thousands of firms. The issue for services partners is to determine how to stand out in a group of such magnitude. The question each SP must ask is, what is our differentiator? An anterior question is, how are we aligned with Microsoft, on a product or a market-vertical basis? While Microsoft's acquisition of these three mid-market players has wrought great changes for SPs, it has also impacted ISVs and resellers. In short, all of Microsoft's partners must co-exist and differentiate themselves to the best of their abilities vis-à-vis Microsoft in order to gain partnering traction, and get more from the relationship.

So how Microsoft perceives your firm—whether ISV, SP or reseller—depends on your firm's efforts but equally on Microsoft itself. Because of Microsoft's dynamism, your partner is a moving target. But recognize that the company has specified criteria for partnership—the partner points system—and instituted new modes and orders for its partners' engagement with the company, and welcomes partners' work on a relationship basis with Microsoft employees. These are all core to the company's culture. So, while Microsoft is in flux, there are structures to your partnership and efforts that can be made to engage with Microsoft in a predictable fashion to help the company's representatives with whom you work perceive your firm as they ought to perceive it. Ideally, this is the same way that your firm perceives itself.

Another facet of Microsoft's perception is timing: what is going on at Microsoft at any given time that might shift or skew its perception of your firm as a partner? Try to anticipate what that perception might be and take pre-emptive action to highlight—or downplay—it, depending, of course, on whether it benefits you or hurts you in Microsoft's eyes. Let us take a case in point: Microsoft is preparing to launch a new product. Make sure that the timing is right for you to jump on the Microsoft-product bandwagon. That determination depends on your firm's capabilities and also on the quality of your current relationship with Microsoft. At times, the issue is not when to jump on the bandwagon but, rather, how high to jump. Consider Microsoft's launch of BizTalk Server. A number of large partners jumped quickly onto that new-product bandwagon, some of them on Microsoft's urging, and sunk time, money and credibility into the new ride. The problem was that the market did not understand the product and thus did not recognize its need, so all of the marketing and the investment were unrequited by the market. In this circumstance, the early-adopter partners were product-aligned and differentiated from the majority of other partners who steered clear of the bandwagon, yet their timing—like that of Microsoft—was wrong and they got nowhere fast for all of their efforts. They could not, of course, have foreseen that the BizTalk initiative would not have been successful; it was perhaps worth the risk, and one that they could afford to take. In some cases, as you will discover in several case studies presented in this book, even failed ventures—particularly those in which partners take a high risk with Microsoft on a strategic technology—can pay dividends. But for the majority of Microsoft partners, the real question in considering new-product alignment and differentiation is when and how high to jump on the bandwagon. Timing is often everything but not always the only thing in partnering with Microsoft.

Mind the Ts and Cs, and Get the Timing Right

Another aspect of engaging in partnership with Microsoft is contractual arrangements, which often hinge on timing. Microsoft has many types of agreements for its partners. Partners must be mindful of the various types, as well as their rationale, principles and the timing involved in executing them. At the time of this writing, the main agreement types are as follows:

- *Master Services Agreement (MSA):* These are customarily executed by and between Microsoft and its services partners. The key to these agreements is to ensure that intellectual property ownership is clearly stated. There are many sub-types of MSA. Perhaps the most commonly executed is the Reciprocal MSA, which specifies terms for both Microsoft and the partner. Again, the key element for the partner is to ensure that the agreement clearly states that the intellectual property that the partner brings to the agreement belongs to it—similar provisions will always be made for Microsoft's intellectual property—and that the partner can live with the provision that any intellectual property developed in the contractual engagement is essentially a work for hire that belongs to Microsoft and the client. Timing is relevant to this type of agreement in that negotiation with Microsoft legal is a lengthy process and ought not be engaged in by partners that are in a hurry. But, because of the potential impingement on the partner's intellectual property, such negotiation is often warranted and can rarely be fast-tracked. It is important to get MSAs right because engagement-specific agreements are executed with reference to the MSA.

- *Work Orders:* These are engagement-specific agreements that are subordinate to the MSA between Microsoft and its partner, and they are the lifeblood of partners' engagement with Microsoft. In work orders, engagement- or project-specific terms are specified. Generally, work orders specify who in the partner firm will be delivering the work and that the work is on a time-and-materials basis, not fixed bid. These can pose difficulties for some partner firms in that they lock in personnel on projects whereas the partner firm may need to switch people in and out to accommodate its workload. Re-negotiating these agreements is also time-consuming, and ought not be attempted by the faint of heart.

- *Technical Assistance Programs (TAPs):* These agreements cover the transfer of knowledge from a Microsoft product group to or collaboration with a software or services partner on a beta release of a new Microsoft product. These are very restrictive agreements that stipulate the exclusive ownership by Microsoft of all of its intellectual property, and—unless the agreement is negotiated for precision's sake, which is, to repeat, time-consuming—may pose the risk of impingement on the partner's intellectual property.

- *Early Adopter Program (EAP):* These are agreements between Microsoft and customers or partners who may be interested in early adoption of a new Microsoft product. Early adoption of a new product is a differentiator for a Microsoft partner in that it can develop competency in the product in advance of other partners, and can author case studies on the new technology in anticipation of its release that can jump-start sales of the product on its release. The same caveats apply to EAPs as indicated in TAPs.

- *Joint Developer Programs (JDPs):* These are very infrequently executed agreements by and between Microsoft and its ISV partners. In fact, they are so infrequent that they are an exception. The advantage for Microsoft is to minimize the cost of development of a new technology while maintaining control of the technology under development. The advantage for the ISV partner is tight engagement with Microsoft. Yet there is a disadvantage, too, in that JDPs stipulate that the developed code is a work for hire and Microsoft by default exclusively owns the resulting work product. While this is a revenue opportunity for the ISV and, as well, an opportunity to work closely with Microsoft to establish mindshare and to demonstrate its talents, there are risks of intellectual property's impingement. Mitigating these risks in negotiation is, as stated, a laborious and time-consuming process.

In short, a partner's contractual engagement with Microsoft is potentially an arduous process of terms negotiation and fulfillment on obligations. While such engagement takes time—and pivots on right timing, especially in the case of early adoption or technology assistance—the potential rewards tend to outweigh the actual risks. In any such case, the partner is advised to be mindful of the agreement's terms and conditions having made a judicious assessment of the time required to execute the agreement relative to its capabilities to see it through, and also the timing of doing so relative to the partner's situation and Microsoft's. There is another way to achieve the same tightness of partnership with Microsoft that is more assured, although doing so entails execution of agreements at times. This is managed partnership.

Become A Managed Partner

Time for a quick quiz. What is the first and foremost basis of partnership with Microsoft? The answer is, relationships!

Without relationships in Microsoft, your partnership is negligible. So how do you measure your relationships with Microsoft?

One answer is, of course, quantitatively—the higher the number of Microsoft employees you actively work with on a regular basis, the better—but the main answer is, qualitatively. This is a holistic measurement composed of two elements, one quantitative and one qualitative.

Measure the viability of your relationship with Microsoft, first, in terms of sales: sales that you help make for Microsoft and sales that you make for yourself as a result of Microsoft's help. That is the primary quantitative component of a holistic measure of your firm's partnering success with Microsoft. It is the bottomline measurement because, after all, you partner with Microsoft to make more money, right?

The qualitative component pertains to the nature of your relationship with your Microsoft colleagues—not simply the number of them that you work with, but the product of that collaborative work. Remember the iron quadrant, which we discussed above? It is good if you can see your firm as Microsoft sees it, and better still if both you and Microsoft see your firm in the same favorable light.

Now, how do you measure the nature of your relationship with your Microsoft colleagues? The best measure of the best relationship is the extent of representation that your firm has in the Microsoft field organization. That is, how many Microsoft field employees do you have serving as advocates within Microsoft—to other field groups, to corporate groups, to other Microsoft partners—of your firm? The higher the number, the better. The more Microsoft field employees you have who take an interest in and actively vouch for your firm, and help you increase your connection points within Microsoft, and refer business to your firm, the better.

Such Microsoft employees raise their hand within Microsoft and say, with confidence, "I am responsible for our relationship with this partner." The more highly positioned they are in the field organization, the better for you. Ordinarily, these are partner account managers (PAMs) but there are other employees in Microsoft field organizations who can manage your relationship with the company and open doors for you, again, in Microsoft, to the market, and with other partners.

This is the essence of the managed relationship, which is not only reserved for partners but for partners who partner in the best ways possible, that is, in terms of building and extending promising, productive relationships with Microsoft based on delivery of results and true-blue Microsoft partnership.

There are managed partners among ISVs, SPs and resellers. There are managed partners in industry verticals, corporate accounts, global accounts and within SMS&P. It does not matter how you slice it—what matters is that you have an actively interested and sponsoring Microsoft field employee that helps your firm be more productive in its partnership with Microsoft. And that the productivity of the partnership is measured tangibly in sales derived by Microsoft as a result of your partnership and accruing to you as a result of your partnership's very productivity.

So one core objective of the ambitious Microsoft partner may be to have a given number of managed relationships with Microsoft field—and even corporate—employees, and to grow that number annually by a given percentage. Do not fear having too many sponsors within Microsoft because it is a large company and the more helping hands your firm has in the company, the better. Become a managed partner and you will have achieved the apex of partnership, you will have realized the spirit of the partner points system and reached the pinnacle of the Microsoft Partner Ecosystem.

Vest Microsoft's Interest In Your Success

Having Microsoft colleagues who help and sponsor—who take responsibility for "managing"—your firm within Microsoft is of fundamental benefit: it vests Microsoft's interest in your firm's success. It is possible to vest Microsoft's interest in your firm without being a managed partner, but the advantages accruing to a managed partner far outweigh and are more comprehensive than those possessed by unmanaged partners. So, too, is the limited extent to which Microsoft can invest itself in an unmanaged partner's success.

The clearest indicator of Microsoft's investment in your firm's success is, of course, the opening of doors by your Microsoft sponsors—within Microsoft, to the market and with other partners—in a manner that brings your firm more business and with a view to your firm's bringing more business to Microsoft. This is partnering symbiosis at its best, and in subsequent chapters you will read case studies of firms that have mastered this approach to partnering with Microsoft.

Another indicator of Microsoft's investment in your firm's success is its investing capital, human and financial, to help your firm. Microsoft funds certain partner projects and it equally designates its own human resources for certain partner initiatives. The general rule of thumb is to ask Microsoft for funding, and often. Managed partners clearly have the advantage here, or at least get priority treatment over unmanaged partners. It is best to seek funding around specific account projects or definite opportunities in order to get Microsoft's skin in the game to the fullest where an outcome is tangible and the benefit to Microsoft and its customer is specific. The best approach for funding or resources is your firm's PAM, if you are a managed partner, or the AM if you have a solid relationship with that person in your field office.

Of course, Microsoft gets requests for funding from partners all the time. The primary impetus for its funding a partner boils down to who within Microsoft that manages partners competing for funds has the most clout or, if applicable, what competitive threat in a customer account might be neutralized if the partner were funded. This means that if your PAM is well-positioned within Microsoft and your request for funding is to counter an imminent competitive threat in a customer account—reversing, for example, a Linux solution that is being considered—chances are very high that you will secure your requested funding. This is opportunity-related funding, and it is a good idea to secure it from as many sources as your firm and PAM can manage from Microsoft—get what you need but do not be afraid to ask for more if you need it. Your ability to get such funding also depends on the available programs from which funds would be administered and, again, your PAM will know the path of least resistance and the best opportunity to help your firm secure what it seeks.

There are also marketing-related funding sources within Microsoft. Generally, marketing funds are available at the beginning and during the middle of Microsoft's fiscal-year calendar (roughly July/August and February/March) so it is best to plan your marketing drives for the months subsequent to these in order to leverage such funds. Bear in mind, though, that in the middle of the fiscal year the company makes adjustments to its funding—how much and what it can be given for—and refines its set of funds for specific purposes. The best rule of thumb is to work through your PAM and other Microsoft counterparts to establish and sustain relationships with corporate marketing personnel who are sufficiently placed to provide insight on where and why marketing-related funds are being invested throughout the fiscal year.

A material benefit of being a managed partner and of getting Microsoft's skin in your game is the compounded ability to expand your network within Microsoft and to pursue—and win—better account opportunities under Microsoft's auspices and with its representatives' help. For many clients, Microsoft's perceived backing of a partner is sufficient for them to partner more closely with the partner itself. In this circumstance—the Holy Grail, as it were, of partnering with Microsoft—the partner is in a position to reduce its cost of sales substantially and to earn a premium on its product or service. But in such circumstances the pressure to deliver is intense and one slip can damage the clout the partner has earned. Still, with Microsoft invested in your firm's success—overall and on specific projects—the likelihood of problems is reduced because the managed partner with Microsoft's backing will be in a prime position to succeed.

Extend the Scope of Your Partnering Success

As you extend your network of relationships within Microsoft and move up the ladder of the partner points system to managed partner status, you will discern improvements in your partnership with the company and measure these improvements in terms of bottomline benefits, such as more referrals and greater funding opportunities. You will also be in an enhanced position to capitalize on your partnership by extending your sphere of operations and influence, potentially regionally or even globally, under Microsoft's auspices and with its facilitation. This extension of your success will bring with it new challenges—pitfalls of partnering with Microsoft that are common to all partners but more acutely so for Microsoft's closest partners—and introduce you to the rarified heights of Microsoft partnership. There, the air is clear and the panorama of partnership is expansive. From this vantage point, you can see clearly which Microsoft partners to emulate and which ones to steer clear of as you advance your firm's success as a partner with Microsoft. This book is meant to get you to this point and to position you to capitalize on your partnership with Microsoft to its fullest.

Expand Into Markets on Microsoft's Coat-tails

The most common benefit for Microsoft's closest partners is their ability to leverage their relationships within the company to identify, pursue and secure extended market opportunities. These can vary from new industry verticals to new geographic markets, and Microsoft can help open the requisite doors to the partner's extended success. Historically, Microsoft has done a poor job at this sort of partner facilitation. It has most often been the case that this enviable position was reserved for the largest partner firms with the most resources and the most clout, and most of their success in extending their opportunities was due to their own investment of human and financial capital.

This reality was due in large measure to Microsoft's lack of a partner pull-through system, which is an innovation in the current partner ecosystem, and to the relative insularity of its subsidiaries from one another. The saying is, that, "if you know one Microsoft district, you know one Microsoft district." Fortunately for partners, this is no longer entirely the case. While Microsoft districts still call their own shots—because "all politics are local"—their personnel are provided due incentives for partner pull-through. And Microsoft corporate has also taken a more nimble approach to help not only its district offices work more capably together but its partner firms to expand their sphere of influence and opportunity among territories. The PAM's role is essential in this latter regard, and smaller firms—no longer just the largest partners—are key beneficiaries of Microsoft's new partner-leaning and partner-moving organization, which are attributes true to the company's culture.

So Microsoft's innovation in partner pull-through and the provisions that the company makes for its organization to help partners more actively also extend to another facet of its culture: it is relationship-motivated. Simply the best way for a partner to expand into new markets, whether vertical or geographical, is through the professional facilitation of Microsoft employees with whom it has productive relationships. That is, relationship-based references to other groups within Microsoft and to new accounts in various verticals or geographies is the single most effective way for a partner to ride Microsoft's coat-tails into expansive opportunity. Doing so, of course, begins in the field and entails finding a local champion to make connections for your firm in the most promising areas for expansion. Once these connections are made on the partner's behalf, it behooves the partner to make the most of them—to deepen the new relationships quickly and to manage and sustain them productively over time. In due course, these relationships will spawn others, and this constant expansion of one's connection points within Microsoft is the key to a partner's growth within Microsoft and its growing opportunities with the company's help. Of course, the perils of such intimacy with Microsoft are potentially profound. The overriding imperative is thus always to deliver—on your promises, on your obligations—and constantly to advance as a value-adding partner. Another imperative is to stack up successes based on new connections and broadcast them as quickly. The principle here, true to Microsoft's culture, is to *make a splash ... or sink.*

Avoid Common Pitfalls

Many firms have indeed sunk in their partnership with Microsoft. And there are common pitfalls of partnering with the company to which all partners are subject and of which many are oblivious. As you deepen your partnership with Microsoft, you will see these pitfalls and their opposites more clearly, especially as this deepened partnership enables you to understand Microsoft's culture. The pitfalls themselves violate the principles of partnering with Microsoft by virtue of being contrary to the pillars of Microsoft's culture. For most partners, the following pitfalls are common and must be avoided for at least the stated reasons:

Do not tell Microsoft you can do it all. No one can. Just as Microsoft specializes—it makes and sells software, period—so do its employees and so must its partners. Specialization, accountability and expert delivery are core to Microsoft's culture.

Do not be just another XYZ. For example, Microsoft has many infrastructure partners, such as Dell and HP, custom application-development partners and broad-based systems-integration partners. Your firm needs to stand out, be differentiated and be known for its particular skills, successes and contributions to Microsoft's bottomline.

Do not spread your messaging in too many markets. While it is important to convey your firm's capabilities to as many Microsoft employees as possible, it is preferable to restrict your Microsoft marketing to the field offices and vertical groups in which you are actively engaged. Over-extending your messaging to Microsoft can incur the risk of dilution of your impact in letting Microsoft know who your firm is and what it does. In other words, be discriminating about whom you tell your firm's story to at Microsoft, and respect the organizational boundaries and purviews of the company, which is core to the culture. It is always best to build a strong base from which to expand through Microsoft-facilitated introductions, and then to expand from there when those new connections are established.

Do not change your messaging to Microsoft too often. Remember, Microsoft employees deal potentially with many partners. They need a "handle" to grasp partners by, and they need that handle to be reliable. If your firm does one thing one day and another on a different day, your handle for your Microsoft counterpart will be weak if not entirely broken. Remain consistent in your messaging to Microsoft and in your delivery of results based on your messaging. In this way, you will establish a track record of success that fosters immediate recognition and, soon enough, you will not need to deliver your messaging to new Microsoft employees because your current connection points will do it for you, more crisply and effectively even than you can do for your firm.

Do not burn bridges. Never, ever contact your PAM or another Microsoft counterpart and accuse Microsoft of competing with or under-cutting your firm. It takes potentially years to build a vibrant partnership and only one call to destroy all the work that goes into it. Always assume goodwill on Microsoft's part and work constructively to resolve any issues that may arise. Common courtesy goes a long way in working with Microsoft.

Do not have uneducated representatives in your firm and, if you do, never let them represent your firm to Microsoft. This gets back to the virtue of univocality—your firm's employees must speak as if with one voice, one mind—to Microsoft. If your Microsoft counterparts sense dissonance in what your firm does or what you can contribute to Microsoft's success through partnership, they might distance themselves from the relationship, especially if what they hear from some of your people is contrary to what you tell Microsoft. While it is a true challenge to educate all of your relevant personnel—and it is desirable to educate every member of your staff—on the purpose and objectives of your partnership with Microsoft, and what your firm brings to the table and has achieved for and with the company, it is essential that your firm commit to and succeed in such education.

Again, these are just the most common pitfalls. There are others to avoid. As you read this book, you will infer others. The more prudent and more effective mechanism for succeeding in your partnership with Microsoft, however, is to identify and emulate those Microsoft partners that have succeeded and to deepen your understanding of their partnering principles and practices.

Emulate Others' Successes in Partnering with Microsoft

One need not be Machiavelli to know that the surest way to succeed in a venture is not by itemizing and steering clear of pitfalls and dangers but by imitating the success of those who have come before. "Above all [the prince] should do as some virtuous man has done in the past who found someone to imitate who had been praised and glorified before him," Machiavelli writes. In so doing, "a wise prince must observe such modes and never remain idle in times of peace but, with his industry, make capital of them in order to be able to profit from them in adversities so that when his fortune changes it will find him ready to resist those adversities."

This extended quotation from Machiavelli's *The Prince* indicates certain themes that you will find in ensuing chapters: partnering with Microsoft can be difficult, like warfare, and it can seem easy, too, as in times of peace; the strongest partners are those who properly assess their firms' situations and know the culture, strategy, organization and modes of engagement with Microsoft; they will know the experience and the causes of success of those who succeeded in partnering with Microsoft, and will be able to apply those to any situation; they will work hard and constantly to perfect their standing and their ability to partner and to succeed with and through Microsoft; they will capitalize on their partnership with Microsoft based in large measure on having studied the successes of others.

We believe this book can do a great deal for you and your firm in your partnership and engagement with Microsoft and get you on your way to success. But, as importantly, it will equip you with the principles of partnering with Microsoft—in this and foregoing chapters—and the best practices of doing so depending on what type of firm yours is—in the subsequent three chapters. And we will orient you to the opportunities of tapping fully into the Microsoft Partner Ecosystem, in Chapter Seven, to extend your partnership to other Microsoft partners and thus your success as a result of partnering with Microsoft.

Chapter 4

ISV Tactics for Successful Partnership with Microsoft

Microsoft has achieved exponential growth due in large part to its symbiotic relationship with Independent Software Vendors (ISVs). The development of thousands of popular software applications for the Windows platform by third-party software developers—as well as by Microsoft—has undoubtedly driven adoption of the company's platforms and products well beyond any measure of that accomplished by mainframe, mini-computer or UNIX vendors.

Microsoft's success in recruiting ISVs to deliver applications for the company's platforms and products over the past 20 years is a result of widespread adoption of Microsoft products and a symbiosis that formed between the company and its software partners. Mr Gates' roots as a programmer fostered a developer-friendly culture that quickly attracted a following of eager ISVs.

This symbiosis reverses many myths identified in Chapter One, notably one specious argument that Microsoft is solely self-interested. Proponents of this myth claim that Microsoft will at first adore and then ignore its ISV partners. That is, the perception is that it will court ISVs with false promises of licensing their technology, only to co-opt their intellectual property or to buy them at less than market value.

There are many compelling arguments against the set of myths that Microsoft is solely self-interested and views its singular success as the goal. Microsoft recognizes that its growth depends on the continued growth of its ISV ecosystem that extends its platforms and applications. Without a healthy ISV partner community, the Windows platform would die. Microsoft knows this.

There are thousands of ISVs that have become successful owing to their equal focus on *innovation* and *symbiosis* in partnering with Microsoft. These are the two drivers in Microsoft's ISV-partnering model, and the two principal themes whose corresponding tactics we focus on in this chapter to explain ISVs' success in partnering with Microsoft.

There is a special affinity between Microsoft and its ISV partners, of course. Microsoft, like its ISV partners, is a software developer and continually looks for ways to add value to its client and server platforms and products. The key for an ISV is to form a strong Microsoft partnership with a healthy balance between collaboration and competition, and a commitment to innovation, in a manner that benefits yet also preserves its own technical lead over Microsoft. Remaining close to the market, too, is essential as this has accounted for Microsoft's success not only as a company but as a magnet for ISVs over the past 20 years, since its inception, of growth into the most powerful software company in the world. A brief review of the company's historical partnering with ISVs will shed light on Microsoft's growth through symbiotic innovation with its high-affinity ISV partners.

Microsoft's Historical Partnership with ISVs

The company inaugurated its first ISV partner program with the launch of Windows 3.0 in the early 1990s and swiftly updated that program as the MSDN ISV Program following the release of Windows 3.1. A handful of early ISVs that wrote applications for Microsoft's original MS-DOS platform, WordPerfect and Lotus, also developed the first Windows desktop applications. Microsoft's Application Programming Interfaces (APIs) enabled software developers to build applications that leveraged internal Windows-system calls and became *de facto* standards in the software industry. Within two years of its debut, 720 independent software vendors, also known as third-party ISVs, delivered more than 1,200 applications for the Windows operating system. Among the most successful application developers was Microsoft itself, whose Word for Windows and Excel for Windows steadily gained market share against more established software developers in the word-processing and spreadsheet markets, WordPerfect and Lotus, respectively.

A more sizable group of ISVs developed server applications in advance of Microsoft's first server operating system in 1993, known as Windows NT. The initial release of the server platform was accompanied by the debut of 5,000 applications from several thousand ISV-partners. Since then, more than 11,000 ISVs shipped many thousands of server applications for Microsoft's next-generation server operating systems, Windows 2000 and Windows Server 2003.

Microsoft's APIs remained the mainstay of application development on the Intel and x86-compatible platforms for more than 15 years. By the mid-1990s, the company's share of the desktop-PC market exceeded 95% and its server operating-system market share was climbing rapidly against entrenched platforms such as Novell's Netware and its UNIX competitors. Microsoft has maintained more than a 95% share of the desktop operating-system market to date and its Windows server operating system runs on more than 50% of all new servers shipped worldwide.

In 2000, Microsoft made two strategic moves of great importance to ISVs. First, it ushered in a new era of software development with the launch of its .NET programming model, language and framework. Second, Microsoft acquired two large ISVs in the business applications market. In 2000, Microsoft acquired Great Plains Software for US$1.1 billion, taking a bold step into the business applications software market. Two years later, Microsoft acquired Navision, of Copenhagen, Denmark, for US$1.45 billion. These moves were designed to expand the depth and breadth of Microsoft software in the enterprise, mid-market and small business customer segments. The deals significantly augmented Microsoft's number of ISV and services partners, and increased the number of available business process-oriented applications for its platforms and products.

Although Microsoft launched its first mainstream partner program in the early 1990s to support partners that provided value-added products for its platforms, it was not until 2000, that Microsoft decided to consolidate its separate partner programs—including its ISV program—into the mainstream Microsoft Partner Program. In 2004, ISVs were officially inducted into the Microsoft Partner Program. Today, there are more than 63,000 Microsoft ISV-partners that develop value-added applications for the Windows desktop and server platforms, including Microsoft's own Office and Information Worker product add-ons. There are approximately 59,000 "breadth" ISVs, another 4,364 that are account-managed and more than 200 that are Global ISVs, including Citrix, Symantec, Epicor, Siebel, Quest Software and Meridio.

ISVs know that doing business with Microsoft, as with any other platform vendor, is a risk. They may incorporate an ISV's functionality directly into their platforms or products if it is deemed in their customers' interest. For example, ISVs such as Netscape suffered when Microsoft integrated web browsing into its operating system. Server ISVs such as Plumtree, which developed portal software for the Windows platform, were adversely affected when Microsoft released SharePoint Portal Server, as were ISVs Pivotal and Onyx following the debut of Microsoft CRM. Symantec and McAfee are long-time Microsoft Global ISV partners that have survived and prospered as Microsoft integrated their utilities into every Windows upgrade. They will undoubtedly face a major challenge to their core security-software business line when Microsoft ships its planned anti-virus software products and services in 2005 and 2006. Countless other ISVs have been impacted when the SS Microsoft shifted course and sailed directly in their course. Some have survived, others have capsized or been crushed. So there is always some basis for concern that Microsoft, like any platform vendor, will decide to compete with its partners. But ISVs that innovate and collaborate with Microsoft often benefit from the wave of growth that inevitably follows Microsoft's entry into their market. There are many ISV success stories that highlight this principle.

ISV Success Stories

Consider, if you will, the following successful ISVs that have grown as a result of partnering with Microsoft through a focus on innovation and symbiosis with the company.

Veritas is one of the 10 largest software companies in the world, having built a US$1.7 billion business from licensing a scaled-down backup-software product that has come bundled with every version of Windows since NT 3.5. Its flagship Back-upExec extends Windows' functionality in a manner that Microsoft values and seeks from its partners. Moreover, the ISV also became a major provider of storage software that integrates with the Windows platform. Veritas is a case study that illustrates the benefits of giving ground to take ground, a subtle principle of warfare, with Microsoft as a mutually benefited partner. It merged with Symantec in December 2004, in a stock-swap deal valued at US$13.5 billion.

Citrix has built a US$725 million business on top of a server product originally called WinFrame that was developed based on a cross-licensing deal with Microsoft in 1997. In a joint development pact, the Ft Lauderdale, Florida-based software vendor made licensed modifications to Microsoft's NT 3.51 kernel and then licensed back to Microsoft those kernel modifications to enable the multi-user capabilities (widely used on UNIX systems) in Windows NT 4.0. Microsoft released Terminal Services as a result of its joint-development and licensing pact with Citrix, a successful partnership that continues to pay handsome dividends for Microsoft and the ISV today. Citrix has extended its strategic alliance with Microsoft several times since 1997. The latest deal, signed in late 2004, further extends and expands the scope of their cooperation: it calls for the two to conduct broad joint-development on the forthcoming "Longhorn" version of Windows server and establishes cross-licensing provisions for patents that provide broader access to their respective safeguarded intellectual property. Citrix's success in developing a mutually beneficial technology and partnership with Microsoft is a promising case study that demonstrates the independence, interoperability and success that is possible in partnering with Microsoft.

Executive Software partnered with Microsoft to deliver system-management tools and capabilities that complemented the Windows operating system's native functionality. Its manual disk-defragmentation tool has remained bundled with Windows to this day. Diskeeper—along with Executive Software's other products—has been separately available in more extensive versions directly from Executive Software and its partner-suppliers. Like Veritas, Executive Software is a case study in partnering with Microsoft to help it address a need and to create a demand that only the partner can best supply. Executive Software remains a privately held, global and very successful ISV as a result of its symbiotic partnership with Microsoft.

Meridio (an Irish firm), *SourceCode Holdings,* originally out of South Africa, and *CorasWorks,* of McLean, Virginia, are representative of a new class of Microsoft ISVs that have established successful partnerships with Microsoft on emerging technologies for the next generation of Microsoft platforms. These ISVs have developed electronic document and records management, workflow, business process automation, and vertically oriented business applications for the next major upgrades of Windows and Office systems for the 2006-2007 timeframe. These three ISVs, all founded after 2000, ascended to the coveted status of Global ISV in relatively speedy fashion. Case studies of these new ISVs as well as established partners demonstrate that the principles of successful ISV partnering with Microsoft remain consistent and predictable despite the shifting course of the SS Microsoft.

———■———

Microsoft advocates a strong third-party ISV partner model but acquires ISVs whose niche technologies fill gaps in Microsoft's product portfolio or that address specific and urgent market needs. But there have been a number of more sizable, established ISVs whose culture and technology were so complementary that they they were pursued, acquired and folded into Microsoft. Figure 4.1 is a representative listing of such Microsoft-acquired ISVs.

Take, for example, *Great Plains Software,* a developer of mid-market business software from Fargo, North Dakota, that was acquired by Microsoft in December 2000, for US$1.1 billion of Microsoft common stock. The ISV was a dedicated Microsoft software provider whose culture and vision closely mirrored that of Microsoft. The CEOs of both companies viewed it as a marriage made in heaven.

YEAR	ACQUIRED ISV	TARGET MICROSOFT PRODUCT BENEFIT
1996	Vermeer Technologies	FrontPage
	eShop	Windows IIS Web Server
1997	Hotmail	MSN Hotmail
1998	Visio	Office Visio
2000	Great Plains Software	MBS Great Plains
2001	NCompass	Content Management Server
2002	Navision	MBS Navision, MBS Axapta
2003	Connectix	Virtual PC, Virtual Server
	PlaceWare	Office LiveMeeting!
	GeCAD	Forthcoming anti-virus solution
2004	Giant Software	Windows AntiSpyware
	ActiveViews	SQL Server 2005 Reporting Services Report Builder
2005	Sybari Software	Forthcoming anti-virus solution
2005	Groove Networks	SharePoint

Figure 4.1: Representative List of Microsoft-Acquired ISVs, 1996-2005.

Great Plains CEO Doug Burgum observed on the announcement of the acquisition that the sum of the whole would be greater than the individual parts. "We weren't looking to be acquired but ... the more we talked about the needs of our partners and customers, the more we realized how much we could do together," Mr Burgum said. Microsoft CEO Steve Ballmer commented on the good cultural fit between the two companies, and highlighted Great Plains' innovation and symbiosis with Microsoft when the deal was announced. "In 19 years of operations, Great Plains has proved to be one of Microsoft's most innovative partners," Mr Ballmer said. "Microsoft and Great Plains see the future of business applications for small and medium-sized companies in the same way."

In this case, Great Plains' strategy and culture, in addition to its products, were deemed so complementary that Microsoft folded its vision, executives, market approach and partners into the company. Indeed, while CEOs often depart after their company is acquired by a larger entity, Great Plains' Burgum, by contrast, has ascended Microsoft's corporate ladder quickly. In 2004, he was named senior vice president of Microsoft Business Solutions (MBS), one of only seven executives in charge of the company's business units who reports directly to Mr Ballmer.

Visio was also a long-time partner that Microsoft acquired in September 1999, for US$1.3 billion so that it could include its popular Visio business drawing and technical graphing software as a component of Microsoft Office. Visio is another example of a firm that worked closely with—and then was acquired by—Microsoft on equitable terms, and for the right reasons.

One need not dwell only on such large ISVs. There are many examples of smaller software manufacturers that have succeeded in partnering with and even been acquired by Microsoft. In fact, they make up the overwhelming majority of Microsoft's 63,000-ISV partner community. The list includes ISVs that cooperate and compete with Microsoft. What Microsoft prizes in its most successful ISV partners is their collaborative commitment, like Great Plains, to advance innovative solutions and to work very closely with Microsoft. How these companies actually execute on these principles varies widely. The approaches of Visio and Great Plains were similar, for example, and yet strikingly different from those of Executive Software and Veritas. Citrix's model is distinct from those four.

Yet the prime differentiators among these firms reside in *how* they have executed on innovation and symbiosis with Microsoft, not *if* they have, and this is an important distinction to appreciate. For these two elements—innovation and symbiosis—are necessary for Microsoft ISVs to attain any level of success. The tactical differences must be viewed in the context of what binds these firms as Microsoft partners: they work tightly with Microsoft to innovate their respective products. And they are growing wildly in number and in the scope of solutions they offer. Their tactical differences are a function of their adoption of one of two models commonly employed in ISVs' partnering with Microsoft, but the aim of successful ISV-partners is uniform and instructive, as evidenced by the case studies in this chapter.

ISV Partnering Models: Tangential or Targeted?

Before considering the tactics that ISVs should employ in partnering with Microsoft, it is essential, as underscored in Chapters Two and Three, that ISVs understand the field of play and the principles of partnering with Microsoft. As such, ISVs ought to grasp Microsoft's culture and mirror its customer-focused and product-centric mission. They must also be in control of their own ship and their own destiny—or risk being crushed by the SS Microsoft. Knowing Microsoft's culture and strategy, and learning to work its organizational maze—which is dynamic yet consistent—are paramount obligations for Microsoft partners that wish to succeed.

Your tactics—what you do as a Microsoft ISV-partner—will fail if your understanding—what you know about Microsoft, and who you know there—falter. The successful Microsoft ISV-partner factors into its market strategy and tactics the same focus on innovation and symbiosis with Microsoft that has made other ISV partners successful.

This includes the selection of a business model to structure innovative and symbiotic work with Microsoft. In Microsoft's world, there are two generic ISV models to choose from: tangential and targeted. The models are defined by the nature of the ISV's product relative to Microsoft's. An ISV can manufacture and market software products

1. for a specific technical or business solution that is *not* directly tied to a Microsoft product, called the *tangential approach*, in which an ISV's product is meant to solve a technical problem or fill a business gap *and* may leverage or be leveraged by a Microsoft product—but need not be in order to be successfully brought to market; or

2. to fill a void in or to complement one or more specific Microsoft products, called the *targeted approach*, in which an ISV's product is meant to provide functionality lacking in a Microsoft product, and intentionally gets developed as an add-on or as a bundled element of the Microsoft product itself.

In the tangential approach, the ISV focuses on addressing a technical or business problem that Microsoft has not addressed in any of its own products. It can be, for example, an enterprise resource planning (ERP) tool or a customer relationship management (CRM) solution for a particular industry vertical that is not in Microsoft's product suite. The solution addresses a distinct technical or industry-specific problem that may benefit from the integration with the Microsoft product but does not require it in order to succeed. It may also be a wireless or mobility solution that *can be* integrated but *need not be* integrated with Microsoft products in order to work; that is, the third-party solution can be modified or integrated with another operating system platform such as Linux or Solaris. Executive Software got its start by developing disk-management utilities for Digital Equipment Corporation's legacy VMS operating system and only later developed the disk-defragmentation utilities that are bundled with Microsoft operating systems. Veritas' (and its acquisition Legato's) software is marketed and sold as a multi-platform product. NetIQ also falls into this category. These products solve technical and business needs not addressed by Microsoft yet they do not *require* Windows to be brought to market. In spite of the tangential nature of this approach, these products sold much better once they were integrated with Windows.

The targeted approach, by contrast, represents a tighter integration—and symbiosis—with Microsoft. Consider Citrix, for example, whose inaugural WinFrame and successor product MetaFrame would not function apart from their target Windows Server version, and MetaFrame has since become even more integrated with the platform by requiring Windows Server 2003's terminal services to run in order to function. Citrix's technology extends Microsoft's operating system for multi-user capabilities that had long been considered *de rigeur* on UNIX platforms.

Several other ISVs examined in this book, including Meridio and CorasWorks, fall into this category, as do all of the ISVs that Microsoft has acquired. Visio ran only on Windows and integrated tightly with Office when it was sold as a stand-alone product. It was specifically designed and intended to address a deficiency in Microsoft's product suite, whereas other applications in the same category offered similar value but not *exclusively* to the Microsoft platform. Similarly, Great Plains Software was developed to run on Microsoft's operating-system and SQL database platforms as well as to leverage Office functionality in order to apply Microsoft technology to the needs of small- and mid-sized business management operations.

These products, unlike those created as a result of the tangential approach, were specifically designed and optimized for Microsoft platforms to address specific shortcomings in or to extend the functionality of Microsoft's products to resolve specific technical or business problems.

ISVs with either of these operating models need to take appropriately different approaches to partnering with Microsoft. And firms that employ a hybrid of these models need similarly to tailor their partnering approach. Consider two ISVs, one that has adopted the tangential approach and another, the targeted approach.

NetIQ Rides the Waves of Microsoft's Success

NetIQ (www.netiq.com)—a Microsoft Gold Certified Partner based at San Jose, California, founded in 1995—is a publicly listed ISV with annual revenues of US$261.6 million (2004), that makes and markets systems- and security- management and web-analytics solutions. Through dynamic growth—a merger with Mission Critical Software and the acquisition of complementary firms (WebTrends, PentaSafe Security Technologies and Marshal Software)—NetIQ has consolidated its leadership position in innovative, cross-platform products for Windows, UNIX and Linux. Under the leadership of Olivier Thierry, senior vice president for worldwide marketing and alliances, NetIQ has sustained a vibrant relationship with Microsoft, its strategic partner, and capitalized on its cross-platform solutions strategy and tangential Microsoft-partnering approach.

It has not been easy. Recall from Chapter Two Mr Thierry's analogy of Microsoft as a battleship cruising the high seas. NetIQ has positioned itself to ride the waves of Microsoft's wake to mutual success despite shifting seas at market and the SS Microsoft's re-steered course over the nine years of its partnership with the company.

There is a dedicated Microsoft strategic alliance team and field team assigned to work with Microsoft technical and sales personnel, often with daily communications among them. NetIQ has other partners—Microsoft and Cisco fall in the category of "center of gravity" partnerships, while many systems integrators (SIs) and original equipment manufacturers (OEMs) are "satellite partners." Some of these, like NetIQ, provide solutions for both Microsoft and its competitors, such as UNIX or Linux platforms and products. Yet NetIQ has been able to leverage its Microsoft relationship to extend its cross-platform strategy. Other ISVs have failed in this. Mr Thierry accounts for NetIQ's success by pointing to the depth and strength of the firm's Microsoft relationship and Microsoft's own realism: "Part of the agreement that we signed in 2000 (it expired in 2003) for Microsoft to license and acquire our Operations Manager code, which became Microsoft Operations Manager (MOM), was that NetIQ would build cross-platform capabilities to help Microsoft extend Windows and its platform solutions. Microsoft knows that it is not the center of the IT universe. And it wants partners that will help it develop cross-platform solutions so that Microsoft can inter-operate with competitive platforms and products out there. Microsoft always protects its own code. Microsoft needs its partners to extend its solutions to competitive platforms. NetIQ has been able to do this for Microsoft with Microsoft's backing." So NetIQ's collaborative innovation with Microsoft extends the company's reach into enterprises by expanding its platforms' and products' operability with competitive solutions.

Such collaborative innovation would not be possible without a measured focus on symbiosis. NetIQ capably works Microsoft corporate and field teams. There are quarterly executive meetings and daily communications with Microsoft employees. In addition, NetIQ has an office on Microsoft's Seattle campus for regular contact with Microsoft corporate and field teams.

As we have heard from other ISVs, regular communication with Microsoft corporate and field personnel contributes to symbiosis but it also makes evident an interesting reality: the SS Microsoft looks a lot more pristine from corporate than it does from the field. The structured communications at corporate pertain to product roadmap alignment meetings and annual GTM meetings, respectively, to coalesce NetIQ's products with Microsoft's and to coordinate the two firms' market-messaging to amplify each other's GTM success. Mr Thierry refers to the product roadmap alignment meetings as "collision avoidance" get-togethers because product teams, in their exuberance to craft an all-in-one, do-it-all platform, will blithely ask "did we hit anything?" in the ISV's product roadmap. These meetings can be tense at times due to the elitism of Microsoft corporate personnel that many ISVs have noted. By contrast, the "GTM tuning" meetings are far from contentious, generally coordinating and celebratory events once the product and marketing strategies have been defined.

As we noted earlier in this chapter in another context, the corporate product teams' exuberance to craft all-in-one, do-it-all platforms may be due to their compensation structure that encourages a siloed, stove-piped approach: the Exchange product team will want to absorb all possible functionality into its platform, the SQL team will want to do the same, and they are not encouraged as structured product teams to collaborate. Consequently, while Microsoft's upper-echelon management discerns the advantages of what the company touts—integration of "back office" platforms (*eg*, Exchange and SQL) and "front office" products (*eg*, Office)—in reality the very exuberance on the part of the product teams that inclines them to build out their products to suit all possible needs, even if doing so excludes or obstructs partners' products, is encouraged by their operating structure. Such product-team exuberance accounts for the rosy-picture view from Seattle of Microsoft platforms' and products' impact on the market, and it can frustrate ISV partnering efforts.

NetIQ has managed to balance the mentioned flexibility—adjusting with Microsoft and positioning its products to fill gaps in Microsoft's strategy—with firmness—staying focused on areas of accentuated value to Microsoft. So NetIQ's message to Microsoft is consistently that its solutions extend Microsoft's focus on core platform functionality. NetIQ has done so by riding the waves of Microsoft's initiatives—"Trustworthy Computing," for example—and putting product-level disputes in that context. These Microsoft initiatives set the tone for Microsoft's GTMs but the product teams' exuberance always bleeds through not only in the so-called "collision avoidance" meetings but in Seattle's marketing about new product releases. Microsoft corporate marketing inevitably hypes new product and platform releases to reflect this exuberance of their market potential.

In the field, where sales and competitive pressures apply, the reality is often quite different from the marketing hype. The tension in the field is to deconstruct the rhetoric about a new product release and to emphasize the core features that will account for sales. So NetIQ's strategy in working with the field is to equip Microsoft teams to make sales. NetIQ's field teams engage with their Microsoft counterparts to understand the needs and specific GTMs of the districts, factoring in their compensation model—Microsoft field-team financial interests and motivations—and communicate regularly with them. The issue is not what Microsoft thinks about NetIQ but how much NetIQ thinks about Microsoft, and how effectively it demonstrates this thoughtfulness.

The result is measured in joint sales activities, where NetIQ shines. The firm measures—and tracks—its joint sales traction and success with Microsoft. In addition, NetIQ trains its personnel, especially its field teams, with "lunch and learn" sessions on Microsoft GTMs, on Microsoft-partnering tactics and on how Microsoft field teams are compensated. And the firm encourages the preparation and dissemination of "battle cards" among NetIQ and Microsoft field teams to outline potential customer-buy objections and how to reverse them.

The corporate-to-corporate strategizing and field-level tactics to shore up and advance collaboratively with Microsoft fosters NetIQ's symbiosis with Microsoft. It helps, too, that the companies have broader shared interests. For example, Microsoft and NetIQ are each other's customers: NetIQ uses Microsoft platforms and products, and Microsoft uses NetIQ's systems- and security-management solutions. Microsoft has also engaged NetIQ to develop elements of its products and, in fact, to develop entire products, such as the Active Directory Migration Tool. And, in Microsoft's largest in-licensing deal (US$178 million), the company contracted with NetIQ for the use and marketing of Microsoft Operations Manager (MOM), which—true to Microsoft's bias that it is the "only software company in the world that gets it"—has been rewritten by Microsoft.

In brief, NetIQ has mastered the tactics required to partner with Microsoft in a manner that expands the terrain of shared interests between itself and Microsoft, and NetIQ personnel work that terrain daily, intensively to extend its symbiosis and innovation with the company.

Panorama's Targeted Approach

Panorama (www.panorama.com)—a Microsoft Gold Certified ISV-Partner based at Toronto, Ontario, Canada—makes and markets business intelligence (BI) software that is explicitly developed to extend Microsoft platforms. Microsoft's SQL-bundled Analysis Services product—an OLAP implementation—was developed by Panorama's Israel-based development team and later sold to Microsoft. The firm decided at that point to refocus the company on front-end BI solutions that would add additional value to the SQL database and Office Systems platforms. Partnership with Microsoft to develop and bring Panorama's solution set to market was essential.

According to Lee Ho, Panorama's director of worldwide marketing, the key to Panorama's early and subsequent sales growth was aligning and mapping Panorama's organization to Microsoft's, and to orchestrate their working together to foster the sort of innovation Panorama sought.

Panorama hired former Microsoft employees or other BI manufacturers' employees and trained them intensively on Panorama's strategy and go-to-market approach. Then they organized them in a mirror image of Microsoft's organization: Panorama's partner alliance manager would be assigned to a Microsoft partner account manager, a technical specialist at Panorama would have interface to one of Microsoft's, and a sales specialist at Panorama would work closely in the field with a similarly positioned Microsoft colleague. In the firm's main North American office, there is a working map of Microsoft's team and a mirror image of Panorama's.

The firm created a "cook book" on engaging and working with Microsoft. As Microsoft's field organizational structure shifts, so does Panorama's in order to remain matched to its partner. Panorama puts its field personnel through training on tactical partnering with Microsoft, and annually holds a firm-wide GTM webcast and meetings at the beginning of each Microsoft fiscal year, after Microsoft announces its GTM strategy for the fiscal year, to train all of its employees on the joint strategic initiatives and tactics between the two companies.

Panorama's approach appears to be working. The privately held firm announced that its revenue for the first half of 2004 had increased 200% and that Microsoft has agreed to showcase Panorama's BI solutions and dashboard at Microsoft Technology Centers worldwide.

It is sometimes important to state the obvious: Panorama's approach is targeted at extending a Microsoft product (innovation), and Panorama's organization and strategy mirror Microsoft's (symbiosis). This approach is quite appropriate to Panorama's Microsoft-targeted model, and it accounts for the strength of their partnership.

———■———

Both NetIQ and Panorama enjoy Microsoft-partnering success by employing two different approaches, respectively, tangential and targeted. Their partnering approaches and their shared objective—successful partnership with Microsoft—express, as well, two other elements of their success that are absolutely essential for any Microsoft partner:

- their products are complementary to Microsoft's, and

- Microsoft perceives these products—and these companies—as enhancing Microsoft's own value in the respective markets in which they are collaboratively engaged.

Without product complementarity, no ISV can succeed in partnering with Microsoft. That is perhaps obvious, but bears some consideration. An application developed by an ISV that is interoperable with a Microsoft platform yet runs on

Linux exclusively will not be treated by Microsoft as a complementary product. Microsoft sees value in its ISV's products to the extent that they promote sales of Microsoft's products. If an ISV cannot demonstrate this, a partnership with Microsoft is not possible. In Microsoft's view, the fact that an ISV's product runs compatibly with Windows is simply a market requirement since Windows is pervasive; it does not make an ISV a complementary partner. Microsoft looks askance at any product that runs exclusively on a competitor's platform, particularly Linux.

Without Microsoft's perception of the product or the company's added value, the partnership cannot even commence. This consideration begs the question the following questions: what does Microsoft seek and prize in its ISV–partners? How should ISVs position themselves to be perceived as value-added partners?

The answers to these questions will help ISVs define appropriate tactics for building their businesses in partnership with Microsoft. Partnering is a two-way street and there is no one way down it. Microsoft wants its ISV-partners to collaborate with Microsoft but working with a company of that size and complexity can be a challenge. Not only is there no one, right way to do it, but there are many ways to fail at it. A key is to find the balance between collaboration and competition with Microsoft.

Find The Competitive-Collaborative Balance: Innovation and Symbiosis

While partnering with Microsoft may appear on its surface to be a straightforward affair, it is often quite challenging due to the company's aggressive, even arrogant, attitude and its potentially competitive posture. This potential for direct competition is a unique challenge for ISVs among Microsoft's vast partner ecosystem. Every successful ISV knows that partnering with Microsoft is a time-consuming, challenging and sometimes risky endeavor that can pay significant dividends if the partnership is executed correctly. Partnering effectively with Microsoft is lucrative: Microsoft sees a US$55 billion partner opportunity in the small to medium-sized business sector over the next several years, according to optimistic predictions by Microsoft's Orlando Ayala, senior vice president of the Small and Midmarket Solutions & Partner (SMS&P) Group.

How you choose to partner with Microsoft or any other vendor is highly subjective and unique depending on a variety of factors. Nevertheless, it is worth observing that successful Microsoft ISV-partners employ similar tactics and corporate traits that are instructive for other aspiring ISVs. Their successful tactics and traits include the ability to

- strike a balance between competition and collaboration with the emphasis on the latter;

- execute through innovation and symbiosis, respectively, in products and culture;

- build and optimize multiple connection points into Microsoft;

- align locally, expand globally;

- weigh risks and rewards in partnership with Microsoft;

- remain urgent, flexible and firm to accommodate Microsoft's dynamic nature;

- demonstrate clear value to Microsoft through sales of Microsoft licenses, and articulate that value in financial terms;

- provide consistent, concise messaging about their core value proposition to and revenue generation for Microsoft;

- stay present with Microsoft, temporally and in a locative sense; and

- address Microsoft's pain points and vulnerabilities, especially in a market characterized by tightening competitive pressure.

It is essential for ISVs to mix these tactics and traits to strike a competitive-collaborative balance with Microsoft that works for both. First and foremost, ISVs must innovate, which is to say, add value to and extend the Microsoft platform by continually developing software that helps sell Microsoft licenses and that is customer-focused. In addition, ISVs must exhibit cultural affinity with the company that enables them to sail briskly alongside the SS Microsoft, including an ability to be urgent, flexible and firm, and technically adept. As indicated, it is essential to work and extend connections points into Microsoft to build a base for symbiotic innovation.

Beyond the complementarity of ISV solutions with its platforms and products, Microsoft expects ISVs to be comfortable with creative tension in the relationship. The partner must thrive in a competitively collaborative environment. An oyster will produce a pearl only after processing an irritant, such as sand. In much the same way, a partner lodges itself in the Microsoft ecosystem and the resulting tension and collaboration foster the production of something of value. The most successful ISVs recognize that a healthy dose of tension in their relationship with Microsoft is both to be expected and mutually productive.

The question is, though, how much tension is productive? Many ISVs have found that they are naturally competitive with certain groups in Microsoft and that the ensuing tension detracts from their progress in jointly bringing to market value-added products. With other groups, however, they are less competitive and enjoy a productive collaboration in spite of occasional, even inevitable, tensions. ISVs are thus challenged to strike a comfortable balance between competition and collaboration, with the scale tipped to the latter. In other words, collaboration—and not competition—ought to be the primary characteristic of an ISV's working relationship with Microsoft. If there is too much competition and tension in the relationship, it will be difficult to stike a balance and will generate only more tension. Of course, the proper balance between collaboration and competition is difficult to gauge and varies for each ISV depending on the level of partnership sought. ISVs then must find the right balance in the relationship, as Citrix and NetIQ, which is case-studied above, have done so well.

Citrix Balances Collaboration and Competition, Delivering Value

Citrix Systems (www.citrix.com) is a Microsoft Gold Certified, Windows Embedded and Global ISV Partner based in Fort Lauderdale, Florida, that develops access software products under its MetaFrame brand name. It counts more than 160,000 corporate customers and 60 million user licenses to its credit worldwide. With annual revenues of US$841 million and 2,700 employees, Citrix—founded in 1989—has an enviable partnership with Microsoft, which named Citrix its Global ISV Partner of the Year in 2003.

Microsoft and Citrix have partnered closely for 15 years. The two announced a significant cross-licensing and joint-development pact in 1997 to develop the Windows NT 4.0 Terminal Server Edition and Windows 2000 terminal-services technology. The pair signed another in 2002, giving Citrix access to the Windows source code. In December 2004, an expanded collaboration agreement was signed for Citrix to provide input on the Terminal Server for Windows "Longhorn." This new pact is effective until 2010, and adds a new provision that grants both parties broad access to their respective patents and Citrix access to the Windows source code once again. The partnership has been lucrative for both parties and is expected to remain so. Citrix aims to be a US$1 billion software company and is well on its way to achieving that.

As we have pointed out, some ISVs have been adversely affected by Microsoft's decision to integrate certain features of their products into Windows. Browser developer Netscape is an obvious example of an ISV hurt by Microsoft's operating system integration strategy with Internet Explorer, for example. Citrix, on the other hand, is an example of an ISV that has prospered from Microsoft's integration of that ISV's terminal services technology into Windows.

Citrix and others thrive as a result of Microsoft's intrusion into their market space while still others have been marginalized or had doors closed on them. Why? How was Citrix able to strike the right balance between collaboration and competition?

According to Citrix's top Microsoft alliance executive—David Jones, senior vice president of corporate development—there are three key strategies that have enabled Citrix to flourish where other ISVs have faltered: sustained revenue generation for Microsoft, articulation of that value through constant communication with Microsoft and aggressive investment in product development. Citrix learned the hard way that an ISV that hopes to be successful with Microsoft needs to execute on all three fronts or risk being marginalized.

Revenue generation is by far the most important metric. But equally important is the ISV's ability to articulate its business value to Microsoft and its customers on an ongoing basis. As Mr Jones explains, "it is important for an ISV to generate revenues for Microsoft, do the math, and constantly keep Microsoft apprised of that value—or risk having its market usurped."

He should know. Citrix let its communications with Microsoft slide during the Internet boom years and learned a hard lesson in that it needs to keep in close communication with Microsoft—constantly—by articulating and proving its financial value to Microsoft in terms of pull-through licenses of Microsoft product sold to Citrix customers. Unlike other businesses, Microsoft will not be lulled with golf outings, social events and personal appeals, Mr Jones notes. Microsoft wants hard numbers and business value. Citrix did just that and it worked. The ISV calculated that it generated US$200 million for Microsoft in 2003, and projected that it would generate US$250 million in 2004, and roughly US$300 million for Microsoft in 2005. "Numbers like these get Microsoft's attention. But it will not mean anything unless the ISV spells it out," Mr Jones said.

Citrix learned that it must prove its value proposition, consistently communicate that value, and persuade Microsoft that the benefits of collaboration far outweigh the potential value of competition. So far, it has worked, according to Mr Jones:

"You have to be relentless in your communications with Microsoft to educate and re-educate them about your business plans, product plans, customer wins and how your product adds customer value. If you step away for any length of time, problems occur. In Microsoft's DNA, in their soul, Microsoft believes it can do everything pretty well. We have to prove our business model to them. Citrix calculated that for every Citrix dollar in revenue, Microsoft gets 75 cents and application revenues from all client deployments. So we not only add value to Microsoft's product but we extend the reach of Microsoft and any devices connecting in. It is a heck of a sweet deal for them." Microsoft will accede to an ISV's greater capabilities if it is deemed in the company's best interest and that of its customers.

In addition, Mr Jones says, good working relationships with Microsoft personnel are essential. Successful ISVs must sustain and extend these relationships, and always remain focused on business, financially and operationally. "It is important for ISVs to form close relationships with Microsoft corporate and field personnel. The more we remain aligned with their ecosystem, the better. We align our own CRM systems and increase dialogue with them in the field and do a better job of calculating the revenues we drive for each other. We quantify best practices. We have a team of two business development people in Seattle and another executive in Fort Lauderdale, as well as people in marketing, business development and people in sales and channel organizations, distribution, product management, and solutions marketing working with Microsoft."

Citrix responded to Microsoft's plan to enter the terminal services market with great urgency and flexibility by partnering with them, licensing the technology to them and making it a platform it could extend with its MetaFrame products. Citrix's partnering strategy strengthened its relationship with Microsoft and its own stock price. But then it let its partnering efforts slide, which had a direct impact.

"In 1997, Microsoft announced what they were doing with Windows remoting and it took our stock from $40 to $6 per share in one day," Mr Jones recalls. "We took up space in hotels in Seattle and worked with them to commission us to write and embed terminal services into Windows and the relationship was extremely strong. But between 1999 and 2001, we were all-out-smoking in our own success and then it crashed and reality set in. But during that whole bubble period, pre-Y2K, we stopped talking to Microsoft. Our stock went back down to $6. We dramatically increased our communications with Microsoft at all levels in corporate and in the field. I built a virtual Microsoft team led by one ex-Microsoft employee from Australia who I moved to Seattle. And so we have a worldwide team in Seattle and each of those people is measured and compensated based on Microsoft satisfaction. Our Microsoft team is very cross-functional. You need one to coordinate with Microsoft and to align your business with theirs. We interface with support, consulting, product management and marketing. We have a PAM, and we know how their partner-facing people are measured. In fact, there are 24 Microsoft personnel worldwide whose variable compensation is based on our success and that of other ISVs."

Citrix also invests heavily to ensure that its MetaFrame software adds significant value over and above what Microsoft's core terminal services technology offers. For example, there are more than 700 Citrix engineers working on access software problems, many of which are based on terminal services technology; Microsoft, by contrast, has around 50 personnel dedicated to terminal services. Citrix ensures that the development efforts of its product teams complement those of Microsoft. It is also committed to continual innovation in terminal services technology and will continue to drive Microsoft server licenses for the foreseeable future. In this way, Microsoft can feel comfortable that customers' needs will be met so it can focus its attentions to areas of the operating system that are lacking and need Microsoft's attentions and resources. "If you do the math, it is not rocket science. Of course, Microsoft could be more competitive with us but why should they make a substantial investment in doing something their partner does?" Mr Jones asks.

So Microsoft considered ramping up its terminal services efforts but was successfully persuaded by its ISV partner to change course. The ISV stated its argument which Microsoft analyzed and then decided to change its direction. In turn, Citrix pledged continued fidelity as a Microsoft-centric partner. Citrix said it decided solely based on customer needs not to develop a Linux server version of its software, as other ISVs have done. "Microsoft changed the roadmap based on a reallocation of resources to other areas. And we are a beneficiary," Mr Jones said. "Adding terminal services functionality that Citrix already does, instead of working on security and patch management, does not make sense for Microsoft."

Mr Jones points to two verities that ISVs should take to heart: Microsoft will accede to a partner's greater capabilities if it is deemed in the best interests of the company and its customers. But it requires firmness on the part of an ISV to stay the course, develop innovative solutions that complement Microsoft platforms and products, clearly articulate its value in hard numbers, and collaborate with Microsoft in order to generate activity and deliver superior value.

Target Microsoft Personnel: Quality and Quantity

Making connection points into Microsoft is equally as important as an ISV's innovation, complementarity and collaboration with the company. The overriding objective is to determine who—and what types of employees—are suitable to pursue in the Microsoft organization in order to form a collaborative, symbiotic partnership.

Knowing whom to contact and work with at Microsoft is essential. ISVs must target appropriate contacts within product groups at corporate in order to gain traction. But the answer depends on the features and function of an ISV's offering and how they can best be leveraged with and by Microsoft to foster growth in markets that they jointly pursue.

The key is to find the product or vertical group within Microsoft that will intrinsically benefit most from what your product offers and will work with you to bring the solution most capably to market. This assumes that you have a solid grasp on your competencies and place in the Microsoft ecosystem, and that your solution advances Microsoft's and your firm's individual and collective causes.

ISVs, then, are more motivated to bond with Microsoft product groups than, say, a reseller partner. But aligning locally should be an ISV's first step; that is, interacting with the local Microsoft field office for insight and facilitated introductions throughout the field and into product groups works best.

Align Locally, Extend Globally

As underscored earlier, "all politics are local" at Microsoft and this applies to ISVs as well as to services partners. The rules of the game are established at corporate but are played out at the local level, and they determine *how* field teams are measured and compensated. An ISV will gain (rewards) or lose (risks) to the extent that it aligns its interests with its local field teams, and to the extent that Microsoft's local field team aligns the ISV with appropriate corporate product teams.

Aligning with your local field team is the first and foremost priority in the majority of circumstances. It may seem more appropriate for a software startup to try to fast-track its success by setting up shop in Seattle and attempting to get close to product groups and engineers at corporate first. But that is a common mistake that many software startups make, according to the CEO of SourceCode Holdings, a Microsoft ISV that originated in South Africa—more than 10,000 miles away from Microsoft headquarters—and yet quickly climbed the ladder to become a Global ISV. It eventually moved its corporate headquarters from South Africa to Seattle, to enable better communications with product groups but only after earning significant customer wins and a track record of strong partnering with Microsoft field personnel at local offices in South Africa.

Adriaan Van Wyk, SourceCode Holdings' CEO, emphasized that aligning locally is a very important strategy for any ISV interested in achieving symbiosis with Microsoft: "If you are building a relationship with Microsoft, you have to make a choice: do I work in Seattle or do I spend time building relationships with the field office? You have limited time and resources. A big mistake companies often make is they decide to camp out in Seattle and that is the first place where they plan to open offices, meet product groups and think the rest will happen. There are no customer purchase orders in Seattle. We took a different approach. We decided to go out and get some traction with 15 or 20 customers and then go to the local office and field office to form relationships. It is an interesting scenario: we saw competitors take the first strategy (go to corporate first), and we went with the second approach, and we have been more successful. We started out regionally and got traction in our home region and then carefully decided which was the next region to approach. It was only after three years of hard work, getting customer wins and maturing our intellectual property that we got traction from Microsoft corporate in Seattle and go-to-market funding." SourceCode moved its headquarters from South Africa to Redmond, Washington, in 2004, after being tapped by Microsoft to collaborate and co-develop workflow technology. But that would not have occurred had the ISV not earned significant customer wins and built a track record of strong partnering with its local Microsoft field personnel in South Africa.

There are exceptions to this principle. It is not entirely relevant to align locally with your Microsoft field team when, for example, your account manager or technical-sales and solutions-sales managers work in different locations than the field team. For example, some ISVs establish sales offices in cities where their opportunities are more prevalent although their partner account managers do not reside there. ISVs often have salespeople who work from different cities or are predominantly on the road. Still, executive management alignment between the ISV and their Microsoft field teams is paramount even if it is not tied to one location.

An ISV should expect only limited support from its local field team if a particular customer account is located outside of that district. In such cases, the ISV sales teams and Microsoft partner account managers are often better served by working directly with corporate product groups if they have the necessary connections into them. This does not, however, negate the need for such ISVs to cultivate and nurture relationships within their Microsoft-designated field teams on a periodic basis, in both the geographies and industry verticals they target.

Since "all politics are local," then, local alignment—the number of interactions your firm has with field representatives, the number of customer calls you make together, the extent of your interaction—is essential to keep your firm first and foremost in the minds of your Microsoft colleagues. Your Microsoft relationships in the field— whence doors to corporate are opened, and where all sales are made—are vital to your firm's success with Microsoft. Working with corporate groups—whether they are product or industry vertical-focused (industry vertical groups are a new breed in Microsoft, and vary among regions but they are evolving in importance to ISVs)— is also very important. Yet we have learned that local alignment is the most important first step because field representatives can open both customer and corporate doors, while corporate personnel can only open doors to the field.

In addition to identifying *with whom* they should work, Microsoft's ISV-partners must also assess *how many* contacts they have at Microsoft and constantly increase their number of connections points into Microsoft to leverage them whenever and as much as possible. As highlighted throughout this chapter, it is imperative for ISVs, indeed all partners, to build and properly manage many relationships at Microsoft in order to extend their networks through introductions and to generate opportunity referrals as a result. This is a critical best practice for ISVs.

Many ISVs hang their hopes for success on one Microsoft connection point—an acquaintance, a relationship—in the particular geographical or vertical markets that they hope to penetrate. Do not waste your time with this limited approach. One, two, three connections points in any given market with Microsoft is not enough! And in some cases, quality is less important than quantity. If you have deep friendships with three Microsoft employees in a geographical or vertical market, your chances of success in penetrating the market may be less beneficial than if you had multiple professional relationships with five or more. Keep your friendships by all means, as they make life meaningful. But this is business. Volume counts.

If you are not actively engaged in professional relationships with at least four or five Microsoft representatives in each market, your firm will not get the traction it deserves. If you intend to go to market and to co-brand with Microsoft, you need to establish multiple points at Microsoft.

ISVs should have at least four connection points in Microsoft in every geographic market, including at least one solution specialist, one business productivity advisor, one account manager, and one MCS representative.

Let us boil this down to particulars: how many Microsoft employees do you know in your local office? How often do you talk to them? How many Microsoft employees in your local field office know you or about your firm's product? What do they think about your product relative to your competitors and their subsidiary's GTM goals? When was the last time Microsoft field personnel brought you on or accompanied you to a sales call? Or referred you a lead or an opportunity? These are important questions that must be answered to ascertain the fundamental health of your partnership with Microsoft.

To recap, it is important for ISVs to take a two-pronged approach, working from field to corporate and from corporate to field, in that order. Align locally first. Field-level connection points are as essential to the success of an ISV as they are to a services partner or a VAR. One can measure the progress of this approach obviously based on the number of leads or referrals, and the size of contract wins, achieved through field-level relationships with Microsoft. But even the quantity of conversations or email messages exchanged with Microsoft personnel is indicative of an ISV's traction within the company. It is important that every communication with Microsoft personnel is an effort to advance Microsoft's cause since it is a results-oriented company. And these communications must obviously be relevant to the contact—never waste a Microsoft employee's time.

In working with any Microsoft personnel, you must also be mindful of something more fundamental: scarcity of time. Microsoft personnel have precious little time in which to achieve challenging sales quotas and product deadlines. Always assume that they are busier than you. Microsoft hires people, as some have said, with the attention span of gnats for whom constant movement from one goal or objective to the next is *de rigeur*, and they are generally wired in this way to switch gears speedily. Others more charitably refer to this reality as the "Microsoft millisecond." What it means for ISVs is that they must be committed to the principle of *carpe diem* with Microsoft. You must be ready and willing to take on a challenging assignment at any moment, without hesitation or indecision. In order to have this urgency, it is essential that ISVs know their competencies, their target market and how Microsoft perceives their products and/or services. One should at all times be prepared to give Microsoft employees an effective, concise and compelling account of why Microsoft should do business with one's firm.

Get the point? It is very simple: *you* have ultimate influence over how many Microsoft field (and corporate) employees know you and your product and think favorably about both. The more of them that you can count, the greater your chances will be to track your progress with Microsoft. This is both about you and not about you. You have the wherewithal to influence Microsoft to your favor, but it is Microsoft's favor for your company and its solutions that counts.

Qualitative measures enter into the calculation once you have a sufficient quantity of Microsoft field personnel thinking and saying good things about your products. You must focus your relationship-management and value-selling efforts on field-level solutions and sales specialists. But you must also penetrate the field-level management tier, from account managers to the general manager. Doing so may not drive more business your way, but it will certainly help you extend your network within the Microsoft field and establish links to corporate. This approach ensures that your account manager need not ask corporate for referrals when they need a solutions specialist at a customer site: they will already know about your capabilities—thanks to your relationship-building efforts.

It is important to determine how managers in the field are compensated and which GTMs rank highest on their list of priorities. Go ahead, ask! But use discretion when broaching the topic. Mike Thomas is vice president of sales for Shavlik Technologies, a Microsoft security ISV based in St Paul, Minnesota, that has a strong connection into Microsoft: his boss Mark Shavlik, the firm's founder, is a former Microsoft developer who served on the original Windows NT Server project and who created a popular utility for downloading patches and updates to Window. The ISV later licensed its technology to Microsoft for the Microsoft Security Baseline Analyzer. Mr Thomas has partnered with Microsoft in various capacities for more than 15 years. He claims that a firm's having a former Microsoft employee as a founder is no panacea; it can either help you or hurt you. In his estimation, it is more important for ISVs to form many connections within Microsoft and glean what objectives are on the GM's scorecard—but be aware that such information is not made public. It must be extracted delicately in the context of trusted relationships, Mr Thomas advises: "Make connections. You need lots of contacts because everyone shifts chairs at Microsoft. If you bet on one person, they will change jobs, so you will need a breadth of relationships and persistence. Microsoft is really good about giving referrals and giving out email addresses, but not phone numbers. You need to be persistent to find out what their objectives are. And Microsoft GMs will not easily make known their Management By Objectives (MBO) status, because it reveals their vulnerabilities. Yet you can ask them obliquely what is important to them and ask how you can help satisfy their needs. And they will give it to you."

It is also very important to sustain the level of communications with Microsoft at a suitably high level in your firm and to measure your progress in discernible ways to advance your firm's objectives in partnering with the company. Consider the example of Pebblestone.

Pebblestone Measures Tactics from the Top

Pebblestone (www.pebblestone.nl) is a Microsoft Gold Certified Partner based in Nieuwerkerk, The Netherlands. The firm develops ERP software for the fashion industry. Founded in 1995, it became a Microsoft partner when the software giant acquired Navision in 2002. Pebblestone employs 100 people in its European and US offices. It has no other corporate partner besides Microsoft.

Pebblestone's CEO Leo van der Grinten and Theo Doelman, vice president of international marketing and sales, manage the Microsoft relationship capably and according to distinct metrics. Pebblestone ensures that it generates as much revenue for Microsoft in product and services sales as Pebblestone itself earns. That gives Microsoft a definite interest in taking Pebblestone's calls.

Of the 100-employee company, five employees are involved in developing the Microsoft relationship although the overall partnership is managed from the top. The primary Microsoft relationship managers for Pebblestone are, in fact, Messrs Van der Grinten and Doelman. They communicate with Microsoft employees—in corporate product groups and with the field organization—nearly every day, averaging approximately 20 phone calls, email messages and meetings per month. Microsoft representatives, in turn, contact Pebblestone employees several times per week.

Despite the high contact ratio of Pebblestone-to-Microsoft employees, Pebblestone has not had to rely on business referrals from Microsoft. This indicates Pebblestone's efficiency in garnering its own business leads, another characteristic that successful ISVs and other partners in Microsoft's ecosystem exhibit. The high contact ratio simply demonstrates that Microsoft and Pebblestone are engaged, and at a personal level with top executives. Again, ISVs are rewarded for dedicating resources to enable the symbiosis. Microsoft has granted Pebbestone co-marketing funds because of its efforts to sail alongside the SS Microsoft.

Pebblestone hopes to extend its network within Microsoft and as a result expand its operations and opportunities globally. Intended expansion through extensive communication with Microsoft is Pebblestone's strategy and, based on initial results, it is working well.

Weigh Risks and Rewards

Knowing whom to contact and to work with at Microsoft is essential. But this, in turn, begs another important question ISVs ought to consider before approaching Microsoft: what are the perceived risks and rewards of partnering with your firm—from Microsoft's perspective? We assume that you have come to terms with your own risks and rewards of partnering with the company. But what are Microsoft's risks in working with your firm? It is important for you to determine your strengths and weaknesses, and to appreciate how Microsoft may perceive your liabilities as well as your strengths. Both scenarios must be addressed before determining the right people to work with at Microsoft. Be prepared to address Microsoft's perceived risks (downplay them) and rewards (play them up) in partnering with your firm.

As a case in point, when Microsoft was developing Windows XP Service Pack 2 (SP2), it had many difficulties with ISV-partners not updating their products to reflect its new APIs, which delayed SP2's release. Consider that some security-focused ISVs, such as anti-virus manufacturers, may have dragged their feet on developing their applications' compatibility with SP2 and yet, poignantly from Microsoft's perspective, they had updated versions of their applications for Linux, Solaris and Macintosh platforms. That is, from Microsoft's perspective, these ISVs would be doing work for the benefit of competitive platforms—pleasing someone else—so the company would appropriately question their loyalty if not energy on Microsoft's behalf. Such an ISV would be perceived as a risky partner as opposed to a rewarding partner by Microsoft. In such circumstances, Microsoft may be inclined to move on—move into the development sphere of—these ISVs' products and co-opt their functionality into its products and platforms. Not that this occurred, but it surely is conceivable from Microsoft's perspective of the risks and rewards of partnering with Microsoft.

A scenario may illustrate the principle. Assume that you are a Microsoft partner in good standing. You have at least one certified product, and your firm plans to launch a new business-intelligence (BI) solution on the Microsoft platform for a particular industry vertical. You want to leverage Microsoft as much as possible to generate more sales of your product under the aegis of Microsoft's brand.

The first question your firm must ask is, which Microsoft group gains the most benefit from your product? The answer points to the area of highest reward from which you must also weigh the risks. In this case, the highest reward area would likely be the Windows Server product group because of its massive sales volume. If your solution runs on Microsoft SQL Server, then the SQL Server group, too, would benefit from your product. Once you have assessed the product groups you would like to target, query your Microsoft field organization for as much information as possible about the players in these groups, what they seek in partners, how they work with partners and what might be the best way to approach their executives. Go ahead, ask! Perhaps Microsoft even has funding available to certify a SQL Server-related solution. You could approach the company to finance a proof of concept with an agreeable customer that demonstrates the success of your solution in combination with a Microsoft product. Perhaps business intelligence is ranked as a high priority on your district's general manager's GTM scorecard. This kind of information drilling can help you determine your best course based on the rewards from your perspective but especially Microsoft's.

Perhaps the situation is more complicated in that you discover that your BI solution is competitive with a similar solution being developed for the same vertical by Microsoft's Information Worker product group on its own or with another partner. In this case, you want to steer clear of that group because your offering is directly competitive with that group's and, therefore, the competitive tension would be too great. There would be little basis for developing a relationship. Your product is not complementary—the risk is too high from your perspective and Microsoft's—so any effort to cooperate would be unproductive, and could impair your ability to partner with a more suitable product group within Microsoft. You should avail yourself of your Microsoft field representative, on whose advice you rely to make an informed decision.

Remember that field teams elect their own GTMs to focus on as a subset of those that Microsoft corporate defines for the fiscal year. It is important for you to ensure that your product and your initiatives are in line with the appropriate corporate product groups and complement the GTM priorities of your Microsoft field team. What are the top priorities on your field team's general manager's scorecard, and how does your solution deliver on those numbers? How many SQL Server license deals will your solution drive? That is, the same rules apply in working with corporate as they do with the field: you seek as much collaboration as possible and try to minimize competition.

It is imperative that the account manager, technical-sales and solutions-sales managers in your field office have a vested interest in driving Windows Server and SQL Server-generated revenue through ISV solutions such as your BI offering. If Microsoft's account, technical-sales or solutions-sales managers are measured and compensated on the promotion of the business intelligence solution that the Microsoft group is developing, on the other hand, you will find yourself in a competitive stance with corporate and field. It is best to avoid this. You cannot win in such a scenario. The risk would outweigh the rewards.

In summary, then, ISVs should assess the collaborative-competitive balance of a possible relationship with Microsoft by determining the interests and priorities of field and product groups. But you need to ask the right questions. The answers to these questions will lead you to the proper risk/reward calculus.

It is important for ISVs to develop a plan for field engagement with Microsoft and to invest in relationship-management techniques in order to achieve the best partnership possible. As many successful partners point out, making joint calls with Microsoft can be very beneficial in persuading a customer to adopt a solution. How ISVs choose to introduce Microsoft's local field team to their customers, however, must be handled on a case-by-case basis. Some ISV–partners opt not to bring Microsoft to meetings with all of their prospective customers because they prefer independence and want to steer clear of any possibility that Microsoft may trump them and swing the deal to a Microsoft product or a competitive partner's product. Some ISVs bring Microsoft in when it advantages them, such as when, for example, the customer is undecided about adopting a Microsoft solution and Microsoft's credibility can help swing the deal favorably.

ISVs must understand that there is also a necessary investment of time and effort to identify the right groups within Microsoft to work with and to establish productive relationships with them. These considerations—the costs of partnering with Microsoft—incline some ISVs not to pursue certification or co-marketing opportunities with Microsoft. This may appear to be a safe way to do business but there are significant opportunity costs attached to this approach. If partnering with Microsoft affords an ISV the stability and power of the Microsoft brand in the market and potentially lucrative co-branding and co-selling arrangements, then of what benefit is it for an ISV–partner to go it alone on prospective deals and lose these valuable benefits? No ISV is an island in Microsoft's partner ecosystem. If Microsoft learns about an ISV's desire for independence, it could frustrate the partnership by steering clear of that ISV, thus helping it to be more independent and perhaps less successful.

From these working scenarios, then, one can see that there are many challenges in assessing one's risk/reward calculus. Knowing Microsoft's culture is quite important but so, too, is factoring in Microsoft's strategy and organizational dynamic as well as the requirements of partnering. These are not lofty, theoretical considerations but practical business judgments about risk and reward. If a newly appointed GM in your district is encouraging more sales of SQL Server, and you have learned that the Microsoft product group will likely scrap its plans for a BI solution, it is a good time to move in. Timing may be on your side, or maybe not. But it is up to you to weigh the risks and rewards, and your Microsoft counterparts can help you.

It is always advisable to go to market with a product that fits well with Microsoft's new release or latest field-endorsed GTM and to make sure that there are a number of Microsoft employees who will recommend your product to customers. Be careful how far you stick your neck out backing Microsoft's early technologies, though; it is important to be first to market with Microsoft, but necessary to ensure that there will be a market into which you can sell your product. Alternatively, dedicating only limited resources to new, more risky Microsoft projects is an option for currying favor with the company while ensuring that your firm can continue earning a healthy revenue stream while it tests these new technologies in your customer base.

Remember innovation and symbiosis? ISVs must be in a position to collaborate with Microsoft from the early stages of product conception through the marketing blitz of a product launch. It is impossible to co-innovate when your firm is not joined at the hip strategically and operationally with Microsoft. This requires field-level awareness of your product and field-initiated ties into corporate product groups. It is important to weigh potential rewards against risks to achieve a proper balance in your partnership with Microsoft. Yet sometimes taking risks—such as backing brand new technologies that Microsoft deems strategic—is a good way to form strong relationships in the field and particularly at corporate. Even if that risk does not pan out immediately, it will likely generate rewards at some point since relationships in Microsoft are so fundamental, as we learn from Apptero.

Evolving with Microsoft: Lessons Learned from Apptero

ISVs (and services partners) who are willing to back emerging, strategic Microsoft technologies take a big risk. But win or lose, they make friends in high places at Seattle. And they learn a lot, too.

Take, for example, Avinon, an ISV in the web-services market that backed Microsoft's .NET platform in a big way. In November 2001, months after Microsoft's .NET was first announced, the San Francisco-based ISV signed a three-year alliance with Microsoft. Originally, Avinon had backed a cross-platform strategy like many of the pioneering web-services startups in the early 2000s. And because Avinon was willing to back .NET exclusively and to dump support for Java, Microsoft responded generously, pledging to provide its ISV partner with financial backing, joint product roadmaps and marketing-development funds. Yet Avinon executives knew they were rolling the dice. "We were a .NET poster child, but also a guinea pig," said David Ruiz, Avinon's vice president of marketing, at the time.

He was not kidding. Roughly a year later, Avinon closed its doors.

Nevertheless, the executives who founded Avinon built strong relationships at Microsoft corporate that continue to pay off. And they learned some important lessons that they carry into their new venture, lessons that are beneficial to all ISVs.

Avinon's founders launched a startup in February 2003, called Apptero (www.apptero.com)—based at Oakland, California—that also bets heavily on the .NET client-side technologies, but that models and prototypes enterprise applications that could run on any platform. Having a past relationship with Dan'l Lewin, Microsoft's corporate vice president of .NET business development, and other key product and program managers has certainly helped the startup. But company executives also built a business model more insulated from the risk of betting on new technologies. Their success was affirmed in May 2005, when the company was acquired.

"Ideally you want a relationship where you are not just one of thousands of partners but something much more strategic. We achieved this in our last company because we started Avinon when web services and .NET were so hot. That helped get our foot in the door and build a base of relationships that we could leverage going forward," said David Ruiz, now Apptero's vice president of product marketing and management.

For example, Apptero's founding executives were able to re-engage quickly with Dan'l Lewin and his emerging-business organization and to get briefings with the Microsoft Office System and Visual Studio product teams because of these relationships. Like other ISVs close to Microsoft, Apptero is informed early about changes on the horizon so they can properly develop and market their add-on products. But that is not all. Mr Ruiz said he learned many lessons from the Avinon experience that have helped him and his colleagues create a company that has a better chance at success in the market. The lessons learned include the following:

Ensure that the technology you embrace has a go-to-market strategy and business interest in the field. Avinon followed a technology strategy that was in its infancy. Back in 2001, .NET was a corporate initiative that had little market adoption at the time. Now with Apptero, the founders of Avinon are leveraging the knowledge and relationships formed when .NET was in its infancy, but are part of a maturing and growing market. Apptero's products leverage .NET and add value to Microsoft's flagship Office and Visual Studio products. In this way, Apptero is aiming for a balanced product strategy that pleases both Microsoft corporate and field personnel: it embraces strategic technologies such as .NET but offers a solution with real value to enterprise customers today.

Apptero has developed business application-planning software for use with Office and Visual Studio—established products—that leverages multiple, well-defined go-to-market strategies for Microsoft sales and partners. Here, Microsoft's ability to provide marketing programs support for partners helps significantly. "The secret to success is having the right go-to-market angle that is top of mind for the Microsoft field sales force, which is increasingly focused on enterprise sales," Mr Ruiz observed. "At Avinon, we had a .NET solution but no enterprise market ready to go there. Now, with Apptero, we offer a compelling solution that solves a real problem: overcoming the gap between business needs for new applications and IT's ability to deliver them. Our Apptero Composer software runs like an Office companion product while at the same time bridging to the world of developers using Visual Studio. This allows us to leverage Microsoft GTMs for both products."

Make sure your solution extends—but does not directly overlap with— Microsoft technology. "We are focused on providing an on-ramp to the application delivery cycle, extending Visual Studio to provide key capabilities for non-developers. With the introduction of Visual Studio Team System (VSTS), Microsoft is expanding the footprint of Visual Studio to include other team members such as architects, testers and project managers. Still, Microsoft's focus is on developers, allowing us to provide software for business analysts that complements and does not overlap with VSTS. We are not concerned about Microsoft providing lifecycle solutions for the business user anytime real soon, so we have a good angle to work with now. We fill a gap in Visual Studio for the business user while the combination of Apptero and Microsoft offers a more complete solution to the marketplace," Mr Ruiz said.

Make sure your solution is Microsoft-friendly but extends to other platforms. Apptero has developed a Microsoft-friendly solution that is based on .NET technology yet allows customers to build application models and prototypes that run on any platform. The strategy is Microsoft-centric yet it dovetails with Microsoft's efforts to extend its reach into heterogeneous enterprise environments. According to Mr Ruiz, "at Avinon, we made a bet on .NET completely for both the client and server. With Apptero, we are still using Microsoft tools, but the models we create are totally platform-agnostic. The application could ultimately run on .NET, IBM WebSphere or BEA WebLogic. This opens up opportunities in both Microsoft-centric and Java-centric enterprises."

Learn from your mistakes. "There is no question, we were too early with Avinon. .NET was too early, web services in the enterprise was too early, and we were too early. And, to top it off, we launched in a down market that was very deep and continues to linger to this day. But there is no one to fault," Mr Ruiz commented. "If you never innovate or take risks, you never give yourself an opportunity to start new software companies that deliver real value."

ISVs need constantly to assess the risks and rewards of their activities with and apart from Microsoft and to seek balance in their collaboration and competition in order for both parties to remain productive in the partnership.

Calculating the risk and reward of partnering with Microsoft is an essential first step in seeking to partner on a product initiative, but be prepared to shift your strategies accordingly when working with a company as dynamic as Microsoft.

Remain Urgent and Flexible, but Always Firm

As in any market, the software market changes and not always for the better. Not every firm has the resources, like Microsoft, to accommodate and rise to the challenges of dramatic change successfully. Still, ISVs must find ways to ride Microsoft's waves in order to succeed.

Take, for example, Microsoft's sudden reallocation of personnel and resources in January 2001, to push Exchange 2000 more aggressively and, in the autumn of that year, to push SQL Server 2000 in similar fashion. The sales numbers for both products were not as high as Microsoft had expected in 2000 so the company invested more personnel and market funding to drive sales in 2001. In the end, Microsoft wildly exceeded its most optimistic revised projections for fiscal-year sales. Microsoft made that investment because both products were deemed critical to Microsoft's overall strategy. Sales of those products got top priority, and everyone in Microsoft's ecosystem—including ISVs—focused on delivering results.

ISVs that developed add–ons for Exchange and SQL naturally benefited. But what happened to the ISV-partners that had, for example, enterprise backup and recovery solutions or other software products that were not directly aligned with Microsoft's targeted product push? They could not shift on a dime and change their product strategy to fit Microsoft's urgent need to sell its enterprise platforms. Microsoft's sudden shifts in focus, as evidenced above, can often stall or derail the market progress and product development of some ISV-partners as Microsoft's available resources are shifted away from peripheral product development and sales to the new priorities.

At times like these, ISVs need good working relationships at Microsoft to be able to shift with the company and make themselves perceived as team players. ISVs must reposition their products and their benefits in order to align with Microsoft's new focus. Many ISVs—even those whose products do not easily fit into the revised game plan—can tap into Microsoft's urgency if their organization is flexible. In the aforementioned case, for instance, an ISV with an enterprise backup solution might respond by investing in an advertising campaign that focuses on new government regulations requiring companies to backup email systems. That messaging helps sell the ISV's product and, indirectly, Microsoft Exchange. By exhibiting a sense of flexibility and urgency, and an ability to react nimbly, an ISV can ride the wave and benefit from the shift in course rather than get pulled by the current and lost at sea. Such tactics will prove your allegiance and preserve your traction within Microsoft as an actively engaged partner that can respond swiftly when the SS Microsoft calls for all hands on deck.

The same principles apply in more routine scenarios—Microsoft's quarterly or semi-annual shifts in personnel assignments. These regular changes of Microsoft personnel among positions can be frustrating because partners invest significantly to build relationships with field contacts, who move on to new roles after a brief tenure. Another Microsoft employee moves into that position and you have to start from scratch to build that new relationship.

What many partners fail to appreciate and seize upon, however, is the opportunity these frustrating organizational changes offer to ISVs to assert themselves and assume the driver's seat in the partnership. For not only do you have an old friend in a new position at Microsoft to serve as an advocate for you and possibly give you an entrée to a new product group, but you also have an opportunity to form another relationship with a new Microsoft representative. Make yourself invaluable as a go-to resource for these novices and form more bonds with Microsoft personnel. The requirement for constant relationship building puts significant demands on ISVs but you should exude the same flexibility and urgency as Microsoft. In nearly all of the case studies presented in this chapter, successful ISVs point to the importance of having numerous connection points within Microsoft and the ability to exploit this revolving door to their favor.

Your job as an ISV-partner is to leverage the Microsoft organization at all available levels to keep your firm at the forefront of strategic, tactical and organizational developments in a manner that is appropriate in the Microsoft culture. You do this by implementing simple relationship management techniques and constantly articulating the value of your products as conduits for selling Microsoft software. Always keep the ball moving upfield. Learn to lead at all opportune moments. Master the art of backseat driving.

Consider another less routine but still applicable scenario that affords ISVs with new opportunities: Microsoft's acquisitions. In recent years, Microsoft acquired Great Plains Software and Navision—both prominent ISVs in their respective markets—and these acquisitions have been accompanied by significant strategic and tactical shifts, more down-market, as well as by changes in the company's platform push. Microsoft's vigorous move into the business-applications market caused concern among some partners who perceived this as an assault on their marketplace. With these changes have come grumblings from many ISVs that Microsoft's CRM and ERP push into the small and mid-sized business market has diluted the value of its ISV-partner products and proved to be directly competitive with them. Perhaps these ISV partners do not want to take Microsoft's suggestion and move down market, or they do not think they have a chance in such a battle. But this is not necessarily true. These ISVs should focus on adding value and extending Microsoft's product lineup, and forming a more complementary—rather than competitive—approach. Here, too, urgency and flexibility are key assets that can help smaller ships move astern of the SS Microsoft and, in fact, benefit from the massive volume opportunities that result from Microsoft's intrusion into their markets.

The key is to learn in advance from your Microsoft colleagues all you can about product and marketing changes on the horizon and to position your firm favorably to rise to the occasion—quickly, effectively—as Microsoft's culture dictates. These are core attributes of successful ISVs. There are no better mechanisms, no more proven tactics, other than to align locally, leverage the field organization, and extend relationships with Microsoft personnel who know you and know the worth of your company and its products. Again, here, ISVs that form a healthy symbiosis with Microsoft's organization and culture can leverage these relationships to extend regionally, nationally and internationally, and continue to innovate their products in a manner that adds value to Microsoft's platform goals. Additionally, successful ISV-partners pattern themselves after Microsoft's culture and practices, as we have seen, but they are also comfortable in their own skin. They know the value of their company and solutions and remain firm—like an oak tree, bending but never breaking—as Microsoft changes course.

Let us consider several Microsoft global ISVs that have demonstrated these traits—urgency, flexibility, and firmness of purpose—and mastered the art of Microsoft partnering.

Apptix Reinvents Itself

Apptix (www.apptix.com) is a Microsoft Gold Certified Partner for Hosting and Application Services based in Sterling, Virginia. The ISV is a software platform and services company that spun off from application service provider (ASP) TeleComputing in 2002. The ISV was named Microsoft Global Service Provider of the Year in the Hosting and Application Services category in 2002, after becoming an independent company. It has enjoyed a multi-faceted five-year alliance with Microsoft.

Originally, the founders of Apptix embraced the application service provider (ASP) model, an outsourcing business in which customer applications are hosted by service providers and paid for on a subscription basis. Microsoft backed this business model and invested in it significantly during the late 1990s. But the ASP market was slow to take off and many ASPs closed doors. The ASP model is still considered viable, and many ASPs are retooling their strategies for a future when software subscriptions are adopted more widely.

Apptix survived by spinning off from its parent company, switching gears and repositioning its TECOS software platform as a private-label service to be marketed to more established network service providers, including Bell Canada, NTT, Verio, Digex, MCI, XO and Level 3. Additionally, Apptix formed partnerships with network-service outsourcers, including HP, which uses Apptix's TECOS platform to manage its application-hosting infrastructure.

Apptix has a multi-faceted relationship with Microsoft. Its connections into the Microsoft organization are numerous and varied, and have yielded great returns. Since TECOS is an enabling software platform for mobile applications, Apptix works with Microsoft's Communications and Mobility Group. Apptix also works with various Microsoft product-development groups including the Exchange product team because of the integration of TECOS with Microsoft's messaging platforms and products. It also partners with Microsoft's Network Service Provider (NSP) team and solutions unit to co-develop other enabling technologies for the application-hosting model. Finally, Apptix works with Microsoft as a customer. Apptix, for instance, hosts Microsoft.com's global online program that allows customers to experiment with Exchange and SharePoint over the Internet.

As such, Apptix has roughly 10 connection points within Microsoft. The relationship is a very valuable asset, according to Apptix's former CEO Alex Hawkinson. It is worth dwelling on Mr Hawkinson's view of the partnership, which highlights the value of Apptix's dynamic approach to partnering with an equally dynamic company: "Our relationship with Microsoft has evolved a lot because, every year, Microsoft switches gears and reorganizes pretty fully. Because Microsoft is a very nimble company, each year our company has to switch gears. We have to reinvent our business and partnership with Microsoft every year. To partner effectively with Microsoft, you have to change as much as they do. The formal relationship is not the asset—it is the history *per se,* and you have got to keep it going."

The formal partner program provides the rules of engagement between Microsoft and its partners. But Mr Hawkinson and others emphasize that one must not confuse the formal relationship with the *possibilities* of partnership.

The partner program allows an ISV to get in the door to partner with Microsoft. But what steps an ISV takes in working with Microsoft's people and organization, and structuring that work in the context of advancing its intellectual property and professional responsiveness, is a more important determinant of success than merely earning points. The objective is to preserve and extend your relationships in order to stay ahead of the curve of change. Partnering is dynamic because Microsoft itself is dynamic, constantly adjusting to position itself more favorably to take advantage of market realities. This dynamism diffuses authority—and accountability—throughout the organization, from corporate to the field organizations. This characteristic, which distinguishes Microsoft from many corporations whose power is more centralized, must be taken into account by aspiring ISVs. Microsoft personnel are expected to work well in this environment and to adapt constantly to changes in responsibilities and resources that are provided them to realize their objectives.

In short, Microsoft's dynamism requires its ISV-partners to be as nimble, to know how to navigate the organization, and build and extend connection points with Microsoft's personnel in the field and at corporate. Mr Hawkinson continues: "To have impact, Microsoft does not just empower senior leadership, but all of its people. So, as a partner, you can work with all sorts of people throughout the organization. And you can have an impact. In other companies, your ability to partner directly correlates to your access to the senior executive team. At Microsoft, there is a far broader array of empowered people. Microsoft is nimble. It is a cultural choice made by Gates and Ballmer. They reorganize every year and they give their people clear, measurable objectives, money and promotions based on success. It is a simple formula that works incredibly well. We have learned to work it."

Apptix's success as an ISV–partner derives in large measure from the firm's nimbleness in building and extending its connection points within Microsoft despite annual strategic, tactical and organizational change. It is also due to the firm's ability to reinvent itself in tandem with Microsoft while keeping its bearings and maintaining constant momentum toward being perceived by Microsoft as a valuable partner integral to its product development groups, network service provider efforts and sales in the field. Apptix, for instance, actively participates in the Joint Devel-

PROGRAM	PARTNER	BENEFITS
Rapid Deployment Program (RDP)	ISVs	Access to pre-release Microsoft software
Joint Development Program (JDP)	ISVs, SPs	Co-development gives ISV strong ties into product groups
Early Adopter Program (EAP)	SPs	Early learning offers competitive advantage Strengthens customer and Microsoft relationships

Figure 4.3: Microsoft's Partner-Collaborative Programs.

opment Program (JDP) for Microsoft Exchange and, as a result, it benefits from Microsoft's technical and marketing support before product upgrades launch.

Microsoft shifts gears and directions on an annual basis, and sometimes more frequently if market trends dictate. As we have noted, ISV-partners must remain nimble and co-evolve in step with Microsoft. Microsoft personnel are seasoned at embracing change and nimble at navigating as new corporate mandates are issued. They expect ISVs to follow suit. In this case, Apptix's ability to change course with urgency has enabled it to prosper. Examples of ISVs failing to do so abound.

In 2004, Microsoft's key priorities shifted to shore up its reputation in security and ensure customer wins in competitive engagements against Linux. ISVs whose products were naturally complementary to these new mandates or that changed course to conform to Microsoft's urgency often succeeded. ISVs that helped Microsoft score points in these important categories include Shavlik Technologies, whose patch-management solution naturally helps that security initiative by allowing customers to download security updates to their Windows server. On the second front, Citrix reiterated its pledge not to develop a Linux version of its server software.

ISVs must react quickly, particularly when Microsoft announces its go-to-market strategy or specific initiatives designed to mobilize its sales crews and partners, too. ISVs should be first out of the gate to align their offerings with Microsoft's GTMs in the field, and must inform as many Microsoft employees as possible how their offerings are of value to those initiatives. For example, if Microsoft's marketing push is concentrated on Information Worker products, assess your solution's fitness for the campaign and craft a pithy message, couched in your competency, that will demonstrate for Microsoft employees its precise fitness for their purpose. Emphasize your grasp of Microsoft's priorities in the context of ROI studies or case studies by employing their language to describe your product and the value of the combined platform. If you win the field with your message, you are on your way. But urgency is essential.

Partnering with Microsoft, then, can be like walking a mile over sand dunes in loose-fitting shoes. It is difficult to keep course and even more difficult to sustain traction. The slippage in part comes from ordinary changes in the marketplace that account for Microsoft's changing strategy or tactics. As a dynamic culture, Microsoft's strategy, tactics and organization are subject to change. Industry consolidation, globalization and outsourcing are mega-trend shifts that have impacted all software and hardware companies. But local markets, likewise, are always in flux. And Microsoft is constantly engaged to seize new opportunities that spring up. Among ISVs that have mastered the spirit and the letter of the law of Microsoft partnering—despite a potentially competitive cross-platform strategy—there are few more successful than NetIQ, whose case study is above. NetIQ and others have also mastered the power of leveraged co-branding with Microsoft, which is a topic that warrants some consideration.

Marketing and the Power of the Microsoft Brand: How ISVs Can Apply It

ISVs such as Citrix, NetIQ, Panorama, Apptix and Meridio invest heavily in their partnerships with Microsoft because they recognize the value of co-branding with Microsoft. It is tough to find a better business partner when it comes to marketing and branding than Microsoft.

According to a July 2004, report issued by *Business Week*/Interbrand, the Microsoft brand is ranked the second most valuable in the world behind Coca-Cola. The annual report estimates the value of the Microsoft brand at US$61 billion, only slightly below Coca-Cola's US$67 billion market worth. The value of the third most powerful brand, IBM, is US$54 billion, according to the survey, so Microsoft is in the top spot for high-technology companies.

Microsoft platforms and products have significant value because of the marketing engine that fuels the desired market impressions. Microsoft's marketing machine is legendary. Here, it would appear that Microsoft needs little help from partners. But this is not really the case. Aside from establishing and maintaining brand awareness, there is an oft-neglected element of branding that ISVs and other partners can assist Microsoft with: *applying* the brand. As a result of its worldwide television advertising, Microsoft is a household name; even computer novices know that Microsoft software enables customers to realize their potential, their goals. But what does this really mean?

Brands must be applied, that is, brought down to products that customers actually use in their homes or businesses. Microsoft relies on partners, to some extent, to translate the benefits of its branded software to select customers and select industries. ISVs can apply Microsoft's brand, for example, by emphasizing the need for customers to use its financial software applications in combination with Microsoft Exchange in order to enable email archiving and storage as required by federal mandates. This is a straightforward example.

This dependency is accentuated as Microsoft's software becomes more complex and requires more translation from bits and bytes into business solutions. As Microsoft's portfolio broadens, the company relies on its ISVs and solution providers to blend attributes of the combined product as applied to their particular need, to get to that level of granularity with customers so as to apply the value of the Microsoft brand to their unique situation. For instance, Microsoft is relying heavily on its Office-contributing ISV-partners to translate—define, apply and extend—the product's business benefits for the small and mid-sized business (SMB) market, for example, in a business process automation-application driven by Office, Microsoft Business Solutions and SharePoint. Enterprise customers have had ample financial resources necessary to build business process applications for many years. Yet for many cash-constrained customers in the SMB market, the combination of Microsoft software and new ISV products represents new opportunities to address their business needs, thus applying the Microsoft brand in new ways. Microsoft's ISV–partners are in a powerful position to market to vertical industries and customer segments by educating customers to the new possibilities offered by their applications in tandem with Microsoft's platforms. That is, they must apply the brand effectively, and co-brand with Microsoft.

ISVs work with Microsoft to develop complementary solutions and bring them to local, regional, national and international markets. They can leverage Microsoft's brand name, logo and personnel to bring a joint solution to customers. This is a powerful responsibility—and opportunity—that many ISVs overlook. Applying Microsoft co-branded solutions at market is equally as important as establishing your own brand. Microsoft needs its partners to help extend and reinforce that brand awareness. Conversely, partners need Microsoft's assistance to help extend the brand and their own solutions into the marketplace.

There are practical ways of doing this that some ISVs have mastered. The most obvious way, of course, is inviting Microsoft personnel into prospective customer accounts for pre-sales briefings and backing. There are other perhaps less known but effective and deliberate approaches. Some ISVs are so successful in navigating Microsoft, for instance, that they are invited to participate in semi-weekly and monthly field-level pipeline calls. That is, these ISVs work alongside Microsoft field personnel to formulate tactics for making the Microsoft solution, and the partner co-branded solutions, relevant to the prospective customer accounts, and to devise tactics for bringing the co-branded solutions to them. This level of collaboration and willingness to share insight not only establishes ISVs as trusted advisors in the GTM process; it also saves Microsoft time and money. It makes the partner an extension of Microsoft's sales force and the sales process more efficient and cost-effective, while proactively soothing pre-sales tensions that can occur when the partners are not in agreement about marketing solutions. Do your best to get on these calls.

Co-branding in local markets also affords an ISV—especially startups—greater insight into Microsoft's ways of thinking and go-to-market approach. It allows ISVs to discern relatively quickly the strengths and weaknesses of applying the Microsoft brand to local markets. Armed with this information, successful ISVs are able to adjust their approach to complement and extend Microsoft's approach.

Getting to this stage can be difficult, as we have seen. And it requires empathy on the part of the ISV-partner as well as a seasoned awareness about how to partner with Microsoft to build and extend the edifice of shared interests, to collaborate on innovation and to realize symbiosis in operations, vision of the market and the seizing of market opportunities.

Another essential element of successful partnering with Microsoft is staying abreast of market trends. It is important for ISVs to keep tabs on local, regional and global markets, and to understand Microsoft's dynamic approach to market shifts. How is Microsoft moving to capitalize on opportunities that emerge in cities, states, regions, nations and throughout the global market? How does Microsoft's shifting course impact your opportunities and your own movement? Do you get out of the way, or hitch your boat onto the SS Microsoft and ride the waves as skillfully as possible?

What opportunities do you see on the horizon? Should you share your experience and insight with your local Microsoft field office, or corporate? It depends, of course, on the nature of the opportunity. But the point is that the ISV, like Microsoft, must keep its business dynamic and constantly ask itself, "Where Do I Want To Go Today?" An ISV must constantly address how it can best align itself and its brand with Microsoft.

There are branding tools available from Microsoft that may be of some use. Microsoft offers a Windows logo program for ISVs whose applications are tested and certified for compatibility, and a partner logo builder that enables ISVs and other partners to create custom logos using the Microsoft brand. Microsoft also provides links and referrals to partners from its powerful online and print brand advertising. How can your firm exploit these branding opportunities? To recap, if your timing is right with Microsoft and in the market, and you are working in tandem with Microsoft field and corporate to bring your product to market per their GTMs and powerful brand name, then you stand a good chance of succeeding.

Staying Present with Microsoft

As we have seen in the case studies above, successful ISV-partners develop and maintain a consistent presence to Microsoft. Presence has two dimensions—temporal (pertaining to time) and locative (pertaining to place)—and the most successful ISVs dwell with Microsoft in a specific time/space continuum that accounts for their symbiotic innovation with the company.

They stay current with Microsoft's thinking, which may be defined as the changing corporate strategy in the field or field-level tactics designed to drive sales. In order to ride the Microsoft wave, partners keep their products current and their marketing aligned with that of Microsoft. They are present—current—with Microsoft's initiatives and solutions on a daily, weekly, monthly and annual basis. They are willing to take judicious risks on Microsoft's future technologies yet protect their firms from too much risk by delivering solutions that they can sell into an installed base of customers today.

They keep in mind the "Microsoft millisecond" and are concise and deliberate about articulating their value to Microsoft by enumerating how their product sales fuel Microsoft license sales. Successful ISVs know that time is short and pressures are great for Microsoft personnel, so they make the most of their time to achieve their mutual objectives. Yet ISVs must speak regularly with Microsoft personnel in the field, and at corporate, and routinely leverage their existing relationships to extend their network and presence within the company. They know what go-to-market initiatives are most important to their Microsoft counterparts and how their success is measured (*eg*, Management By Objectives, or MBOs, and compensation models for field and product teams).

Successful ISVs articulate their business value to Microsoft by quantifying their product pull-through rate of Microsoft licenses. They educate all staff members about its value proposition and stay on message with Microsoft. They constantly deliver and reinforce this message to Microsoft. And these messages must be updated at least annually to couch them in the context of Microsoft's latest GTMs. ISVs should align their new product launches with Microsoft's fiscal-year start, on 1 July, or coincident with Microsoft 's own product launches in order to ride the marketing buzz and publicly align their products with Microsoft's initiatives.

ISV-partners must also know Microsoft's rules of engagement with partners. These rules, like all other cogs in the Microsoft wheel, are reviewed, revised and changed each year. As a result of folding ISVs (and other partner types) into its mainstream partner program in 2004, Microsoft introduced a new partner points system that requires ISVs to meet certain standards, qualifications and ISV/Software Solutions Competencies to earn and maintain their ISV partner designation as Gold or Certified partners. Keeping abreast of such changes in the Microsoft Partner Program is a responsibility and an opportunity for ISVs to enhance their partnership with Microsoft.

In short, successful ISVs practice ordinary human virtues for building strong relationships. They empathize with and experience the successes and pains of their Microsoft counterparts and become part of the virtual team. They position themselves to be of service to their Microsoft colleagues. Successful ISVs stay in the present with Microsoft because doing so is what successful partnership requires. It pays dividends.

Successful ISVs also stay present to Microsoft in a *locative* sense. That is, they work in the same actual or virtual space with their colleagues. They go on joint calls with Microsoft to specific markets, customer accounts and buy-side decision makers. The market itself is of varying scope—local, regional, national and global—and ISVs must determine their optimal market fit in partnering with Microsoft. They need to define how their presence is most likely to be profitable and foster the best partnership with Microsoft. Citrix, for example, maintains a staffed development center at corporate offices in Seattle. Other partners set up shop in the same corporate complex as their local Microsoft subsidiary to enable close day-to-day engagement.

Thanks to virtualization of sales and globalization of markets, ISVs wish to sell their products in all markets and geographies. Many ISVs highlighted in case studies in this chapter made explicit and specific choices in this regard to enable maximum partnering with Microsoft. That is, ISVs avail themselves of Microsoft's global reach but first embrace a local focus in order to drive their solutions on a field-by-field basis. The most successful ISVs, then, extend globally, but always align locally.

Geographical presence with Microsoft fosters expansion into new countries and continents and promotes penetration of new industry–vertical markets for both ISVs and Microsoft. If an ISV is working with Microsoft in Chile, for example, it will tailor Microsoft's message and branding, and modify it with the partner's expertise in a manner that is appropriate for prospective clients in that market. Once penetrating the Chilean market with their combined solution, the two software partners focus on a specific vertical industry—banking, for example, or manufacturing—and then bring the same solution for banking there over to the banking industry of Argentina. Solutions can then be re-purposed by ISVs and Microsoft for similar geographical markets with little modification and customization apart from language and dialect, of course. The re-usability of these Spanish language-based banking solutions, which are developed by Microsoft in concert with its ISV and services partners globally, usher in a new era of mass customization, in which software is sold according to a traditional mass volume model but one that is customized, tailored and targeted for specific customer sets.

The truest difficulty is to align locally on multiple fronts, not only with Microsoft but with markets *per se*. Core alignment with Microsoft, being present with Microsoft in its product trajectory (time) and its field- and corporate teams (location), is a prerequisite as we learn from AVIcode, which has overcome challenges of both time and place to position itself to fill a unique niche in Microsoft's product set.

AVIcode Drives Results By Deepening Its Relationship With Microsoft

AVIcode (www.avicode.com)—a Microsoft Visual Studio Industry Partner based at Baltimore, Maryland—was founded in 2001, and has branch offices in Hartford, Connecticut, Paris, France, and St Petersburg, Russia. It is a privately held ISV that makes and markets solutions "designed to protect software investments by simplifying application maintenance and troubleshooting," and to extend the features and functionality of certain Microsoft platforms, including .NET, into the universe of custom-developed enterprise applicatons.

A high ratio of the firm's employees—seven of 23—are engaged in the Microsoft relationship, which is managed by Steve Pelletier, vice president for business development, from the firm's Hartford office. Because Hartford is located between two major Microsoft markets—Boston and New York, where AVIcode's PAM is located— Mr Pelletier spends a significant amount of time at Microsoft's Manhattan office and oversees the company's continual communications with Microsoft field and corporate personnel. Specifically, there are weekly meetings with Microsoft and typically more than 100 phone calls or email messages exchanged between AVIcode and Microsoft personnel per month.

Other ISVs are challenged to keep their messaging to Microsoft consistent among all of their employees—as indicated, doing so is fundamentally needful for Microsoft partners because one's value needs to be expressed crisply, consistently and unambiguously—but AVIcode manages to keep its personnel on the same page and speaking with one voice. It does so by using the equivalent of "playbooks" or, in its case, PowerPoint presentations that distill what it does and why it matters to Microsoft and its customers. A great deal of care and deliberation go into developing these presentations, and AVIcode personnel engaged with Microsoft have a hand in developing them. They also play off of these presentations in making Microsoft consistently aware of the firm's value and contributions; sometimes this is in face-to-face or on-the-phone meetings, at other times key points are the subject of email distributions to major relationships within Microsoft just to keep them up-to-speed on the firm's achievements and to keep in front of Microsoft. This basic coordinated–communication approach has paid off as 10% of AVIcode's business is directly attributable to Microsoft and another 50% is indirectly acquired as a result of the partnership. While AVIcode has other partners—and is developing partnerships with other companies, including HP, BMC and IBM—Microsoft is and always has been the firm's main strategic partner.

It has not always been easy for AVIcode to partner with Microsoft, Mr Pelletier advises. He recounts the story of several years ago—before the current partner program—when there were widespread press attacks of Microsoft's taking advantage of its partners and profiting from them. Microsoft responded vigorously, holding partner get-togethers to assure its partners that Microsoft was committed to them and was investing in a revamped partner program to demonstrate this commitment. The head of the Microsoft partner program at that time took the stage and promised that the company would demonstrate its commitment, offering her direct telephone number and email address, which she gave to the assembled partners, should anything go wrong with them in the process. Mr Pelletier took down her number and, when she left the stage, approached her. He thanked her for the offer and told her he would take her up on it someday, promising that he would not contact her except as a last resort. Nearly two years later, after many months of trying to get one product group's attention, he did so with an email message outlining the need, the problem and what he hoped the outcome would be. "Within minutes," Mr Pelletier says, "I had a reply from her thanking me for bringing the problem to her attention, indicating the person she copied on the message as being responsible for resolving the problem, and promising a resolution within 14 business days. Soon after that, the product group that we had been trying to contact for 18 months actually reached out to us. And that is when our partnership with Microsoft became strong. After that, things have been great." On other occasions, Microsoft's Emerging Business Team, with which AVIcode works on an on-going basis, has proved to be an invaluable gateway and door-opener into product groups and relationships within Microsoft and, indeed, an outstanding voice in the venture–capital community for its partner AVIcode.

The relationship has progressively tightened as AVIcode jumped on the .NET bandwagon, which has also extended the firm's opportunities not only with its customers but with Microsoft and other Microsoft partners, as well, says Mr Pelletier: "In 2004, AVIcode established its Alliance Partner Program (AAP) for solution providers, who develop and sell solutions built on the .NET framework. The AAP is aimed at allowing AVIcode product users to protect their software investments by substantially reducing application maintenance and troubleshooting costs, while eliminating the need for pre-deployment QA instrumentation. AAP features a reseller discount schedule, advanced training, product support and licensing models that fit with the needs of our partners, whether they are resellers or integrators. Consistent with that model, AVIcode is working with Microsoft to make its offerings available in an integrated fashion with Microsoft products."

The firm's principal Microsoft product integration solution pertains to Microsoft Operations Manager, or MOM (versions 2000 and 2005), and a forthcoming solution will integrate with Visual Studio 2005. AVIcode's solutions extend the functionality of these Microsoft platforms by serving as a middle tier for quality control between them and custom .NET applications; in MOM's case, AVIcode's solution detects exception errors and performance degradation issues affecting any custom .NET applications' faulty code in real time, feeds alerts to MOM for instantaneous monitoring and reporting, and collects root cause information for engineers and developers who are responsible for application maintenance. In essence, then, AVIcode's solution is a bridge between custom .NET applications and Microsoft's platform(s) that optimizes software defect resolution response time. Similarly, AVIcode will soon release a version of its monitoring agents that will provide the same always-on monitoring with root-cause fault and performance bottleneck analysis for J2EE applications. As we have seen in other case studies, Microsoft knows that it is not the center of the IT universe in the enterprise so it embraces its partner ecosystem to help its solutions integrate with other manufacturers' products.

Savvy ISVs walk a fine line with Microsoft, then, especially in product roadmap discussions (what one ISV called "collision avoidance" get-togethers). That is, they must determine where Microsoft's product groups are moving and discern where the product or function gaps are that the ISVs can fill. "In every case, ISVs have to put forward complementary solutions and always work to collaborate—never compete—with Microsoft. Otherwise, they cannot win," observes Mr Pelletier.

Such product roadmap meetings are essential for ISVs to stay abreast of where

Microsoft is moving with its products and thus to stay close to Microsoft itself. Another venue is the nearly constant string of events that Microsoft puts on—from TechEd to MSDN seminars and, of course, the worldwide partner conference. While these are often expensive to attend and lack customer prospects, there are few better opportunities to liaise and work with Microsoft employees, who must attend these and who do so without their usual day-to-day work distractions. Mr Pelletier expresses better than most the need to drive results by deepening relationships with Microsoft: "Hang in there and work your network. Get to know as many Microsoft people as you can and help them help you. You will get your chance as a Microsoft partner if what you have matters to Microsoft, when you make them aware of it and as you work with them toward your joint success."

Challenges of Aligning Locally

Aligning with Microsoft, especially locally, is a challenge for ISVs on two fronts. It is costly in terms of time and energy since software developers must work with Microsoft field teams in each district where their sales are driven. Also, ISVs, like Microsoft, must localize their solutions, where applicable, to account for language, cultural and legal requirements of each region. The investment is significant for both parties: French and Spanish language versions of Microsoft applications may not appear in the European marketplace for months after the English version debuts in the US. Local alignment with Microsoft field teams is by far the most effective and rewarding localization initiative to pursue. Yet ISVs and services partners must be mindful of the time lag involved in delivering international versions of Microsoft software, and must plan their own product launches and services appropriately, as ISVs and services partners in Montreal and Lebanon point out later in this book.

Microsoft has thousands of feet on the streets—sales teams and field teams in local offices worldwide that can bring your solutions to customer accounts. As you are an extension of Microsoft's sales force, so, too, is Microsoft's sales force an extension of yours. This provides you with a tremendous advantage. It extends your sales force (assuming that you have the requisite personnel to support Microsoft's sales initiatives). In addition, Microsoft's local marketing engine, which drives GTMs in each local subsidiary, is a powerful tide for you to ride to get your solutions to market. But taking advantage of those benefits depends primarily on your efforts. You must work with field teams in each subsidiary to understand what is important to them in their markets and to sell them on how your solution helps them drive Microsoft product revenue.

As we have stated and seen, you can leverage field-level relationships to escalate the visibility of your solutions at regional and national levels. You can further extend your fortunes by working field and corporate teams to extend globally. But because

Microsoft parses the world in various ways—by regions and countries, by industries, by product segments—determining the right relationships to build takes its cue from where your product is likely best to fit within Microsoft's view of the world. An ISV that develops software for hospital administration, for example, should attempt to make contacts with sales personnel in Microsoft's Healthcare vertical and in districts with the highest concentration of health care facilities.

Remember that Microsoft is product-centric and customer-focused. Although it is possible for a Microsoft ISV to grow its business by extending Microsoft products into non-Windows environments, the targeted business model—that is, a Microsoft-centric strategy—is valued increasingly as Microsoft faces its most serious competition to date. Customer demand for Java and Linux offerings has forced several key server-focused ISV- and OEM-partners into cross-platform strategies that consist of supporting Windows and Linux. In such a competitive environment, the value of being a Microsoft-centric ISV increases, particularly if that software partner can sell Microsoft licenses into competitors' environments or persuade customers using or considering alternative platforms to embrace the Microsoft platform. ISVs that help Microsoft confront competition effectively and soothe its pain points (*eg*, Linux and security) earn great rewards from the experience.

Consider Citrix's successful experiences in partnering with Microsoft, based on its high volume of Windows server licenses sold and its commitment to provide MetaFrame on the Windows server platform only. Citrix provides multi-platform client support for its server, but the ISV—which co-develops terminal services with Microsoft—will remain purely Microsoft on the server side. "IBM is an important partner and wanted us to do more. But we explained to the Linux-server support team at IBM that a Linux server was not something we were going to do," recalled David Jones, Citrix's senior vice president of corporate development.

This targeted approach is echoed by the successful Irish ISV, Meridio, which climbed the ladder of success in Microsoft's ISV ecosystem quickly.

Meridio Draws a Line in the Sand and then Takes Ground ... from Linux

Meridio (www.meridio.com)—a Microsoft Global Partner based at Belfast, Northern Ireland, with offices in Washington, DC, Houston, Boston, Toronto, London and Sydney—develops and markets enterprise document- and records-management software exclusively for Microsoft platforms. A spinoff of Kainos, a large UK systems integrator, Meridio was founded in 2001, and quickly ascended Microsoft's ISV-partnership ladder to become a Global ISV Partner only three years after its incorporation. That is an extraordinary feat considering that Microsoft has only 213 Global ISVs in its roster of nearly 4,500 managed ISVs, most of which are far more established firms. How did this little-known international ISV capture such a prized position with Microsoft so quickly? Meridio's fast-track success was achieved by adhering to three key ISV tactics identified in this chapter, and executing on them with urgency, flexibility and firmness. Specifically, Meridio

- adopted a Microsoft-centric strategy;

- articulated and demonstrated its ability to generate sales of Microsoft's desktop and server solutions; and

- aligned its GTM priorities to match those of Microsoft while addressing competitive pain points for the company.

Meridio decided early on to embrace a Microsoft-only strategy. This foundational decision distinguishes it from many large ISVs in the document-management space, such as Documentum and OpenText, both of which have cross-platform strategies. Becoming a pure Microsoft ISV carries with it significant rewards as well as risks. Due to its solid execution, however, the rewards for Meridio have outweighed the risks, notes Roger Johnston, Meridio's vice president for the North America sales office: "We do not compete directly with Documentum or OpenText. Meridio will never go head-to-head against those ISVs because we are Microsoft's compliance partner and we are a Microsoft capability. So it is Microsoft-Meridio up against IBM and Documentum. If we cannot partner with Microsoft on an opportunity, we turn down the opportunity, no matter how big. If someone tells me they will give me a 100,000-seat deal if we go to Oracle, I will walk away from it. Meridio pitches its product as an add-on to Office 2003 or SQL. That approach has been a unique differentiator for Meridio in a category that is primarily cross-platform."

Like Citrix, Meridio also spells out its value to Microsoft in a very concrete manner. During its annual joint-planning meetings with Microsoft, Meridio executives set specific revenue targets: for every dollar Meridio earns on a deal, Microsoft sees two-to-three dollars in desktop and/or server revenues. Then Meridio delivers, and continues not only to meet its targets but to exceed the promised revenues for Microsoft each quarter. "For every US$50 million in sales for Meridio, it means US$100 million to US$150 million in Office and SQL revenues for Microsoft," Mr Johnston pointed out.

This essential ingredient, articulating its value to Microsoft in terms of dollars and cents, is one of the most effective strategies for ISVs. In this way, Meridio emulates Citrix's model. And Mr Johnston maintains that all ISVs should do so—but not many do: "I do not think a lot of ISVs can show their value to Microsoft, or break down for their Microsoft sales representative how they will generate X amount of revenues for Microsoft. They have got to do that."

So Meridio's go-to-market urgency is tied directly to Microsoft's interest. That Meridio delivers on its promises and is a very urgent, results-oriented company has enabled it to prosper in Microsoft's vast partner ecosystem.

Meridio also demonstrates its flexibility and urgency by focusing on markets in which Microsoft has experienced vulnerability, such as the public sector. In recent years, advocates of open-source solutions have successfully persuaded some public-sector organizations and governments that Linux is more cost-effective than Windows. Meridio stepped up to the plate to defend Microsoft's value message. It made a pitch to one major US government agency that was increasing its use of Linux: the US Department of Defense. By refocusing its energies on the federal government as its key vertical, Meridio generated enormous goodwill among many at Microsoft who are concerned about its top competitor—Linux—taking root at its largest global customer, the US government.

Like other ISVs and solution providers that have developed strong partnerships with Microsoft, Meridio also played a major role in helping Microsoft save a significant deal in Europe that was all but lost to a competitive IBM-Linux-Documentum solution. In an urgent attempt to reverse that outcome, one Microsoft executive called Meridio and asked the ISV to collaborate on a revised proposal to save the deal. It worked. Within eight weeks, the Microsoft-Meridio team won back the 27,000-seat deal! "Those kinds of saves are not forgotten," Mr Johnston observed with satisfaction. Meridio continues to work on other federal-government opportunities worldwide based on a cost-effective, combined Microsoft-Meridio solution for records management. The ISV is growing rapidly and now employs more than 100 people.

Meridio sees itself as a partner in Microsoft's competitive battle with Linux and other antagonistic vendors. This is a strong position for any ISV looking to align closely with the Microsoft organization.

Connect Where You Can, Advance Microsoft's Cause Globally

Meridio got called into the European deal because of its strong capabilities as an ISV and its deep connections into Microsoft. Citrix and many other ISV executives have intimated that great rewards await ISVs that align closely with Microsoft at both the corporate level and the field level. Align locally, extend globally is their mantra.

Be aware, however, that Microsoft views its organization on a national level and draws lines in the sand. The United States is treated as one market, admittedly huge and diverse; France is another market and Mexico still another, for example. Microsoft assesses its market penetration on a relative basis. In an interview, Mr Ballmer said he "wants the world to look like Denmark" (CNET, 13 July 2004), meaning that Microsoft would be in an ideal position if its product penetration in each geography were as deep as it is in Denmark. Software partners should take note of this goal and help Microsoft penetrate deeper into the software stack and further into national, geographical and vertical markets with their complementary solutions as selling-points. In Microsoft's new world, depth and breadth are both important.

Like Microsoft's organization, ISVs must be customer-focused and product-centric, fixed on satisfying customer needs and extending Microsoft products into non-Microsoft environments. Successful ISVs can do this if they are aligned with Microsoft yet they can also remain neutral in its competitive battles. This is an important balancing act for ISVs. It requires an ISV to factor Microsoft's top priorities into its business plan, to play strategically yet not in a manner that appears biased to customers. Executives from ISVs and services partners concur that Microsoft partners must be firm in their primary mission: be customer-focused. As Citrix's David Jones observed: "Our strategic advantage is that we are Switzerland. We do not recommend or demand that customers favor one operating system over the other. We do not get in the center of anyone's crosshairs. We have always gone left-right-left. We work with IBM on the Windows piece and we have a good and growing relationship with IBM WebSphere. And we have a Linux client."

Although Citrix—like NetIQ—maintains a platform-agnostic posture, it is indeed tightly aligned with Microsoft, both at the corporate and the field levels. And the ratio of its Windows business relative to other platforms is overwhelmingly high: more than 95% of Citrix's revenues are derived from Windows sales, while the remaining five percent is derived from other platforms. Similarly, 90% of NetIQ's revenues are derived from Windows platform sales.

One might reasonably conclude from these examples that approximately 90% to 95% of an ISV's partnering energy should be spent in aligning with Microsoft, as Citrix and NetIQ have done at both corporate and field levels. However, ISVs should consider spending the balance of their corporate partnering energy diversifying solutions for Microsoft-competitive platforms—with or without Microsoft's backing. This complementary and competitive balancing act seems to make the Microsoft relationship interesting at the very least, and it may in fact provide ballast for the ISV while remaining amidship to the SS Microsoft. It is important to note that this approach, so successful for powerhouses like NetIQ, is rarely achieved without deep field-level tactical collaboration as well as corporate-level strategic alignment.

Symbiotic Innovation and Protecting Your Intellectual Property

Microsoft is the world's largest software developer and will continue to innovate its platforms to deliver more value to customers. ISVs need to be realistic early on that Microsoft will continue to innovate and grow their existing platforms and products,

MICROSOFT DOs	ISV DOs
1 Focus on software and the channel	1 Decide priorities: what, why and when
2 Keep exposing roadmaps	2 Invest time and money
3 Generate demand with partners	3 Work Microsoft at multiple levels
4 Train, educate ad evangelize	4 Review and revise regularly
5 Think "value creation" in the channel	5 Work for the long term
MICROSOFT DON'Ts	**ISV DON'T's**
1 Assume the market is what you say it is	1 Expect Microsoft to know your business
2 Allow partners to waste time or money	2 Look just for the next deal
3 Do everything	3 Ignore certifications, GTMs and programs
4 Eat into the ecosystem	4 Under-estimate time and effort
5 Forget today's products	5 Forget why you partner

Figure 4.4: Top 10 DOs and DON'Ts For Microsoft and Its ISV Partners.

and to develop or acquire new offerings. The risk for any ISV is that Microsoft might move into the market space in which it operates and compete with it head-on.

Microsoft has made strategic moves that have impacted many ISVs, including its acquisition of Great Plains Software, and several anti-virus and security ISVs in 2004. Microsoft will step up to the plate and will openly compete with its ISVs if it deems it in the best interest of its customers and the company's platform strategy. Financial analysts agree that Microsoft is under pressure to protect the value of its powerful platforms and brand by enhancing security and responding to competitive threats, such as Oracle's purchase of PeopleSoft, a Microsoft ISV. Microsoft publicly acknowledged that it had talks with enterprise application-software manufacturer SAP following that merger.

So how do you respond if Microsoft considers a move into your firm's turf? Run and hide? Ignore it? Hope Microsoft fails? These are options, but not strategies. As we have pointed out, Microsoft typically succeeds in most markets that it enters. So these options would not be advisable.

The challenge is to develop a strategy to deal with that competition in a complementary manner by innovating your product set and leveraging your existing relationships within Microsoft. The next logical step is to determine how much of the functionality of the planned product overlaps with your product, and what gaps exist that may be filled by your product. Try to get a product briefing and a roadmap of planned products and services. Begin testing the alpha or beta versions. Ask Microsoft executives to provide guidance about how you can integrate your offering with Microsoft's product and extend and add value to enable your mutual success.

Whether or not Microsoft competes directly with you, you must innovate in step with Microsoft and advance Microsoft's platform and your own. In order to protect and preserve your intellectual property, you must innovate and form a symbiotic relationship with Microsoft. And collaboration must outweigh the competitive aspects of that partnership. You must embrace the qualities that have accounted for Microsoft's own success. Duplicate the blueprint: be dynamic, product-centric and customer-focused.

ISVs worry about commoditization of their intellectual property and competition from other ISVs and from Microsoft itself. But they cannot control these factors. So prudent ISVs cannot think of their intellectual property as a static piece of property. They must innovate their platforms in step with Microsoft and continue to leapfrog the functionality offered by competitors, whether they are other ISVs or Microsoft. This is how successful ISVs such as Citrix protect their intellectual property.

Another younger ISV that knows the complexity of aligning with Microsoft in a potentially competitive situation is SourceCode Holdings, of South Africa, that conducts business with Microsoft as a global ISV in many regions of the world. Like Citrix, the ISV formed a close partnership with Microsoft that entails co-development and collaboration on a workflow system service planned for the "Longhorn" release of Windows. SourceCode's enterprise workflow and business process automation software, known as K2.net, is representative of a new class of ISV software that is designed to advance Microsoft's ambitions in business process automation, vertical applications and establishing Office as a next-generation platform.

SourceCode Goes with The Flow and Focuses on Symbiotic Innovation with Microsoft

SourceCode Holdings (www.k2workflow.com)—a Microsoft Global ISV originally based in South Africa that moved its headquarters to Redmond, Washington in 2004—is a privately held firm, founded in 1998, that started off as a Microsoft services and solutions provider developing enterprise workflow and business automation software for its customers. It decided to formalize its intellectual property, switch business models and become a "true ISV" in 2000, according to its CEO, Adriaan Van Wyk.

The ISV has enjoyed a significant amount of success due to the strength of its K2.net platform and its smart partnering strategies. Rather than reinvent the wheel, SourceCode decided to emulate the partnering strategies of other successful Microsoft ISVs. What better choice than Citrix? SourceCode followed Citrix's partnering playbook like a recipe. The results have been impressive. In a relatively short time, the ISV has successfully established itself as Microsoft's key development partner for enterprise workflow and business process automation for the .NET era and the next generation of Windows and Office.

In 2004, Microsoft CEO Steve Ballmer publicly discussed plans for a Windows orchestration engine (WinOE) designed to help corporations orchestrate business processes and business workflows among workgroups. (Microsoft's BizTalk team developed an orchestration workflow for the BizTalk integration server and is leading the WinOE effort.) Like Citrix, SourceCode faced a dilemma when Microsoft decided to integrate its technology into Windows.

But the ISV opted to emulate Citrix's successful model of collaborative development, and is currently working with Microsoft to develop the Windows workflow services planned for the "Longhorn" version of Windows. Yet it is also working to ensure that its own intellectual property advances and extends the value of that future platform and sells Microsoft licenses.

Mr Van Wyk said his partnering approach was not accidental. "Citrix has done a brilliant job packaging and delivering a solution on top of terminal services and there are a lot of parallels there with what we are going to do with Microsoft. Citrix is still growing. When the relationship with Microsoft was announced, we thought it would kill Citrix but it has really accelerated their business. We learned from this. We have a healthy relationship with Microsoft and a healthy ISV engagement. If you engage Microsoft as an ISV there are a number of things you have to realize and take responsibility for and ownership of in order to get respect on both sides. It is really up to ISVs to deliver solutions and to be responsible for building their own business so the partnership will accelerate. At the end of the day, there is customer adoption and ROI on both sides, instead of one leaning on the other. We strike that balance perfectly."

SourceCode has taken somewhat of a different approach from Citrix, though. It did not license its technology to Microsoft. Instead, as part of their partnership, SourceCode is co-developing the workflow services for the operating system. It is a major undertaking: Microsoft's workflow APIs and technologies will be embedded into Microsoft's Windows and Office platforms. Aside from the strong symbiosis formed with Microsoft on workflow services, SourceCode plans to innovate on top of them and add value to the overall platform. The workflow technology is strategic, and essential to making Windows, Office and SharePoint more suitable platforms for business process re-engineering, management and automation in the future. This is a massive opportunity for Microsoft and its key ISV partner.

The collaborative approach enables a more symbiotic relationship, which will benefit both parties. SourceCode's co-development work with Microsoft places it in an ideal position to exploit the new APIs and Windows workflow system for optimal innovation. "We need to make the workflow engine useful across all Microsoft products while we continue to build advanced solutions on top of it like business process definition," said Mr Van Wyk.

SourceCode's response—firm, flexible and urgent—mimics other successful Microsoft ISV-partners that are confronted with competition from Microsoft. Source-Code's CEO is convinced that this partnership will reap rewards for Microsoft and his own firm.

SourceCode climbed to the top of Microsoft's ISV community rapidly for the same reasons as other successful developers. SourceCode's current offering—the K2

Enterprise Workflow Server and business process automation platform—delivers a high pull-through rate for Microsoft platforms and products. The product, for instance, requires customers to have licenses for SQL Server and for other Microsoft products, including Visual Studio, Office 2003, Windows Server 2003 and Share-Point. There is no doubt that the ISV's workflow platform will help evolve Microsoft's next-generation business initiatives, including making Office a platform and establishing Microsoft's increasing role in vertical industries and in business applications, business process re-engineering and business process automation.

Like Apptero, SourceCode offers limited support for non-Microsoft platforms but its core technology is Microsoft-centric, according to Mr Van Wyk: "We have a unique model. We require use of SQL Server and the operating system to run our core functionality. If you want to do a document–centric approach, it requires Share-Point. We require all Microsoft products, including Visual Studio. We are Microsoft-centric. We have web services API so you can co-exist with J2EE but we rely on the Microsoft platform and .NET."

Regardless of who you know at Microsoft, you need to have "good intellectual property," articulate that value in the context of Microsoft's goals and you need to align locally, Mr Van Wyk also observed. "We see a lot of startup companies that believe they will move Microsoft software but they cannot prove it or articulate the business value to Microsoft. There is a lot of good software and technology developed but ISVs struggle to sell the value proposition. SourceCode delivered its first product six years ago and had a business plan and strategy. We got a big customer win for Microsoft. Microsoft gave us assistance and backing and recommended us to customers but we built our own relationships with customers. There are no customer purchase orders at Seattle. Get traction in your own region, in your home region, then approach new regions."

Mr Van Wyk counsels that determining whom to work with in the field office is a challenge but ISVs should avail themselves of their PAM for guidance. "It is difficult for an ISV to determine who you should talk to in the field office. Our initial traction came from MCS. MCS had an engagement with a customer on an early proof-point and we had a certain piece of the technology puzzle that Microsoft did not have, and they had to engage an ISV. That happened because we knew the individuals in that office and we communicated our value proposition within that subsidiary and when they needed to do work related to business process automation, they knew us. Our traction came out of MCS. It is classic relationship building. Our PAM is significant to our success."

———◆———

Of course, SourceCode has realized rewards in its partnership with Microsoft but it has recognized and accounted for the risks, as well. The firm has agreements with Microsoft to protect its intellectual property.

ISV agreements with Microsoft can make or break you. Recall that one of the partnering myths is that Microsoft will steal your intellectual property. Although this claim is frequently over-stated, it is indeed the obligation of any business partner to protect its own interests when entering into a contract. Doing so is of paramount importance for the ISVs because, in the software market, of course, intellectual property is the key asset of the firm. You need to make sure that your firm is covered legally when working with Microsoft's product groups and field staff.

Microsoft has several types of agreements for ISVs that have evolved in recent years. They include Master Services Agreements, Technology Access Programs and Early Adopter Programs. These have traditionally specified that software code that the ISV brings to the agreement is owned by the ISV, yet code that is jointly developed under the agreement is owned by Microsoft. This is similar to the type of agreement that systems integrators sign when they collaborate with Microsoft on solution accelerators.

There are, for example, occasional disputes posed by customers whose solutions are a by-product of joint-development by Microsoft and its ISV partner. In those cases, who, indeed, owns the solution—the customer, Microsoft, or Microsoft and the ISV, or all three? And what if the ISV intends to perform further custom development for the customer on this co-developed code base—who, then, owns the further customizations?

These considerations need to be hashed out. Focus your agreements with Microsoft on the issue of anterior ownership of a code base that will be jointly developed for a mutual customer. Determine the line of ownership of code, if Microsoft has access to your code under an agreement, which is subsequently jointly modified by or with Microsoft. And where does the line of ownership then reside relative to your originally owned code base? Addressing the particulars of intellectual-property ownership will alleviate misunderstandings or future headaches. Further, ensure that your proprietary code is patented properly to prevent Microsoft—or any competitor—from adopting the core idea, crafting it in a different way or co-opting it into one of its own products. In short, get a good intellectual-property attorney.

Again, ISVs need to be mindful that Microsoft will add value to its platforms as it sees fit or as customer demand suggests. And Microsoft generally claims ownership of code that is jointly developed for the company's purposes or needs. However, there are discussions and agreements ISVs can spearhead with Microsoft to reduce their risks in engaging with Microsoft. These are not simply academic questions for the paranoid. These are questions that would be posed by judge and jury in mediating or adjudicating any disputes in the event that a lawsuit is filed. These matters are better resolved upfront in a manner that is not prejudicial to your interests. Do not neglect legal services when entering an agreement with anyone. This applies to agreements entered into with Microsoft, as well. And it is an element of your risk/reward calculus in partnering with the company.

These considerations apply not only to joint-development agreements but also to royalty arrangements. Registered partners with tested applications have recourse to royalty arrangements with Microsoft. These can be lucrative depending on the extent of negotiated pull-through for elements of your products or the products themselves that are sold with Microsoft products and platforms. Recall that Veritas and Executive Software have products—Backup and Defragmenter, respectively—that have shipped with Microsoft Windows for more than a decade, and these are subject to pull-through revenue.

So, too, are ISV solutions that field teams sell as a bundle with other Microsoft products and platforms. In 2004, Microsoft expanded its ISV Royalty Program to academic customers and reduced requirements to encourage more ISVs to embed Microsoft's core technology in their software applications and to package it for resale. This enhanced version of the ISV Royalty Licensing program, available as of 1 August 2004, eliminates the need for an ISV to apply for licensing through a separate Product Integration Program (PIP) and reduces the ISV's revenue-producing requirement to US$10,000 over a two-year period (Windows and Office sales are not included). In the past, ISVs would not qualify for royalties unless they generated sales of US$50,000.

One question emerges, though, in entering such royalty arrangements with Microsoft: will such an arrangement negatively impact how a field-account team views a prospective deal with the ISV? At the time of this writing, the answer appears to be no. The Microsoft account team in the field will still get credit for the bundled sale and the ISV will get the royalties. But if you are contemplating such a royalty arrangement, ensure that your product is based purely on—or is exclusively operable—with Microsoft technologies. If you want Microsoft to sell your product to a customer in the hope of royalty revenues and your product runs on SQL as well as Oracle or IBM's DB2, you run the risk of alienating the field sales team and drying up the potential royalty-revenue opportunity.

As we have noted, ISVs can advance in Microsoft's ecosystem with either a targeted or tangential approach. In this case, however, ISVs need to ensure that their products are complementary and exclusively targeted at Microsoft's products. An ISV cannot offer cross-platform support and invariably expect royalties from Microsoft.

ISVs that dedicate their development to the Microsoft platform—or any platform for that matter—worry about protecting their intellectual property. As discussed above, there are many ways that ISVs can work with Microsoft and other partners to insulate their firm from risk. SourceCode's CEO Mr Van Wyk provides four practical points of advice to ISVs:

Adhere to Microsoft's intellectual property guidelines in a mutually benefi-cial, executed Master Services Agreement. "Yes, you can protect your intellec-tual property. Guidelines are in place. Intellectual property guidelines have matured over the last three-to-four years as Microsoft's own business has matured. Microsoft's model in building intellectual property into its platforms has matured significantly. Microsoft has a partner agreement model that is the same for ISVs and systems inte-grators. It is a standard partner engagement model and it is important, especially if you talk to Microsoft product groups and groups that deal with Microsoft's intellectual property. You talk to them subject to non-disclosure agreements and intellectual property agreements that protect both parties. Sign the agreement only when you get to the engagement level. Never hand over any source code. If we share ideas that are not publicly known, because we need to do joint planning or joint strategies with Microsoft, there is an agreement. But protection is more about the relation-ship and how you manage it than what code you have."

Always innovate—intellectual property is not static. "We are an intellectual property-contingent organization and that is our real asset. It is really two separate things: our historical intellectual property and our ability to innovate. No one can copy your ability to innovate going forward. Your ability to innovate on the platform is based on the availability of Microsoft's two- and three-year product roadmap and vision. We address problems by making ourselves well–aligned with Microsoft's product groups."

Hire a law firm and get support from Microsoft's ISV partner team. "We have a legal team out of Chicago that looks after our intellectual-property interests. It is the responsibility of any management team to have those controls in place. Just like you would have a good set of financial accounts you need a healthy intellec-tual-property management policy. We also have a team of people within Microsoft that looks after our intellectual property. Microsoft has personnel that manage ISV engagements that can handle it. They are our advocates at Microsoft, not our legal watchdogs. There are a number of good disciplines in Microsoft's ISV program that assist with the protection of intellectual property on both sides."

Stay close to product groups and aligned with their product roadmaps. "We spend a lot of time making sure we manage our relationship with Microsoft and we plan out 18- to 36-month engagements very carefully. Microsoft has a team of peo-ple managing global ISVs in this regard."

———■———

The success of many ISVs demonstrates that the principles and tactics of ISV partnering with Microsoft as outlined in this book are consistent, even if the world of software is ever-changing. Like any partner segment, ISVs must follow impor-tant principles when doing business with Microsoft, and must form a partnership based on innovation and symbiosis. These include remaining firm, urgent and flexible; extending the value of the Microsoft platform, generating pull–through of Microsoft licenses, articulating the business value to Microsoft and playing close to home. And ISVs must also stay present with the company's product and marketing roadmaps and protect their intellectual property by improving it in revolutionary ways, always innovating, as does Microsoft itself. As the SS Microsoft sails in new directions, so, too, must its software partners. It is not surprising, but it is instructive, that the new class of global ISVs that are emerging to meet new demands in the .NET era—such as SourceCode, Meridio and CorasWorks, as we will discuss next—are using the same partnering tactics and principles of veteran ISVs such as Citrix.

Follow Microsoft's Lead Toward Vertical Solutions, and Lead It There

As we have seen, Microsoft is a product-centric company. Yet the software giant has been evolving its organization to deliver *solutions*—as well as standalone products—that solve business problems for its customers and address the *specific* needs of vertical industries and unique customer segments.

Recall from Chapter Two that Microsoft's cultural dynamism enables the firm to *evolve* its organization—its strategy and field accountability—in a manner that is tightly focused on its product segments. The products are the focus of *revolutionary* change, while the cultural engine that drives the product revolution is *evolutionary.*

Microsoft purchased two business-application companies and developed products to move it into the business solutions arena. Purchasing and marketing the new products was revolutionary, for example, while the transformation of its organization—and its partner ecosystem—was evolutionary. Let us look at how Microsoft's approach has differed from that of its competitors'.

Since 2000, Microsoft has expanded its vertical practices internally and hired key executives from IBM Global Services to help it expand its reach into the enterprise and to develop a solutions delivery model in conjunction with its partners. Yet, unlike its competitors—"left-handed" organizations such as Oracle and IBM that internally combine products and services to deliver a full solution to customers—Microsoft does not have a large consulting services arm. It is primarily dependent on external partners to deliver solutions. As a right-handed organization, Microsoft is product-focused and does not currently plan to build a large services organization. Microsoft's product-focused and partner-driven culture dictates that it must rely on ISVs and services partners to build custom business solutions. So while it is primarily a partner-driven company, the nature of product and service integration necessary for the delivery of custom solutions has necessitated another evolutionary change to the

Microsoft organization that is consistent with its business model: a tighter integration with its partners and the refinement of its partner ecosystem to deliver full end-to-end solutions to customers. This will be discussed in depth in the following chapters. Suffice it to say for now that Microsoft has invested heavily in its partner base to achieve tighter integration and alignment of its partners into its sales and services organizations and processes. To achieve this solutions delivery model, Microsoft has also unified all partner types under its one partner program to encourage cross-pollination among different partner types which enables delivery of integrated solutions. In this way, Microsoft is *evolving* its product-centric, customer-focused and partner-driven organization and strategy to meet new market requirements with revolutionary solutions—all of which is true to its culture. This increased reliance on its extended partner sales force is good news for all Microsoft partners, particularly ISVs and services partners.

Let us consider Microsoft's advance into solutions and vertical industries. In August 2003, Microsoft revealed a realignment of its business model based on verticals. The number of Microsoft vertical practices (for classic products and Microsoft Business Solutions) has expanded to address the unique needs of many industries, including healthcare, financial services, government, life sciences, retail, electronics, oil and gas, automotive-manufacturing, professional services, wholesale and distribution, industrial equipment, high-technology and electronics, not-for-profits, food and beverage, construction and contractors, manufacturing, and media and entertainment.

Microsoft's culture remains focused on its technology. But we see how Microsoft is evolving its internal organization and its partnership model for the solutions era. Microsoft's partner-driven model remains intact, then, with a conscious focus on nurturing the creation of a partner ecosystem that delivers revolutionary new solutions based on Microsoft platforms and products. It was imperative for Microsoft to integrate ISVs and services partners tightly into its sales and technical organizations to enable the solutions delivery model. During the early 1990s, Microsoft publicly discussed the need for the creation of this revitalized, solutions-emphatic partner ecosystem and hoped there would be a spontaneous grassroots effort among partners to realize it. While some partners signed on, Microsoft soon realized that it would need to evolve its internal and partner organizations in order to drive its revolutionary solutions agenda. As discussed earlier, Microsoft ramped up its internal investment in partner support and partner account managers worldwide and made wholesale changes to the Microsoft Partner Program to encourage cross-pollination and specialization through partner competencies.

In addition to those programmatic changes, Microsoft increased the number of partner advisory councils and established a Worldwide Service Partner Executive Council of 20 partners to evolve the services delivery model. Microsoft also appointed partner account managers to systems integrators and solution providers to maintain control of their own enterprise accounts.

As we pointed out earlier, Microsoft is a dynamic company that is willing to take risks and experiment with different executives, management philosophies and business models in order to achieve the most efficient and optimal solutions for its customers. In 2000, Microsoft decided to deliver packaged solutions called Office Accelerators in conjunction with its services partners in order to help customers meet federal mandates for compliance imposed by Sarbanes-Oxley, for example. After all, Microsoft had successfully developed and deployed several solution accelerators for its BizTalk Server that enabled customers to comply with HIPAA and RosettaNet. Why should not the same approach work for the enterprise solutions opportunity?

As part of its Office solution accelerator plan, Microsoft developed 75% of the code and turned it over to its services partners to complete the remaining 25% of the project—the last mile—to customize it for specific industries and customers. But there were several problems with this model that ran counter to its partner-driven approach to solutions delivery and its customer focus. First, it left ISV-partners out of the business equation and in some cases competed directly with their product offerings. ISVs expressed their dismay. It also concerned services partners, many of which wanted neither to take ownership of nor to be accountable for Office-solutions code that was primarily developed by Microsoft. More significantly, the solutions did not catch on in the marketplace (BizTalk accelerators, on the other hand, are still available). Customers expected the Office solutions to work out-of-the-box like other Microsoft products and were disappointed with the amount of customization needed. So, to address the grievances of its customers and partners, Microsoft reversed course, gave away the source code to its partners and allowed ISVs and solution providers to work together to build highly targeted custom solutions. In this case, Microsoft shifted back to a more traditional course whereby it delivers products and prescriptive guidance to a network of partners upon whom it relies to collaborate and deliver customer solutions.

So, in much the same manner as it evolves its own internal organization for a new era, Microsoft is evolving its extended sales force—its partner ecosystem—in order to deliver optimal results for its customers. This is good news for ISVs, services partners and resellers because once again it validates Microsoft's product-centric, customer-focused and partner-driven business model. Proving Citrix's point, Microsoft will accede to the wishes of its partners if it is convinced that customers are better served—and its talents are better invested—and that its focus on product development and partner-enablement pays a higher premium for its customers, who get better solutions and services.

Microsoft's implementation of solution accelerators was a failed experiment yet it paved the way for the company and its partners to realize the optimal way to deliver solutions to customers. It also got ISVs and services partners to start collaborating in truth. Might such experiments be conscious and deliberate efforts to motivate collaboration among partners? It is not clear whether Microsoft believed that its Microsoft Solutions Offerings (MSOs) follow-on to Office accelerators would be successful, or whether they would serve as lightning rods to get its partners more active in solutions delivery. It is clear that Microsoft has made a monumental investment and taken an active role in linking ISVs and solution providers to deliver those solutions for customers.

In many ways, which will be discussed later in Chapter Seven, Microsoft is incubating and nurturing the meshed development of its partner ecosystem in order to carry forward its vision of distinct solutions for vertical industries. SourceCode's CEO suggests that Microsoft depends on feedback from its partners to refine its model and to stay on course. It worked in this Office accelerator crisis. "What was missing was getting ISVs involved and drawing lines around the value proposition," said Mr Van Wyk." The end result is that it moves from a Microsoft-led solution to a partner-driven solution, which results in lower costs."

CorasWorks, another Global ISV, considers Microsoft a good company to partner with because, while it may experiment with new approaches to solutions and partnering, it chooses what is most effective for satisfying customers. CorasWorks partners with specialized systems integrators and solution providers, including RDA Associates, Booz Hamilton, IBIS, Greystone Solutions and ExtraTeam to deliver a full solution that integrates with existing business processes and the applications of customers in specific vertical industries. "The beautiful thing about Microsoft is that, as its model evolves, if it finds that something is not in the company's best interests, it stops doing it," observed William Rogers, CorasWorks' CEO. "Now they tell partners to create the intellectual property and own it and build applications around it and Microsoft will focus on bigger-picture marketing and education. Microsoft's decision to walk away from the solutions-development business is good for ISVs because it accelerates ISVs into the solution stack. ISVs offer off-the-shelf intellectual property and so we can take what we have and build more complex applications for verticals, including military and government customers. The Microsoft platform is the enabling element for solution providers and ISVs because it reduces their investment costs in having to build platforms and lets ISVs focus on applications and provide value at the business-application level while service and solution providers extend their knowledge in implementing customized solutions for customers. It validates the success of Microsoft's partnering approach in the market."

Partners help Microsoft evolve according to its culture. As ISVs and services partners become more integral to solutions delivery, they free up Microsoft's resources to focus on the development of revolutionary products. The launch of Microsoft

Business Solutions, Office 2003 and SharePoint Portal Server are foundational technologies for this revolution. Aside from those efforts, Microsoft is increasingly developing unique products or several versions of a single product for distinct customer segments. In the small business space, for instance, Microsoft has targeted offerings for small business customers including Windows Small Business Server 2003 and Microsoft Operations Manager 2005 Express.

Finally, we can see how Microsoft's shift from desktop products to server platforms, and the tight integration between the two, is reflected in its revolutionary/evolutionary cycle. As Microsoft attempts to move into solutions and vertical markets, for example, it must evolve its *mass volume* business to accommodate the specific needs of verticals and customer segments. This evolving *mass customization* approach is further discussed in Chapter Six.

By assigning solutions delivery to ISVs, Microsoft can develop more prescriptive guidance for implementing Microsoft software in vertical industries. For example, Microsoft delivered a dozen or so Office accelerators between 2003 and 2004. In 2005, it expects to deliver prescriptive guidance for as many as 50 solutions that ISV-partners can use to build financial, pharmaceutical, healthcare and even horizontal solutions. These include guidance for creating performance-review, project-management and invoice-management solutions from Microsoft's base products and horizontal accelerators for vertical segments, such as specific accelerators for investment banking and the pharmaceutical industry.

As it spearheads a product revolution based on .NET, Microsoft is evolving its organization and, by extension, its partner-driven model in step. To achieve this evolution toward vertical solutions, however, Microsoft needs ISV partners. For ISVs not only innovate on Microsoft products and platforms to make them applicable to specific vertical markets, but also help to create mindshare for Microsoft by crafting enticing branding and messaging appropriate to the targeted industries. Pebblestone, for example, was instrumental in applying Microsoft's brand in the fashion industry. CorasWorks is a successful Microsoft ISV that sees this shift in course as largely opportunistic for ISVs—and customers in the small and medium-sized business (SMB) market. For it expands not only the role of ISVs and services partners into vertical segments but also their role within specific customer segments, moving from one of pure technology advising to business consulting for the masses. Until recently, only enterprises could afford such services and solutions. Now, ISVs and services partners, as we will highlight in the next chapter, are evolving into mini-systems integrators that can deliver revolutionary solutions for SMB customers in the same way that Accenture delivers business process re-engineering services for Fortune 500 customers.

Mr Rogers of CorasWorks sums up this trend nicely: "What we see is a shift from software architecture to business architecture. It is not the code you write but how you design and implement your customer's refined business processes. This is the first time a mid-sized customer can do this and structure their objectives and business processes and have what it wants within weeks."

Such ISVs that offer Microsoft an in-road to specific verticals are eligible for resources to capitalize on those opportunities. The opportunity can be doubled if a solution in one vertical is leveraged for another vertical. In other words, an ISV that develops a product designed for the Information Worker product segment—a workflow and process automation offering for the insurance industry, for example—could then tailor it for the healthcare market. It is no great stretch to hopscotch from insurance to healthcare; solutions re-usability has been done before. Microsoft has a healthcare-focused industry vertical group that can be leveraged by ISVs to identify opportunities as well as appropriate guidance and market intelligence about how to penetrate those markets.

The caveat above about the need for significant Microsoft opportunity in vertical markets points to a tactical obligation of ISVs that few partners have mastered. In your dealings with Microsoft, you must help the company perceive you as augmenting its success. If you do so, Microsoft will help augment yours. That is, help Microsoft vest its interest in your growth and expansion by making Microsoft understand that you are working—tirelessly, ubiquitously, constantly—to help them drive the company's platform and product sales in existing and into new markets, industries and accounts. You can do this, as Meridio and Citrix have done and do consistently, by demonstrating more revenue and product pull-through for Microsoft than your own solutions sale. A strong sales-to-sales team relationship is vital for this to work, and the technical credibility of your team with Microsoft's product groups and technical sales personnel is absolutely necessary.

Concerted communication and collaboration with Microsoft—at multiple levels in the organization, with a singular message—is the best tactic to employ to realize this objective. And this is the key objective for ISVs to pursue in partnering with Microsoft in the future, to drive Microsoft and ISV products into targeted customer segments and vertical industries.

Let us consider one ISV that is trying to evolve in step with the SS Microsoft. Like SourceCode Holdings, CorasWorks, of McLean, Virginia, is representative of a new class of ISVs developing solutions for vertical industries that are designed to advance Microsoft's next-generation client and server platforms.

CorasWorks Evolves In Step with Microsoft's Vertical Focus

CorasWorks (www.corasworks.com) is a Microsoft Gold Certified ISV founded in February 2003 that has created a workplace-development environment for Microsoft SharePoint. Given the tight integration between Office, on the front-end, and the Sharepoint Portal Server, on the back-end, CorasWorks is committed to advancing Office as a platform to enable business process re-engineering and automation for vertical industries. As such, it is evolving in step with Microsoft's new business model and key priorities, which aim to drive *extensible solutions* that solve *business problems* for *vertical industries.*

CorasWorks employs fewer than 30 people, but it has created a big name for itself for its integrated add-on to SharePoint that allows customers to snap together components and create instant workspaces for typical business processes used by IT, and sales and marketing divisions within corporations. The list of traditional business processes addressed by the platform includes project management and helpdesk workspaces for IT staff, sales pipelines and proposal management for the sales force and partner extranets and marketing campaign-management tasks. It is in some ways a component-driven version of Lotus Notes for SharePoint that integrates well with Exchange and Outlook. CorasWorks acquired 250 enterprise customers within the first year of launching its new product, in December 2003, CorasWorks Workplace Suite.

From the perspective of its top executive, Microsoft must rely heavily on its ISV- and services partners to realize its ambitions. For CorasWorks' CEO William Rogers, Microsoft struggled for more than five years to determine the best way to deliver business solutions to the marketplace. After numerous experiments, Microsoft has concluded that its integrated software stack must include the Windows Server System and Office System. On top of that, ISVs create business logic. After ISV-partners build solutions for verticals, the solutions are customized by services partners for each client.

The integration between Windows and Office on the desktop, the front-end, began the evolution to solutions. Following that, the integration of Windows and Office with infrastructure services on the Windows-Server back-end evolved the process further. ISVs such as CorasWorks are focusing on the next generation of integration between desktop systems and server systems to deliver solutions.

The integration of more and more features into Windows, and their integration with Windows and Office on the desktop, began the drive to integrated innovation and the revolution to solutions. Following that, the integration of Windows and Office desktops with back-end infrastructure services running on the Windows server evolved the process even further. Office and SharePoint exemplify this approach. As IBM evolves WebSphere as a central computing platform, Microsoft, likewise, is developing a revolutionary new middleware stack to compete with its rivals.

As Microsoft tries to re-brand Office from a products suite into a complete system, smart ISVs such as CorasWorks are jumping in to help advance Microsoft's agenda as well as their own. The Office system, for instance, is composed of a whole set of products including Office, OneNote, InfoPath and SharePoint that are designed to deliver solutions to business problems. Microsoft is essentially applying the same recipe for establishing Office as a platform as it did for Windows.

"We see Office as a platform that is designed with hooks for modularity that purposely allows ISVs to build on top of it," Mr Rogers said. "We built our application development environment on top of Office and SharePoint so that customers can snap together our components to create instant program-management, helpdesk and marketing campaign-management workspaces out of the box with no programming. Microsoft cannot scale into building a thousand business solutions for hundreds of verticals. ISVs and partners are maturing enough to 'productize' solutions."

Again, CorasWorks is an example of a new class of ISV that demonstrates the same characteristics as other successful Microsoft ISVs, such as Citrix. It is firm, flexible and urgent. And it formed an innovative and symbiotic partnership with Microsoft based in part on collaboration. Maybe that is why the firm was named a Global ISV shortly after being founded. It certainly responded to a competitive challenge from Microsoft by partnering in a manner that balanced competition and collaboration, and that pleased both parties. Shortly after hitting the market, CorasWorks learned to its dismay that Microsoft would introduce solution accelerators for sales proposals for Office 2003 that would compete directly with its offering. But CorasWorks neither capsized nor drowned. Rather, it survived by innovating ahead of Microsoft and staying close to Microsoft throughout the process. Fortunately, Microsoft got out of the sales-proposal business after canceling its solution accelerators. And, when it did, Microsoft cited CorasWorks as a reference to explain its exit. Given Microsoft's success in so many software categories, observers sigh when ISVs claim they stand to benefit when Microsoft publicly announces it is moving into their market space. While it is true that some capsize as a result, other ISVs do in fact benefit when Microsoft validates and grows their market category. CorasWorks' experience with Microsoft, for example, reverses a key myth identified earlier in this book: that Microsoft is solely self-interested and has no interest in the success of its ISVs. CorasWorks also echoes a point made by SourceCode Holdings: its ability to innovate is valued more than its historical intellectual property and Microsoft wants it ISVs to innovate, not stagnate in its shadow. CorasWorks grasps that it must be dynamic, stay abreast of product roadmaps and continue to evolve its product offering on top of Office and SharePoint in order to survive.

"Whatever Microsoft releases or plans to release in SharePoint, we are three years down the road. An ISV protects its intellectual property by innovating ahead, leapfrogging Microsoft and adding value the software giant cannot offer," Mr Rogers said. "Microsoft has to look at the lowest common denominator and figure out how to support 100 million users. CorasWorks currently integrates global menus and dynamic tabs as part of its navigation pane for business applications; Microsoft has informed CorasWorks that some features will be integrated into SharePoint in 2006. So we are focused on project collaboration. Microsoft may add a project-collaboration template but they will not do a dashboard or group technology so customers can build very sophisticated business systems for all the collaborative elements in a single application. When they do that, we have plans to be much further down the road. It is a nice model where Microsoft stair-steps and partners launch capabilities on top of that and it keeps moving the value of the Microsoft platform full steam ahead."

Microsoft keeps its ISVs apprised of its plans but it leaves it up to partners to sink or swim. ISVs like Citrix and CorasWorks can not only survive but prosper if they innovate and ensure that their technology leapfrogs Microsoft, while ensuring that it adds value to and extends the Microsoft platform. It can be a win, win, win for all three parties: Microsoft, the ISV and customers.

CorasWorks, for instance, acted urgently and launched four upgrades of its flagship product in its *first* year on the market. Here, once again, CorasWorks exemplifies the value of a Microsoft ISV remaining firm in the face of a challenge from Microsoft while having the urgency and flexibility required to deal with—and exploit—competition from Microsoft. CorasWorks has mastered many of the key principles for successful ISV partnering with Microsoft. Not bad for a startup.

In such a fashion, Microsoft's partner ecosystem evolves in step with the SS Microsoft. It is no accident. When it first launched its .NET model, Micosoft anticipated that its ISVs and services partners would have to collaborate to deliver solutions. Yet these ecosystems did not spring up naturally. Microsoft helped jumpstart the process. The company made a number of conscious and deliberate moves—and launched experiments—designed to arrive at its partner-driven delivery model. As outlined in Chapter Seven, Microsoft is also active in "match making" for its partners to bolster this new model of collaborative solutions delivery.

ISVs that fail to heed Microsoft's new product roadmaps and company charter will sail off course and be forced to steer clear of a strong ship leading the way. Unlike many ISVs that focus exclusively on Windows client and server as the core Microsoft platform, CorasWorks and others are heeding Microsoft's new direction to establish Office and server applications, such as SharePoint and Microsoft Operations Manager, as respective business process automation and collaborative management platforms upon which ISVs and solution providers can develop solutions.

Fold Into and Stand Out In the Microsoft   Partner Ecosystem

Insofar as Microsoft is strategically evolving toward the vertical industry-specific application of its platforms and products, it will do all it can to bring its partners along for the ride. ISVs that let go of the reins, or whatever it is that binds them to Microsoft, risk falling by the wayside as the company accelerates in any direction. True, the company will continue to develop its platforms and products—Office, for example, or Exchange and SQL—but it is increasingly clear that the future of Microsoft's software revolves around tailoring software to industry verticals. ISVs that can help Microsoft along the way—that eschew generic products and tailor solutions for target markets—will stay ahead of the curve. The Microsoft Partner Ecosystem has been enhanced in a manner to serve as the structural context for engaging with Microsoft to ride this trend, as well as the mechanism that Microsoft, through its field organizations, will hit its targeted opportunities.

To recap, then, ISVs must implement a number of partnering techniques in their day-to-day interaction with Microsoft. It is imperative for ISVs to articulate their value to Microsoft succinctly, delivered in terms and business language that Microsoft personnel understand—your competency, your vertical, your market wins and their value to Microsoft—in a consistent, energetic, unwavering manner. Refinements of your messaging are, of course, acceptable in this dynamic partnership, but do not substantially change your message or you will run the risk of confusing your Microsoft representatives. For ISVs that are inclined to change their messaging substantially, a better alternative would be to re-brand themselves with Microsoft's guidance so that the company has some vested interest in their new identity or focus. If you are so inclined, do so cautiously.

In any case, your message to Microsoft must be consistent with its corporate GTMs—its focus for sales in any given year—and especially with your field-team's subset of corporate GTMs. You do not want to stand out as an ISV-partner that does not know its niche and cannot clearly, concisely state its value to Microsoft. You want, rather, to deliver to Microsoft a message that lets it know where you stand in the ecosystem and what that means to the company.

You need to make and work many connections across the organization, ultimately in corporate product groups, but you should align locally first. Like other partners, get to know how your Microsoft counterparts are rewarded and help them fulfill their mission. Set up shop locally first. It is a long way to the top, and camping out in Seattle will not make you successful any faster; in fact, it will likely work to your disadvantage—if not kill you. Remember the wise words of another successful ISV: there are no customer purchase orders at Microsoft.

Microsoft's name recognition (for co-branding) and its marketing engine (for go-to-market power) are central to your success. Given Microsoft's focus—solely on software, undiluted in hardware or services—your co-development work with Microsoft and customized products can be lucrative if you leverage strong relationships at Microsoft and ensure that there are appropriate legal protections for your intellectual property. First and foremost, though, is to work toward symbiotic innovation with Microsoft directed toward business results, as SourceCode Holdings has done.

You can protect your firm's intellectual property by scrupulous attention to agreements with Microsoft, and by working with the company to innovate and add value to its platforms and products, working symbiotically with appropriate corporate product groups and your Microsoft field representatives. To be successful, you must be comfortable with creative tensions and strike a nice balance between competition and collaboration with Microsoft. Remember the metaphor about the oyster-like creation of a pearl of great value from tensions in Microsoft-partner symbiosis? The partner-driven solution-delivery model is a grand example of this process. Always remain firm, flexible and urgent. If there is a dramatic shift in course on the SS Microsoft, re-orient your firm quickly to avoid capsizing, and position your firm to benefit from the changing winds.

ISVs must consequently fold seamlessly yet prominently into the ecosystem. Networking with Microsoft and other partners—ISVs, service providers and resellers—is of paramount importance. Doing so enables ISVs to exchange information and ideas on how best to engage Microsoft in specific vertical markets. And it provides opportunities for ISVs to refine their marketing message to Microsoft.

Networking in the ecosystem and engaging Microsoft also helps you to stay informed, to remain up-to-date on what appropriate product groups are doing and what competitive forces in the market are shaping your field team's approach. These three factors—an expanding ecosystem, as well as constant changes in product positioning and competitive pressures—make ecosystem-networking extraordinarily difficult. For example, ISVs with reporting solutions, even in industry verticals, can find themselves in a quandary when other such ISVs join Microsoft in partnership and Microsoft turns around and gives Reporting Services away for free to respond to competitive pressures.

In ecosystem networking, one must keep a constant eye on changes while putting them in the context of Microsoft's culture, strategic intent and organizational flux. It is by understanding Microsoft's culture and all that follows from it that one can thrive in the ecosystem because it, too, emanates from Microsoft's culture. Keeping informed and gaining cultural insight to Microsoft, the evolving company, will help you stay centered and to adjust your approach to partnering with Microsoft and your go-to-market strategy and tactics accordingly.

Focus where you can on decisively reversing competitive threats to Microsoft's position—and be sure to promote these victories within Microsoft—in order to stand out in the ecosystem and to earn Microsoft's continued favor. Meridio did this in countering the Linux threat in the US government, and helping Microsoft win a 27,000-seat deal away from its Linux competitor. This is a sure way to win Microsoft's favor.

Foresight—thinking ahead—can also pay dividends, and help you lead Microsoft into profitable new markets. Seeing where Microsoft ought to go, and communicating that up and down the chain of command in your network, can help your firm immensely in its partnership with Microsoft. It can also help Microsoft shine a more favorable light on your solution.

Being perceived by Microsoft as having market foresight can help you go to market with Microsoft's marketing engine behind you. The more Microsoft knows that you are forward-thinking for its benefit and that of its customers, the more likely the company will seek you out as a trusted advisor and put its marketing muscle to work for you and your solutions. But be forewarned: if you put yourself in this position, make sure that you communicate your position to the appropriate people at Microsoft so that they can help you to the utmost. And always deliver on Microsoft's heightened expectations of your performance.

This brings us back to managing your relationship with Microsoft and managing your network in the company. You need to master this art of management in order to reap the rewards—and mitigate the risks—of the partnership. You may take the aggressive lead in the relationship or take a more collegial approach that other ISVs have found workable. In either case, managing your partnership is a top priority if you want Microsoft as a partner. You must foster innovation with Microsoft by working collaboratively, symbiotically, with its people. And this job is up to you. You hold the key to your success as an ISV in partnering with Microsoft.

As emphasized throughout this book, it is most important not to neglect your Microsoft relationships. Leverage them to extend your network within the company, increasing your relationships to expand the sphere of your opportunities and influence. Doing so is true to Microsoft's culture—it is relationship-motivated and results-oriented—and alignment with the the company's strategy and market posture of being the largest partner-friendly software firm in the world. You may have the best Microsoft application on the planet, but without connections into Microsoft and an appreciation of its organization, culture and inner workings, you could end up stranded on an island, alone with a treasure that bears no benefit.

We know that all this advice is easier written than realized. But you must do these things at minimum in order to engage Microsoft effectively as an ISV partner. Such partnering strategies and tactics have accounted for the financial success of many of the firms case-studied in this and other chapters.

Let us move on to the next class of partners in Microsoft's ecosystem that interface closely with Microsoft and ISVs: services firms. Their experience and partnering tactics are instructive for ISV partners, too.

Chapter 5

SP Tactics for Successful Partnership with Microsoft

The morning rush hour in Manhattan is a hectic, frenetic time. On the same block as Microsoft's office in midtown is a Starbucks where Microsoft employees stop for a coffee between their morning commute and settling into the office. One sage sales manager at a service provider (SP) that partners with Microsoft made it a habit to stake out the Starbucks between 7:00 and 8:30 every morning to happen, coincidentally, upon his Microsoft counterparts in a relatively relaxed atmosphere. Light chats over coffee generated in this casual environment quickly turn to business, mutual understanding, leads and opportunities.

Sales in the Microsoft services arena are primarily relationship-driven. To establish these relationships, one must go to considerable and sometimes extraordinary lengths to make Microsoft connections on a personal level, not only with sales but also technical personnel.

Microsoft defines services partners as systems integrators (SIs), custom application development firms and technical training firms. This is a diverse assembly of partners totaling more than 329,000 firms. It should not be surprising that their success as Microsoft partners is driven—and can be measured—by their relationships with Microsoft on many levels.

Making these personal connections and establishing rewarding relationships takes time, energy and effort. But doing so is well worth the investment, as many services partners have found. Investing your time with Microsoft employees—personally and professionally—will yield reliable introductions to qualified clients and referrals to viable opportunities. It is important for any partner in Microsoft's ecosystem to form these relationships but perhaps more so for services partners due to the massive number of firms competing for Microsoft's attention.

Microsoft corporate has worked diligently to shift this relationship-driven partnering model for its services partners into a more systematic, predictable structure. But, given the size and scope of Microsoft—and its relationship-driven culture—the company's interactions with services firms are based predominantly on relationships and networks.

So using creativity in making and expanding your connection points in Microsoft is essential to your business and, like ISVs, your business goals must correspond to Microsoft's and your firm must align with its culture, organization and strategy.

Microsoft Needs Its Services Partners

As we learned in Chapter Two, Microsoft is a product-centric, customer-focused, partner-driven company. It needs the customer-facing salesmanship and implementation services of its SP-partners in order to drive its platforms and products to market. As discussed in Chapter One, Microsoft is a right-handed organization and, as such, it lacks the combined products-and-services approach of a left-handed organization, such as IBM and Oracle. Partnering with service providers is, according to Chairman Bill Gates, "in our genes to use that model." (CRN Online, 14 July 2002)

Microsoft's relatively small consulting-services arm—Microsoft Consulting Services (MCS)—of approximately 5,000 people supports its platforms and products. But it could never scale efficiently to support the thousands of consultants that would be necessary to turn Microsoft into a services organization for the masses, Mr Ballmer has said. Besides, he has said that Microsoft is not meant to become an IBM Global Services because the profit margins are better in selling software. At the company's worldwide partner conference in Toronto in 2004, Mr Ballmer maintained that the company has one mission and one mission only—to sell software—and will not veer from that course. So, again, while Microsoft is dynamic, its core culture is predictable, focused on making, selling and delivering its software. Meanwhile, the technical services business has experienced wild ups and downs during the past decade. Microsoft has on occasion caused ripples for its services partners in, for example, its joint venture with Accenture called Avanade and, of course, MCS. Yet, notwithstanding market volatility and Microsoft's own forays into the services business, an astounding 40% of Microsoft's ecosystem continues to be composed of services partners.

As Microsoft faces the first significant competitor to its operating-system platform since its founding, Messrs Gates and Ballmer have turned up the volume of the company's investment in—and appreciation of—its SP-partners. The top executives appropriately view the company's partner ecosystem as a competitive advantage against its key competitors in the software market, even more so now than in the past. And all indications are that it will continue to shower SP-partners with resources to help drive the company's next-generation business in platforms, products and solutions. Company executives spend more time publicly discussing software, but in recent years they have emphasized its 841,000 firm-strong ecosystem of partners as Microsoft's main line of defense against Linux and the open-source movement.

It is clear that Microsoft's top executives recognize this vast ecosystem as a distinct, competitive advantage over rivals IBM and Oracle, which back Linux and Java. As Microsoft works to keep partners loyal—and away from IBM, Red Hat and Novell—the company is nurturing its ecosystem in much the same way as when the company was founded. Yet doing so is a challenge, even for Microsoft, which has occasionally handicapped itself with its SP-partners. Again, MCS' creation and its touted build-up as an internal services organization, which was ultimately deemed contrary to Microsoft's DNA, fostered tensions with its SP-partner community. Another complicating factor is the very size of the SP-partner community. Consider that each services partner must have at least two salespeople and two technical people to be certified as a Microsoft partner. With roughly 329,000 services partners, this translates into 1.3 million outside-sales people and personnel on the streets driving Microsoft business free of charge. Still, Microsoft employs roughly 55,000 and, of this number, perhaps one-quarter, or 14,000, have some partner-facing responsibilities. So for every Microsoft partner-facing employee, there are potentially 94 SP-partners that must be communicated with, helped and managed, a huge ratio even for a company of the size and with the resources of Microsoft.

Microsoft's organization has evolved with the needs and aspirations of its partners, especially service providers, in part governing its very structure and trajectory. And for good reason, as its partner ecosystem has accounted for driving Microsoft's low-cost-software marketplace success. The company devotes 3,000 fulltime employees to advancing the cause of its SP-partners and has roughly 300 that provide pre-sales and technical support to them. There are more than 30 position titles in the company with the word "partner" in them, and likely more with peripheral partner-facing responsibilities yet without the titular indication. The compensation of thousands of field personnel is based in part on partner satisfaction, specifically the partner pull-through metrics—partner assign and partner attach—as we have seen in foregoing chapters.

So Microsoft's SP-partners are quite integrated to the company's organization and strategy. Indeed, they are core to its culture, and always have been as Mr Gates himself commented: "Microsoft is totally reliant on partners. We have been forever. We do not have the services or training or solutions-oriented capacity to do everything the customer expects. In the same way, when we came up with the vision of the PC, we did not do microprocessors or manufacturing, and we did not do broad sets of applications to get a critical mass. We initiated an approach totally dependent on partners, and that is very unusual in the computer industry. So this is a key group for us. It is so hard to say [who came up with the idea]; it was like 20 years ago. The idea we chose was not to be like Oracle in services or IBM in services. Very, very early on, we said when we work with PC hardware, we came up with a way that focuses on designing just what we are good at designing: software products." (CRN, 2001)

So Microsoft simply cannot afford to alienate its SP-partners because doing so would jeopardize its success. More affirmatively, services partners are an extension of the company's culture, organization and strategy, and are integral to Microsoft's leadership position in the market.

In short, Microsoft needs its SP-partners, especially in a Linux-competitive climate in which Microsoft aims to drive its platforms and products, packaged increasingly as distinct solutions, into vertical-industry markets. How its SP-partners satisfy this need and capitalize on their doing so is the topic of this chapter.

SP Business Models

Before we consider the tactics that SPs employ in partnering with Microsoft, we must consider the generic models of their doing so. But, first, we must urge you to review the field of play in partnering with Microsoft explained in Chapter Two, and particularly to master the principles of partnering with Microsoft that are elaborated in Chapter Three. Like Microsoft, your firm must be customer-focused and product-centric. You must learn to drive, or you will be driven, in your relationship with Microsoft. Knowing Microsoft's dynamic culture and strategy, and learning to leverage its organization, are paramount obligations for partners.

Your tactics—what you do as a Microsoft partner—will fail if your understanding—what you know about Microsoft, and whom you know there—falters. The successful services partner factors into its market strategy and tactics the same Microsoft-centric approach in driving sales that has made other partners successful. This includes the selection of an appropriate model to structure your engagement with Microsoft. The model that you choose must work for you and address Microsoft's expectations of a services partner.

What Microsoft seeks from its services partners is relatively straightforward: expertise with Microsoft platforms and products, consistent quality in implementing them and energy in driving Microsoft solutions to market. Any attribute beyond these that an SP can offer—creativity in designing solutions, for example, or innovations in delivering them—is additionally valuable, icing on the cake. In order to gain expertise on its expanding portfolio of platforms and products, most services partners agree that it is best to be Microsoft-centric. Ironically, as Microsoft and other major software vendors work to provide some level of interoperability for companies with heterogeneous systems, many services partners say the days of supporting all operating-system platforms are over, that most customers have already made the

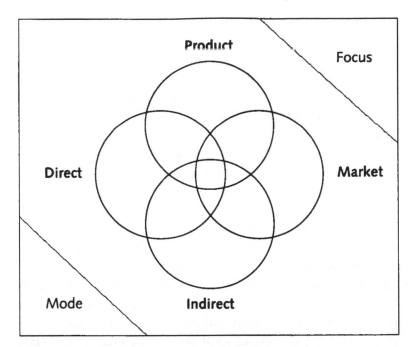

Figure 5.1: Service Providers' Business Models for Partnering with Microsoft.

choice to base their future on either .NET or Java, Windows or UNIX/Linux. So there is no market need, from this perspective, to be a cross-platform solutions provider. Moreover, as software stacks grow in complexity, services partners need to devote more internal resources in order to gain a high level of expertise on Microsoft's expanded software portfolio and enhance their reputations as well as that of Microsoft. So selling your firm—its qualifications, its achievements—to Microsoft is a fundamental imperative to succeed as a services partner. To err is human, but to forgive ... is unlikely for Microsoft executives who have a wide roster of capable partners to engage. Given its past challenges in stability and current challenges around security, Microsoft has little patience for partners who mess up an installation and cause customer dissatisfaction. If problems occur, and they will, do not walk away or deny responsibility. It is important, with all due haste, to address problems at customer sites regardless of where the fault lies. As one solution provider noted, one negative report card can wipe out dozens of "attaboys."

Despite the relative simplicity of what Microsoft expects from its services partners, partnering models admit of some complexity. The services business has historically worked on a value-added reseller (VAR) model but, since the 1990s, it has been transformed into a multitude of models. There are four generic services models to choose from, as shown below, which are defined from the perspective of the partner's work with Microsoft relative to its situation. This is a depiction of the available models:

Note that there are two diagonal axes, corresponding to an SP's *focus* as a firm (either on a product or a function that represents a set of products, or on vertical markets with a negligible or secondary product-set competency) and its *mode* of engaging with Microsoft (either directly or indirectly). Let us drill down on this for the sake of clarity.

The focus of a services partner's business can be either on a product or a technical function of business importance that represents a set of products, or on vertical markets. Either type of focus requires a particular set of attributes and a distinct cultural driver in order to be successfully managed. A discussion of how these partners can be complementary and drive business for each other, such as a typical case in which a contractor subcontracts work to a specialty firm, is offered in Chapter Seven.

Services partners that focus on providing services around particular products or on a technical function that encompasses various products require a great deal of urgency in order to succeed. Some services partners may specialize in database design, implementation and development—a technical function with a business impact—and may focus, for example, on Microsoft's SQL Server as a product. But, like ISVs that develop cross-platform applications, this type of services partner may also include in its focus such competitive products as MySQL, Oracle and DB2. The same applies to services partners with a specialty in messaging, who may offer services for Microsoft Exchange exclusively, or include in their scope of services support for competitive products such as Lotus Notes, iMail, SendMail and other messaging platforms. Services partners that specialize in designing, deploying and managing eCommerce sites may include a focus on IIS and Apache as well as other platforms in their services' scope. And so on.

A services partner's focus, however, need not be defined solely by its specialty in back-office products or functions. Some focus on providing desktop-related or end-user application-development services, or on the integration of client-side products with "back-office" platforms. These, too, can either focus on Microsoft solutions—Windows XP, Windows Server 2003, Active Directory and such back-office platforms as Exchange, SQL and IIS, among others, whether exclusively or inclusively along with competitive products such as Linux, Novell and other manufacturers' solutions.

In any case, a services partner that focuses on a distinct product or a set of products that address technical functions of business importance must aggressively drive volume in services sales and stay abreast of new product releases. Their livelihood depends on the currency of their skills with respect to the products that they provide services for, and they depend on the amount of sales generated in a necessarily mass market with finite sales potential. Such services shops will rarely walk away from business because a customer that has a technical need requiring the partner's competency represents a potential sale and customer relationship. These partners operate on the basis of volume of sales because their competencies are not so differentiated from others as to command a premium for services. Urgency is the core cultural driver for these services partners.

On the other hand, services partners that focus on providing services to a particular industry-vertical market—for example, healthcare, financial services, insurance—or a recognized market sector—such as Fortune 1000, mid-market or small business—inherently specialize in unique or cross-platform solutions' provision, generally with a particular technical function as a core competency. For example, some services partners provide technical services—infrastructure and application development—only to a particular industry or set of industries (eg, manufacturing, retail or hospitals) while others focus on providing services to market sectors, such as the middle market or Fortune 1000 firms. These services partners deliberately narrow their market to a vertical or a customer segment and, therefore, concentrate their sales efforts on a more finite number of companies that need their services based on Microsoft technologies. They must exercise great ingenuity in defining progressively higher-level services based on particular technical functions with industry- or sector-specific applicability, usually of a cross-platform nature (eg, process re-engineering and workflow automation or business intelligence, for example, that draw on various platforms and products), to command premium bill rates. They must also orchestrate their marketing, sales and delivery teams to drive high-value solutions to market. So orchestration is the core driver in such firms.

Services partners also embrace what is commonly called a hybrid model for developing software products in specific industry vertical markets. These are fundamentally services firms that choose to leverage their knowledge in a particular software area to develop software for a customer and then wish to market the application more broadly. Unfortunately, Microsoft occasionally has difficulties (along with customers and others in the industry) in understanding and embracing the hybrid model: is the firm a services partner or an ISV? If such an SP has three or more software products, for example, Microsoft's incentive to work with it may be diminished simply because Microsoft cannot ascertain the partner's true business model. Microsoft relies on its partners for strong and clear messaging about their competencies. The hybrid model, then, is riskier because it makes it more difficult for the partners to communicate, clearly and succinctly, their value propositions to Microsoft.

But there is a solution. In order to circumvent this confusion, hybrid-services partners should establish a separate company for their ISV product business. A services partner, then, can have it both ways—a vibrant services business and profitable software products—as long as the partner splits those separate efforts into two companies to make it easier to partner with Microsoft. This is the consensus among partners that have embraced the hybrid model. And, as we learned in the case study of

SourceCode Holdings (Chapter Four), a pure Microsoft services-firm-turned-ISV, the requirements for such business models are so vastly different that they cannot—or should not—be merged under one roof. Like any product manufacturer, an ISV must operate a call center and documentation division. A services partner has other requirements.

—■—

The mode of engaging with Microsoft can either be direct or indirect. The direct mode entails building one's services business upon Microsoft platforms and products, whether exclusively or predominantly, as suggested. Relationship- and consensus-building are core cultural drivers for services partners that rely on Microsoft as their primary partner for the viability, strength and growth of their business. On the other hand, some firms only indirectly leverage Microsoft as a partner. They are Microsoft partners, but may only opportunistically bring Microsoft into prospective customer accounts, or build only a portion of their practices around Microsoft's platforms and products. They likely partner with other firms, offering Microsoft-competitive platforms and products in their suite of services. Most recently, we have seen dedicated partners that once worked exclusively on Microsoft platforms support Linux for a small minority of customers. Deliberation is a core cultural driver of such services partners because they must constantly weigh whether or not partnering with Microsoft on an opportunity is to their advantage. Providing services based on competitive solutions will harm their opportunistic partnership with Microsoft or working with competitive solutions will dilute their image as a Microsoft partner.

As you can see, the circles in the diagram (Figure 5.1) overlap. This is because some services partners move from one focus model—product or market—to another, or combine the two focus models in their practices. Other partners work directly with Microsoft to advance either their product or market focus, or indirectly, to achieve the same goal. A firm's partnering model with Microsoft depends on its history, its present growth-trajectory, the aptitude and attitude of its management, and the particular markets in which it engages. So there are complex factors that partners must consider when defining their preferred business model and in adjusting their positioning with Microsoft for optimal market engagement. Regardless of its unique circumstances as a firm and at market, a services-partner's engagement of Microsoft as a partner is a definite competitive advantage. Of course, Microsoft owns more than a 95% share of the desktop operating-system market and more than 50% of the server market. This explains, in part, why there are 329,000 SPs worldwide that partner with Microsoft in one form or another.

In the following sections, we elaborate on the decision points and variables that services partners must come to terms with in order to partner with Microsoft, and the particular tactics that services partners of varying models employ to advance the partnership. Again, despite the relative simplicity of what Microsoft expects of its partners, the calculus involved in determining the best model—and choosing the optimal tactics to pursue—are quite complex, as should be clear from the foregoing discussion.

Partnering Is a Two-Way Street...There Is No One Way To Get Down It

Microsoft demands a great deal from its services partners and expects their delivered services and solutions to reflect well on the company's platforms and products, to enhance its reputation in reliability and security. Of course, it also wants services partners to understand its organization, culture and strategy so that they can work synergistically with Microsoft. But working with such a demanding company, as we have seen, is a significant challenge. There is no one way to do it, but many ways to fail at it. Many services partners get less than they should from their partnership with Microsoft because they are simply unaware of the strategies and resources available to—and exploited by—savvy services firms. You may not even realize the extent to which you are short-changing your firm if you do not take advantage of what Microsoft offers its services partners. We hope that this book will be of help. You must deliberate on the factors that make a partner successful, and find successful partners to emulate. In this chapter, we examine the strategies and tactics of many types of services partner—regional and local systems integrators, large systems integrators, Gold Certified Partners, Certified Partners and MBS partners—that have adopted successful models of partnering with Microsoft to make your task a little easier.

Recall the SS Microsoft analogy from Chapter Two—a ship with all hands on deck, steering aggressively ahead while supported on all flanks by a flotilla of allied crafts positioned optimally to protect and defend the mission of their benefactor, while countless other craft steer afoul of the battleship and constantly risk getting scuttled or overrun. There is an important observation contained therein that partners should not overlook: Microsoft is the most powerful ship on the sea because of its superior design and elite crew. As Microsoft's vision is impressed on the global IT market by its employees and allies, there is seemingly no end of resources to move the ship forward aggressively to realize its goals and priorities. One can love or hate Microsoft—or entertain a love/hate relationship with Microsoft—but, at the end of the day, Microsoft simply cannot be ignored. Services partners need to come to terms with the company.

As we have emphasized, you need to know Microsoft's culture, strategy and organization, and appreciate the company's dynamism. And you need to understand the Microsoft Partner Ecosystem, and its related Partner Points Program. But, more importantly, you have to grasp and master the relationship-based, results-driven basis for advancing as a partner (Chapter Two). You need to master the principles of partnering with Microsoft (Chapter Three). Tactically, the successful services partner must speak Microsoft's language, know its go-to-market strategies, products and platforms, and craft appropriate, timely messaging to Microsoft personnel about its services at the right time and in the right way. In addition, the successful services partner must maintain a good sense of balance because partnering with Microsoft requires it, as we explain in the following sections.

Successful Services Partners Speak Microsoft's Language

Seeing the world as Microsoft sees it and using terminology used by Microsoft personnel are necessary first steps in a successful partnership with Microsoft. As the company expands to seize new market opportunities, it is increasingly segmenting its customer accounts and markets, by size and industry, and focusing its field personnel on penetrating these domains. There is more depth, and breadth, to its sales strategies. Microsoft relegates its approach to the small and mid-sized business (SMB) markets to its Small and Midmarket Solutions and Partners (SMS&P) group and the company also focuses, on the other extreme, on the enterprise market, which at the time of this writing is divided into two categories: corporate accounts and global accounts. Microsoft has traditionally segmented these accounts by revenue, headcount, or number of licensed users, and is considering future segmentation based on the number of servers at customer locations.

Each services partner's strategy for dealing with each of these customer segments is slightly different yet relies first and foremost on the relationships developed in the Microsoft groups that serve each segment. The approach to Microsoft in each account segment varies, of course, since the relationship you may have with one Microsoft representative covering 1,000 SMS&P accounts is very different from the interactions you have with five Microsoft representatives covering one global account. But both approaches rely on a set of well-developed professional connection points within Microsoft that are specified in precise terms.

The playing field within the services market is important to understand since a firm's potential entry into a new market depends on the extent of competition and

Small Business	Such firms have one or fewer servers, fewer than 25 PCs and between one and 49 employees. (Microsoft believes there are 40 million such firms.)
Mid-Market	These firms have between 25 and 500 PCS, and between 50 and 500 employees.
Corporate	These companies have between 500 and 1,000 PCs, and between 1,000 and 5,000 employees.
Global/Strategic/Major Accounts	Enterprises with more than 1,000 PCs and 5,000 employees.

Figure 5.2: How Microsoft Segments Its Customer Accounts.

the quality of competitors in that market. Sibling rivalry—partner competition—in Microsoft's services ecosystem is a constant source of tension for the company.

Successful services partners must know how Microsoft refers to the various partner groups in its vast services ecosystem and in any market, and how they fit into that network. First, there are the Global Systems Integrators (GSIs), which, by definition, have a global presence and many relationships with Microsoft on many levels and in many different markets. Generally, they are managed accounts and will have core areas of technical expertise such as application development, a business focus such as financial services process automation or several vertical practices. From a delivery perspective, however, their skills and models may vary from market to market. Competing against a GSI in one market may be different from competing against it in another market.

Regional Systems Integrators (RSIs) often have a strong presence in a specific country or region of a country and engage with Microsoft based on their geographical/services delivery approach. RSIs are also generally managed accounts and typically have more than one Microsoft representative monitoring their business. Most of these players are very well defined and strong in their particular areas of technical expertise. Competing against an RSI will likely be difficult if it operates in a geographical area and specialty that a startup or another services firm is looking to enter.

GSIs and RSIs focus primarily on the enterprise customer market (as opposed to the SMS&P space) where competition—against MCS or other GSIs and RSIs—is fierce. They often find, as do smaller services partners that, despite successful partnering with Microsoft on a particular opportunity, Microsoft will strategically commit various types of opportunities to other large players. So GSIs and RSIs know—and smaller services partners should also realize—that it is essential to understand this core facet of Microsoft's enterprise business and keep abreast of Microsoft's global relationships, and to focus their partnering and customer-focused energies in the right areas. For instance, services partners should target upper mid-market customers that fall just below Microsoft's opportunity radar for corporate accounts, which cuts off at 1,000 desktops.

By mid-2004, Microsoft counted 525 partner account managers (PAMs) assigned to serve roughly 2,000 services partners that work in enterprise-customer accounts. Many of these partners are Gold Certified, either regional or local players, who work exclusively in enterprise accounts or serve primarily mid-sized customer accounts and occasionally have an enterprise engagement. These services partners either subcontract through MCS or have engaged customers on their own.

Of these 2000, approximately 30 services partners—mainly large systems integrators with global operations—are designated as capable of serving as prime contractors, which means they are responsible for the full scope of an enterprise engagement. These include 18 global alliance partners, including the likes of Accenture, Avanade, BearingPoint, Capgemini, Computer Sciences Corp. (CSC), Dell, EDS, HP, IBM Global Services, Infosys Technologies, Unisys and Wipro, among others. All of these global partners participate as Gold Certified partners but they are managed separately under Microsoft's Enterprise and Partner Group. Microsoft holds an Executive Partner Summit at corporate headquarters annually to brief large systems integrators on business plans coming for the next fiscal year, and the top executives of large firms such as Capgemini fly to Seattle for private two- or three-day engagement-planning sessions. So larger players often get preferential treatment—and more resources—from Microsoft than smaller partners, yet smaller players have a massive backyard to play in with more potential customer accounts.

Increasingly, Microsoft is improving its treatment and resource allotment to smaller services partners, who can compete effectively if they ride the tide of the company's go-to-markets to seize opportunities. For example, Microsoft is expanding deeper into the SMS&P market and business-applications sector and thus needs appropriate services partners to address that customer segment. LSIs are primarily interested in large enterprise accounts and specialize in one-to-one engagements, while smaller services partners often have one-to-many marketing efforts and relationships in their districts. Microsoft built much of its platform business in the midmarket with the help of its early services partners and now wants to extend its breadth, depth and reach into distinct customer segments within SMS&P as well as deeper into the software stack—beyond the OS layer and into business logic and processes. There are either global or regional systems integrators that have a particular focus or specialty in Navision, for example. Such firms get extra attention from Microsoft given the company's SMS&P focus and expertise.

When entering new markets, therefore, services partners must size up the global and regional systems integrators in their targeted markets, as well as specialty services boutiques, and plan accordingly. Microsoft's acquisition of Great Plains Software and Navision, as well as the 6,000 services partners that serve them, expanded potential opportunities for mainstream Microsoft services partners yet it also introduced a more complicated competitive landscape for partners going forward. This consideration begins with recognizing who the competitors are on the basis of how Microsoft identifies them, and referring to them by the name that Microsoft gives them.

The ideal position for a services partner is to be certified as a go-to–market player with Microsoft in a particular geographical or, ideally, in a specific market area such as financial services. It is easy as such for Microsoft personnel to differentiate this partner from the pack of other more general services partners in that area or sector, and steer leads to it. But it is fruitless to hope for such preferential treatment from Microsoft if the services partner does not understand Microsoft's partner universe and naming conventions for its various partner types, and if it fails to use those designations to identify itself and its competitors in a manner familiar to Microsoft.

Most often, the failure to grasp Microsoft's business language is most prevalent among Local Systems Integrators (LSIs), who by definition have only a local presence in one geographical market. They are obviously smaller than GSIs and RSIs, and lack resources for building business and their Microsoft partnership. LSIs represent the majority of services partners in Microsoft's partner ecosystem, and often aspire to become RSIs in order to enjoy more benefits afforded to partners higher up in the SI ranks, including more funds, account management and cross-districting rights. To climb the ladder, services partners may try to grow their expertise by acquiring smaller firms, build up organically through new hires, or seek acquisition by another partner to expand their presence. But, as noted previously, there are other methods to distinguish one's firm from the pack of local services partners, including using Microsoft's partner designations, business language and selling tactics. Doing so demonstrates that the LSI views the IT world as Microsoft does and has a deeper grasp of its business than the average partner. There are many ways to learn the ins and outs of the Microsoft universe. Services partners might try to find an effective guide to help steer their business down this path by hiring a former or current Microsoft employee or by surrounding themselves with Microsoft personnel in their territory, setting up in the same office complex, for example, or frequenting the local Starbucks to "happen upon" key Microsoft personnel. Another significant strategy for LSIs to improve their Microsoft partnership is to assign employees to pass Microsoft's solutions selling course.

One LSI in the southeastern US has employed some of these tactics and is successfully moving in the direction, with Microsoft's help, of becoming an RSI as a result.

Intellinet Blankets Microsoft in the Southeastern US and Looks Beyond

Intellinet (www.intellinet.com)—a Microsoft Gold Certified Partner and Local Systems Integrator founded in 1993, that is based in Atlanta, Georgia, and has offices in North Carolina, Washington, DC, New York and Florida—is striving to become an RSI, providing for a bigger footprint and more integration points with Microsoft in a number of geographies, and access to more benefits. It employs roughly 65 people, most of whom work at company headquarters, which until recently was strategically located in the same building as the Microsoft office in Atlanta. The proximity allowed for a generous amount of communication and collaboration, coffee breaks and business leads. The firm moved to another building in late 2004.

Over the course of a decade, Intellinet has developed deep relationships with Microsoft sales, consulting and partner executives in the Southeast as well as with product groups at Seattle. Braden Barras, director of partner alliances for Intellinet, said the complex web of relationships between Intellinet and Microsoft's sales account representatives, Microsoft Consulting Services and partner representatives is a key asset that has been consistently nurtured. This mirroring technique is employed by several successful ISVs and services partners that aim to optimize their partnership with Microsoft.

"Our business development teams work closely with counterparts at Microsoft to put together next-generation plans for named accounts. We work jointly with Microsoft account representatives to understand their strategies. These are the sales folks. We have built relationships over time and we had a physical location in Microsoft headquarters in Atlanta that strengthened our connection with Microsoft. The relationship between our consultants and Microsoft consultants has developed over time by working on services engagements and impacted us in a very positive fashion. We sell a deal with MCS and we deliver those services alongside MCS. The more trust that is built, the better our relationship grows."

Intellinet used many of the aforementioned strategies and tactics to grow. In 2003, Intellinet hired a former Microsoft sales and channel veteran to expand its services business into the Gulf States region. The firm has ties into the partner organization and a designated LSI PAM in the Southeast, Gulf States and Mid-Atlantic Districts. Mr Barras said deep relationships with Microsoft on all tiers of the sales, product and partner groups are a significant asset. "Microsoft proactively engages us. A significant part of our business is referred by Microsoft."

In order to continue nurturing its partnership with Microsoft, Intellinet—like most other solution providers—is undergoing a significant change in its business model to accommodate Microsoft's changing business. To do this, the firm is expanding into the Northeast. In 2004, for instance, Intellinent opened up an operation in Washington, DC. This year, they have opened operations in New York City. The firm is also ramping up its vertical domain expertise. "As Microsoft focuses more on becoming a solutions company, Intellinet has had to adapt its business in providing true business solutions or get left behind. We have not officially set up vertical practices but have attained vertical domain expertise," Mr Barras noted. Intellinet is trying to emulate in some respects the Big 4 (Global) SIs and is building a separate line of business focused on strategy-based consulting targeted at CXOs. "We focus on how we can help companies impact their business by aligning technology investments with their business drivers and helping them build technology roadmaps rather than just deploying software." In one case, Intellinet helped build a wireless roadmap for one CIO of a corporate client, which could one day revolutionize their business and cut significant costs. Like other services partners, Intellinet is recruiting "consultants that have experience at the management level and business process consulting instead of hiring folks only versed in bits and bytes."

"We are helping clients build cases for ROI and craft methodologies for their businesses." As Microsoft dips into vertical practices, such as healthcare, manufacturing, and oil and gas, partners are following suit. "We are looking for a different profile—we are looking to build separate lines of business to augment our technology services," said Mr Barras. "If we can broaden the spectrum of our services and offer more business and operational consulting, to illustrate more value for our clients while increasing the size of our engagements."

———■———

From Intellinet we see that being aligned with Microsoft means mirroring the organizational dynamic, speaking the same business language and being present and "on time" with the company. That is, the timing of a services partner's initiatives must correspond to those of Microsoft's marketing plan. And they should ideally be structured so as to work synergistically with local offices in order to anticipate any tactical or strategic moves under consideration by Microsoft. Intellinet has positioned itself favorably for a vertical thrust with Microsoft and expansive growth to accommodate Microsoft's down-market, cross-country sweep.

Intellinet's goal to become an RSI benefited from significant consolidation in the Microsoft services business in the Southeast, since two of its key competitors—Extreme Logic and GA Sullivan—were acquired by larger systems integrators. In August 2003, HP acquired Extreme Logic, and St Louis-based Microsoft services partner GA Sullivan became part of Seattle-based systems integrator Avanade in May 2003. These are just two of many acquisitions and mergers that have occurred in the Microsoft services ecosystem following the slowdown in overall IT spending.

2005
Interlink Group acquires Equarius
ePartners acquires YET
YET merges with In2Gr8
2004
Vis.align acquires Econium
Avanade acquires en'tegrate
Trinity Expert Systems acquires The Computing Practice Limited
Resolute—the product of a merger between Pacific Solutions Group and Resolute Business Solutions—acquires Hunt Interactive and The KIS Group
Tribridge acquires CXO Technology

Figure 5.3: Representative Mergers And Acquisitions Consolidating The Microsoft Services Partner Market, 2004-2005.

Dell led the charge in June 2002, with its controversial buyout of Plural, a former New York web integrator. Unisys, a Microsoft OEM partner and systems integrator, acquired ePresence's security services in June 2004. Many services partners have merged to grow their market share, a trend particularly evident in the Microsoft Business Solutions sector. Tectura, of Tempe, Arizona, made 11 acquisitions in two years. There have been other acquisitions, too, further consolidating the Microsoft services-partner market.

Craft and Constantly Deliver Your Message, and Value, to Microsoft

Make sure Microsoft knows who you are and keep your messaging simple. Remember, most Microsoft personnel are constantly bombarded by partners who want to work with them but who deliver confusing and complex messages about who they are and what they do. A typical and extreme case of complex messaging that usually works against a services partner is the jack-of-all-trades approach. The core messaging is that such a firm "can do just about everything ... except sell your software." This is bad messaging on two counts:

First, no partner can do everything and be all things to all customers, given the expansive scope of Microsoft's products and platforms. This is why Microsoft has stratified partners by defined competencies that place them in manageable buckets, ripe for quick picking by Microsoft personnel who seek a specialist for specific opportunities. Microsoft does not know how to position itself with services firms that have vague "everything-but-the-kitchen-sink" messaging. As indicated, Microsoft—in the field, and at corporate—has so many partners to work with that you cannot expect the company to keep the identity of each partner straight as its personnel work feverishly to meet their sales quotas. It is critical for services partners to come up with a "handle," a clear identity, for Microsoft employees based on their competencies, geographical or market focus and how best to engage with them. This "handle" must be sales-oriented since Microsoft is sales-oriented.

Second, a services partner must always be willing to resell Microsoft software even if that is not its core competency. Firms that say they cannot or will not sell Microsoft software violate a cardinal rule—and the core mission of Microsoft itself—which is to sell as much software as possible. Microsoft personnel—technical sales, account management and consulting services—are first and foremost focused on their sales. The challenge for them is to deliver sales at volumes defined from above, often a seemingly impossible goal since their quotas increase regularly regardless of the business climate. Microsoft personnel are under constant pressure, challenged for time, and they must rely on their partners to help them meet their quotas. So they must have a crisp, clear recall of partners that are a best fit in any given customer situation. A Microsoft sales representative will have at most five go-to services partners whose specific strengths the representative understands. And, because each of those services companies will have as many as five opportunities at any given time in their territory or preferred market, it is possible, through its partners, for the Microsoft sales representative to handle up to 25 opportunities simultaneously. This is only possible with effective teaming between Microsoft and its partners. But such a level of project management is not easy to master. The services partner that aligns itself with and leverages its Microsoft connection points with a focused and pointed message enhances its prospects of becoming one of those five go-to partners.

Score Points

Microsoft has attempted many methods and matrices over the years to establish an objective partner evaluation system but historically has lacked an effective mechanism to measure partners. The point system is yet another attempt at this goal to help partners evolve in step with Microsoft. Services partners should, of course, factor in the partner point system as a guide to position themselves in the best possible light in the partner ecosystem. Although there is some skepticism about the practical value of the still unproven system, it is by all accounts an improvement over what Microsoft previously had—or, more accurately, what it did not have—in place to grade and reward partners. This has changed in part due to the partner point system but, as we noted in Chapter Two, there are shortcomings that will likely be refined over time. For example, there is currently no clear way to map how much revenue is influenced—as opposed to caused—by a partner, so it becomes problematic for Microsoft to assess objectively which partner or agent should be credited for a sale. Your success will boil down to customer wins, references and certifications. The partner point system is Microsoft's mechanism for keeping its partners organized, identified, and up-to-date on information about its services partners' expertise so that Microsoft can act fast if an opportunity emerges that requires a specific skill set.

So it is in services partners' best interests to communicate their identity and value to Microsoft personnel. Microsoft cares about services partners to the extent that they contribute to its livelihood but what it knows about a particular services partner comes from the partner itself. Microsoft does not pick names out of a hat, so it is your job to make your value known. The first rule that partners must observe, as indicated, is to steer clear of the message that your firm "does everything ... except sell Microsoft software." Microsoft is encouraging all of its partners—ISVs, services partners and resellers—to specialize. Generalizing is out; specializing is in. The best approach for a services partner, then, is to communicate specifically what its competencies are and how much Microsoft software it can sell. Here is a simple template you can fill in and have ready should you encounter a Microsoft representative on the street or at a meeting: "We hold X, Y and Z competencies and we sold US$X worth of Microsoft software in A, B and C customer categories and industries, and have built a demonstrable reputation for excellence in implementing them." In addition to scoring points in the partner program based on your Microsoft-designated competencies, you will score points with your Microsoft colleagues with such succinct, effective messaging.

Verticals: "Customer Categories" Are Red Hot

In this context, "customer categories," which refers to their placement in industry verticals, have become more significant in Microsoft's overall strategy. As Microsoft strives to address the unique needs of its customers and to move deeper into business applications and business process automation, re-engineering and the management arena, it requires greater expertise both internally and externally. Microsoft is evolving its organization to meet the challenge while also enhancing its extended sales force and remaining committed to its partner-driven culture. Microsoft retained top sales and enterprise services executives from IBM Global Services and strengthened sales and support for established vertical practices in many industry sectors, including healthcare, financial services, communications, retail, automotive, public sector, manufacturing, and still others. The company's Business Solutions division (MBS) separately supports numerous verticals, including automotive, construction, food and beverage, government, high technology and electronics, industrial equipment, life sciences, metal fabrication, not-for-profit, professional services, retail management, and wholesale and distribution.

The company is building out global implementations for all of its vertical practices and has appointed global managing directors for each subsidiary's verticals and solutions maps within the US. Customer-segment marketing is being enhanced from Seattle and in each subsidiary. Microsoft Consulting Services handles roughly 20,000 projects per year; it needs partners to penetrate deeper into the verticals globally. If current trends continue, almost all corporate-level accounts will be classified within some vertical. Partners must shift their own product-and-service plans to accommodate this growing trend at Microsoft. And planning is essential before moving into a vertical market that may be crowded.

It is, therefore, important for services partners to create vertical messaging and to promote that messaging to target Microsoft vertical personnel at corporate and in the field. You must continue to train your sales and delivery teams to deliver your firm's message to Microsoft as if with one voice. Review your firm's Microsoft messaging once a month if not more often to determine how it can be refined, and update messaging annually to couch it in the latest GTMs. And always align your new product launches with Microsoft's fiscal-year start—again, in July—as well as shortly after Microsoft's new product launches to take advantage of marketing buzz and to align your product with Microsoft's initiatives. These are basic co-branding principles that cannot be overstated. Your message can be effectively delivered at Microsoft's annual worldwide partner conference.

Like other partners, services partners must make the most of their Microsoft connection points. We have seen the imperative of doing so in case studies throughout this book, and we will see it again. This means networking with Microsoft and building relationships with the right Microsoft personnel—ideally, for you, in this order: field, then corporate—and managing those relationships, developing them so that you begin to extend your Microsoft network through introductions and referrals as a result. This is a critical best practice for services partners.

Many SPs will establish one Microsoft connection point—an acquaintance, a relationship—in a geographical or vertical market that the services partner hopes to penetrate. Do not waste your time with this limited approach. One, two, three connection points in any given market with Microsoft is not enough! And quality is less important than quantity. If you have deep friendships with three Microsoft employees in a geographical or vertical market area, your chances of success in penetrating the market are far fewer than if you have multiple professional relationships with five or more. IBM Global Services generally has more seasoned executives working within its vertical practices. Microsoft is hiring more partner account managers to help its services partners in the field but some are fairly young and inexperienced, which can make it difficult for a more seasoned business person. These PAMs can help you access resources available more generally but it is your responsibility to target and pursue Microsoft sales and consulting personnel working in your vertical markets.

As part of building your connection points within Microsoft, get to know the sales and technical staff that work for specific industries. If you are focusing on a particular vertical, you must get to know the sales executives, solutions specialists, consultants and technical staff that work with customers in your domain expertise. What vertical priorities—if any—are on your general manager's scorecard? When was the last time Microsoft field personnel brought you on or accompanied you to a sales call that is vertical-related? Or referred you a lead or an opportunity?

Again, like ISVs, services partners are the masters of their own destiny and can influence how Microsoft field (and corporate) employees regard your firm and its services quality. The more of them that you can count, the greater your chances will be to track your target market. You need to work the people in the local trenches. You need to get exposure to their managers or find a way to make yourselves known to them. If possible, you also need to establish connections to Microsoft's top vertical executives in Seattle. One enterprising systems integrator based at Montreal, Canada, who was formerly an Oracle partner, is spearheading its evolution to verticals and has made it a point to get to know the sales executives who work in financial services, healthcare and manufacturing. The experience of Nexxlink highlights the need—and some tactics—for services partners to pursue industry verticals, as we see in its case study.

Bell Business Solutions Banks on Verticals, Evolving as a "Mini-SI" In Canada

Bell Business Solutions (www.nexxlink.com) is a systems integrator that employs 1,100 people and generates roughly CA$125 million in revenues annually. In 2005, Bell Canada acquired Nexxlink and Charon Systems, combining them to form an IT services firm to serve SMB customers in vertical markets across Canada. Long before the acquisition, the former Nexxlink had moved away from turnkey IT services and began focusing on providing more advanced business process re-engineering services for vertical markets in Canada, including financial services, manufacturing and healthcare. Reginald Howatson, an account manager for Nexxlink, said the choice of verticals was easy: Montreal has a sizable healthcare community and the federal healthcare system is being revamped at a cost of CA$18 billion. There are no secrets about where the next opportunities lie. Mr Howatson said he is comfortable partnering with Microsoft because it is exclusively a software company and, in spite of its attempt at solution accelerators, does not have a general-purpose solution, as does IBM Global Services. This gives services partners many more opportunities in the vertical sector that are served by IBM, Oracle and Sun. "It is good that Microsoft has people with a vertical focus like municipalities and healthcare," Mr Howatson said. "Microsoft Montreal has financial representatives who deal with the big banks and take care of partners that work in the industry. It is important for Microsoft to have PAMs and account people and technology people but vertical people are important as we try to take MBS into manufacturing and distribution or services companies."

"Unlike IBM and Oracle, Microsoft does not have a strong arm of professional services internally so they rely on partners for specific skill sets," he said. And the evolution of services partners, solution providers and value-added resellers into IT business consultants to add value to their technology consulting skills is inevitable as Microsoft focuses on specific verticals and builds solutions that solve real business problems or address the business processes of enterprise, mid-market and small-business customers.

Notice how Microsoft's ISVs such as CorasWorks and services partners such as Bell Business Systems are evolving in the same manner. Echoing the words of Coras-Works' Mr Rogers, Mr Howatson said SPs are likewise blending in business consulting practices to supplement their technology expertise.

"I predict that more and more IT shops will become business consultants as Microsoft has more of a business solutions focus. The large SIs, like KPMG and

Deloitte, and big shops, like Accenture, will decrease in importance and go the way of Enron and more Microsoft services partners will become like mini-Arthur Andersons. This can happen. I get CA$500 per hour for preparing my clients for financial compliance and offering financial consulting services. I have on staff a production engineer and a certified public accountant and I am doing implementations of business processes and business process re-engineering. There will be more Microsoft business solutions moving forward in which I can offer the highest value-add by getting closer to the center of customer business processes. The closer you get to the center of business processes, the better. It is like lawyers, doctors and other professionals; you get to the heart of the matter."

Build Bridges with Microsoft at Multiple Levels

Having ties in Microsoft corporate is an asset but services partners must think globally and act locally. And you need to climb all steps of the ladder at your local office. Again, here is where qualitative measures enter in once you have sufficient quantity of Microsoft field personnel thinking and saying good things about your services. You must focus your relationship-management and value-selling efforts on field-level solutions and sales specialists, but you must also penetrate the field-level management tier, from account managers to the general manager, who is the boss of the local district. Find out what GTMs are of the highest priority on his scorecard or, at the very least, what his major goals are within his territory. Sit down and do a business plan with local Microsoft executives that span a two-year time period. It is important that you be kept apprised of product roadmaps in order to prepare your staff for training and certification and the rollout of your new services based on Microsoft's new products and platforms. This to-management approach will also ensure that when the account manager calls a solutions specialist into a customer, the account manager will already know that your solution is best for that customer—thanks to your relationship-building efforts.

Mirroring is one organizational tactic that several successful ISVs and services partners have employed to partner successfully with Microsoft on multiple levels. In order to maximize communication and coordination, partners structure the organization of their firms to mirror that of their Microsoft local office. We have seen Intellinet employ this tactic with great results. Resolute is another Microsoft services partner based in Microsoft's backyard of Bellevue, Washington, that has mirrored both Microsoft's corporate organization and the internal organization chart. Resolute's CEO John Fallou is a former MCS and Avanade executive who is leading the firm's charge into verticals and business consulting. The firm, for example, established 17 offices nationwide to correspond to Microsoft's 17 subsidiaries in the US, and devised an executive organization that corresponds precisely to that of Microsoft—GM to GM, sales to sales, services to services—in order to maximize efficiencies.

Timing is also important to your firm. Go to market with a service that fits with Microsoft's new release or the latest field-endorsed GTMs and ensure that there are several Microsoft employees who will vouch for and recommend your product to customers. Services partners that participate in early adopter programs (EAPs) can gain advance expertise on a new technology, which gives them a wide competitive advantage. Others get trained on the new technology and start building solutions to establish expertise while they wait for the market for that technology to grow. It is important to note that international partners including Nexxlink of Montreal and Softflow of Beirut, Lebanon, point out that localized versions of any new software typically lag the US version by more than one year. Therefore, they must account for that lag when formulating marketing plans. Ensure that your set of service offerings is updated as Microsoft's products come to market. Also, tap into Microsoft's marketing engine if it works to the benefit of your services portfolio. In order to be in synch with Microsoft on new product releases, you have to be in synch with Microsoft personnel.

Remember what Microsoft seeks most from its services partners? Expertise, quality and energy. Microsoft is a product-centric, customer-focused, partner-driven company. You also need to be innovative in designing solutions, and ought to collaborate with Microsoft from the conceptual inception of a new product through the marketing blitz that favors its products and your services. Microsoft depends on its partners to relay information about the business problems that customers face, and the capabilities and processes they want to implement, so that its R&D teams can develop features and products appropriately. Partners are co-developers. It is impossible to co-innovate when you are not joined at the hip strategically and operationally with Microsoft. This requires field-level awareness of your firm's services and field-initiated ties into corporate product groups. Ensure that this two-tiered communication works on your behalf. This is why it is important to stay on top of your relationships and constantly to extend them. This approach is of utmost importance in Microsoft's culture and fits in with their strategy—but it must come in Microsoft's timing. Doing so requires a great deal of flexibility in services firms, as well as their products and personnel.

Large systems integrators, especially of the global variety, which pioneered services delivery, fully grasp the need to engage at multiple levels with Microsoft and all other software companies. All Microsoft services partners pushing into vertical markets can benefit from the experience and knowledge of two major Microsoft GSIs, Capgemini and Unisys, in working Microsoft's organization to extend into markets that the company is targeting.

Capgemini Allies and Aligns with Microsoft

Capgemini (www.capgemini.com)—a systems integrator founded in 1967, and based in Paris, France—has been a Microsoft Global Alliance Partner since 1997. It employs 60,000 employees worldwide (more than 5,000 of whom interface with Microsoft personnel and accounts) and reported revenues of US$8.2 billion in 2004. In mid-2004, Microsoft and Capgemini extended their seven-year alliance, which has generated more than US$2 billion in sales of Microsoft-based solutions and services, and driven sales growth of more than 47% since 2002. Roughly 25 Capgemini employees globally are dedicated to the Microsoft partnership.

Capgemini works with all leading software companies. One key differentiator that Microsoft offers is that there is neither conflict nor competition from the company's consulting services, said Deanne Handron, vice president and global Microsoft alliance executive at Capgemini. "We do not view MCS as a competitor to us and we have more than 12 Microsoft consultants working fulltime to help us with various sales and marketing, solutions development and client engagements. We view them as an extended part of our team. And I can say IBM Global Services is a very big competitor of ours and so is Oracle's consulting team for certain kinds of work," she said. In addition, most systems integrators have different business units that work with different vendors. "We keep our vendor alliance teams separate so that I do not know what our IBM or Oracle teams are doing. Microsoft is very competitive. So it is good to be ignorant because you are not pressed to divulge competitive information."

Like other systems integrators, Capgemini has noticed Microsoft's improved and streamlined manner in working with its large SI partners. "As Microsoft moves into more vertical markets and extends its reach into the enterprise, it has become more sophisticated in how it engages large systems integrators on many levels," said Ms Handron. In mid-2004, the two companies announced a combined investment of US$50 million to push Windows Server 2003-solutions into specific vertical segments, including healthcare, the public sector, energy, chemicals and utilities, automotive, manufacturing and retail.

There is also much cross-pollination between Microsoft and SIs given its size, scope and vertical focus. Jon Arnold, who joined Microsoft in late 2004 as worldwide utility industry manager, for instance, served as a communications consultant to Capgemini in the creation of Capgemini Energy, a 10-year, US$35 billion IT and business process outsourcing agreement with TXU in May 2004.

Most significantly, Microsoft has established more connection points with Capgemini and enabled its participation in the worldwide partner program. Ms Handron noted that the Microsoft partner programs of the past were more friendly to smaller firms working in the SMB Space, but it has evolved over the past decade in a more balanced way to serve both the SMB channel and enterprise SI players very well. "It is a much better program and Microsoft now accommodates input from the large partners." Ms Handron said that vendor-partner programs are important because partners need training, marketing support, differentiation through certification, different branding levels and each offers different competitive advantages. "Since 1997, Microsoft has learned to listen to partners in general and all the partners told them the same thing: we need alignment with Microsoft in marketing. Microsoft is a very good marketing company and we want to ride its coat-tails in the market and, in order to do that, there has to be a message you can all stand behind. They are refocusing their marketing messages into GTMs and stabilizing them over time."

Ms Handron observed that Capgemini's connection points to Microsoft are varied and numerous; Capgemini interfaces with Microsoft's product development teams, Microsoft Consulting Services and the Enterprise and Partner Group executives. This is a significant improvement. In the past, Capgemini had one business development manager who reported to the Enterprise Customer and Partner Group.

Additionally, the inclusion of SIs in the mainstream partner program and go-to-market campaigns has added structure to an otherwise *ad hoc* partnership. Before, there was little consistency or predictability in how the two collaborated, Ms Handron noted, and systems integrators now have the best of both worlds. "At the start of each fiscal year, Microsoft sends its systems integrators a list of GTMs and Capgemini meets with the GTM marketing teams to discuss what solutions and offerings we have and what things we can do together. Now Microsoft's marketing is based on GTMs. Additionally, Microsoft continues to work to refine its approach to solutions selling. "What we would do was up to our imaginations and every SI had a unique way of going to market with Microsoft. That had advantages and disadvantages because you had to blaze a trail for everything you did. We still have that but we see people putting together programs we can all use, especially around GTMs. Before, we would deal directly with product teams but there is a huge gap between BizTalk guys and the systems integrator who is responsible for doing connectivity and integration projects. We just do not speak the same language. Now there is a GTM team between us and those guys that figures out a solutions message for Microsoft. They are part of the product teams."

"We do business with MCS in enterprise accounts. We have two GTM approaches: named accounts have partner account managers and may or may not be Microsoft-friendly; and then there are transaction accounts, where we sell through a more programmatic approach, such as campaigns and events. We do one-to-many marketing, where we attend executive partner summits in the US, Europe and Asia. Then we have specific and unique events. Once or twice per year, we have a custom event with Microsoft designed by our business development manager to build a more intimate relationship between the two companies. Bill Gates participates. We talk about products that are a couple of years out and we tell Microsoft what kinds of business problems we are trying to solve and what we need the technology to do. We have discussions with Microsoft about what is a business issue. It is a way to get more intimate relationships between the technical teams so our people know more about where Microsoft is going and where we can provide input. We have our regional CTOs attend and our technical architects and, from Microsoft, they have group product managers, even Bill Gates."

For Ms Handron, "the relationship is a very important asset, it is critical for our business. Each year our CEO, who is French, comes to Microsoft to meet with top executives including Steve Ballmer, and our regional CEOs meet with Microsoft's vice president for sales. I do not think I could get that level of interaction with Microsoft executives without a strong relationship." One way to keep the relationship strong is to respect Microsoft's strict cultural norms. "I never go above the person I am working with unless I absolutely cannot get it done any other way. Microsoft follows a strong chain of command," notes Ms Handron.

Unisys Sails High in the Data Center with Microsoft, and Tests Linux Waters

Unisys (www.unisys.com)—a Microsoft Platinum OEM Partner, Global Partner and Gold Certified Partner—has 35,000 employees and is headquartered at Blue Bell, Pennsylvania. For its fiscal year 2004, Unisys reported US$1 billion in server revenues. The firm formerly established an alliance with Microsoft in 1999. Initially, the pact involved Unisys' Systems and Technology division but rapidly spread across all the Unisys operations, including systems integration and security services as well as applications development and desktop deployment.

"We have a sophisticated and well-established communication model with Microsoft and a corporate alliance group responsible for coordinating and managing the overall relationship," said Peter Samson, vice president and general manager of enterprise server market development at Unisys. "Microsoft has a new and enlightened enterprise partner strategy and measures the value of their partnerships not only by Microsoft product revenues that flow through the Unisys channel but also by 'affected revenue,' the top-line integration services value to Unisys based on our implementation of the Microsoft platform within our customer base. Our major initiative with the US Transportation Security Administration was largely built on Microsoft technology and Microsoft sees that as a leading indicator of the value we bring them."

Mr Samson continued: "Microsoft understands the value of the enterprise partner ecosystem much better than it did in the late 1990s and early 2000s, and they are putting their money where their mouth is. This integrated and extended community is the biggest differentiator Microsoft has over open-source competitors. Moreover, they are compensating their field people on partner satisfaction. I have found that Microsoft has been much easier to deal with and are empathizing more clearly with our requirements in the field."

Unisys currently employs more than 30 executives and managers whose primary responsibility is to coordinate and manage the firm's complex relationship with Microsoft. Included in this are Microsoft Relationship Executives, or MREs as they are known, are based in major cities throughout the world to ensure that the two partners communicate effectively, identify opportunities on which to engage and develop local marketing campaigns. "The touch points between the two partners are extensive: Unisys also has in its Redmond, Washington, Technology Center a large corporate alliance team that works on business development, joint marketing activities as well as the development of Unisys-Microsoft portals."

Unisys works closely with Microsoft's advertising and public relations team and key go-to-market programs such as server application re-platforming, server consolidation, mobility solutions, desktop deployment and business intelligence. Also, Unisys engineers collaborated with Microsoft on development of the Data Center Server Program. The Unisys Solutions Alliance Technology Center in the Redmond office works closely with Microsoft on systems integration work around BizTalk and e-business suite of products and other solutions as part of our 3D-VE initiative. "So, at headquarters, we have many touch points."

"In the field, we have dedicated Microsoft consulting practices with teams of technical specialists that focus entirely on delivering and implementing Microsoft solutions. There are sales and marketing teams that specialize on local execution of the programs. There is also joint funding of local and regional seminars and marketing events," Mr Samson noted.

With respect to funding, Mr Samson stated that "Microsoft co-funds us in a number of ways, such as advertising, collateral and demand generation. They also help fund strategically important customer-related pre-sales activities. We do joint road shows and sports marketing events."

Microsoft is investing heavily in their PAM and business development organizations. In North America, Microsoft has at least three people dedicated to the partnership and, in each major subsidiary, they have dedicated people that work closely with Unisys. "Three years ago, I did not think Microsoft had the same emphasis on supporting us globally. While we did have PAMs assigned to Unisys around the world, Microsoft has improved the quality and quantity of these people and raised the visibility of these partner managers within their own organization."

Matching Microsoft's urgency in tightening its interface to Unisys is Unisys' own urgency in penetrating verticals markets with Microsoft in order to align with the company's overall strategy. "Microsoft is going after verticals and they are matching up with systems integrators that can deliver. We have domain expertise in many areas including federal and local government, justice and safety, health and human services, financial services, publishing, transportation, telecommunications and supply chain work."

Mr Samson also observed that it is rare for Microsoft to ask Unisys to work with an unknown partner in an existing opportunity. Microsoft likes to replicate the process and framework of engagements. "Usually when Unisys teams with Microsoft on an opportunity, very early in the process the extended ecosystem of partners is identified. For example, on a big SAP implementation, we would involve SAP and we would need an integrator like Unisys' own Transformation Services, Accenture or RealTech to team with." That is, Unisys has established relationships with systems integrators that have specialties within larger technology competencies, such as Real-Tech's SQL expertise.

There are indeed opportunities for small integrators to get in on these opportunities but vertical expertise is generally necessary. "It is happening this way because as the Microsoft product stack gets deeper and broader, almost by default there is a requirement for more specialized integrators. If they are horizontal integrators that know Active Directory or Content Manager, they should also know a vertical like healthcare." The fact that Microsoft is driving more into a complete solution stack drives new intersections between the horizontal line-of-business and a vertical technical domain specialty. Unisys has an organization as part of its global commitment to Microsoft to work closely with ISVs and systems integrators. Partners can go to this organization directly. "We have a triangular proposition between Microsoft, systems integrators and ISVs. For example, Microsoft, Unisys and MicroFocus partner on IBM MVS migrations. We rely on our global partner team to identify best-of-breed application vendors and integrators in the high-end space. They should be knocking on our door if they are not engaged. We have an organization that is the clearing-house for point skills so, if we lack talent in-house, we go to this organization to identify a services vendor. For example, if the company is a regional systems integrator in New Jersey, they should get introduced to Unisys through their local PAM or through local Unisys office. This is easier than trying to work through the Unisys switchboard. The integrator should try to leverage its relationship with Microsoft to interest Unisys."

From Mr Samson's perspective, Microsoft does not yet enjoy a large market share in high-end solutions but he expects the company to get more aggressive. "Microsoft's Data Center Server program is a well-kept secret but we have many proof points that Microsoft has scalability and reliability. In my opinion, they are not being as aggressive as I would like in driving this to market.

"The high-end is actually counter-cultural for Microsoft. In the high-end enterprise, it is more of a one-to-one marketing model and requires a different sales and support mentality. Microsoft's Enterprise and Partner Group has a team of people addressing this issue and they are bringing in expertise from established computer companies." In the short term, Mr Samson sees this as the next level of partnering with Microsoft.

In response to the same market pressures that incline Microsoft to shift its go-to-market approach to win big deals, Unisys itself has shifted its approach in a direction counter to Microsoft's interests. In mid-2004, Unisys publicly announced at LinuxWorld Expo that it would start shipping Linux on its high-end servers. This is a big gamble for Unisys, just as it has proved to be for HP and Dell. Unisys executives were aware that Microsoft would not be happy. So they went to Microsoft directly and explained the situation roughly a month in advance of the announcement, which according to Mr Samson, is "what good partners do." The deal means Unisys is willing to migrate companies from UNIX to Linux, where before it only provided UNIX-to-Windows migration services. Unisys executives deny that the move will sour relations between the two companies. Unisys was among few dedicated Microsoft SIs and OEMs for many years.

"All of the large systems integration companies, including Microsoft's close ally HP, have Linux service practices. Microsoft understands: we are reacting to market pressures. We have large clients that are moving to Linux, they want to stay with our products and we are not in a position to lose them," said Leo Daiuto, Unisys' president of Systems and Technology. "We have had a lot of customers coming to us about the possibility of going to Linux. Most have been in UNIX environments and they want to go to Linux. There are some in the proprietary RISC world tied religiously to UNIX that do not want to move to Windows so now we can play in open UNIX space. We cannot afford to turn business away and Linux is definitely making a play with the Linux 2.6 kernel."

So compounding Unisys' urgency in accommodating Linux is the firm's urgency to shore up its Microsoft relationship, to stay close to the company—aligning at the corporate level and locally in the field, and extending globally pursuant to Microsoft's GTMs.

"I predict that more and more IT shops will become business consultants as Microsoft has more of a business solutions focus. The large SIs like KPMG and Deloitte and big shops like Accenture will decrease in importance and go the way of Enron and more Microsoft services partners will become like mini-Arthur Andersons. This can happen. I get $500 per hour for preparing my clients for financial compliance and offering financial consulting services. I have on staff a production engineer and a certified public accountant and I'm doing implementations of business processes and business process reengineering. There will be more Microsoft business solutions moving forward in which I can offer the highest value by getting closer to the center of their business processes. The closer you get to the center of business process, the better... you get to the heart of the matter." —Reginald Howatson, Nexxlink

---

Score Points by Aligning Your Priorities with Microsoft's Top Priorities

Central to the success of Capgemini and Unisys are partnering tactics that any LSI can master and use to its advantage: many connection points, strong relationship management, strong messaging and proper alignment of your firm's goals with Microsoft's GTMs. Urgency is another imperative. If Microsoft's team has been instructed to focus on pushing email (Exchange), and your firm's messaging is about corporate portals, your alignment is off kilter. Your messaging is of little utility. If you want to strengthen your partnership with Microsoft, consider Microsoft's current initiatives, go-to-markets and determine how best to map your service offerings and competencies to help Microsoft reach its goals for any given quarter, or to help them meet their annual GTM goals. Of course, you can market any service, but if you want to gain traction with Microsoft, hone in on the types of services Microsoft is pushing or perceives as urgent. In 2004, security and Linux were hot-button issues. In 2005, we are seeing increasing focus on the forthcoming "Longhorn" release of the Windows desktop and server platforms, collaboration, and business solutions. Microsoft is a dynamic ship that shifts course frequently, and quickly. It is best to map your Microsoft business annually and review it quarterly, that is, as you plan your annual go-to-market campaign, you must factor in Microsoft's yearly GTMs and revise it on a quarterly basis depending on Microsoft's shifting priorities at corporate and within your geographical area or market sector. Keeping tabs on those shifting priorities is easier if you remain close to your Microsoft connections as you develop and refine your marketing plans and messages. But remember "the Microsoft millisecond": be concise, direct and stay on message.

In addition, there is the need to jump on the bandwagon when Microsoft announces its go-to-market strategy or sudden jihads and needs to mobilize its crew. It is said at the polls, "vote early and often." And so it is with Microsoft: be first out of the gate to align your firm's offerings with Microsoft's priorities, most importantly in the field, and let every Microsoft employee you meet understand how your service offerings are of value to them in terminology they understand. For example, if the push is on for Information Worker products, assess your services' fitness for the campaign and craft a pithy message, couched in your competency, for Microsoft employees that will demonstrate that you are ready as a go-to partner who will help a sale. Situate your message and its delivery in the context of Microsoft-published ROI studies or case studies, where appropriate. This will let them know that you are speaking their language to describe your product. If you tell Microsoft an opportunity your firm is pursuing is at "60%," know what 60% means in Microsoft's sales nomenclature. It means something very different from 50%. Microsoft cannot ascertain what support or resources to provide your firm if you cannot size up your prospects accurately.

If you win the field with your message, and your grasp of the Microsoft business, you are well on your way. If your business-intelligence services are driving a strong run–rate for a recently introduced version of SQL Server, do not keep that a secret from Microsoft. Microsoft values results-oriented partners that can demonstrate—and articulate—the Windows or BizTalk license sales your firm generates. There are too many partners for Microsoft to keep score; you have to keep reminding Microsoft of your value to their business to solidify and hopefully increase your stature in the ecosystem. These tactics will keep you in front of Microsoft as a services partner that has a solid grasp of the company's goals, culture and the way its organization—and field force—works. It also helps you to remain close to Microsoft so that you are well informed about the victories and battles in the field that affect Microsoft and perhaps your own firm. Doing so could result in a lead or tip from well-placed sources about a competitor that is having problems on a particular account. What if a competitor of yours has not informed Microsoft that it is working a customer account? Either of these dilemmas for your competitor can place you in favor with Microsoft and position your firm to be called in as a relief pitcher. There are other ways to score big points with Microsoft. Saving the day at a customer site, or a deal from ruin, certainly improves your stature in Microsoft's eyes. But saving the day in the context of undoing Microsoft's rivals in the market, or scoring a defection from Linux or winning a last minute SQL-Server deal away from Oracle are strategic wins that are not forgotten. Achieving this requires extraordinary initiative and a willingness to go the extra mile to prove Microsoft's case against a competitor, but the rewards outweigh the risks if you can get it done. Security and Linux were key pain points for Microsoft in 2004. A partner that can convince a Linux customer that Windows offers a higher return-on-investment or lower total-cost-of-ownership over its open-source rivals, and persuade a conversion, gets noticed in Redmond—regardless of size or ranking. This level of aggressiveness and commitment can extend your connections into Microsoft, and can pay dividends, as we see in the cases of Bayshore Solutions in the US and IDE of Sweden.

Bayshore Lands Big Wins with Microsoft

Bayshore Solutions (www.bayshoresolutions.com)—a Microsoft Certified Partner and Microsoft's 2004 Global Business Partner, based at Tampa, Florida—knew that it needed to make a connection with the local Microsoft office after years of collecting business cards from a never-ending stream of partner account managers who called once and never called back.

The Internet development firm had survived the dot.com bust and opted, in 2001, to become a Microsoft- dedicated solution provider due to the high percentage of

SMB customers in the Tampa area. But it had no connection to its only partner. When the next eager Microsoft account representative gave him a call, Bayshore's CEO Kevin Hourigan pounced. The web developer challenged the Microsoft partner account manager (PAM) to spend some time with his company and develop a working business relationship. That was in early 2003.

Eighteen months later, after faithful meetings with his PAM every month, exchanging business ideas and discussing potential solutions for clients, the partnership has begun to pay off. Bayshore Solutions has delivered custom web applications to more than 1,000 clients in 54 countries. Its client roster includes Outback Steakhouse, YMCA, Grand Expeditions, Holland and Knight Consulting, Gevity HR, Tampa Bay Lightning, Z-Tel, Hyatt Hotels, Tampa Bay Convention and Visitors Bureau, BankUnited and the State of Florida.

The new level of support and nurturing from Microsoft gave Bayshore more confidence to go after accounts it normally would not touch and do more general prospecting. Mr Hourigan said having the full resources of Microsoft behind him was the factor that cinched the deal a number of times. "If we have an opportunity where we do not know if we have the support necessary internally to handle the objections of a client, Microsoft can demonstrate a proof of concept and offer technical assistance especially with new technologies," Mr Hourigan said. "They have been there as backup. I have not had to use them but I have been ready to pull the trigger. You do not want to walk into a large account without the horsepower behind you. If you say you are coming in with Microsoft behind you, you get a confidence boost on the customer side."

By mid-2004, the Internet applications development firm reported a 50% up-tick in sales and an increase in traction and the length and size of projects. But what propelled Bayshore from obscurity to the corporate spotlight was a customer win of strategic importance to Microsoft: the conversion of a travel web site running Oracle/Red Hat Linux to an integrated Windows and SQL solution. Like most vendors, Microsoft loves competitive wins. At a time when open-source advocates were trumpeting the reliability and cost advantages of a Linux/Apache web solution over Windows and IIS, one Microsoft solution provider came in and proved otherwise with a customer case study, not benchmarks. Bayshore's win publicly challenged a powerful perception that Apache is infinitely more reliable than IIS and gave Microsoft standing in the highly contested web server realm if only for a moment. Bayshore's solution demonstrated that the Oracle-Red Hat Linux solution was not flexible enough to accommodate the constantly changing price, scheduling data and content edits of a commercial travel site. The fact is, Bayshore developed the intellectual property called SiteManager that allows administrators to edit content on a web site from a Microsoft Word interface. Such integrated innovation—the marrying of Bayshore's IP with the Microsoft platform—is the business model Microsoft endorses as the cornerstone value-add of the partnering relationship.

The project was a "decent-sized" win that generated hundreds of thousands of dollars for the firm but it also stirred up new business. Bayshore's Mr Hourigan was able to convince two of three large publicly traded companies that sent him RFPs for an Oracle implementation that the Microsoft SQL story was a better solution. He won the two new clients in the banking and HR training industries but lost the RFP submitted by an existing client, who is wedded to a vertical industry that strongly backs the Oracle platform. Later, that client joked that the Oracle proposal was twice the price of the Microsoft bid but his firm had to stick with the *de facto* standard. The competitive wins against Linux and Oracle earned Bayshore accolades from key Microsoft corporate executives, including Kevin Johnson—Microsoft's worldwide vice president of sales, services and marketing—who touted the firm's Grand Expeditions coup at the annual partner conference. Bayshore's CEO met with Microsoft's third-ranked executive at the conference and says he now carries Mr Johnson's business card with him in case he needs help.

But Mr Hourigan recognizes that the continued success of his firm depends on how well he nurtures the relationship with his PAM and his local Microsoft offices. Bayshore generated revenues of between US$1 million and US$2 million in 2002, doubling business after the Microsoft relationship was formed in spite a major downturn in the economy and high-technology spending. To him, the relationship with Microsoft is hard currency. "I definitely think the relationship is an asset. It did not exist before. I believe you get what you put into a relationship. Once Bayshore and Microsoft committed to this relationship, we were able to share in some great success stories."

IDE Scores Big Points with Microsoft by Converting Two Linux Shops

IDE Nätverkskonsulterna—a Stockholm, Sweden-based Microsoft Certified Partner founded in 1992—specializes in advanced infrastructure and network infrastructure services. For more than a decade, CEO Per Werngren has had relationships with various executives at Microsoft Sweden, which employs roughly 500 people. Like other European solution providers, IDE is getting more attention from Microsoft partner account managers these days due to Microsoft's ramped up partnering activities worldwide. But IDE is certain that the increased attention it is getting from Microsoft stems from two key Windows wins over Linux. IDE's wins have extra impact in Europe, the open-source movement's backyard and where Linux has grown most quickly. IDE gained Microsoft's notice after signing two deals to convert Linux sites to Windows, most notably the Royal Opera House. As part of the deal, IDE converted three Linux servers to Windows and also consolidated tens of servers down to seven. Like other services partners profiled that used tools to persuade customers of the value of Windows over competitors, IDE performed a study that demonstrated that an integrated Microsoft software stack would be less expensive for the Royal Opera House to maintain than an open-source environment.

"They had a huge dependence on consultants and it was very tough to maintain," said Mr Werngren. "It was tough to get figures for their current standing on Linux but we showed them what was the right way to move forward, and have it all integrated instead of having isolated islands. We went in with Windows XP, Windows Server 2003, Storage Server and ISA Server 2000. And we showed them that they do not need consultants for maintenance."

IDE scored another, albeit smaller, coup when it converted SAP consulting firm Stretch Consulting from Linux to Windows Small Business Server (SBS). The 25-consultant firm had been running Linux for two to three years and was spending US$8,000 per month to support the infrastructure. IDE demonstrated that using SBS 2003 instead of Linux would realize significant cost savings. IDE's study and its resulting intellectual property—backed up by Microsoft's argument that Windows provides better TCO than Linux—is precisely the kind of activity Microsoft needs from its services partners. IDE learned that one way to cull favor at Seattle is to win decisive contracts in markets where Microsoft is most vulnerable.

IDE has had relationships with the Microsoft subsidiary in Sweden since its inception. But the firm finds that it has gotten more attention since becoming a dedicated Microsoft partner in 1997. "Microsoft is a small organization—it has only 50,000 or 60,000 employees—so they need their partners to be able to get close with the end–customer. It is always easier if you are a dedicated partner because they know you will only sell a Microsoft solution."

IDE's local ties to Microsoft in Sweden are most important. Microsoft has one office in Sweden, four offices in Germany and two offices in France, including Microsoft's EMEA headquarters in Paris. However, Mr Werngren says, like most other solution providers IDE sticks close to the executives at the local office for business: "the local relationship is paramount."

Microsoft increased the number of PAMs in Europe since 2002, and now assigns a PAM to each Microsoft Certified Partner while smaller partners get "tele-PAMs." IDE has had a PAM for two years, who meets with the firm on a monthly basis. "Having a PAM take an interest in our business is vital for us and it is a relatively new experience for us. The value is huge. It is our small company going to market with this big software giant and we are both playing on the same team. That enables us to speak to customers with confidence so we can be a trusted advisor to them. There has been an exponential curve in business. Microsoft's partner activity has really picked up in the last two years because we have shown we are ready and willing to be engaged and that we always try to sell Microsoft solutions."

IDE is also very active in the International Association of Microsoft Certified Partners (IAMCP), of which Mr Werngren is the international president and which was originally a pro-Microsoft lobbying group that has become a business network for Microsoft partners (see Chapter Seven for more on IAMCP). The association helps services partners to form virtual corporations, or "circles of trust," a collaborative partnering model endorsed by Microsoft as a way to provide complete, end-to-end solutions to customers. The organization's three-tiered membership structure enables all partners in Microsoft's channel to participate. "It is a business network where partners locally get to know each other, trust each other and start to do business together. Being part of the association allows partners to provide a more complete solution to customers. It is important for our business in Sweden. We give deals away and we get deals from other members."

———■———

Three themes emerge from these two case studies that should be instructive in helping you understand a services partner's success in partnering with Microsoft in an aligned fashion and in a competitive market. Both partners

- manage the partnership at the executive level, and are not averse to taking risks to extend the partnership;

- stake out a niche within the high-technology sector and within Microsoft's ecosystem, and clearly communicate their position in it and value to Microsoft while networking with other Microsoft partners; and

- deliver real value to their clients, which can account for big wins for Microsoft in seizing opportunities from rivals, by going the extra mile and using resources to help sell and advance the Microsoft platform against competitive platforms.

On some sunny days, partnering with Microsoft is smooth sailing, but on other days riding the SS Microsoft's wake is choppy and perilous. A prudent services partner never rests on its laurels because Microsoft is a dynamic company that can shift on a dime: you must find balance in order to ride the waves, weather the storms, and arrive safely, prosperously to port.

Compete and Collaborate: Innovate, Negotiate, Advance Together

Partnering with Microsoft may appear easier for services partners than for ISVs because SPs do not compete directly against Microsoft on the product side. Yet all partners must come to terms with the firmness, even arrogance, of the Microsoft crew. Balancing out this inequity with ISVs, however, is the staggering amount of competition Microsoft's 329,000 services partners face. ISVs, on the other hand, number in the thousands. And some of these partners, maybe even their competitors, may be competitively positioned for Microsoft's favor. Microsoft sales representatives work directly with between five and 10 partners and others vie for opportunities. Additionally, Microsoft Consulting Services (MCS) must also be viewed as a potential competitor in some markets for services provision. These competitive factors contribute to the complexity of a services partner's engagement with Microsoft.

Like ISVs, services partners must know Microsoft and be comfortable with creative tension in the relationship. That is, the partner must thrive in a competitively collaborative environment. This should remind you of an oyster's producing a pearl by processing an irritant, whether sand or another foreign object. The partner is the foreign object that lodges itself in Microsoft's environment, and the resulting tension fosters the production of something of value. The most successful services partners recognize that a healthy dose of tension in their relationship with Microsoft is both to be expected and productive of great results. Systems integrators that work in the enterprise space may have to compete against Avanade, for example, the joint services firm funded by Microsoft and Accenture that is dedicated to Microsoft technology services. On other days, Microsoft services partners may be called into an engagement they bid on that Microsoft doled out to a global systems integrator.

Negotiating and executing legal agreements with Microsoft entails some amount of collaborative tension. Both parties want to advantage their position and, in theory anyway, both want an agreement that will help them advance together in whatever initiative they are contracting about. This you should know: it goes without saying that Microsoft will draft the agreement. Microsoft rarely, if ever, executes a contractual document drafted by a partner. The company has the usual variety of agreement templates ready for customization: non-disclosure agreements, master services agreements, technology assistance program agreements, early adopter program agreements, and so on. These variously specify the terms and working relationship of Microsoft and its services partners on client engagements and with respect to the clients themselves.

The most important thing for services partners to understand about Microsoft agreements is that they are virtually set in stone. That is, it is inadvisable for services partners to seek undue modifications to them because, in so doing, Microsoft's legal department must get involved. The legal department's focus is rightly spent on customer agreements for software licensing, and it will back-burner any services partner requests for agreement modifications. There have been instances in which a services partner's requests for changes to an agreement have delayed an agreement's closure and execution for as long as six to nine months. But that kind of wait time is impossible if a services partner wants to engage contractually with Microsoft on a deal. It is rather advisable to take your chances with Microsoft's agreements as written and, if you cannot do so, do not engage with the company unless you have sufficient time and are willing to invest substantial legal fees to press your case should the engagement go afoul of intentions.

It is possible to negotiate certain provisions in agreements with Microsoft, although it takes time. Such negotiations are, in fact, common and commonly pertain to the intellectual property of a services partner. It is essential for all services partners entering a legal agreement with Microsoft to protect their intellectual property, so all due attention to and negotiation of provisions surrounding the appropriate provisions in the agreement are essential. For example, if an agreement does not have a clause pertaining to pre-existing intellectual property, it must be introduced and, thus, its terms must be negotiated with Microsoft. The property for which the parties respectively entered the contract is the focus, after all, and distinct provision must be made in the agreement to this effect. One common fear is that a services partner's intellectual property—a code modification, an add-on feature set for a Microsoft product or a novel way of implementing a product that might be co-opted in setup binaries—might appear in the next release of a Microsoft product. There is little recourse to the services partner after the fact in such a scenario, so there is every reason to stress upfront the need for intellectual property protection.

In addition, and as suggested, another potentially important (or at least opportunistic) subject of negotiation with Microsoft is involvement in one of Microsoft's early adopter programs (EAP). Participation in these programs can be very beneficial for services partners. It pivots on timing and urgency—services partners must keep their skills current and there is often no better way to do it than participating as an early adopter—but it begs the question of negotiating agreements to protect one's interests. The challenge here is in knowing when to jump into a new or emerging technology and when to hold back. Microsoft has a series of programs that encourage customers and, therefore, partners to jump on the new-product bandwagon. In practical terms, a services partner must have a customer willing to experiment with new technology (and agree to a case study) before approaching Microsoft as an early-adopter applicant. Do not bother approaching Microsoft if you do not have a customer lined up. These programs, identified by the alphabet soup of acronyms that have evolved over the years, have had many names but most commonly they are known as early-adopter (EAP) or technology-adopter programs (TAP). Microsoft product groups will create these programs as they approach the launch of a new product or just the new version of an existing product. A services partner's alignment in time (opportunity) and contractual interests (negotiated collaboration) with Microsoft in such programs can yield it three key benefits: first, it trains the staff of a services partner on a new technology early (on a practical level, they can then train the rest of the firm's personnel); second, it affords the services partner an awareness within Microsoft that the firm is capable of implementing the technology; and, third, it gives services partners a jump in the market over competitors and thus competitive advantage. All are potentially invaluable. Again, though, the question is when to jump on the bandwagon—balancing current (business-as-usual) requirements with potentially new (latest technology) opportunities. There is a risk with every reward. It behooves services partners, then, to consider the experience of other Microsoft partners in their area and to factor in the firm's own readiness to devote personnel to new technology initiatives before committing, and then to decide on how much staff time to invest in such programs. Again, though, you must consider not only the time invested in the technology implementation but also the time of executive management needed for negotiating and executing the agreement.

All such negotiations with Microsoft are the subject of potentially productive— at least, protective—tension. (But the early adopter program is usually the least tense negotiation because its scope and intent are so integral to both Microsoft's and its partner's interests). And the more productive the tension the better as there will likely always be cause for tension in any partnership, and it can in fact help the partnership flourish.

The question is, though, how much tension is productive? Many services partners have found that they are naturally competitive with other services partners, or even with certain groups within Microsoft, as mentioned. This tension detracts from their progress in jointly bringing to market value-added solutions. With other groups, however, they are less competitive and enjoy a robust collaboration, though still marked by creative tension. You need to identify and work with the groups in Microsoft where the balance between competition and collaboration can be achieved in the latter's favor. In other words, collaboration should be the main characteristic of your working relationship with Microsoft, not competition. If there is too much tension in the relationship, it will only beget more tension. You need to find the right balance, and services partners must evaluate where it lies based on different criteria than ISVs since the risks and rewards are unique to each group and their business models differ. Doing so entails identifying the right group of people within Microsoft with whom to build relationships and, for services partners, these are almost certainly in the field offices of the markets in which the SPs engage.

Target Microsoft Personnel, Factor In Their Interests

The right competitive/collaborative balance is hard to gauge. But the overriding question is, whom do I work with at Microsoft? The answer, of course, is that it depends both on your firm's professional focus and services–partnering mode, and how your services can best be leveraged with and by Microsoft Consulting Services or Microsoft sales personnel, to foster your collective sales of their products and your services. It also depends on how various Microsoft groups perceive services partners as perceptions may vary from group to group.

Some groups view services partners merely as a channel to close business for Microsoft. One of the best examples of this is the former Great Plains organization, which—as of this writing (Microsoft nomenclature and acronyms change often)—is called Small and Midmarket Solutions and Partners (SMS&P). The SMS&P group is, at present, a pure partner-driven model for the products that it delivers. That is, partners are certified to sell and service specific products such as Great Plains, Navision and Axapta. However, it is not always so simply partner-driven. There are products in the SMS&P space that are not; for example, Microsoft platform and CRM products are driven to market by their respective field-level groups. But they are partner-driven in the respect that there is no competition with Microsoft resources although services partners are often competitive with one another in this space, by design. Services partners must recognize how each Microsoft group views them and realize the partnering limitations entailed in the market in which they operate. Services partners must direct their energies toward a goal that works for them and works within the Microsoft Partner Ecosystem.

The key is to find the industry-vertical or regional market group that will intrinsically benefit from what you have to offer and that will work with you to bring the solution most capably to market. Most services partners interviewed for this book that do not have a presence in Seattle wish they did. But, as in the case of ISVs, aligning locally—that is, working the Microsoft field office in each of your markets for insight and facilitated introductions—is the first step any services partner should take. This assumes that you have a solid grasp (and certifications) on your competencies and place in the ecosystem, and that your Microsoft-marketing message is well-tuned and consistently, effectively delivered by all relevant personnel to as many Microsoft personnel as possible. Consider the steps that services partner Tectura climbed to determine its messaging and alignment.

Tectura Aims High in the Middle Market with the Help of Friends in High, Far Away Places

Tectura (www.tectura.com)—a Microsoft Business Solutions service provider targeting middle-market firms and Microsoft's Global Partner of the Year in 2003—was originally founded in Tempe, Arizona in 2001, by CEO Terry Petrzelka, a former executive at enterprise management consulting firm Scitor Enterprises. Mr Petrzelka befriended former Great Plains CEO—and current head of Microsoft Business Solutions (MBS)—Doug Burgum while the two executives were on an *Inc Magazine* industry review committee in 1995-1996. The committee—to identify the "Best Companies Under US$100 Million Focused on Customer Satisfaction," including Scitor and Great Plains—served as a launch pad for Tectura.

Mr Petrzelka seized the moment. He saw bubbling opportunity in the middle-market business applications space and formed Tectura through a management buyout of Scitor Enterprises in September 2001, nine months after Microsoft's US$1.1 billion acquisition of Great Plains Software. Despite the startup's poor timing, Tectura has quickly grown into one of Microsoft's top MBS solution providers globally. Tectura has achieved impressive growth through a series of acquisitions with the intention of building an MBS empire, and a clever strategy of combining an MBS powerhouse with the Microsoft classic practice of another significant services provider office in Seattle.

Since its founding, Tectura has won several top honors from the MBS Division, including Microsoft Business Solutions US Partner of the Year in 2002, and it belongs to the Microsoft Business Solutions Inner Circle, which represents the top 1% of more than 2,200 partners. Following its merger with Aston Business Solutions in Copenhagen, Denmark, in mid-2004, Tectura claimed to be the largest partner serving the Axapta and Navision product lines and one of Microsoft's top partners in the Great Plains, Solomon, and Microsoft CRM space. The solutions provider, now headquartered in San Mateo, California, projects that it will generate more than US$500 million in revenues and employ 2,500 by 2007.

Having friends in high places at Microsoft is a big and growing asset to Tectura: Burgum was promoted to senior vice president, MBS Business Group in 2004, after Orlando Ayala, former top sales chief at Microsoft, was moved from that MBS post to become senior vice president of the SMS&P group. At the corporate level, Tectura's CEO has also developed a strong relationship with a key Microsoft ISV executive. While those heavy-duty corporate connections are invaluable to Tectura, the company has also invested heavily to align itself with Microsoft's ramped-up aspirations in the middle-market business applications space.

Since its founding, Tectura has acquired 12 companies that focus exclusively on Great Plains Software and other MBS software, including Select Systems, Sensible Solutions, Concord Business Systems and The Morrison Group. In 2004, Tectura launched its international expansion with two other sizable acquisitions of MBS service providers in Europe, Cosmo Consult AG and Aston Business Solutions along with an acquisition of Optus Software of Canada. The merger with Copenhagen-based Aston, the largest deal to date, has knitted Tectura's acquisitions into an MBS powerhouse with combined revenues of US$150 million in FY2004 and 22 offices in the US and Europe.

Ironically, one of Tectura's most strategic if unlikely acquisitions took place in June 2002, when Tectura executives agreed to buy the Bellevue, Washington office of BORN, a traditional Microsoft solutions provider with vertical expertise in and vast experience with Microsoft classic infrastructure applications, including Windows Server, Exchange, Active Directory, BizTalk and .NET. A group of BORN executives pitched themselves to Tectura after learning that its parent company wanted to let go of its Seattle area operation. BORN's local ties to Seattle as a Gold

Certified Managed Partner in the Pacific Northwest was another quality that Tectura found appealing in BORN. And the BORN executives pitched Tectura on their local ties, vertical specialty and expertise in BizTalk and SharePoint. It worked. The deal not only gave Tectura an aerospace practice, ties into Boeing and experience with competitive application platforms such as JD Edwards but, most significantly, it gave Tectura an opportunity to establish itself as a leading integrator of Microsoft's classic infrastructure applications with MBS applications. For the acquisition not only filled a gaping hole in Tectura's portfolio—in-house expertise with Microsoft's classic applications—but also the additional skill sets to offer full end-to-end integration services between MBS applications and classic Microsoft applications.

Tectura quickly honed in on an emerging opportunity area. Microsoft plans to offer improved integration between its MBS and classic applications over the next few years but executives say they do not expect full integration until the Longhorn wave of products in the 2006-2007 timeframe. Microsoft views this as a core area of opportunity for solution providers. For Tectura, it is a unique differentiator in Microsoft's separate and distinct partner ecosystems for MBS and traditional offerings.

"We were a VAR with a classic practice and today we are more of a full-service mid-market integrator," said Pat Langowski, previously the BORN Seattle branch manager and now director of business development for Tectura Northwest. Michael Kean, director of the Tectura Eastern region, said, "The biggest growth area is for people who find a way to create sizzle. Classic applications integrate with MBS fine but when you can get to the next level where it works out of the box, you will really be there. Right now, most companies are still in the traditional MBS business but we are starting to see companies with vision saying that they want BizTalk and SharePoint to serve our ERP customers," said Mr Kean.

Tectura's many acquisitions have specific industry/vertical focuses, in step with Microsoft's increasing push into vertical markets. Currently Tectura offers expertise in several industries including aerospace, food and chemical process manufacturing, packaging, manufacturing, equipment rental, agriculture, public sector (state and municipal), healthcare, life sciences, consumer packaged goods and advanced distribution. Aside from equipping itself with the right technology expertise, Tectura has also hired knowledgeable consultants who have business process experience and expertise in select verticals. "You need vertical, vertical, vertical. Tectura is now more of a consulting organization. It is a different model for Microsoft because customers do not want to just download bits, they want us to run their business better. They want to hear you say that you understand the jewelry business and their tools," said Mr Kean, who serves in Tectura's Eastern office in Marlborough, Massachusetts.

As an international service provider, Tectura has strong ties to Microsoft corporate yet it aligns itself with Microsoft locally with operating offices in each of Microsoft's regions. It is evaluating a move into the mid- Atlantic and Gulf States regions. Microsoft has appointed a partner engagement manager (PEM) for Tectura for services contracts with Microsoft's named accounts. Tectura enjoys the attention it gets from its PEM, who may serve only 10 or 11 SPs as opposed to PAMs, who may serve hundreds of VARs. The firm's interaction with its PEM focuses on its pipeline and problem resolution. But the PEM is also an enabling relationship for Tectura's vertical business-process drive, which complements and extends its technical expertise, and the partnership increasingly helps Tectura help its customers run their businesses better.

Tectura is making the most of market conditions to grow and expand strategically in tight tactical alignment with Microsoft at all levels, from the top out to the field. At any time, though, there could be a reversal of fortune. As in business, so at Microsoft and also with your firm: things change and not always for the better. Not every firm has the resources, like Microsoft, to accommodate and rise to the challenges of dramatic change successfully. But partners can survive, even thrive, if they are flexible, urgent and have many connections points in Microsoft.

Given Microsoft's dynamism and market volatility, services partners need good working relationships at Microsoft in order to shift gears with the company and make themselves perceived as team players. Growing MBS is for Microsoft a significant challenge of great strategic import. Microsoft's increasing expansion and diversification of products in its portfolio, as well as serving distinct customer segments and verticals makes the juggling tougher for all partners. It requires a great deal of flexibility to keep ahead of the curve, to reposition one's services to align properly with the changing winds and priorities. You need to tune your message of their benefit to match the newfound focus of Microsoft personnel. Compounding the need for such flexibility is a great sense of urgency. And not just to preserve your traction within Microsoft, but to be perceived by Microsoft as being on board and actively engaged with the company's interests at heart and its initiatives at hand when the all-hands-on-deck call goes out on the SS Microsoft.

The same principles apply in a more mundane, routine scenario: the quarterly or semi-annual shift in Microsoft personnel from position to position. The re-assignment of sales and consulting personnel, partner managers and solutions specialists is inevitable. Use the game of musical chairs at Microsoft to your advantage, make and sustain as many connection points as possible. Assume the driver's seat in the partnership. Your job as a services partner is to work the Microsoft organization at all available levels to keep your firm at the forefront of strategic, tactical and organizational developments in a manner that works in the Microsoft culture. You do this by simple relationship-management techniques, and constant selling of your firm and its services. Remember: always keep the ball moving up field. Learn to lead from wherever you are. Master the art of backseat driving.

Consider another, less routine but still applicable scenario: Microsoft's acquisitions. In recent years, Microsoft has acquired Great Plains Software, Navision and Axapta. These acquisitions have been accompanied by strategic and tactical shifts, more down-market, as well as platform-push changes ultimately intended to provide seamless, out-of-box value to customers. The moves have hurt some services partners who maintain that Microsoft's decision to develop CRM and related functionality and move into the small- and mid-sized business market has diluted the value and impact of their service offerings. The core complaint is that Microsoft is positioning itself to compete with or to dilute the value of services partners, who fear they will not stand a chance in such a battle. Here, too, urgency is key and flexibility, too, to be able to learn in advance from your Microsoft colleagues all you can about change on the horizon and to position yourself favorably to rise to the occasion. Consider Tectura's ability to stay ahead of the curve, and steer a course that is complementary to Microsoft's even as it anticipates and fills the market needs that Microsoft cannot satisfy.

Successful services partners know the value of their competencies and remain firm on their value in light of market changes. There is no better mechanism—no more often proven tactic—than to align locally—work the field organization, extend relationships with Microsoft personnel who know you as people and know the worth of your firm and its products—and to leverage these relationships ideally to extend regionally, nationally and internationally.

Knowing whom to contact and whom to work with at Microsoft is essential. We assume that you have come to terms with your own assessment of the risks and rewards of your partnering with the company and that these are reflected in your mode of engaging with Microsoft. How do you determine whom to work with at Microsoft Consulting Services? With its vertical groups? With its sales and marketing arms? What are their perceived risks and rewards of partnering with a services partner?

In mapping out your commercial strategy, do not neglect to map out whom you best align with in the Microsoft field organization. For example, if your consulting services are focused on email migrations from Lotus Notes and Microsoft-competitive platforms to Microsoft Exchange, you would be best served to build relationships with field-level technical sales specialists who focus on Exchange and Active Directory, and with MCS managers, as well, since they are exposed to many infrastructural projects like this. If, on the other hand, you focus on the healthcare market, for example, and provide workflow-automation, business-intelligence or knowledge-management solutions, you would be best paired with the Microsoft field-teams that work in the healthcare sector and Information Worker groups.

Perhaps your firm's professional focus does not have a corresponding field-level group—suppose you are focused on the retail sector but the field office does not have specialists dedicated to that vertical—and your firm's strategy dictates a direct

Microsoft-engagement mode. In this case, you can work with MCS to identify opportunities in your target sector and develop relationships with field-level specialists in technology or sales whose purview is in products required to make your delivered solutions work, such as Exchange, SQL and SharePoint. Collaborative selling of your solutions that promotes substantial sale of these and other Microsoft platforms and products may very well get the attention of the field office to dedicate personnel to work with you. How do your services and solutions generate sales of Microsoft licenses? You need to spell it out ... with a number. Often a necessary first step is to validate the success of your solutions—demonstrate customer wins, develop case studies—but, first and foremost, develop solid working relationships with personnel in the field office who know and trust you and who know and vouch for your firm's services, both within Microsoft and to prospective customers in your target market.

There is a risk in formulating your Microsoft-engagement strategy, just as there are rewards in doing so. Recall that field teams elect their own GTMs as a subset of what Microsoft corporate defines as the company's GTMs for the fiscal year. It is important that your solutions and your go-to-market initiatives complement those of your field team's priorities. If your Microsoft field office's account manager, technical-sales and solutions-sales managers have a vested interest in driving Windows Server and Exchange Server-generated revenue through your solutions, they have an obvious cause to support you. However, if the account, technical-sales or solutions-sales managers are measured, compensated on the promotion of Microsoft platforms and products that are not in your professional focus, you may find yourself in a more competitive stance or at least in a position that does not foster collaboration. The risk of your strategy in this instance outweighs the rewards.

So the question of whom to work with at Microsoft draws on the anterior question, what is the right collaborative-competitive balance given the respective Microsoft groups' interests? The answers to these questions lead you to the risk/reward calculus.

Balance Risks and Rewards in Your Relationship with Microsoft

One must know Microsoft's culture but also Microsoft's strategy and organizational dynamic in order to partner effectively with the company. The calculus of risk and reward in partnering with Microsoft—especially from Microsoft's perspective—is an essential first step in seeking to partner on a product or service initiative. This is where the rubber meets the road in terms of the big game, knowing the rules of Microsoft partnering, which Microsoft itself sets. A rule of thumb in working their nexus and positioning your firm for successful partnering is to find out who gets paid to do what.

For, again, the rules of the game get their teeth at the level of how field teams are measured and compensated. You will gain (rewards) or lose (risks) to the extent that you align your interest with your local field teams, and to the extent that your local field team can help you align with appropriate corporate product teams. Remember that Microsoft's sales force is compensated in part on partner pull-through and partner satisfaction. So aligning with your local field team is your first priority in the majority of circumstances. But there are inherent risks in partnering locally, and one failure or misstep can overshadow years of partnering success very quickly. The key reward of partnership is a lower cost of sales and winning new customers. Reducing the cost of acquiring new customers and providing additional solutions to existing customers through the Microsoft ecosystem can enhance business success, to put it mildly.

Some services partners choose not to bring Microsoft to the table with all of their prospective customers because of the perceived benefits, especially independence, and to avoid Microsoft's potential to swing the deal to MCS, Avanade or a competitive partner. There is also the clear investment of overwhelming time and effort that is required to identify the right groups within Microsoft to work with and to establish productive relationships with them. These considerations incline some services partners not to pursue certification, competencies and co-marketing resources from Microsoft. But why? Like ISVs that try to go it alone, there are significant opportunity costs. Services partners lose out on the power of the Microsoft brand and potentially lucrative co-branding and co-selling deals if they pursue prospective deals indepenendently.

Services partners must constantly assess the risks and rewards of their activities with and apart from Microsoft and to seek balance in their collaboration and competition with the company in order to remain productive in partnership. These considerations, too, are part of the overall risk/reward calculus.

Again, Microsoft is known for its dynamism. Its culture, strategy and tactics and its organization are all prone to change. Global mega-trend shifts aside—industry consolidation, globalization, outsourcing—Microsoft engages in local markets and these are always in flux, with new opportunities springing up and Microsoft scrambling to seize them.

Another element of the calculus of partnering with Microsoft is keeping tabs on the local, regional and global markets, and understanding Microsoft's dynamic approach to them. How is Microsoft moving to capitalize on opportunities that emerge in cities, states, regions, nations and even among nations? How does Microsoft's movement affect your opportunities and your own movement? Do you get out of the way, or latch on and take a ride?

The services partner, like the ISV, must constantly ask itself, "Where Do I Want To Go Today?" And the answer to this question is guided by the partner's answer to two other questions that pivot on risk: if you tell Microsoft about an engagement that you are trying to win, might they alert another services partner, thus opening a bidding war for the project? If MCS learned about your project, could they execute on it for no cost and knock you out of the engagement? Microsoft's official rules of engagement say MCS cannot price lower than its services partners but it happens in the marketplace anyway. Where you want to go with Microsoft depends on what they will do on the way or when you get there. And these factors take into account the renowned flexibility and change-friendliness of Microsoft and its people.

Yet Microsoft personnel are highly selective in whom to partner with on client engagements. They are mindful of their risks and rewards in partnering with services partners. Microsoft risks the value of its brand name every time it recommends a services partner for a client engagement. In an era in which the company faces more customer scrutiny then even before, Microsoft personnel are very selective about the partners they assign and attach to client engagements. Among the criteria Microsoft personnel weigh in making this decision are: to what extent does the services partner use 1099 (contract) personnel on its engagements? Is the services partner certified in relevant competency areas, and has it demonstrated client successes in similar engagements? Has it delivered on former engagements referred by Microsoft, as promised? Is the services partner self-managing or does it require hand-holding? Does the services partner have clout with Microsoft as a result of risk-taking and rewarding business experience with the company? Your track record and reputation count at Microsoft. One services partner took a great risk in adopting a Microsoft-endorsed business and won Microsoft's favor and its trust: Bedrock Managed Services & Consulting.

Bedrock Builds a Managed Services Platform for SMB Clients, VARs on Stable Ground

Bedrock Managed Services & Consulting (www.bedrock.com)—a Microsoft Certified Partner based at Neenah, Wisconsin—provides professional and managed services to the small and mid-sized business (SMB) market. Bedrock focuses on providing IT infrastructure consolidation, optimization, monitoring and management services for firms that cannot afford to support an internal IT infrastructure. Founded in 2004, Bedrock emerged from its CEO's experience with Goliath Networks, a former Microsoft Application Service Provider (ASP) partner. Its CEO Mark Bakken was also CEO of Goliath Networks, where he built a strong relationship with several top Microsoft executives based on his firm's commitment to pursue the emerging ASP model that Microsoft backed in the late 1990s. At Bedrock, Mr Bakken has been able to leverage his Microsoft relationships to help the new firm get off to a strong start.

He is gambling once again on the subscription services model but this time he is insulating his firm from risk by aggregating—rather than hosting in-house—managed services based on Microsoft's infrastructure. The new model—described as a customer premise managed service—frees up Bedrock from having to operate a data center, a hefty expense that doomed many services partners in the dot.com heyday. "Goliath Networks spent US$8 million on a data center because Intel, Sun and Cisco said this was the future. But as we zigged, the market zagged," Mr Bakken said.

In his new company, Mr Bakken has partnered with nine independent service providers, including McAfee Anti-Virus and Procuro's remote monitoring solution. The managed services provider has tested and certified those services as robust and compatible with Microsoft's solutions stack. This is the essence of Bedrock's intellectual property, the "secret sauce" that assures customers that its managed services can be deployed reliably and quickly in their IT environments. This model of certifying and delivering aggregated managed services is the firm's value-added intellectual property and service. Some open-source companies take the same approach: integrating, certifying and testing various open-source stacks such as LAMP for customers. But Bedrock goes two steps further by delivering managed services to its customers and by handling all the service level agreements (SLAs) and contracts with service providers. Bedrock has also negotiated favorable SLAs and contracts on behalf of its SMB customers. This, too, is an important element of its value-added service.

Like many services partners in the new era, Bedrock has embraced a hybrid model to hedge risk in the still-lagging ASP market for SMB customers. Bedrock, for instance, offers traditional bread-and-butter technical consulting and implementation services locally that generate the bulk of its revenues. This year, for example, Bedrock expects to generate roughly 85% of its revenues from traditional planning, building and deploying software services at customer sites. Hence, the firm specializes in foundational, or "bedrock," IT infrastructure servers such as Windows and Exchange. The anti-virus and management services are also offered separately at the tail-end of the process. Ultimately, Bedrock intends to establish its managed services—and its intellectual property—as its core revenue source. Bedrock generated roughly US$400,000 from managed services in its first year, accounting for roughly 15% of its total revenues.

So, as a startup, Bedrock is getting extra attention (for the same reason as the ISV Apptero) because of Mr Bakken's past ties to Microsoft and his willingness to embrace new and risky business models. Mr Bakken learned a great deal about the services provider business and got close to Microsoft executives, who continue to help him today. The pre-existing relationship allowed him to consult with Microsoft product teams and executives so that he could refine his version 2.0 business model and access Partner Advisory Councils (PACs) before launching his new venture. Mr

Bakken leveraged his relationships at Microsoft but he also worked to ensure that the blueprint for his new company matched up with Microsoft's vision. This time around, for example, Mr Bakken chose to focus on SMB customers, whereas Goliath honed in on enterprise customers. Mr Bakken points out that EDS and Capgemini provide outsourced services for the enterprise and mid-market but these large systems integrators will not touch anything under 4,000 seats. "The rest is up for grabs," he claimed. In this way, Mr Bakken is helping to advance Microsoft by pushing into the small business and mid-sized market segment that Microsoft has targeted and deemed under-served.

His keen attention to relationship management continues to pay off. In fact, Bedrock was able to get the software giant to cooperate and publish a Microsoft Project Guide based on Bedrock's managed services formula in a white paper entitled "Remotely Managing and Securing Small and Medium-Sized Organizations." The project guide, written in conjunction with Silicon East Inc, a solution provider in New York, is the template that describes the benefits that solution providers can realize by deploying a remote management and security service offering to their customers. It is a strong endorsement from Microsoft supporting Bedrock's new model.

In addition, Bedrock's access to Microsoft may extend it into the entire Microsoft partner community for its benefit. Bedrock's business model is unique in that it plans to make its intellectual property available to other service providers who want to resell the nine managed services to their small business clients, as if it were their own service. "We provide the framework, method and the service level agreements and then solution providers can resell it all under their own name. I am starting a network with IPremise in Denver and a bunch of classic integrators who want to do this but do not have the time to get the SLAs done and certify all the third-party providers. We worked out all the kinks with the services and got SLAs between the service providers and us so the resellers will not have to worry about SLAs. So we are acting like a distributor." Microsoft's services–partner community is an ideal distribution channel for its service.

Microsoft's backing gives Bedrock a higher level of credibility out-of-the-gate than another startup might enjoy. There is no doubt that Mr Bakken's personal connections at Microsoft were instrumental in giving Bedrock this kind of jumpstart. He clearly recognizes that his relationships at Microsoft are a key asset. Goliath Networks took a risk with a Microsoft-backed ASP model that did not pay off. But that risk ultimately paid off. Bedrock was able to reap the rewards of Goliath's tight relationship with Microsoft executives to get itself going and is now trail-blazing ahead on its unique business model. "Microsoft recognizes that this is a good model," Mr Bakken said. "But the relationships are huge because it helped me network with all the right people."

Calculate Risk and Reward: CPE vs PCE

One component of the risk-and-reward calculus in partnering with Microsoft is the relative importance of customers and partners to Microsoft. Corporate tends to view it in that order, the Customer-Partner Experience (CPE), whereas the SMS&P organization, which lives and dies by its channel, views Partner-Customer Experience (PCE) as paramount. It is important to note that CPE and PCE only come into play when there is an appeal for Microsoft's resolution of a conflict between a customer and a partner. Corporate-backed groups will favor the customer first, SMS&P will favor the partner first.

Not that either of their respective views is inconsequential, but services partners must in all circumstances seek the best interest of their customers while balancing their own interests as partners with Microsoft. Depending on where your firm stands in the ecosystem—an MBS partner, for example, subject to the SMS&P view, or a more classic partner, aligned with the corporate view—your firm's own perspective on the subject should be informed by simple realities: if you have unsatisfied customers, you run the risk of going out of business; if you go out of business, you lose your partnership with Microsoft. So which has higher priority, your customers or your relationship with Microsoft? You know the answer and, in fact, so does Microsoft.

Because it is a customer-focused company, Microsoft wants the best for its customers first and foremost; because it is a partner-driven company—the means to this end—Microsoft highly favors its partners' success, as well. In fact, as demonstrated in Chapter Two, Microsoft views its products, customers and partners as essentially three legs of a stool on which it sits, so to speak, and their stability and equilibrium are very important to the company. Partners should so assess their situations, as well, favoring their customers and working favorably with Microsoft, too. But keep them in the right order, an approach that has its risks, of course, but potentially great rewards, as well. One such partner that banks on this approach is Internosis.

Internosis Takes a Firm and Favorable Stand on Customer Satisfaction with Microsoft

Internosis (www.internosis.com)—a Microsoft Gold Certified Partner based at Greenbelt, Maryland—was once the technology services division of Corporate Software, a large account reseller. In 2003, Internosis earned Microsoft's North American Infrastructure Solution Provider of the Year award and was named partner of the year more than five times during the 1990s, when it operated as CSI and then as Stream. Internosis has carved a strong niche for itself as a Microsoft partner in the federal government/public sector.

Internosis' founder and president Robert Stalick tries to remain as objective as possible in his role as independent advisor to his customers, though 98% of his business is Microsoft-related. Microsoft's high rate of change—the continuous change in the way the operating systems and solutions are updated—creates modernization challenges at customer sites, particularly in the public sector, which in the past hummed along running the same UNIX servers relatively unchanged for years. In the past, this rate of change has been good for Microsoft and its partners because it created new revenue opportunities. However, when it comes to updates, Internosis' primary focus is on meeting the requirements of its customers by recommending what is best and most cost-effective for their particular situations. More recently, though, we see that Microsoft has slowed the rate of change by lengthening its product upgrade cycle: Windows was upgraded roughly every 18 to 24 months during the 1990s. Five years will have elapsed between the time of Windows XP's release in 2001, and a major Windows upgrade expected in 2006 (aside from Windows XP SP2, which was primarily a security upgrade).

Mr Stalick reminds services partners that it is their professional obligation to serve the best interests of their customers first. There are times when he may have to recommend an open-source solution over a Microsoft solution for a particular task; and he will, if the customer's interests are best served. Serving the customer, rather than the vendor, should be the partner's paramount concern.

For him, that firmness works in Microsoft's favor: Internosis has been named one of Microsoft's partners of the year three years in a row. "The challenge for service providers associated with any vendor is learning how to pay attention to what the customer wants and to become their trusted partner while still honoring the relationship with the vendor. We feel that we have done that well with Microsoft," Mr Stalick said.

———■———

While few would question Internosis' stand vis-à-vis its customers and Microsoft—the former come first, the latter second—fewer still may have the resolve to stand up for what is right against Microsoft and weather a storm. Firms that do have mastered, at the very least, conflict-management principles and tactics, which are more attributes of partnering successfully with Microsoft.

Observe How You Handle Conflicts with Microsoft

Microsoft's longtime services partners appreciate a fundamental truth: services are neither in Microsoft's DNA nor in its core mission. The company's field and corporate teams are focused on selling Microsoft product. Period. To a services partner, MCS can be friend or foe. But armed with just about 5,000 consultants, and a non-profit charter, it is not, at the time of this writing, being groomed to grow into an IBM Global Services.

MCS is a division of Microsoft that provides services to Microsoft customers. But it is certain that the vast majority of Microsoft sales personnel view services as a necessary evil they need in order to seed Microsoft's emerging technologies and serve large customers. In fact, many Microsoft sales personnel encourage customers to be self-sufficient in keeping with the company's low-cost volume model and ease-of-use promise to customers. Salespeople in some cases steer their customers away from partner-provided services unless such services are essential to the customer's well-being. So services partners have an ambiguous relationship with Microsoft in that

- they provide a value (services) that the company is not dedicated to provide;

- this value may diminish the perceived value of what the company does provide (its products do not work simply, they must be implemented, developed and supported); and so

- this value is held suspect by some Microsoft personnel and services are seen by some as less valuable than software itself.

As the company expands more deeply into the enterprise, verticals and deeper into the software stack, however, most Microsoft sales personnel are becoming more enlightened about the need for partner services as an effective tool for breaking down barriers to the sale of Microsoft software.

Still, it is inevitable that conflicts will arise between Microsoft and its services partners. Many partners recall the clashes between MCS and services partners between 2000 and 2002. Conflict may also pivot on customers' discontent with certain features or functions of Microsoft products, or on a services partner's recommendation of a third-party product to meet a customer need. In any of these cases, Microsoft field teams may take issue with some services partners or actively engage in conflicts with them.

It is highly advisable, therefore, that all services partners have a strategy for resolving conflicts with Microsoft. Such a strategy governs the airing of conflicts, and ensures clear, fair and effective communications to resolve them. By having a strategy in place before conflicts arise, services partners can minimize the risk of alienation and prevent their loss of Microsoft as a partner as a result of an ineffectively managed dispute. A conflict resolution plan is your insurance policy to stay in the partnering game with Microsoft. Perhaps the best way to short-circuit conflict is to act graciously with Microsoft when conflict arises, which has put more than one services partner in a favorable light with Microsoft as we see, for example, in the case of Nortec.

Nortec Gets Acclaimed for Claiming Ground with Microsoft Consulting Services

Nortec Communications (www.nortec.com)—a Microsoft Certified Partner and Microsoft's 2004 VAR Partner of the Year, based at Falls Church, Virginia—was founded in 1991, with an advanced infrastructure solutions competency for enterprise systems. The company derives roughly 70% of its revenues from its Microsoft-related business with the remainder made up of security hardware, telephony systems, Voice Over Internet Protocol (VoIP) and Veritas storage services.

In one year, between 2003 and 2004, Nortec increased its revenues to US$5.2 million (from US$3.2 million) by skillfully finessing a cozy relationship with Microsoft Consulting Services and by aligning its business goals with Microsoft corporate. In many ways, Nortec had been priming for growth for some time. But it was one gamble that sealed the firm's fate, the proverbial roll of the dice that led to a powerful payback. Nortec spun platinum out of gold after bidding on a NetWare migration deal it was confident it would win on its own—but then opted to invite MCS to collaborate on the deal. That served two purposes: working together with MCS nailed the customer win and also paid off in strengthening its partnership. That wise relationship-building maneuver worked: it also earned Nortec a new batch of influential Microsoft friends. Nortec CEO Andrew Grose said Nortec's willingness to collaborate with MCS on a customer account Microsoft deemed strategic was a win-win for both parties.

And that has paid off more handsomely than either Mr Grose or his second-in-command executive—COO and executive vice president George Hammerschmidt—ever imagined. "We made some friends and it gave us a strong champion in Microsoft," Mr Grose said. "MCS wanted to be involved in the project. I would say 99% of the VARs in the world would have said 'No' because they do not have the vision. We knew this would be a big relationship builder."

It worked. Since then, MCS has invited Nortec in on a number of deals and, in turn, the solution provider has brought Microsoft in on an additional four of five deals. His advice for solution providers is to work with—not against—MCS.

But this did not happen by chance. Nortec's CEO had been leading the company for more than a decade but wanted to grow his business beyond the SMB space. In late 2002, Mr Grose hired Mr Hammerschmidt, then a vice president of sales for a London-based telecom company, who had experience in partnering and forming alliances with large vendors such as Cisco, Juniper Networks and Newbridge. By April 2003, Nortec had climbed the ranks from being a Certified Partner to a Gold Partner and, in July, became a managed partner.

Nortec wanted to move beyond its SMB heritage and started cold-calling larger accounts. While the company got in the door based on its advanced infrastructure expertise, having an experienced sales executive to deliver a polished, professional presentation, negotiate it skillfully and recognize the MCS partnering potential were big differentiators. Bidding against MCS and then opting to form a partnership with MCS was a "leap of faith," Mr Grose said, but the company knew it would pay off. He advises other services partners to get smart about forming alliances with MCS or to hire someone with expertise in forming partnerships. In 2002, Nortec was a Microsoft Certified Partner with annual revenues of between US$3 million and US$4 million. It has since doubled. Today, 70% of Nortec's business comes from the SMB space including software, hardware, support and security business and more than 30% is derived from its enterprise accounts. "Many of those deals came from Microsoft. We did not focus on our partnership before and we tried to be all things to all people. Partnering with Microsoft has been extremely successful for us. Our success is snowballing. We want to be at between US$10 million and US$15 million next year or the year after." But Mr Grose also emphasized that cross-pollination is essential in keeping the relationship strong. "Nortec continues to bring deals to Microsoft as they are rewarded with enterprise gigs. Microsoft does not want VARs with their hands out," Mr Grose said.

Nortec also advises services partners to align their business models to help Microsoft in key areas of importance to the software giant. Nortec honed in on two of Microsoft's ambitions for 2003-2004: licensing/software assurance (SA) contracts and migrations from older departmental operating systems to Windows 2000/2003 with Active Directory. On the migration side, Nortec focused on getting NT customers and Novell NetWare customers to migrate to Windows 2000/2003. In 2003-2004, Nortec migrated 50 companies to Windows Server 2003. Nortec's partnering guru George Hammerschmidt wrote a succinct letter to Microsoft CEO Steve Ballmer informing him of their growing success in the Microsoft ecosystem. That letter made the rounds in a company accustomed to scrutiny and public criticism. It was passed on to Allison Watson and her team. At Microsoft's Channel Summit in May, Nortec was named Microsoft's 2004 National VAR Partner of the Year. It is the first year Microsoft bestowed this award. The letter was also read in its entirety by a key Microsoft executive on stage at the company's 2004 Worldwide Partner Conference. Positive feedback can pay off nicely with Microsoft in publicity and building credibility.

———■———

Balancing risk and reward, and achieving equilibrium in competition and collaboration with Microsoft, is possible when partners adopt approaches such as those employed by the services firms highlighted in this chapter. While predictability seems unlikely when partnering with such a dynamic company, prudent services partners must nevertheless strive for balance in their relationships with Microsoft. As indicated in Chapters Two and Three, the embrace and the pace of change at Microsoft— in its corporate strategy, market tactics, products, culture, organization, acquisitions and response to market trends (*eg*, globalization, outsourcing)—makes for a potentially moving target as a partner. The market itself, though, is no less fluid, and a competitor can enter your space and change the business equation for your firm as quickly as Microsoft can move.

In this dynamic environment, you can only control your firm, and how it responds to change. While you cannot control your market or competitors, you can control your engagement in and with them, respectively, as well as the quality of service you provide to your clients.

While you cannot control Microsoft, you must understand its culture and accommodate shifts in its approach to the market, with its customers and in your partnership. There is some level of predictability in Microsot yet the constant shifts can inject volatility into its relationship with services partners.

Consider, for example, a large corporate customer of Microsoft that decides to outsource its IT operation to an independent hosting services provider. The hosting provider happens to be a Microsoft partner. The corporate customer wants to outsource but that direction runs contrary to Microsoft's goal to "own" and manage the relationship with its corporate customers. Microsoft wants to exercise exclusive influence on its customers' software licensing and technology solutions, and it provides incentives to its account management to make sure that happens. If this happens, Microsoft loses some control of this customer relationship to its outsourced services partner. In this case, the partner must bend and accommodate Microsoft's wishes to exert some influence over this customer's fate, while at the same time pursuing its interests and attempting to expand the number and scope of such corporate IT outsourcing arrangements without alienating Microsoft. This is a visceral example of the kind of competitive tensions that develop between Microsoft and its services partners in the field, in which an opportunity that favors the latter can prejudice the needs of the former—Microsoft—which sets the rules of the game. If you were in this services partner's shoes, how would you navigate this tension and retain a valuable partnership with Microsoft?

How, in other words, can you convert inauspicious events to your favor in partnering with Microsoft or make auspicious events for your firm seem favorable—or at least not detrimental—to Microsoft? One effective way is to leverage your highest-level friends and connections within Microsoft. As we pointed out in Chapter Four, savvy ISVs and services partners can exploit such competitive tensions in either direction to their favor. For instance, perhaps this service provider agrees to subcontract some of the services work back to MCS. Determine which services should be provided by Microsoft—and which services by your firm—in order to serve your customers optimally.

If you are aligned with your customers and with Microsoft at all levels, you can exploit your sphere of influence to generate a services deal that pleases all three parties. In this case, it is essential to work with your local field office first, and then approach corporate, for conflict resolution. It is important to realize, however, that the quality of partner care varies from office to office, from country to country. And there are communication, localization and cultural problems that arise between Microsoft corporate and local offices—particularly outside of the US—that can adversely impact services partners whose business relies upon the local office. There are occasions when communications between the local Microsoft office with its local partners is lacking, or lag behind US trends, and the services partner must bypass that office and go to corporate to achieve its objectives with Microsoft. Consider SoftFlow, a services partner from Beirut, Lebanon, which flew the long distance to Microsoft's partner conference in Toronto in 2004, to help build a bridge of communication between corporate in the US and its offices in the Middle East, and communciate to Microsoft some unmet and specific needs of partners in that region.

SoftFlow Leaps Beyond the Field in the Middle East to Extend Connections to Corporate

SoftFlow (www.softflow.com.lb)—a Beirut, Lebanon-based Microsoft solutions provider, which has been in business for more than 15 years—was named the first Microsoft Gold Certified Partner in the Middle East. Founded in 1991, SoftFlow and its 30 employees focus on advanced infrastructure solutions and the delivery of MBS solutions to leading vertical industries, including banking and manufacturing.

Bachir Zoghbi, SoftFlow's managing director, has local relationships with Microsoft's subsidiaries in Dubai and Turkey, yet he finds it frustrating that the general managers (GMs) of these offices continue to be driven by Microsoft corporate to deliver on quotas and are less inclined to foster the solutions-selling approach with their partners. For example, Mr Zoghbi needed the help of the Microsoft office in Dubai to get customized versions of Microsoft software that adhere to unique local government regulations but he had a hard time getting any local Microsoft manager to respond. In 2004, Mr Zoghbi traveled to Microsoft's worldwide partner conference in Toronto, Canada, to make connections with other Microsoft solution providers and Microsoft corporate executives. His goal was to discuss the needs of partners and the local offices in the region and advise Microsoft corporate to communicate its GTMs and solutions approach more effectively outside of the US. He also wanted to start an IAMCP chapter in Beirut. But, more importantly, he aimed to make essential connection points with Microsoft and partners to help Microsoft deliver better results in the Middle East.

Like other non-North American partners, the Beirut-based SP finds that subsidiaries around the globe typically lag by a year or more in terms of getting localized products and new messages and GTMs from corporate headquarters to the field. He is proactively trying to get the local districts to become more engaged in the solutions-selling approach with services partners, of which there are roughly 35 in Beirut but fewer than 10 of professional quality. Mr Zoghbi's extraordinary efforts may pay off in moving his local subsidiaries forward with corporate momentum.

While this approach may ruffle the feathers of some executives in the local office, such a move will benefit them over the long term and generate more product sales. This approach was risky, yet it abides by the cardinal rules of the partnering game, which is to ensure customer satisfaction and move the ball forward with Microsoft. Mr Zoghbi's initiative also highlights the importance of constantly expanding market opportunities with Microsoft.

Expand the Brand and Opportunities with Microsoft Regionally and Globally

The most tangible way for services partners to expand their opportunities is based on access to Microsoft's brand. Successful services partners use the brand to their advantage, though quite differently from ISVs and OEMs, of course. Services partners apply the Microsoft brand when reaching out to customers with co-branded marketing material and collateral. Partners simply attach their own logo and get it out to market. This allows Microsoft to promulgate its brand and it eliminates the need for partners to reinvent marketing. Microsoft is a huge marketing machine that prudent partners take advantage of in their go-to-market strategies.

Microsoft continually refines its marketing process and the joint leverage it affords its partner channel. There are many leveraged marketing schemes and, at present, the best scheme is known as the channel campaign tool. This tool allows a partner to create a marketing campaign based on the Microsoft brand.

Again, all politics are local. From a marketing perspective, whoever owns an account—whether it is the Microsoft field office or the partner—manages the account and decisions pertaining to it. Still, with respect to services partners, regional relationships with Microsoft are becoming more important. In years past, a regional model *per se* did not exist; all business activity was characterized as either local or national, in the US only. With Microsoft's emerging industry verticalization push, however, regions have taken on decidedly new importance since vertical solutions for financial services, government, retail and manufacturing can be penetrated and applied to entire geographical regions. In some cases, services partners or ISVs push a solution developed for a Mexican bank throughout the Spanish-speaking world. This trend has proved favorable for some services partners that are aiming to move their business and solutions from local to regional scope, as we see in the case of Interlink.

Interlink Grows Wildly As A Western RSI ... with Microsoft

The Interlink Group (www.interlinkgroup.com)—a Microsoft Gold Certified Partner and Regional Systems Integrator (RSI) that was founded in 1989—aims to become the largest Microsoft solution provider in the western region of the United States. The Englewood, Colorado-based solution provider—which once claimed to be Microsoft's largest LSI—successfully attained status as a Regional Systems Integrator (RSI) in November 2004, and is betting its future on its partnership with Microsoft, said CEO Bart Hammond.

Interlink endeared itself to Microsoft in the late 1990s by scoring a million-dollar deal with Titanium Metals Corp. for a major Windows-Exchange infrastructural renovation that rivaled the scale of projects handled by only the largest system integrators. The contract earned Interlink a worldwide partner award from Microsoft and continues to generate recommendations from Microsoft on other subcontracting deals involving infrastructural opportunities in the upper mid-market space. Interlink proved that it could push the limits of NT and Windows 2000 and was hired to upgrade the same customer's 7,000-seat IT infrastructure to Windows Server 2003, Active Directory and Exchange Server 2003. Interlink has earned Microsoft's respect but, like most other services firms, it is growing to fit into Microsoft's evolving ecosystem. That is, Interlink is fine-tuning its business model and is expanding geographically to achieve its next-generation objectives.

First, the services firm—a former Sun iForce integrator—decided to become a dedicated Microsoft partner and made its bet on a single platform. Mr Hammond maintains that it is rare for a customer to look to a technology-agnostic outside services provider to give it wholesale platform recommendations. Many customers have made their platform choice based on IBM/Java or Microsoft/.NET and do not need partners for platform choices as much as they have in the past. Instead, Microsoft's customers need deep expertise further up the software stack and sophisticated mid-tier knowledge of Microsoft's server applications and .NET technologies. "Create mindshare in Microsoft's community as a real go-to-market partner. Show them you are 100% committed to their platform."

In order to qualify as an RSI, Interlink has also engaged in a significant expansion in both headcount and territory. By the end of 2003, Interlink had achieved four gold competencies in collaborative solutions, security solutions, enterprise systems and eCommerce solutions. However, it needed more competencies and geographical coverage in order to qualify as an RSI under Microsoft's rules. In June 2004, Interlink acquired Bellevue, Washington-based Equarius, a deal that gave it local ties to Microsoft headquarters as well as unique technical expertise and new territories. With this first acquisition, for instance, Interlink gained Equarius' office location in Microsoft's backyard and another office in San Francisco. It also gained two new competencies in enterprise application integration and business-to-business (B2B) solutions and Microsoft Business Solutions. Equarius was very attractive because of its MBS and CRM expertise. In addition to adding new service offerings and geographic diversity, the deal allowed Interlink to address under-served needs of companies in the US$200 million to US$2 billion sector who want an end-to-end capable partner on the Microsoft platform.

Mr Hammond expected the acquisition would enhance Interlink's services portfolio and its partnership status with Microsoft, and he was right. During the course of this book's writing, Interlink attained RSI status. "The RSI benefits are a plus," he said. RSI partners are eligible for more Business Investment Funds (BIFs) and a national partner account manager that acts on behalf of the services partner, Mr Hammond said. "We will get more up-front planning, co-marketing agreements and the opportunity to participate in national rollouts and go to markets."

Interlink also distinguishes itself by embracing alternative business models and revenue streams such as offshoring and operating a network operations center. While other partners have closed down their development practices, this services firm continues to derive revenues from an outsourcing operation it established in India five years ago. Interlink also offers full end-to-end management and monitoring services by supporting a network operations center, or NOC. Interlink's NOC—now five years old—provides 24x7x365 monitoring and management support based on Microsoft Operations Manager, as well as NetIQ products and HP OpenView Suite. Interlink does not have an in-house data center but offers managed services for customers—either in their environment or in the co-location facility of their choice.

The firm does not support a hosting co-location model but a customer premise-based management service that reduces the cost for customers to maintain and support Exchange and Windows. Mr Hammond says the network operations center is a "proven model and has been a strategic differentiator for us." Yet Interlink is committed to maintaining focus on areas that are important to Microsoft.

Microsoft's more focused, and ever-changing, customer-segmentation push into vertical markets is also requiring a significant retooling by partners such as Interlink. That trend is forcing partners either to choose a focus on the SMB market or to make increasing investments to play in the middle market, where there will be ample opportunity for SIs. Mr Hammond explains that Interlink must show its extended reach to Microsoft in order to ensure that Microsoft's money spent with partners is used in many markets. "In the small and middle-market space, Microsoft wants to push one-to-many marketing. In their enterprise space they continue to focus on one-to-one interactions. It is tough to make money in SMB because they buy at low volumes and with little repeat frequency. Our sweet spot is upper mid-market customers, those that are big enough to have broad and complex needs but still small enough to value a trusted relationship with a key partner."

Mr Hammond knows the math and sweet spots to approach in the upper mid-market, those accounts that fall just under the 1,000-desktop radar of MCS. Microsoft's positioning works in Interlink's favor in this respect. And Mr Hammond knows that

Microsoft is encouraging partners in the direction of ERP and is moving in that direction. But he is cautious about moving too quickly. "It is a different business model and we have to be careful about skill sets, and need more vertical and financially-oriented consultants than technical consultants."

The CEO says that what Microsoft wants most from partners is to fulfill the last difficult mile of selling the .NET story. "Microsoft wants you to come up with business solutions." To accomplish this, Interlink used a framework provided by Microsoft to develop a Return-On-Investment (ROI) study for a client that showed a Microsoft platform could save the customer US$1.1 million over a comparable solution mixing UNIX, Linux and J2EE. "That kind of intellectual property and partner work generates excitement at customer sites and at Seattle and is viewed by Microsoft as a valuable addition," Mr Hammond noted.

———◼———

At times and in certain engagement opportunities, Microsoft will discount a partner if it is local or regional only. Some services partners have formed alliances or acquired companies that allow them to deliver globally with other like-minded organizations. While partnering with other Microsoft partners is discussed in detail in Chapter Seven, it is one mechanism for expanding the scope of your business and your profile with Microsoft—particularly if you are expanding in territories of great strategic interest to Microsoft such as Europe and Asia Pacific. In any event, successful services partners exercise the partnering posture—firm, urgent and flexible—to extend their work with Microsoft and the scope of their success, in the field and across the globe. GrapeCity is a great example of a Microsoft partner that was founded in Japan and is now operating across a vast area of vital importance to Microsoft: Asia Pacific.

GrapeCity Harvests Hybrid Opportunities with Microsoft in the Asian Fields

GrapeCity (www.grapecity.com)—a Microsoft Gold Certified and Business Solutions Partner that has been in business in various focus areas since 1980—was among the earliest adopters of .NET technology. It was founded in Japan by a core group of Americans and expanded throughout Asia with a presence in Japan, India, China, Vietnam, Malaysia and Mongolia. It is considering expansion in Thailand and the Philippines. It also opened an office close to Microsoft corporate in Kirkland, Washington, in 2002.

With 645 employees and approximately US$25 million in annual revenues, GrapeCity has overcome complexity in its hybrid-operating model—part ISV and part solutions provider—and in navigating diverse Microsoft field organizations in disparate countries. Microsoft has recognized GrapeCity's talents, too, and in fact outsources technical support for its developer tools division to GrapeCity's India operation. Here, too, as in the case study of NetIQ (Chapter Four), among others, we see the multiple connection points within Microsoft and the shared terrain of interests that has worked so well for other partners.

According to Paul Dyhr, GrapeCity's Shanghai-based vice president for business solutions, the firm has come to terms with significant challenges in order to grow in Microsoft's ecosystem. The Microsoft organization is also evolving for the massive wave of business opportunities growing throughout the Asia Pacific region. In fact, Microsoft in 2004, hired an ex-IBM Global Services executive to head up its Asia Pacific operations who had formerly served with IBM and had strong ties in the region.

Overcoming those challenges is the direct result of its intense interaction with Microsoft. "We work with all levels of the Microsoft organization, from corporate downward. But, day-to-day, we do business with our partner account managers. We work with people in Microsoft's large Shanghai office, but China's headquarters is in Beijing where we liaise with the top folks. Linux is not GrapeCity's challenge in China. It is rather the complexity of working with Microsoft in local markets. Often, details are overlooked in execution simply because of overlapping responsibilities within Microsoft and there is very little transparency how leads get disbursed."

Mr Dyhr continues on the complexity of doing business in China and, indeed, other countries in Asia: "In theory, the Microsoft channel in China works the same as in the US or Singapore. But, in reality, it is different because things here are complex and relationships within Microsoft can be ever changing." For GrapeCity and other ISVs in Asia and elsewhere it requires a full-time liaison for all activities with Microsoft. "Because the relationship—or *guanxi*—is so critical in China, a partner needs to have a full-time person who only handles the relationship with Microsoft and nothing else while working with the sales team to make sure sales revenues goals are being met. In Asia, programs are very complex and no one will make a decision that might possibly be out of the boundary even if very slightly. It is very programmatic and not prone to risk taking."

Microsoft appears to be bringing in more western high-level managers to its Asian subsidiaries to ensure that corporate methodologies are consistent in the field. In the past, GrapeCity tried to rely on mostly local personnel in these methodologies but this knowledge transfer may have been incomplete, Mr Dyhr said, so it now appears Microsoft has injected key western managers into Asia to do more direct knowledge transfer. As a result, there have been noticeable improvements in partner satisfaction, he added. But their challenge is to acculturate Microsoft partners in Asia as much as it is to re-orient Microsoft offices there. Microsoft looks to GrapeCity as a model partner in the Asia Pacific region, not only for its growth and the intertwining of their interests in .NET solutions and outsourced support for Microsoft's developer tools, but also for its partnering approach to Microsoft.

GrapeCity, unlike many ISVs, maintains offices that are physically close to Microsoft in its various countries of operation. This makes close personal interaction possible. GrapeCity also has a unique perspective on the partnering relationship itself. "Many ISVs in Asia seem to want to partner with Microsoft," Mr Dyhr says, "but they will not invest the time or money required to do so. They need to show Microsoft their capabilities. Only then will Microsoft recognize them and invest time with them."

GrapeCity's approach has rather been to "be in Microsoft's presence, garnering mindshare and delivering projects on the Microsoft platform. It is only when you do that that projects—opportunities—will follow." GrapeCity's field-level alignment approach has set it apart from its competitors, enabling it to expand throughout Asia with Microsoft despite some of the very partnering complexities that are still in the process of being resolved in the region. Microsoft has made major improvements in the past few years to achieve a more satisfactory experience for its partners, Mr Dyhr said.

As Microsoft increases its investment in international partners, its business grows. Another up-and-coming Microsoft services partner, from South Africa, has expanded its opportunities with Microsoft: Symetrix.

Symetrix Works Microsoft in Sub-Saharan Africa

Symetrix (www.symetrix.co.za)—a Microsoft Gold Certified Partner for Support Services and Enterprise Systems that was officially incorporated in 1999, in South Africa—is an outsourcing partner that employs more than 100 people. It formed as a combination of the former ARC Computers, which specialized in distribution of computer hardware and software, and Compatible Computing that specialized in Support and Development.

South African business normally impacts several southern African countries, including Namibia, Botswana, Zimbabwe, Mozambique and the land-locked countries in South Africa itself, Swaziland and Lesotho. Most of the economic presence there is dominated by South Africa, the business powerhouse of the sub-Sahara with over 65% of the businesses focused in Gauteng Province, which contains the interlinked cities of Johannesburg and Pretoria. Microsoft South Africa concentrates mostly on Gauteng and the Western Cape (*ie,* Cape Town).

Warren Machanik is operations director for Symetrix and he estimates that there are more than 5,000 Microsoft resellers in this market, of which 2,000 to 3,000 are registered partners, roughly 400 are certified partners and 40—including his services firm—are Gold Partners. Partner account managers are available for the "select few" in South Africa but this is changing, and partners are getting shared, non-dedicated PAMs.

Symetrix started building a Microsoft relationship at the field level. That changed in 2001, when the services firm became a Gold Partner in Support Services, which escalated its stature in Microsoft's South African subsidiary. Over the past few years, the company has begun working more closely with corporate. But the field is where the action is. Symetrix gets good care: it has participated in joint-marketing initiatives with Microsoft, including seminar and exhibition hosting, and Mr Machanik was invited to participate in the Rapid Deployment Program (RDP) of Windows Server 2003.

In this market, the firm could not operate its outsourcing business without the premier support offered by Microsoft's technical account manager from the local office. Mr Machanik has observed an increasing number of partner account managers being deployed to work with partners, most of whom are shared among several services companies.

Microsoft South Africa has two models: one in which it works directly with the customer and another in which it works through partners, though the latter is less common. The 400 certified partners find this frustrating. They do not blame Microsoft South Africa, and the local office does provide resources when partners are persistent—but the local office does not drive business for partners. Microsoft is the dominant player in this market, but Novell has issued a rallying cry around Linux, and partners there are taking notice but not losing much business. Mr Machanik believes that Bill Gates' visit and substantial donations to Africa were well-received and enhanced Microsoft's image in the region.

Mr Machanik echoes the same strategy. "You need to understand your role and your niche. Once you do that, you can engage with Microsoft. Find out who your partner account manager is, or whatever engagement person you have, and spend time with them, get to know them. Explain to them the value-add that you can bring, and they will soon be helping you by ensuring that the relationship is reciprocal."

Maximize Connection Points

Part and parcel of expanding opportunities with Microsoft is maximizing your connection points within the company. If you only have one or two people you know in Microsoft and those people change roles every three to six months, then you are never going to be connected enough to get business referrals from the company. But quantity is not everything; the quality of your Microsoft connections matters, too. Symetrix found its champion in a technical account manager at the field office and has scaled its outsourcing operation so capably that it has its own partner account manager as one of 40 Gold partners in South Africa, and new touch points into corporate.

Potential connection points in any given market include at least the following types of Microsoft personnel: local marketing specialists, solution sales specialists, MCS personnel, account managers, technical sales specialists and, yes, even licensing specialists (although many services partners do not sell licenses, licensing specialists know which partners are assigned and attached to deals and which qualify for or will be getting BIFs).

These are the types of Microsoft personnel in the trenches—the field office—that successful services partners need exposure to, in addition, of course, to the managers of these personnel so that they, too, are aware of the services firms' capabilities and commitment. One Boston, Massachusetts-based Gold Certified services partner called Trinity Consulting volunteers free programming services to local Microsoft office representatives when there is downtime in his firm. This not only enables his firm's employees to hone their technical skills at no charge and form personal relationships with Microsoft personnel but it also gives his firm an opportunity to showcase his most talented engineers to the local Microsoft office. This tactic has enabled his firm to form tighter relationships with Microsoft and more contacts in the local market, as well. It can be a risk unless you send your best talent to represent your firm.

Of course, it is always advisable to establish professional connections in Seattle with product or support teams and, of course, in Microsoft marketing. Most services partners have or want a presence in Seattle. And there is good reason for this. But services partners vary in their success in working the field and working corporate, although field-level connections are essential for services partners and corporate connections are secondary. We see this clearly in the case of BORN.

BORN Works the Field and Struggles with Corporate

BORN (www.born.com)—a Microsoft Gold Certified Partner and Regional Systems Integrator based in Minnetonka, Minnesota with offices in Dallas, Denver, Atlanta and Milwaukee—was founded in 1990, and has 600 employees. A full-service systems integrator, BORN had been a Microsoft partner for nine years, but it also had 40 other partnerships, none of which were driving significant business. Four years ago, BORN hired a dedicated partner manager from Microsoft to see if it could establish itself in the Microsoft ecosystem.

That move elevated BORN's brand name within Microsoft marketing. The firm has become a Regional Solutions Integrator, with a Microsoft business manager at Seattle along with partner account managers in each of the firm's field locations. Its collaborative approach to a full-scale campaign with Microsoft delivers on average three to four referrals from Microsoft per month. There are daily communications between Microsoft and BORN, and consistent information flow about accounts and activities that go beyond the direct referrals.

So what are the challenges with this relationship and the lessons learned that other partners should be mindful of as they approach Microsoft?

Managing the Microsoft relationship is a challenging and important process—

make sure that everyone in your firm communicates on a daily basis about your collaborative initiatives with Microsoft, that your people are trained on how to represent your firm to Microsoft and that Microsoft's personnel understand your firm's competencies and goals.

Do not put your IBM-facing sales person in front of Microsoft, even when a well-known customer insists on sticking with an IBM (or any Microsoft-competitive) solution (eg, WebSphere). In the interest of preserving your Microsoft partnership, your firm must explain the customer's decision to Microsoft. Keep the communication lines open and lead with your strongest people and message or else you risk those lines being cut permanently.

BORN sees as its weakest point its lack of a permanent presence in Seattle (Tectura acquired that office). The firm has great relationships in the field but is not as strong at Microsoft corporate. Its incomplete relationships from corporate product groups to the field organizations is a weak link in its Microsoft partnership.

BORN's growth and success, like other firms whose cases are presented above, is due to its extending connection points within Microsoft's organization according to the rules of the partnering game and, more importantly, with a view to winning.

Although Microsoft has established the rules of the partnering game, the game is played out in the open marketplace. Microsoft is a software company and it needs services firms to implement and extend its products. While it is true that MCS once attempted a buildup and competed against partners briefly, the conflict has since diminished. The notion of Microsoft as a services giant is antithetical to its core mission and culture. In some countries, one finds vestiges of MCS. But in Microsoft's culture and partner ecosystem, the relationship between Microsoft the software manufacturer and its services partners in services delivery is essential. In the IT industry, it is also unprecedented.

There is perhaps no more symbiotic relationship between Microsoft software and integration partners, whose purposes are mutually aligned, except, of course, for resellers of Microsoft's products, which is the subject of the next chapter. The tightness of Microsoft's relationship with its resellers is instructive, too, for SPs and, for that matter, ISVs, as well.

Chapter 6

Reseller Tactics for Successful Partnership with Microsoft

Partners that are independent software vendors (ISVs) and service providers (SPs) comprise a large portion of the Microsoft Partner Ecosystem. These two groups have accordingly received substantial treatment in this book. But there are other types of partners in Microsoft's vast and complex ecosystem that focus, quite importantly, on reselling Microsoft's products. These include original equipment manufacturers (OEMs) that license and pre-load Microsoft software on PCs, servers and mobile devices, as well as a large channel of software resellers that sell Microsoft software to business customers and end-consumers. Like ISVs and service providers, resellers are evolving in step with Microsoft to address significant shifts in software acquisition and distribution practices as well as to accommodate changes in Microsoft's business.

From a Product-Delivery to a Value-Delivery Model

Microsoft's original business decision to embrace an indirect business model—that is, to build a channel of resellers by licensing its operating-system and other software to third-party computer manufacturers and software resellers—is one of the key reasons for its overwhelming success and market dominance. Apple Computer—which preceded Microsoft to market with its own graphical operating system—squandered the same potential by rejecting the indirect model, opting instead to control all of the Macintosh-related hardware and software business rather than license it to OEM partners and resellers. That decision cost Apple dearly: Microsoft today owns more than a 95% share of the operating-system market while Apple's share is less than five percent.

Given Microsoft's culture, strategy and organizational dynamism, resellers must evolve in step with the company. They must employ the same urgency and flexibility as other partners in order to survive. And, in recent years, the Microsoft reseller business has undergone significant transition as software spending slowed dramatically and Microsoft took enterprise licensing direct, essentially embracing a mixed indirect/direct model. In response, software-reselling business models have moved from pure product distribution—that is, the delivery of software products and licenses—to value delivery. The trends toward multi-year licensing and software maintenance and Microsoft's movement closer to enterprise customers have required its reseller partners to evolve and support a mixed model of product sales as well as licensing-support and deployment services to ensure that customers derive the most value from their software purchases. In this way, resellers are evolving into services partners, too. Resellers, like other partners in the ecosystem, are also moving toward specialization, offering unique services for distinct customer segments. Microsoft believes that the distribution of its products and delivery of value to the market through the reseller channel is a fundamental wheel in the Microsoft machine, especially in the small and mid-sized business (SMB) sector. Microsoft has an amazing marketing machine to drive the volume of its product and solution sales. But resellers are the driving force for the delivery of its products and their value proposition to Microsoft's customers.

Risks Accompany Rewards in Reselling for Microsoft

From Microsoft's perspective, the rewards and risks of working through its reseller channel are obvious: resellers may not succeed for a variety of reasons—distraction by services-related opportunities, pushing competitive products that run on Linux and market downturns—in driving an increasing volume of Microsoft sales and especially license renewals.

For resellers, clearly, Microsoft is a must-have partner. But because margins overall in the Microsoft software business are not significant, volume of sales is the key success factor. Pull-through of other products is also a major plus, although the strongest resellers have learned that pull-through of a broad range of products with better margins is possible only when the relationship between resellers and their corporate customers is established.

As product margins evaporate, some observers predict the end of the software reselling business. But as of late resellers are embracing new models such as software agency as endorsed by Microsoft to ensure that partners are compensated for value delivery to customers.

The same risks that Microsoft senses apply to resellers themselves, and the virtue of partnering tightly with Microsoft and taking full advantage of its marketing muscle is an antidote to these risks.

The Reseller Community

Microsoft sells the vast majority of its software through OEM sales and organizational licensing. OEM channel revenue represents license fees from original equipment manufacturers that pre-install Microsoft products primarily on PCs. OEM sales represent roughly one-third of Microsoft's revenues. In Microsoft's FY04, for instance, OEM sales represented US$10.2 billion of Microsoft's US$32 billion in annual revenues. Organizational licensing and packaged product sales in Microsoft's Americas, Europe/Middle East/Africa (EMEA) and Japan/Asia-Pacific (JAPAC) regions accounted for two-thirds of Microsoft sales for the year. Licensing and some packaged sales accounted for US$22 billion in FY04.

Microsoft originally sold software in standalone, shrink-wrapped boxes. In the 1990s, licensed software on CDs became the predominant method of product fulfillment. The gradual transition to multi-year licensing with software maintenance and support now constitutes the majority of Microsoft's software revenues. This includes annuity-based licensing and one-time transactional licensing deals.

Microsoft estimates that more than 60% of its software is sold through licensing arrangements. It also offers Enterprise Agreement (EA) subscriptions but the vast majority of enterprise customers opt to purchase their software on a perpetual basis. Microsoft also supports a number of network and application service providers that host Microsoft software for customers based on monthly or annual subscriptions but these "leasing" and "rental" models have not yet been widely adopted.

Before discussing these emerging trends in models of software acquisition and consumption, we first explore how Microsoft sells its software and provide a brief description of the community of resellers and a history of the reseller channel.

Microsoft's reseller-partners can be broken down into two categories: computer manufacturers and pure resellers. By way of itemization, they include the following reseller types:

Computer Manufacturers
- Original Equipment Manufacturers (OEMs) of PCs and Servers

- Systems builders (white-box manufacturers)

- Windows Mobile/Embedded OEMs, Independent Hardware Vendors (IHVs) and Original Device Manufacturers (ODM)

Software Resellers
- Large Account Resellers (LARs)

- Value-Added Resellers (VARs)

- Value-Added Providers (VAPs)

- Direct Marketers

- Distributors

- Network/Application Service Providers

The roles of these various reseller partners in relation to Microsoft and its services partners is explained in this chapter, which primarily deals with the business models of OEMs and large account resellers that serve enterprise and mid-market customer segments, as well as their counterparts that serve the SMB market: systems builders and value-added resellers, and the distributors that serve them.

We discuss the role of direct OEMs and software marketers that bypass the distribution channel and sell directly to customers. In addition, thousands of specialty resellers focus on selling PocketPC personal digital assistants (PDAs) and SmartPhone mobile communication devices pre-installed with Windows Mobile operating systems; as well, there are manufacturers of thin-client terminals, appliances and other embedded devices that ship pre-loaded with the Windows XP Embedded operating system.

Microsoft operates unique partner programs for these reseller partners that are discussed later in this chapter.

Who Are Microsoft's Reseller-Partners?

The Microsoft product reselling community is commonly broken down into the classifications below.

OEMs and Systems Builders

Microsoft supports three tiers of manufacturers that pre-load Windows and Office on PCs and servers sold to customers. These include:

Original Equipment Manufacturers

These are "Tier One" partners that ship the highest volume of Microsoft software. Microsoft licenses software directly to its 20 tier-one OEM partners, including brand-name computer manufacturers such as Dell, HP, IBM, Unisys and Fujitsu. Dell is the only OEM to offer a purely direct model, selling exclusively to its customers. Other OEMs support a mixed indirect/direct model.

OEM Gold Systems Builders

These are "Tier Two" partners to which Microsoft also licenses software. There are approximately 1,000 of these, and they straddle the line between OEMs and systems builders. They ship high volumes of Microsoft software on custom-designed PCs and servers.

Systems Builders

These are considered "Tier Three" partners and are also known as "white-box manufacturers." They buy Microsoft software through distribution and pre-install it on unbranded or private-label PCs and/or servers. Microsoft counts roughly 150,000 systems builders globally. Systems builders build custom systems that are sold predominantly into the SMB market, although some also sell into the enterprise-customer segment.

Windows Mobile/Embedded Systems and Appliance Manufacturers

This class of OEM is also referred to as original device manufacturers (ODM), which develop and sell PocketPCs and Smartphones as well as thin-client devices and other appliances pre-loaded with specialty versions of Windows. PocketPCs and Smart-phones ship pre-loaded with Microsoft's Windows CE, or Windows Mobile 2003/2005, operating systems. Thin-clients and other embedded devices ship with Microsoft's Windows XP Embedded, a highly componentized and customizable operating system. The continued expansion and increasing specialization of the Windows operating system family continues unabated. Microsoft released, in 2004, a version of Windows XP Embedded For Retail, and other specialized versions of Windows Embedded are expected to follow. These manufacturers typically have specialized distributors and channel partners who focus on selling mobile and wireless solutions and embedded solutions, respectively.

Software Resellers

Large Account Resellers (LAR)

The term LAR originated with Microsoft's Select License program, which debuted in 1993. This class of software reseller sells the highest volume of Microsoft software. LARs formerly sold all Microsoft software to large corporate accounts. They no longer sell Enterprise Agreement licensing in major markets but continue to sell Microsoft Select and Open Licenses to enterprises and SMB customers. LARs also function as Enterprise Software Agents (ESA) that provide transactional support and software asset-management services for Enterprise Agreement customers on behalf of Microsoft for a commission.

Value-Added Resellers (VARs)

This class of reseller sells software and services predominantly to SMB customers. Like LARs, VARs typically support a mixed business model in which they depend on services revenues in conjunction with Microsoft product sales. What distinguishes VARs from services partners *per se* is their business model, which is product-driven in contrast to that of services partners, whose business model is services-driven. VARs provide services but only for the products they sell.

There are three types of Microsoft license that authorize customers to use its software:

Packaged Product: shrink-wrapped/boxed for retail distribution

OEM License: legally installed by Tier-One OEMs and Systems Builders

Volume Licensing: for multiple copies; sold by Microsoft Direct, LARs, VARs and distributors

There are various types of Volume License for companies with more than 250 PCs:

An **Enterprise Agreement (EA)** is best for companies that standardize on Microsoft software. It includes Office Professional, Windows Professional desktop operating system upgrade and a core Client Access License (CAL) based on a three-year agreement term. The core CAL replaces the former BackOffice CAL and currently includes CALs for Windows Server, Exchange, Systems Management Server, and SharePoint Portal Server. Software can be used in perpetuity.

An **Enterprise Agreement Subscription (EAS)**, whose license expires at the end of the contract period. Microsoft handles negotiations, sales and billing of EAs through its Microsoft Licensing online subsidiary in Reno, Nevada. A handful of Enterprise Software Agents (ESAs)—formerly known as Large Account Reseller (LARs)—are authorized to handle the contract paperwork and licensing asset management services for EA, in exchange for a fee.

A **Select Agreement** is designed for companies with mixed software needs; they can get a volume discount for each pool (applications, systems, or servers) of software, also based on a three-year term. At the end of the term, the customer can continue to use the software if it is properly licensed and paid for, and renew any Software Assurance (SA) that was acquired to continue receiving the associated benefits (eg, upgrades). ESAs and LARs are authorized to sell Select licenses.

For companies with fewer than 250 PCs, the following options are more favorable:

The **Open License Value** is the EA-equivalent for small businesses, and includes Software Assurance for five desktops and the ability to spread payments over a three-year period.

The **Open License Volume** provides, as suggested, a volume discount for customers that earn 500 points on a select pool of software paid for in advance.

The **Open License Business** requires the purchase of only five licenses.

For such smaller companies, there is

■ a broad channel base of retail stores, solution providers, and online vendors; and

■ product upgrade rights (Software Assurance) purchased in advance at current prices, with payments spread over a three-year term.

Figure 6.1: How Microsoft Licenses Software Through Its Reseller Channel.

Value-Added Providers (VAPs)

This class of reseller has the same business model as a VAR but it focuses exclusively on small businesses.

Distributors

This class of reseller distributes technology products from vendors and sells to services partners and VARs. Ingram Micro, for example, sells thousands of IT products from 14,000 suppliers, including Microsoft, to more than 165,000 resellers around the world.

Direct Marketers / Retailers

Direct Market Resellers (DMRs, or Direct Marketers) acquire products from Microsoft or distributors and sell directly to customers in niched market segments, generally to businesses. CDW, PC Connection and Insight Direct are Microsoft's top US DMRs, and some have become ESAs as well as authorized LARs.

Retailers acquire products directly from Microsoft and re-sell them to consumers. CompUSA and Best Buy are US-based partners of this type.

Not Just a Volume Business Anymore

The reseller business is all about volume, volume, volume: generating profits based on selling high volumes of hardware and software to business and consumer markets. This is true for both computer manufacturers and software resellers. While the volume model remains intact, there have been significant changes in software supply, customer demand, and Microsoft's business model that have impacted all partners in Microsoft's reseller community.

Severe pressure on profit margins forced a major consolidation in both OEM and software reseller channels from 2000-2005. The remaining resellers are assessing new ways of competing on value and customization in addition to price. Hardware manufacturers have historically generated the bulk of their revenues by selling PCs pre-loaded with Microsoft Windows and/or Office products but now they pre-install a wider variety of Microsoft software on an increasingly diversified mix of computer systems and form factors, ranging from 64-way Intel servers and blade servers to single-purpose appliances, laptops, tablet and desktop PCs as well as PocketPCs and Smartphones.

The product-driven model of large software resellers and value-added resellers (VARs) remains largely intact, although it has evolved from one of pure product distribution to one in which value-added services and solutions are essential for driving margins. Increasingly, resellers also serve as agents that do not engage directly with customers in the negotiation and sales process but do receive commissions from Microsoft and other vendors for influencing product or license sales and generate additional revenues by providing licensing support services on those sales.

Significant corporate spending on technology during the 1990s, and the subsequent slowdown and shrinking in IT budgets refocused customer attention on the costs of software purchases and the value derived from those investments. The emergence of Linux and other alternatives has provided customers with choice and a basis of comparison for demanding more value from Microsoft and all software vendors. This provides new opportunities for software resellers.

Microsoft is a product-centric company that is also customer-focused and partner-driven. The company seeks to improve its direct relationship with customers as it refines the features and functions of its platforms and products in order to deliver the most value, or at least more value than its competitors. Microsoft recognizes that its ample supply of resellers worldwide is a competitive advantage over its primary competitors, so it is more dependent on that channel to translate the benefits of Microsoft software over competitive offerings to drive sales. Given Microsoft's shift from a purely indirect model to a mixed indirect and direct model for software sales, which is discussed later in this chapter, some question the long term viability of the software reseller business model. Yet these partners continue to play a pivotal role, advising and helping customers derive the most benefit, *eg*, reducing the total cost of ownership (TCO) and maximizing return on investment (ROI) from their Microsoft purchases and licensing contracts.

Microsoft is also dependent on its resellers to translate the benefits of its increasing portfolio of software offerings, licensing, maintenance and purchasing mechanisms to customers. In this new world, the reseller's ability to deliver value-added services to complement its core resale function is vital.

As margins dwindle, resellers cannot expect to survive solely on product sales alone. There has been a significant amount of consolidation in both the OEM and software reseller markets, and many others have closed doors. Yet still others are evolving to develop product and service offerings that address distinct customer segments and vertical industries that enable customers to derive the maximum value from their Microsoft software purchases. In order to accomplish this, resellers are increasingly partnering with other Microsoft ISVs as well as services partners to enable customers to achieve more value from their Microsoft software. For instance, resellers are pairing up with developers of desktop-management software to ensure that Microsoft client updates are deployed after purchase, and they are forming alliances with certified learning partners to ensure that customers are properly trained on the Microsoft software they purchased.

The Enterprise Resellers: OEMs and LARs

As indicated, two classes of reseller partners—Top Tier OEMs and LARs—sell the highest volume of Microsoft software. Roughly 96% of Microsoft software was once sold through the reseller channel. OEMs' and LARs' sales represented a disproportionate amount of these sales since they served large enterprise and corporate accounts.

As Microsoft's growth soared between 30% and 50% annually throughout the 1990s, the growth of OEMs kept pace. Compaq, IBM and HP recorded hundreds of billions of dollars in revenues for PCs and later enjoyed strong revenue growth on more expensive server hardware pre-loaded with Windows NT Server or Windows Server 2000. Intel and Compaq are representative of the class of early OEMs that built huge fortunes based on reselling Microsoft Windows and Office on their PCs, and later on servers, to business customers and consumers.

In the OEM category, consider the following examples of companies that, through partnership with Microsoft, have succeeded:

Intel, the other half of the famous "WIntel" pair, has built a US$30 billion per year-business by making microprocessors and chips as well as computer, networking and communications products for Microsoft products. It is the largest such manufacturer in the world. Intel's growth and success have corresponded with that of Microsoft, since sales of personal computers and server equipment pre-loaded with Windows operating systems and Intel processors and chipsets have experienced the same volume and trajectory. This is an example of OEM/Microsoft symbiosis at its best.

Compaq, before being acquired by HP for US$25 billion, was arguably Microsoft's closest computer equipment OEM-partner. Its server and storage family of products, most of which survived the merger, were co-engineered and certified by Microsoft, a major user of Compaq server equipment for its own internal IT operations. Microsoft's symbiosis with Compaq verged on legendary.

HP has also long been a Microsoft partner, especially since the merger with Compaq. The merged firm has quickened the pace and scope of partnering activities even as HP, in order to keep pace with IBM, has branched out into Linux-based server systems. HP's services arm, too, has historically been focused on systems-integration services for Microsoft software, although HP markets Linux-related services, as well.

Dell has long been a darling of Microsoft for its proven ability to move standards-based personal computers and server equipment—all with only Microsoft operating systems until recently when Dell partnered with Red Hat Software, a Linux distributor—steadily and aggressively. True to this partnership, Dell's recent endeavor to move low-cost servers down-market to help Microsoft move its Small Business Server product into the small and medium-sized business market has boosted the partnership, which has worked favorably for both companies.

Apple—despite its early combativeness with Microsoft—accepted US$150 million from the company in 1997, to address Apple's cash constraints in exchange for making Internet Explorer the default browser on its MacOS. Internet Explorer is no longer the default browser on MacOS X yet Apple continues to distribute the latter's products—especially Office for the Mac—on Apple computers. Microsoft Office is the *de facto* standard Office suite on Macintosh computers, in spite of widespread anti-Microsoft sentiment among the ranks of its users.

LARs are software resellers that sell the most volume of organizational licenses and packaged product to commercial accounts. Unlike OEMs, which ship brand-name

PCs and servers to all customer segments, LARs exclusively target multi-national corporations and other large corporate accounts that purchase or license Microsoft software in large volumes. During Microsoft's heyday, LARs followed the same growth trajectory as their OEM counterparts. For example, Software Spectrum grew from a small retail operation in Dallas in the early 1980s, to a US$1 billion giant two decades later. ASAP Software, another US-based LAR out of Chicago, also surpassed the US$1 billion revenue milestone.

Continued strong growth of the PC, server and Windows/Office businesses fed the OEM and software reseller channel very well for a long time, aided at the end of the 1990s, by an excess of Internet-related business purchasing and a burst of Y2K spending. While the turnover to the new millennium proved to be largely a non-event on system clock cycles, time was indeed ticking on the explosive levels of growth that Microsoft and its top resellers had enjoyed for many years.

Resellers—and, indeed, the technology industry at large—braced for a slowdown. Rising saturation rates of PCs throughout the developed world lowered forecasts by Intel and PC vendors, and, of course, Microsoft's growth rates began moving downward. The frenzy in PC and software spending by business customers throughout the 1990s and early 2000s, began to decline as did software margins for resellers.

LARs faced more margin pressures because they did not play in the consumer space that propped up the earnings of their OEM counterparts and because of the role of rebates in relation to their margins. In many cases, the rebates and discounts offered to LARs by Microsoft for achieving volume sales exceeded the product margins. Declining volumes led to diminished rebates and, of course, shrinking profits. As the market became increasingly saturated, LARs battled over the diminishing number of enterprise licensing deals and engaged one another in price wars. LARs undercut one another and sold software below market as they battled over customer account control and volume deals that qualified resellers for Microsoft's coveted rebates and discounts. Worried about price erosion and the commoditization of its software business, Microsoft decided on a mixed indirect/direct model.

Microsoft's Direct/Indirect Model, and the Impact on Resellers

In 2001, Microsoft announced that it would take EA licensing sales direct. This was a major shift for Microsoft, which sold the vast majority of its software through the channel. And it represented a considerable portion of all licensed software: Microsoft will not publicly reveal what percentage of its overall licensing revenue it assumed control over when taking EA sales direct but observers conservatively estimate that it represents at least 25% of all Microsoft licensing sales (although the impact on each LAR varies).

In the aftermath of this decision, LARs continue to be authorized to sell Microsoft

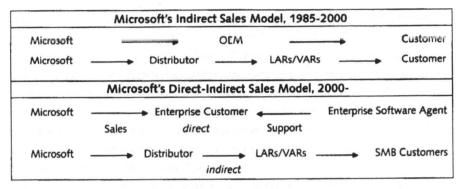

Figure 6.2: Microsoft's Direct/Indirect Model Impacts Its Reseller Channel.

Select and Open licenses but also play a role in customer accounts by being reassigned by Microsoft as ESAs. In this additional capacity, ESAs would provide licensing support services for Enterprise Agreement customers and, in exchange, would receive a commission from Microsoft. But many resellers eyed that move as a prelude to Microsoft's going direct with its entire software business. And the signs at that time appeared somewhat ominous for the channel. The announcement followed another major move by Microsoft as it launched a joint venture in the IT services space with Accenture, called Avanade. Dell's enormous success in selling PCs directly to consumers had enormous impact on the consciousness of business executives everywhere. The consulting services arms of IBM and Oracle provided additional profits as margins on software declined. Why would Microsoft's thinking not be affected by these market realities?

Product Distribution Is Guided by Market Forces

There has been a great deal of attention paid to Microsoft's moving from a purely indirect software reselling model to a mix of direct and indirect reselling. At the furthest extreme of the channel model, Microsoft has a direct sales channel with its largest customers that purchase Enterprise Agreements. Naturally, this has caused significant stress to the reselling business model and an undercurrent of animosity between Microsoft and some of its larger partners. Many former resellers have abandoned the reseller business for other opportunities in the partner ecosystem.

Yet Microsoft's mixed reselling model is not unique. The Internet has revolutionized the way all products are distributed and re-sold across all industries, and fundamentally altered the relationship between manufacturers, distributors, dealers and customers. Traditionally, products have moved from vendor or manufacturer to distributor to dealer. The ability of customers to use the Internet as a tool for negotiating, buying, acquiring and selling product has shifted more power to consumers and turned the traditional model of distribution on its head. This problem has been compounded in the software industry by the fact that the software product itself can be downloaded, or distributed, via this new mechanism. As the Internet opened the floodgates and more channels globally, customers gained leverage in the purchasing equation and in some instances pressured Microsoft—and all manufacturers—to have a direct relationship in monetary terms so the customer can have more influence over the vendor and the price.

The impact of the Internet has been felt across all industries, including software, banking, travel, automotive—even farming and agriculture. According to a report issued by *Farm Industry News* (1 January 2000: "Golden Age of the Buyer"), four factors accounted for a rethinking of product and service distribution in agribusiness and, indeed, across all industries in recent years: a fragmented customer base, higher customer expectations, increased competition among suppliers and, of course, the advent of the Internet, which has been discussed. Similarly, Microsoft's product distribution cycle has been impacted by these factors. Its customer segmentation and verticalization initiatives recognize that the market is not monolithic but pervasively niched.

- *Fragmented customer base:* As a volume supplier, Microsoft traditionally embraced a one-size-fits-all Windows desktop and server approach to product packaging and reselling. Yet, like its counterparts in the agriculture world, Microsoft is evolving its distribution to address the needs of a fragmented customer base, including SMB and enterprise customers, and end-consumers. Customer segmentation and verticalization have also influenced Microsoft's increasingly diversified software portfolio, most notably in its stepped-up moves into the business applications, enterprise software and SMB software markets. These offerings also reflect the shifts and diversification of its product reselling and distribution strategies.

- *Customer Expectations:* Microsoft also faces higher customer expectations in terms of improved IT efficiencies and TCO as well as better ROI on their software purchases. Moreover, there is increased pressure for Microsoft to put more "skin in the game," that is, for the company to assume greater accountability for enterprise customers that are more accustomed to the integrated product-services delivery model of IBM and Oracle. Microsoft cites this as a key factor for its direct moves, including launching Avanade with Accenture and taking enterprise licensing direct, although the reasons for those decisions are far more complex. Microsoft is also responding to customer demands for increased efficiencies by cultivating an ecosystem of services and software partners that can deliver a fully integrated solution, and provide more advanced business process automation, re-engineering and consulting services in addition to standard product delivery, installation, implementation, support and management services. Resellers in the partner ecosystem are accordingly evolving their business models to support

Microsoft's customer segmentation, verticalization, value proposition and new delivery models.

- *Increasing competition from suppliers:* Microsoft has also encountered increased competition in the operating-system software market for Intel and AMD-based servers, and this is having a significant impact on its product-reselling and distribution strategies. Microsoft once dominated this market with no serious competition. Advances made by Linux and open-source software in recent years, however, have shifted the business for resellers, indeed, for all partners in Microsoft's ecosystem. Defining elements of the PC industry have shifted as a result of increased competition: the so-called WIntel "duopoly" no longer exists. Intel has formed alliances with Linux distribution vendors and Microsoft has executed partnerships with Intel-rival AMD. Intel and Microsoft remain close partners but that pairing is no longer exclusive.

Microsoft's decision to support a mixed indirect/direct model in opposition to channel needs is offset by its increasing, rather than decreasing, reliance on channel partners to help the company stave off new competitive threats. The presence of a viable operating–system alternative in the Intel, x86 and 64-bit market has shifted more power to the customer, and to reseller partners, on whom Microsoft relies for the delivery of product and value.

All of these factors account for Microsoft's evolving approach to product distribution and reselling, and the indirect/direct model, which has had a ripple effect across the channel of services and reseller partners in a variety of ways. To begin, the changes have significantly impacted the vendor/manufacturer-distributor-partner-customer relationship. This is significant not only to OEMs and large resellers that serve enterprise customers but also to systems builders and VARs that serve the SMB market. The significance resides in customer-relationship ownership, an important consideration for Microsoft and its resellers. When customers demand that vendors go direct, the reasons are many but can essentially be boiled down to this: the perception that the distribution channel, not the individual distributor, is failing to meet the needs of the customer. A second reason is that the customer may perceive a lower cost of procurement by having a direct relationship to the vendor.

There are mixed views on the impact of the indirect/direct model on resellers and customers. On the hardware side, Dell has achieved enormous efficiencies selling exclusively directly to customers. Microsoft historically enjoyed great efficiencies selling exclusively indirectly. Still, taking enterprise licensing direct has given Microsoft a closer relationship with enterprise customers and undoubtedly more account control. There are some positive aspects to the direct relationship for customers. Some enterprise customers cheered Microsoft's decision to go direct with EAs. They wanted to license directly from Microsoft so that they might negotiate more custom, value-added deals and better pricing. On the one hand, customers have in some cases been able to negotiate better deals and extract price concessions from Microsoft. But at what cost? Was this direct move positive for customers?

The results appear to be mixed. Shortly after taking EAs direct, for instance, Microsoft announced a controversial Licensing 6.0 program and revised mainte-nance program called Software Assurance that some say increased software pricing and forced customers to pay higher maintenance fees. Microsoft contested those claims. Yet there is no doubt that there was a strong backlash from customers after Microsoft took EAs direct and revised its licensing approach.

While licensing continues to represent the bulk of Microsoft's revenues—the com-pany claims that more than 60% of customers continue to renew EAs—the increas-ing number of transaction-based and OEM sales that have been recorded in recent quarters suggests that a good number of customers are opting against multi-year deals and maintenance, and are upgrading their software only as part of a regular PC-refresh cycle.

It remains unclear whether Microsoft's indirect-selling approach, or direct model, is best for customers. Some studies indicate that the direct relationship with the ven-dor often results in a negative impact on the customer and the channel, and that even-tually the channel that the customer severed relations with comes back into play. It appears highly unlikely as of this writing that resellers will regain control of Enterprise Agreement licensing, and more likely that Microsoft will continue to support both indi-rect and direct models as the software-distribution evolution marches on.

Consolidation Impacts the Reseller Market

There is no doubt that Microsoft's shift in sales strategy—to one based on a mix of direct sales and channel sales—had severe repercussions on its software reseller chan-nel, and has necessitated significant shifts in reseller business models.

Substantial consolidation in the reseller channel occurred after 2000. In 2002, for example, Microsoft's two largest LARs—Corporate Software and Software Spec-trum—were both acquired by Level 3 Communications. Today, there are roughly 20 Microsoft authorized LARs in the US, although only 10 are considered signifi-cant players (and none of them continue to operate as pure resellers). Microsoft's new model forced LARs to shift to either a hybrid model or a mixed model sup-porting volume software sales and services revenues.

Meanwhile, OEMs struggled with the same issues that led to deterioration in margins and price wars in the software reseller market. If the slowdown in IT spend-ing was not enough to curb the growth of the PC industry, the economic freefall after the 2001 terrorist attacks in New York and Washington, DC, exacerbated the crisis in the channel, indeed, across the US. As the general economy and software industry slowed to a halt, all partners in the Microsoft ecosystem—resellers, solution providers and ISVs—experienced massive consolidation. HP's acquisition of Compaq in 2000, formed the largest computer company in history. In 2004, Gateway purchased eMachines for US$230 million. During the fourth quarter of 2004, following several years of severe pressure on margins and profitability, IBM announced its decision to sell off its PC business to Chinese firm Lenovo, further consolidating the US PC market into a two-horse race between HP and Dell.

—■—

The handful of remaining LARs maintain that the fees Microsoft pays them more than make up for the profits lost when their Enterprise Agreement revenues disappeared. Those that have survived the fallout attribute their successful adaptation to preserving the contractual aspects of licensing services and, therefore, their customer relationships, and accepting while exploiting the change in Microsoft's course. Like some ISVs, resellers faced a serious challenge when Microsoft decided to compete against them in the enterprise market. Like successful ISVs that have survived, however, resellers that have sought to adapt and exploit this shift to their advantage by collaborating with Microsoft have fared well. There is no contention that this shifting paradigm in software acquisition has forced Microsoft resellers to pursue new models—or to fade away. Many have faded away. But those that remain have evolved in step with Microsoft.

Academics note that the Internet is a powerful intermediary that has become an equalizing force for customers, shifting the power from vendors to buyers. But this does not necessitate the erosion of the software reseller and distribution channel, which remains an important conduit through which Microsoft delivers value to customers. In 2001, Eric Clemons professor of operations and information management at the Wharton Business School at the University of Pennsylvania, points to a "seismic shift" in the relationships between consumers, retailers, distributors, manufacturers and service providers occurring as a result of the Internet. But in examining the transformations that have occurred in two industries—securities trading and travel—he discovered many individual companies wondering the same thing as software resellers: will their market share and profitability increase or decrease as a result of business and consumer adoption of direct distribution models? His contention is that the shift to direct distribution implies an obvious challenge for resellers but not necessarily extinction. This is because resellers, like ISVs and services partners, must evolve to provide new value as the PC and operating system have entered a phase of commoditization. (*Inc Magazine*, June 2001)

Expanding on the topic of indirect/direct distribution Mr Clemons suggests that vendors are studying optimal ways of forming customer relationships but will likely add new channels and have a multi-channel strategy rather than a wholesale change to direct sales. Microsoft's indirect-direct mix, then, is appropriate given these market forces. "The channel power [of consumers] presents many companies with the option of reducing or eliminating the role of intermediaries and lets those providers transact directly with their customers. But some observers are questioning whether it makes sense for all companies to take advantage of the new possibilities," wrote Mr Clemons, a professor of business at Wharton. After all, direct distribution can present "numerous strategic uncertainties," he added.

So rather than allow traditional reseller channels to erode, vendors like Microsoft are parsing their distribution strategies into separate buckets based on which channels of distribution make the most sense for certain customer segments. Some software vendors such as SalesForce.com have successfully adopted a purely electronic distribution model enabled by the Internet for software distribution. Yet established software giants like Microsoft will likely use a mixture of online and traditional reselling methods and channels to meet the specialized needs of many different customer segments and vertical industries.

Delivering Value Is the Imperative to Survive and Thrive

Regardless of how software is sold in the future, the new role of the Microsoft reseller is to ensure that software yields meaningful productivity gains and return on investment for customers in order to motivate upgrade purchasing. This is, after all, part of Microsoft's core culture and mission—to sell more software based on a product-centric, customer-focused and partner-driven model. Microsoft's cultural imperative makes it unlikely that the reseller channel will disappear, however. But contemporary resellers' future viability requires continued evolution of their value propositions based on delivering value and solutions, and not just products.

Those resellers that can evolve new services to add value for customers will survive and thrive, while others capsize. As Microsoft embraces this mixed indirect-direct strategy, resellers are also adopting hybrid business models in which they serve as licensing agents for enterprise customers and software resellers for mid-market and upper mid-market customers, as well as managed service providers and software developers.

ASAP Software, for example, is one of seven LARs in the US that has undergone a substantial transformation of its business model based on Microsoft's directive for resellers to focus on software asset-management services. In order to deliver these services, ASAP Software has expanded beyond a licensing advisor and reseller to a software developer and service provider.

Reseller Partner Points: Licensing Competency

Microsoft needs independent advisors to help steer customers to purchase licenses and provide value-added services. To meet increasing customer demands, Microsoft is partnering with its remaining resellers to develop new business models that deliver on customer needs while ensuring maximum return for the company.

In 2004, Microsoft started match-making programs that enable resellers to form alliances with ISVs to ensure that customers deploy the software they license, and pacts with training outfits such as New Horizons to ensure that customers are properly trained on the use of their software. Those services ensure that customers get maximum ROI—and purchase the next version of Microsoft software. In this way, the function of the reseller has shifted to provide new value-added services based on Microsoft's shifting course to meet customers' increased ROI demands.

As integral players in Microsoft's ecosystem, LARs and VARs have been folded into the Microsoft Partner Program and so, too, must earn points to become certified partners. In 2005, Microsoft launched a Licensing Solutions Competency as one of the competencies within the Microsoft Partner program. Resellers must attain that licensing competency in order to become Microsoft Certified Partners.

It is important for all resellers to understand the field of play outlined in Chapter Three and Microsoft's rules of engagement with its partners. Microsoft's organizational structure is most important to this group of partners because of the programmatic nature of how software is sold and licensed, and how partners earn rebates and volume discounts. While services firms and ISVs must also know the programmatic pieces of the partner program to get in the door at Microsoft, they rely primarily on connection points in the field organization to improve their bottomline and evolve into new services delivery. Reseller relationships with Microsoft are important, of course, but it is more important for these partners to stay abreast of Microsoft's constantly changing promotions and rebate offers to make their businesses as profitable as they can be. Consider one LAR's situation in the Microsoft ecosystem.

ASAP Software Evolves with Microsoft

ASAP Software, or ASAP (www.asap.com)—a Microsoft Enterprise Software Agent (ESA) and Large Account Reseller (LAR) that was founded in 1984 and is based in Buffalo Grove, Illinois—employs 600 people and generates US$1.5 billion in annual revenues. ASAP was one of Microsoft's first LARs and that partnership is critical to ASAP: as much as 50% of its business is Microsoft-related. ASAP continues to sell Microsoft's Select Agreements to enterprise and mid-market customers, and Open Licenses to small businesses even as they provide new license asset-management services for Microsoft's Enterprise Agreement customers. ASAP remains independent and is one of seven LARs authorized by Microsoft to serve as an ESA and provide software asset management services to enterprise customers.

Like other successful partners, ASAP continues to have many connection points inside Microsoft. For instance, ASAP has a partner account manager (PAM) that provides ASAP with general marketing and sales support on a day-to-day basis and contacts within many Microsoft sales offices outside of Microsoft headquarters.

ASAP has numerous functional points of contact in Microsoft from operations and contract processing to Microsoft's Licensing subsidiary at Reno, Nevada, as well as individual product groups for strategic marketing purposes.

As it made the transition from a pure reseller model to an agent-reseller-services model, ASAP's connection points into Microsoft helped make the transition easier. The change in Microsoft's business model to direct licensing had the potential to affect sharply the financial performance of ASAP and other LARs. ASAP executives acknowledge that they were concerned that Microsoft sales people would interact less with them after Microsoft shifted the revenue model but those fears have not yet materialized into problems for resellers that have evolved in step with Microsoft. Microsoft, for example, now negotiates more factors with its customers while ASAP can earn commissions for managing all licensing services for those accounts. ASAP observes that its relationship with customers remains strong and its partnership with Microsoft has not changed. In fact, its partnership with Microsoft is expanding due to the expanded nature of its services delivery to customers. For ASAP, it is not simply about delivering product to customers, but delivering value.

Microsoft, for its part, knows that LARs have formed strong relationships with enterprise customers over the years. And it has no motive to eliminate a channel of loyal partners that can add to the value provided to Microsoft customers, particularly in a competitive climate, ASAP executives contend. Microsoft's local and corporate offices are mindful of this. "One of the big concerns when you shift revenues is that salespeople tend not to care as much because they do not see the revenues flow from us. But those salespeople know where their bread is buttered and they keep a good focus on the compensation garnered from doing a deal with those customers. So, from a Microsoft-relationship viewpoint, things have not changed very much. We do not carry revenues on EAs but we do on Open and Select licenses, and we manage a lot of important steps and details and review every contract," observes Roger Moffat, senior director of product marketing for ASAP.

The shift to selling Enterprise Agreements direct and launching Software Assurance (SA) maintenance are among the most significant shifts in Microsoft reselling business to date: most reseller business in the past was based on licensing agreements and now it revolves around selling annuity-based deals and secured renewals. There is more urgency around renewals because Microsoft—and its reseller partners—benefit handsomely from a predictable, and recurring revenue stream.

This puts LARs in the hot seat: conveying the value of SA to customers and then ensuring that the customer deploys the software and enjoys its benefits. Yet it also presents those partners with new opportunities. Said Mr Moffat: "We have to articulate more what a customer gets with SA and, to do this, our salespeople have become more hands-on with customers. We discuss more with customers their strategic needs and discuss deployment alternatives because, after I sell a million-dollar contract, I want to make sure the software is deployed and the return on investment is achieved. Technology support needs evolve as quickly as technology itself. Our goal remains to stay in tune with those needs and to react with our partner network, to exceed our customers' expectations. There are many partners we have cultivated relationships with."

It has also required ASAP to expand its business model beyond its advisory and reselling functions to provide end-to-end software asset management (SAM) services. This propelled ASAP to take on the additional roles of software developer and hosting services provider. In 2001, ASAP developed and launched eSMART, a subscription-based, hosted service that allows companies to manage and track their software and hardware holdings. By 2005, eSMART had evolved into a sophisticated platform offering advanced discovery and license-tracking services for software, hardware, mobile devices and other IT resources connected to the network or via the Internet. The services enable customers to reduce TCO and greatly improve the ROI of their Microsoft software and other software assets. For instance, customers often uncover too many or too few software licenses in use, licenses for software they have not deployed, and licenses for products they did not know they owned. In spite of the obvious challenges to its reseller model, ASAP maintains that resellers can play a more pivotal role in this environment by translating the benefits and value of Microsoft software to customers as trusted advisors, rather than hammering out deals on pricing alone. There is a real need for these services in the current purchasing climate. "Microsoft representatives in the field know less about licensing because they tend to be focused on the product and so they are relying on ASAP Software to provide those services more than before. Microsoft may carry the revenues but they depend on us for renewals, deployments and overall client satisfaction" stated Jeremy Jackson, ASAP's partner marketing manager.

He refutes the contention of some observers that Microsoft is eliminating its software reselling channel. "If there is anyone in the landscape that I would trust, it would be Microsoft. More so than any other IT provider, Microsoft knows and understands the leverage dynamics of the channel and uses it to their advantage. They are a very channel-friendly organization and have been consistent over the years and have always been a voice of reason. Microsoft is always very fair when it comes to working with their channel; they do not take away opportunities. The opportunities reside within the channel."

Enterprise Software Agent (ESA) Model

LARs once negotiated a significant portion of Microsoft's enterprise revenue as authorized resellers of Microsoft's Enterprise Agreements. When Microsoft took the EA business direct, it cut deeply into the revenues of large account resellers and distributors. Yet Microsoft recognized that large account resellers had well-established relationships with enterprise customers who look upon them as objective, trusted advisors. Microsoft viewed this channel of independent intermediaries as an asset to its business, one that distinguished its model from that of competitors IBM and Oracle, whose global services consulting divisions are not widely viewed as impartial or as customer-focused as Microsoft's reseller channel has been historically viewed.

To stem the flow of blood, Microsoft anointed LARs as Enterprise Software Agents (ESAs) that would be paid commissions to provide services, and urged resellers to compete over value-added licensing services rather than product margins. Microsoft viewed the new role of the large resellers as ESAs that would be paid a commission for influencing and educating customers about licensing options, providing software asset-management services, and helping customers realize more benefit from their purchases, while also continuing to sell Microsoft software to small, mid-sized and upper mid-market customers.

So, like many software vendors, Microsoft has instituted agent models that give LARs and VARs commissions for influencing sales. The agent model has had mixed results to date. Microsoft launched its agent model with large account resellers in 2001, and expanded it to its VAR channel in 2003. The model is similar in some respects to the Enterprise Software Agent model that replaced the role of LARs in customer accounts with Enterprise Agreements. In that case, Microsoft assumed direct control of the flow of revenues while large resellers served as agents and licensing advisors, and earned fees from Microsoft for influencing sales and serving customer accounts. In the VAR agent model, by contrast, the responsibilities for the deal are split across two tiers of the channel. In this case, Microsoft has assigned distributors as license providers and solution providers as trusted advisors that get a commission for influencing a technology purchase decision.

Mass Customization Model:
The Next Evolution

Over time, some expect the software reselling business to vanish as customers download software updates over the Internet and pay for monthly subscriptions or per transaction. Such is the model employed by Linux leader Red Hat and, in the past, by mini-computer vendors. Many observers note that new technologies that are better enabling this type of utility computing are falling into place, and will make IT resource allocation—and spending—as dynamic and unit-based as electricity flowing into the home.

Even as it moved directly into the territory of its largest resellers, Microsoft is encouraging its largest OEMs serving enterprise customers—as well as systems builders and VARs—to steer along close to the SS Microsoft as it shifts course. Customer segmentation is a key direction for resellers, as for Microsoft. The emerging use of mobile computers is another key trend. On the horizon are also opportunities for specialization and market verticalization for OEMs, resellers and distributors to exploit. It is apparent that resellers must evolve and grow—or die. Price wars and razor–thin margins have prompted many resellers to walk away but some are evolving their volume business in step with Microsoft or to a hybrid model with products and services to generate margins.

OEMs are exploring new form factors and scenarios for business users and consumers. The future for LARs, VARs, OEMs and systems builders resides in customer segmentation via mass customization. OEMs continue to ship brand-name PCs at lower and lower prices. By 2005, the average cost of a high-powered desktop PC with advanced multimedia capabilities ranged from US$500 to US$1,000. As OEMs strive to move away from such commoditization, Microsoft is expanding its Windows offerings to meet the unique needs of consumers, small businesses, midsized business and customers. In the same manner, Microsoft has pushed OEMs to follow suit and offer customized PCs and new server form factors in order to differentiate their systems and to drive more demand for hardware and, by association, software upgrades.

The mainstream PC and server business has been largely commoditized; as a result, Microsoft is urging OEMs and systems builders to design new form factors based on new features being integrated into the Longhorn version of Windows. These include ultra-thin mini-laptops with auxiliary displays. Microsoft is also making Windows XP clients available at smaller footprints and resource requirements to enable its systems builders to build single-task PCs and new mobile form factors that offer most of the functionality of Windows XP.

Microsoft's Windows platform chief advised 50 top-tier OEMs at the company's executive OEM summit in 2004, to think more like custom-systems builders. During Microsoft's annual OEM executive summit, Microsoft group vice president of platforms Jim Allchin advised OEMs to shift development resources into creating computing "experiences" in order to differentiate their offerings, rather than compete on price and features. Mr Allchin urged a mass-volume customization approach, encouraging OEMs to focus on specific needs in the home, entertainment and small-business markets. Hardware, software and services have to be created more closely in tandem to create such custom experiences, and this requires virtual ecosystems of partners to form, he advised. Many such partnerships exist: Microsoft works closely with Intel and OEMs today to support specialized versions of Windows, such as Windows XP Media Center Edition 2005 and Windows XP Embedded. OEM partners and systems builders have learned to adapt with Microsoft's shifting course from a pure mass-volume model to a mass-customization model.

And this is essentially the same direction Microsoft urges resellers to pursue. It entails a closer relationship with Microsoft and other partners as well as a focus on extending Microsoft's power into the marketplace with new form factors and systems based on next-generation client and server offerings as well as new systems based on specialty versions of Windows and Office for the Tablet PC and Windows XP Media Center Edition as well as niche-oriented systems for storage and security needs. It is interesting to observe that Microsoft is advising its Tier One volume-OEMs to mimic the approach of smaller systems builders and VARs. This mass–customization approach, markedly different from the traditional mass-volume approach of most OEMs, signals the shifting winds of customization based on customer segmentation and verticalization. This model was pioneered and optimized by another type of OEM, the systems builders.

"Microsoft has been very consistent in its distribution and reseller channel, recognizing the fact that in its entirety the channel is its largest customer."
—Dan Schwab, D&H

The SMB Resellers: Systems Builders and VARs

To this point, we have focused much attention on the enterprise resellers: OEMs and LARs. Their counterparts in the small and mid-sized business market—systems builders and VARs—have experienced much the same growth trajectory and subsequent margin pressures as the larger resellers. These resellers do not boast household brand names, such as Sony, Dell or CDW, but they are a vital aspect of the value chain, particularly as Microsoft ramps up efforts in the SMB market.

Systems builders, also known as white-box manufacturers, design and build custom PCs and servers using Windows/Office client and server software as well as standard processor, chipsets and components available on the open market. Now folded into Microsoft's mainstream partner ecosystem, systems builders are forging closer bonds with Microsoft by adhering to several principles and focusing their businesses on initiatives deemed strategic to Microsoft.

Microsoft estimates that systems builders make up roughly 20% of its base of 841,000 partners worldwide. Many of these partners wear multiple hats in the partner ecosystem, first as systems builders and then as value-added resellers, distributors and consultants. For instance, smaller systems builders are also small value-added resellers that tend to be vertically aligned and specialize in specific markets such as education or the public sector.

There are roughly 30,000 systems builders in the US that fall into three camps, Gold systems builders that number in the hundreds; managed systems builders, which number in the thousands; and the broader, less-defined class of unregistered third-tier systems builders that also purchase Windows through distribution. There are other systems builders who acquire counterfeit Microsoft software or illegally copy Windows on hardware, and pay nothing.

According to CRN, revenues for the top 50 systems builders range between US$1 million (True Tech Systems) and US$1+ billion (Systemax Manufacturing/Tiger Direct). On average, most systems builders report sales under US$30 million annually.

Microsoft tracks authorized systems builders that register with large distributors such as Ingram Micro and Tech Data. According to Microsoft, 47% of its systems builders design PCs and servers for small and mid-market customers while 10% sell into the enterprise, and 20% to 25% sell to consumers. Another seven percent sell to the public sector (state and federal governments) and 10% sell into the education market.

Historically, Microsoft has viewed systems builders as commodity manufacturers (hence the reference to white box, deemed by some as derogatory) but the company is gaining more appreciation for this channel as an effective vehicle for reaching SMB customers and its ability to customize and push out differentiated products such as Windows Media Center PC to consumers and Windows Small Business Server to the SMB market.

Systems builders often bemoan the fact that Microsoft offers better volume pricing on its software to its Top-Tier OEMs—Dell, HP and Fujitsu—but many believe that there are increasing opportunities for systems builders to gain an advantage if they deal directly with Microsoft and forge relationships with its executives. Many systems builders interviewed for this book agree with that assessment despite the fact that the number of systems builders is staggeringly large, and fragmented.

Consider this observation: "Several distributors and systems builders said they have picked up skills and expertise, as well as better pricing, by working directly with Microsoft ... Although working with Microsoft is not as arduous as conventional wisdom would have it, many solution providers say the cost structure for the vendor's software still needs to be addressed ... White-box solution providers and distributors that work directly with Microsoft say that obtaining the proper data and surrounding a business with the right people is all that is needed to ensure good pricing and support from the vendor." (CRN Online, 3 October 2002)

Since 2000, Microsoft has sought to forge closer ties with its systems builders. Many industry observers believe that the company's motivation in this outreach is to extend its reach into the SMB and consumer markets, both of which are high-growth targets for Microsoft. Another motivation is increased competition from Linux in the SMB market. This is a positive turn of events for systems builders, who generally consider themselves to have been historically overlooked by Microsoft partner executives. In 2004, Microsoft offered Office 2003 rebates for the first time for consumers who buy PCs through systems builders. Microsoft also opted to open up one differentiated version of Windows—the Windows XP Media Center 2005—to systems builders for the first time. Up to that point, Microsoft made the code available only to top-tier OEMs.

In terms of its structured relationship with systems builders, Microsoft originally structured an OEM System-Builder Partner Program in the mid-1990s. Traditionally, the company has maintained its system-builder relationships licensing programs separate from Microsoft's mainstream partner program. In 2004, Microsoft officially folded its OEM System-Builder Partner Program into the mainstream Microsoft Partner Program. As part of that initiative, Microsoft established an OEM competency in which systems builders must be certified in order to participate in the program. Microsoft officially launched its OEM Hardware Solutions Competency—one of 13 partner competencies—during the last quarter of 2004. The new program extends many benefits enjoyed by Microsoft's ISVs and services partners for the first time to white-box manufacturers. These include Go-To-Market campaigns, project guides, case studies, expert column archives, sales and marketing tools, Microsoft Action Pack Subscription offer, training, and more technical support, including business-critical phone support as well as newsgroups.

Microsoft works with many thousands of systems builders nationally and globally. Still, a good percentage of these manufacturers have no formal relationship with Microsoft and cannot be tracked because they are registered neither with distributors such as Ingram Micro nor with top-tier Independent Hardware Vendors (IHVs) such as Intel. Some access their components through other means, including other systems builders and the "gray" market. Systems builders that are registered with Microsoft and/or its distributors maintain that their relationships with Microsoft PAMs and field account representatives significantly benefit their businesses, as noted above.

The most effective strategies for systems builders to adopt include but are not limited to:

- sourcing software through official distributors;

- increasing the number of touch points at Microsoft;

- developing systems that are tested and certified according to Microsoft-defined criteria; and

- attaining the OEM competency within the Microsoft Partner Program.

Consider the following case studies of four Microsoft system-builder partners to highlight these imperatives.

Columbus Micro

Columbus Micro Systems (www.columbusmicro.com)—a Microsoft Gold OEM

Systems Builder Partner and affiliate of the Intel Product Dealer Program since the inception of these programs in the mid-1990s—is a 25-employee company based in Columbus, Ohio, with US$8 million in annual revenues. The firm is typically ranked among CRN's Top 50 systems builders annually and was named a gold partner shortly after joining Microsoft's OEM program. Columbus Micro is a managed partner and has one dedicated Microsoft account representative.

Steve Bohman, vice president of operations for Columbus Micro, said partnering requires relationships, and having relationships with both Microsoft and Intel is crucial for systems builders. "Both have legitimized the systems builder community," Mr Bohman said. "Systems builders have a lot to gain by building relationships with Microsoft's partner executives and joining their partner program."

Systems builders that are registered with Microsoft, for example, have account representatives they can call to get critical support as well as marketing help for hosting conferences and seminars. Systems builders can get advance warning on product launches, promotions, product roadmaps and Microsoft's annual marketing campaigns. Such advance notice gives them a competitive advantage over the thousands of other systems builders. Mr Bohman continued: "If you are out flying blind, the customer might be coming to you with questions you cannot answer alone. More and more systems builders are realizing the value of the vendors' channel programs out there and the ones who are successful are the ones who have taken advantage of support from the major companies. In difficult economic times, we have had a lot of channel members that fell by the wayside and many of those were the ones who did not know what was going on. Melding certified partners and OEM systems builders into one program is a transition for some but it offers many new benefits." His most important piece of advice to systems builders is to go through official channels when sourcing Microsoft products. "Job number one is to play by the rules. Buy Microsoft products through an authorized distributor so you show up on Microsoft's radar," Mr Bohman advises. "If you buy from another systems builder, you are a nobody. Microsoft is really looking for many new opportunities through the systems builder channel. There has been a big push of Small Business Server into the channel and they want Windows Media Center to be a channel play. I think Intel and Microsoft realize we have a more trusted relationship with our customers than the multinational corporate Tier One OEMs do. They see us more as early adopters of newer technology because we are trying to avoid the commoditization that Tier Ones promote."

Like ISVs and service providers, systems builders that are Microsoft-centric enjoy more help, Mr Bohman notes. "Being committed to Microsoft benefits us in terms of the level of support we get from Microsoft. We can show better ROI for Windows over Linux."

Mr Bohman says that Microsoft has some issues to work out regarding the distribution channel for systems builders, but that it has been receptive to criticism. "There are challenges around having the top 12 distributors trying to service the entire systems-builder channel. Not everyone can go to Ingram Micro and Tech Data to get products. There is a place for sub-distributors."

But these are essentially growing pains in a program that has been successful in marshalling the force of participating systems builders, who benefit more than they suffer from the kinks in the system if they take their relationship with Microsoft, and the benefits of partnership, as seriously as they should.

Technology Execution Network Corp. (TENCorp)

TENCorp (www.tencorp.com) is a Microsoft Certified Gold Partner with a competency in networking infrastructure, a Microsoft Authorized Education Reseller and an OEM Systems Builder founded in 1993. It has 45 employees and US$11 million in annual revenues (46% in services, 18% in custom systems, 36% in systems integration). The Needham, Massachusetts-based company partners with both Microsoft and Apple. TENCorp president Mike Healey observed that the firm's system-builder role is secondary to services, but TENCorp is considered one of Microsoft's Top OEMs because of its volume of systems sales. TENCorp has a variety of Microsoft PAMs that help drive its three respective businesses: services, systems and education. Having many "touch points" at Microsoft is important, Mr Healey commented. "I would not want one person from Microsoft to have all my business. We have to have a lot of touch points with them because of their size. They have so many little programs that we have got to dig into it because we might be leaving dollars on the table."

PC Wholesale

PC Wholesale (www.buypcw.com) is a Microsoft Gold Certified Partner, Microsoft Authorized Education Reseller that was founded in 1991 in San Antonio, Texas. Its executives said that systems builders can grow their businesses and access resources, such as additional training and marketing, by making connection points within Microsoft, participating in the new partner points program and achieving all necessary certifications. For instance, submitting systems for testing by Microsoft's Windows Hardware Quality Labs (WHQL) enables systems builders to participate in co-branding opportunities with Microsoft and to meet criteria required by corporate purchasing departments and retailers.

Systems builders can increasingly leverage the Microsoft organization to gain competitive advantage. "We have three different areas of touch with Microsoft," notes Warren Wilkinson, the firm's president. "We have a good relationship with Microsoft, much better than before. We use our relationship with Microsoft as an asset and promote our standing with Microsoft. It gives us a competitive advantage because we get a lot of dedication from our account representative. We have training for our resellers, and our account representative will send a national strategist here. We get access to those people that our competitors do not and that gives us better standing."

Systems builders may be eligible for significant benefits under Microsoft's Partner Program, Mr Wilkinson noted. "We have been primarily a Microsoft partner and we purchase about US$1 million in software from Microsoft each year. We will be under Microsoft's new Microsoft Gold Partner program. They re-did the whole program and, under the new guidelines, a lot of resellers will not be in it. We will be at a level that a lot of white-box manufacturers will not be able to achieve. It is a point-based thing. You get points for volume and for certifications. It is good that they are doing this and I like what Microsoft has done. It makes people put up or shut up."

Source Code Corp.

Source Code Corp. (www.sourcecode.com) is a Microsoft Systems Builder Partner and components distributor founded in 1992, that is based in Norwood, Massachusetts. It supplies VARs and solution providers with custom, turnkey systems and components as well as inventory-management and product-lifecycle services. The systems builder meets with its Microsoft PAM at least twice per month and advises others to take advantage of Microsoft's increasing interest in the system-builder channel. Source Code vice president of sales David Lebov believes there are increasing opportunities for white-box manufacturers to sell specialized, custom PCs and servers running Microsoft software in the small office-home office (SoHo) market. But he maintains that systems builders need to refocus their business models on emerging opportunities and the new form factors identified by Microsoft.

"Dell, IBM and HP are very good at servicing the mass market so if a systems builder's only core competency is to build a personal computer then it is unlikely that they are going to get that business. Systems builders and VARs have to develop a core competency outside a typical PC in niche areas, such as the Windows XP Media Center, which you cannot just buy off the shelf at Best Buy. They should get into servers and Tablet PCs and unique opportunities that mass manufacturers will not go after, such as clustering. Microsoft sees that. The way the market is going should direct systems builders to what they should focus on but a lot of them do not have the capacity to refocus. Microsoft needs an ecosystem to build those products. And they are right on top of it."

Mr Lebov said systems builders should get their OEM competency certification and take advantage of all training available from Microsoft. Systems builders should also have their equipment qualified according to the requirements of the Windows Hardware Quality Labs (WHQL). Manufacturers that wish to license Microsoft's "Designed for Windows" logo, for instance, must meet requirements for server, desktop and mobile systems running Windows XP Home Edition (32-bit), Windows XP Professional (64-bit and 32-bit), Windows Server 2003, Standard Edition (64-bit and 32-bit), Windows Server 2003, Enterprise Edition (64-bit and 32-bit) and Windows 2000."

———◆———

As noted, many systems builders are VARs and some VARs are also systems builders. As margins on products continue to slide, VARs are increasingly relying on services as their key revenue generator and source of profits. VARs are evolving in step with Microsoft and embracing new opportunities in managed services, security, storage and serving unique small business needs.

———◆———

There are several other categories of Microsoft reseller that span multiple partner categories. A value-added reseller (VAR), for instance, is a Microsoft reseller that sells products and provides value-added services, such as installation and implementation services for customers. A VAR, also known as a solution provider, is often a Microsoft Certified Partner or Gold Certified Partner whose business is based on a product-led services model. That is, VARs endorse a product and provide services only for that product. Value-added providers provide the same product sales and technology services to the smallest customers. A VAR may have a system-builder business just as a technology distributor may. As noted earlier, there are no hard rules that define each of these partner classes. VARs increasingly offer a mix of products and services because declining product margins have made a pure-product business model unsustainable. In one study commissioned by Microsoft and conducted by Management Insight Technologies, several types of partners often ranked as pure solution providers fell under the VAR/VAP heading, including network integrators, application integrators and systems integrators.

As with other service providers, VARs can gain traction in partnering with Microsoft by aligning their go-to-market approach with the company's. Consider the case of Nortec.

VAR Attains Acclaim by Partnering with MCS, Pushing License Renewals

Nortec Communications (www.nortec.com)—a Microsoft Certified Partner and Microsoft's 2004 VAR Partner of the Year, based in Falls Church, Virginia, and founded in 1991—has an advanced infrastructure solutions competency for enterprise systems. The company derives roughly 70% of its revenues from its Microsoft-related business with the remainder made up of security hardware, telephony systems, Voice Over Internet Protocol (VoIP) and Veritas storage services.

In one year, between 2003 and 2004, Nortec annual revenues grew from US$3.1 million to US$5.2 million by skillfully finessing a cozy relationship with Microsoft

Consulting Services and by focusing on a key Microsoft priority: licensing renewals. In many ways, Nortec had been priming for growth for some time. But it was one gamble that sealed the firm's fate, the proverbial roll of the dice, that led to a powerful payback. Nortec spun platinum out of gold after bidding on a NetWare migration deal it was confident it would win—but then opted to collaborate and engage with MCS. That decision to collaborate served two purposes: it ensured a nice customer win and an enhanced partnership with Microsoft. That wise relationship-building strategy worked: it also earned Nortec a new batch of influential Microsoft friends.

Today, 70% of Nortec's business comes from the SMB space including software, hardware, support and security business and more than 30% is derived from its enterprise accounts. "Many of those deals came from Microsoft. We did not focus on our partnership before and we tried to be all things to all people. Partnering with Microsoft has been extremely successful for us. Our success is snowballing." But Mr Grose also emphasized that cross-pollination is essential in keeping the relationship strong. "Nortec continues to bring deals to Microsoft as they are rewarded with enterprise gigs. Microsoft does not want VARs with their hands out," Mr Grose said.

Nortec also advises services partners to align their business models to help Microsoft in key areas of importance to the software giant. Nortec honed in on a couple of Microsoft's ambitions for 2003-2004, one of which is articularly important fr this chapter: licensing/software assurance (SA) contracts. Nortec became proactive about assessing its clients' compliance with Microsoft licensing contracts and brokered many new and updated licensing contracts for Microsoft. Mr Grose said, for example, that Nortec demonstrated an 82% attach rate in getting new SA contracts signed among its customer base—significantly higher than the 40% average rate. They were so successful that Microsoft started feeding Nortec accounts to call for renewals. Nortec aligned itself with Microsoft sales and estimates it influenced between US$3 million and US$5 million in software sales in one year. How did they get those renewals? Cold calling existing accounts to remind them of their need to sign new their Microsoft licenses.

Nortec also shared its success story with the top executives at Microsoft. In 2004, Nortec's partnering guru George Hammerschmidt wrote a succinct letter to Microsoft CEO Steve Ballmer informing him of the firm's growing success in the Microsoft ecosystem. That letter made the rounds, and was passed on to Allison Watson and her team. At Microsoft's Channel Summit in May, Nortec was named Microsoft's 2004 National VAR Partner of the Year—the first year Microsoft bestowed this award. The letter was also read in its entirety by a key Microsoft executive on stage at the company's 2004 Worldwide Partner Conference. Positive feedback can pay off nicely with Microsoft in publicity and building credibility.

In summary, Microsoft is investing more in its system-builder and VAR channel in order to grow its franchise in the SMB market and to fend off competitive open-source thrusts, which pose a greater, more direct threat to Microsoft in a market that is more price sensitive than mid-market or enterprise customers. Some VARs are experimenting with Linux and open-source solutions to determine if they can generate more margins and profits. To Microsoft, it is fruitless to argue the cost of a Microsoft license versus an open-source license. The company argues that its products are easier to use, richer in functionality and more efficient, to say nothing of its well-oiled delivery channel of systems builders and VARs that provide far more value to customers than a comparable Linux solution.

In the end, the systems builders and VARs are part and parcel of the value chain that enables Windows Small Business Server 2003, for instance, to yield more returns for a small business than a competitive Linux solution. And some VARs have adopted Microsoft's agent model in which they can generate fees for influencing a Microsoft product sale. Others are pursuing application server provider (ASP) and hosting models once again. And still other VARs are moving product and pushing new license types that Microsoft has debuted in recent years. In general, as Microsoft moves, so do its partners in this category, and the more successful of them move in the same direction as Microsoft.

Windows Mobile/Embedded OEMs and IHVs

This class of software reseller sells devices with pre-loaded versions of Windows CE or Windows Mobile operating systems or Windows XP Embedded. The resellers channel also includes manufacturers and vendors of devices and appliances that incorporate Windows CE and Windows Mobile operating system software, Windows XP Embedded, as well as retailers who sell Microsoft's home, entertainment and business software directly to consumers and small businesses. It is interesting to note how Microsoft is trying to grow the respective businesses of this class of partners.

Microsoft's Mobile and Embedded Devices and Communications (MED) was formed in January 2004. It combines the Embedded Devices Group and the Mobile Devices Group. It is the smallest but fastest-growing of Microsoft's seven business units. In the first quarter of FY05, MED accounted for just US$69 million of Microsoft's US$9.1 billion in revenues—less than one percent—but it achieved a year-on-year growth rate of 30%. By the end of the second quarter of FY05, its revenues had increased to US$91 million.

Microsoft has significant ambitions for this segment based on the increasingly mobile workforce and demands for ubiquitous access to information from any device–anywhere, anytime, any way. Microsoft is also making steady gains in the embedded-systems space, which caters to a variety of vertical industries that use terminals and kiosks. OEMs and their reseller partners in this market are trying to capitalize on growing opportunities with Microsoft's help.

Microsoft runs specialized programs for OEMs, ISVs and services partners that focus on Windows Mobile and Embedded operating systems. The Mobile and Embedded partner programs offer partners additional benefits and support for these specialized Windows platforms markets. These programs complement the mainstream partner program. Partners in these specialized programs are also required to gain partner certification but are eligible for additional program benefits. Microsoft runs a separate Windows Mobile Partner program that offers unique benefits, yet partners in this group must earn a mobile competency under the Information Worker Solutions competency.

In 2005, Microsoft plans to debut two new server-centric thin-client Windows XP versions for the mobile workforce and task workers. These clients will make it easier for systems builders and OEMs, for example, to build PCs and smaller mobile form factors without having to do their own Windows CE or embedded customization and development work.

Windows Mobile

In June 2003, Microsoft introduced its Windows Mobile brand. Partners in the Windows Mobile partner program include OEMs, independent hardware vendors (IHVs), consumer/enterprise ISVs, mobile Internet content providers (MICPs), wireless carriers, systems integrators (for third-party products), solution providers (for customer products), VARs and application service providers (ASPs).

The Windows Mobile partner program is based on three distinct Microsoft operating systems:

- Windows CE, a standardized 32-bit real-time operating system that is used in small-footprint devices, including industrial controllers, communications hubs, point-of-sale terminals, cameras, telephones, and home—entertainment devices;

- Windows Mobile 2003 Second Edition/Windows Mobile 2005, the basis of the operating system for PocketPC products, Smartphones and Portable Media Center. Windows Mobile 2005 unifies the separate flavors of Windows CE developed for each device into one code base to simplify development for application vendors and device manufacturers; and

- Windows XP Embedded, a componentized version of Windows XP that is largely based on Windows XP Professional. This highly customizable version of Windows contains 10,000 components that developers can use to build operating systems for retail point-of-sale terminals, thin-client terminals and advanced set-top boxes.

The Windows Mobile Solutions partner program encompasses a broad array of partners, including OEMs that develop PocketPC, Smartphones and Portable Media Center devices, as well as ISVs, systems integrators and solution providers. The goal of the program is to build a micro-ecosystem around the development, distribution and consumption of wireless data software and services. Microsoft lists 11,000 Windows Mobile partners and 17,000 Windows Mobile applications. (UBS Global Communications Conference presentation by Melvin Flowers, New York, 18 November 2004) Microsoft is working to unify its mobile effects under a single platform, Windows Mobile 2005, and to offer improved integration between Windows Mobile 2005-based Smartphones and the Longhorn version of Windows. This is define the standard Windows and Windows Mobile devices and software. Longhorn, for example, will feature a new synchronization manager to facilitate Smartphone synchronization with Windows desktops.

There are several programs and resources aimed to help mobile partners:

- *Mobility Partner Advisory Council (MPAC):* This includes representatives from systems integrators, independent software vendors, solution providers and independent hardware vendors that develop solutions for the Windows Mobile products. PAC members include: Tolt Technologies, Accenture, Capgemini, Conchango and Catapult Systems.

- *Windows Mobile Solutions Partner Program (WMSPP):* This is an entry-level program that has few requirements; Microsoft offers a variety of benefits to WMSPP partners, including free software and a partner solutions directory.

- *Microsoft Mobile2Market:* This is a certification and marketing program for mobile ISV applications that helps ISVs increase revenues and simplifies application development; it also provides distribution channels worldwide.

- *Designed for Windows Mobile logo:* ISVs can apply for a Designed-for-Windows-Mobile certification that certifies the compatibility of their applications on PDAs and mobile phones running Windows Mobile software. Microsoft provides the logo testing.

Of course, the benefits of the Windows Mobile Partner Program depend on what partners put into it. In other words, aggressive engagement with Microsoft to drive the success of technology sales is the name of the game, not a listing in the program directory. Iteration2's case makes this point clear.

Iteration2

Iteration2 (www.iteration2.com)—a Microsoft Gold Certified Partner and ISV based at Irvine, California—focuses on Microsoft's MBS and classic products and mobilizing these applications for specific industries. The firm is a service provider with vertical expertise and enterprise mobility practices that complement its core competencies. For example, Iteration2 provides value added services around mobilizing business applications to enable better field service and logistics services for its customers. The company also mobilizes SharePoint data for team workers that are geographically dispersed. Iteration2 is one of roughly 100 partners in the Mobility PAC, and is also on the MBS and RFID PACs.

Simon Chan, Iteration2's director of business development and a founding member of the MPAC, says that adoption of Windows mobility is increasing as an enterprise application platform and a leading application for field-level sales forces. Mr Chan oversees the Microsoft relationship for Iteration2. It is a multi-faceted relationship since Iteration2 works with Microsoft classic and MBS products as well as mobility products. Iteration2 has a PAM for its MBS and classic practices as well as a partner engagement manager (PEM). It also works with Microsoft enterprise mobility sales specialists that work with the firm and others to drive revenue generation. The PAMs drive sales of its MBS business but they "do not touch" the enterprise mobility space, Mr Chan said. In order to engage on mobility projects, partners need to engage with mobility sales teams in the field and with Windows Mobile Group executives at Seattle.

The specialized nature of mobility enables adept Microsoft mobility partners to get substantial support from Microsoft: "They take us right in with them on deals. That is tangible. They are in a customer account and then they bring in the right partners to drive the deals. We get support from Microsoft in terms of funding for customer pilots and support on the marketing side for trade shows and development of case studies. Microsoft is our best partner."

Windows Embedded

The Windows Embedded Partner (WEP) Program was founded in 2000. Its goal is to advance Microsoft's embedded operating-system platforms, Windows XP Embedded and Windows CE. The partner program includes a wide variety of partners that bring these platforms to market. Microsoft created a brand name and logo for its embedded operating system platforms: Windows Powered.

Partner types include systems integrators, enterprise systems integrators, ISVs, silicon vendors, IHVs and original design manufacturers that often wear multiple hats. That is, many of these partners span two or more specialized partner categories. DST Corp, BSquare, Venture Development Corp and Applied Data Systems are systems integrators that develop customized software and build solutions for embedded devices. ADS is also an IHV, TenAsys is an ISV, Fujitsu is an OEM whose point-of-sale terminals run Windows XP Embedded. Intel is a silicon vendor whose embedded x86 processors are designed for many devices, including PDAs, Smartphones, thin-client terminals, gateway devices, set-top boxes and Voice-Over-IP telephones. Arrow Electronics is a top distributor serving this specialized group of partners in the US. Advantech Technologies is a Korea-based partner that serves as a distributor, systems integrators and solution provider.

WEP Gold-level members are considered first for customer engagements, product referrals, and services engagement opportunities with Microsoft's Embedded salesgroup's named accounts and solutions center.

——■——

Microsoft's Windows Embedded group has been traditionally vertically focused because it serves targeted industries that make use of customized, componentized operating-system platforms. Microsoft is trying to make it easier for solution providers and systems integrators to develop robust solutions faster by offering up packaged solutions for select industries as well as plug-and-play features that contribute to Microsoft's unique value relative to other platform providers.

In 2005, for instance, Microsoft introduced its first embedded solution, Windows XP Embedded (XPE) for Point of Service, for specific verticals: retail and hospitality. The specialized Windows XPE platform enables retail and hospitality establishments to simplify the setup, use and management of point-of-sale and point-of-service systems such as terminals and kiosks. BSquare and Venture Development Corp. are systems-integration partners that deploy solutions to the field.

Demand for lower-cost standard platforms has enabled Windows and Linux to achieve enormous growth in the embedded market and to capture market share since 2000. Microsoft faces competition in this market from traditional vendors that have embraced Linux and open-source solutions more generally. The ability of OEMs, IHVs, ISVs and customers to modify the open-source code has been a unique advantage to Microsoft's Linux competitors. Microsoft has responded by making the source code for its embedded operating systems available to partners under specific license agreements that allow partners to modify and distribute the code without revealing those changes. In these ways, Microsoft offers partners and customers unique benefits that are not extended to Windows XP partners. Many of these partners have longstanding relationships with Microsoft. Wyse is one of them, and its case is instructive for partners in this space.

Wyse Technologies

Wyse (www.wyse.com)—a San Jose, California-based provider of network-centric computing solutions that has been named Microsoft's Windows OEM Embedded Partner of the Year for three consecutive years—is a leading provider of thin-client terminals and management software. Wyse has partnered with Microsoft and Citrix for more than a decade. Linux has made significant inroads into the embedded market due to the componentized nature of the operating system, which makes it possible for device manufacturers and ISVs to develop custom versions of the software-optimized terminals and other devices. In 2004, Wyse announced a Linux version of its thin client terminal.

Like Unisys, Wyse finds that it is possible for partners to support alternative operating systems as long as Microsoft remains the top supplier. The emergence of Linux as a competitor has motivated Microsoft to address issues that its embedded partners encounter in the market more quickly, driving new functionality at the operating-system level. Wyse also gets significant support from Microsoft because there are a smaller number of embedded partners than services partners or ISVs. Additionally, the relationships formed between hardware vendors, device manufactures, software developers and systems integrators need to be highly integrated because of the customized, integrated nature of an embedded solution. There are often joint activities held by one or more of these partners in the Windows Embedded community.

Other Resellers

In addition to the reseller-partners discussed above, there are other specific types of reseller that focus on government and education markets. Microsoft has special programs for these resellers. Microsoft's Authorized Education Resellers (AERs), for instance, are specially trained and authorized to sell Microsoft Academic Edition software products and licenses to educational institutions. Microsoft also has an authorized reseller program for partners in the government market, and is promoting more activity by partners to develop services and vertical practices for local, state and federal governments, as well as public agencies and non-profits.

Reselling Remains an Opportunity

Nortec is one example of a VAR that successfully capitalized on Microsoft's call to action to all partners to secure license renewals among its customer base. There are other licensing programs that afford resellers opportunities. In 2003, Microsoft launched a licensing program for SMB customers called Open Value as well as an agent model for resellers that successfully influenced customers to buy in. The option allows SMBs to buy company-wide licenses that yield up to 25% in software savings over alternative pricing schemes, and it allows SMB customers to spread their payments over a three-year term. In some ways, the model replicates the value of the EAs for SMB customers. Microsoft also offers Open Business and Open Volume deals to SMB customers. With additional Open Value payment options, however, SMB customers with up to 750 seats can enjoy the benefits of annuity payments, software savings and upgrade rights via Software Assurance.

Cincinnati-based IT Advisor Group, for example, is one VAR that leapt on this opportunity. IT Advisor Group established itself as one of 20 managed partners in Ohio, as a dedicated Microsoft shop and by forming a close relationship with its partner account manager. The firm formally distinguished itself in Microsoft's eyes in 2003, by selling US$1 million worth of Open Value licenses, more than any other reseller sold during the first 12 months of Microsoft's new licensing program for SMB customer. Matt Scherocman, the firm's director, believes his strong relationship with his PAM enabled him to drive many of these deals. His willingness to partner 100% with Microsoft, embrace the company's solutions selling strategy and understand the different management-by-objectives (MBOs) of partner representatives helped him cultivate a lot of goodwill with the software giant. He also believes the razor-sharp focus on the medium-sized business segment is a good strategy because it firmly places this service provider in one core Microsoft customer segment rather than straddling two segments, as many solution providers do.

Distributors Evolve to Serve Customers' Needs

Distributors also participate in the reseller value chain by delivering value to Microsoft's resellers. Microsoft has historically backed a two-tiered distribution model in which its bread-and-butter software products—Windows and Office, primarily—have been sold by mainstream distributors to large and small resellers. These distributors work closely with value-added resellers and solution providers. At one point, three top distributors—Ingram Micro, Tech Data and Merisel—were responsible for distributing nearly all Microsoft products.

Like solution providers and ISVs, distributors are evolving to meet the specialized needs of their reseller customers. Globally, Microsoft counts roughly 370 authorized distributors worldwide that provide specialized services for partners in select geographies, customers and verticals. In the US, Microsoft works with fewer than 10 distributors. Like LARs and VARs, the distribution industry has experienced consolidation; those firms that remain standing have become more specialized and focused in their offerings in order to serve the changing needs of the flotilla of large-account and value-added resellers that sail alongside the SS Microsoft.

"Microsoft used to have more distribution partners and it entertained an all-for-one and one-for-all strategy instead of picking out each distributor's strengths and weaknesses," observed Jodi Honore, vice president of vendor management for Ingram Micro North America. But the business has changed, and distributors are evolving in step with resellers and ISVs to serve Microsoft's customer-segmentation and verticalization initiatives. Microsoft has pared down the number of distributors and now assigns business opportunities according to their competencies. Naturally, as the nature of selling software changed dramatically from packaged products to licensing, so, too, has the role of all players in the channel, including distributors and their customers.

Ingram Micro and Tech Data remain Microsoft's top global distributors and Synnex has recently emerged as a major distributor. D&H Distributing is a specialty distributor. Each of these distributors is shifting with the winds of change in the SS Microsoft's reselling business. Distributors are Go-To-Market partners with Microsoft and have refocused their energies on the company's 11 GTM strategies and on vertical markets, such as financial services and the retail sector. Ingram Micro, for instance, is taking an active role in distributing Microsoft Business Solutions and CRM products in the US. A handful of specialty distributors are forming alliances with software vendors in select markets for select products. D&H Distributing, for example, signed up to help Microsoft gain greater penetration in two markets that have proved challenging for Microsoft: education and customer relationship management (CRM).

Microsoft's agent model has also impacted distributors. When Microsoft took its enterprise-agreement licensing direct, many distributors lost up to 20% of their revenues. To grow their businesses, some distributors are focused exclusively on serving the needs of value-added resellers and solution providers who serve the SMB market. Many are specializing in licensing services and vertical markets. For instance, distributors provide account-management services for resellers and online tools that alert resellers when customers' licenses are due for renewal.

So the same sort of full-service potential exhorted for downstream providers applies upstream, too, with a corresponding meshing of relationships between both sets of resellers. This integration benefits the channel and tightens the reins of supplier and distributor orchestration. But it is a challenging response to market changes and Microsoft's adjustments to its reseller-relationship working model. Microsoft has steered distributors toward providing specialized services based on its agenda for SMB partners.

Consider some of the tactics employed by Ingram Micro and D&H to meet new challenges through its refined partnership with Microsoft and the evolving needs of its customer base: the value-added resellers and systems builders who serve the SMB market. Ingram Micro, for example, has adjusted its business model to focus on value-added resellers that serve SMB customers.

Ingram Micro (www.ingrammicro.com)—a global distributor of software and hardware products with US$22 billion in annual revenues, of which 50% are Microsoft-related—continues to serve as a top Microsoft distribution partner globally and wears a number of hats in the process: authorized license distributor for OEMs and classic distributor for licensing packaged products.

The firm has also retooled its business to focus on Microsoft GTMs, the SMB market as well as industry verticals in order to serve the evolving needs of Microsoft VARs and systems builders. In this way, Ingram Micro is helping to push Microsoft forward and to fend off competition by taking a more active role in attending to the needs of systems builders and VARs, which serve the SMB market. They can choose to pre-load their systems with Linux or Windows and thus need special care from distributors on behalf of Microsoft.

Most distributors have multiple revenue streams. D&H Distributing (www.dandh.com), for example, is a distributor and systems builder based at Harrisburg, Pennsylvania, that has been in business for almost 90 years and serves the needs of resellers and VARs. The future of distribution is customer specialization and vertical focus, said Dan Schwab, vice president of marketing for D&H Distributing. Over time, as Microsoft identifies and pursues vertical opportunities, distributors such as D&H Distributing have to achieve a higher-touch model with Microsoft to provide appropriate products to their vertical customers. For instance, distributors need different touch points at Microsoft for various Windows offerings being developed for SMB customers and end-consumers, such as Windows Small Business Server and Windows Media Center Edition, respectively. "Historically we had one person who was our conduit across all segments and they separated that out so we have two dedicated people now, an account manager for home/systems builder and a dedicated marketing person to drive software revenues. We also work with product groups."

Systems builders and VARs are better positioned to partner with Microsoft now than in the past because it is in the SMB market that Microsoft is most vulnerable to Linux. "These guys compete with the gray market and naked PCs that ship without the operating system," Mr Schwab said. "One thing that is clear is that Microsoft wants to touch the influencers and those that influence purchasing decisions, whether they are consulting, VAR or reseller, and that is who they want to engage with and we see that as a good effort on our part to sell more products."

Distributors also partner closely with Microsoft and are launching programs and services such as managed services to move their value propositions forward. For this class of partner, the level of engagement is also intense. "Whenever you engage with companies at the level of Microsoft or Intel, it is never a one-to-one engagement. It is a team-on-team engagement—sales, marketing, accounting, and so on—so it is a full-course endeavor. You are never half-in and half-out. You are committed. We have people who are dedicated to the Microsoft partnership. We have four people whose sole job is to work with Microsoft," Mr Schwab said. "Microsoft has been very consistent in its distribution and reseller channel, recognizing the fact that in its entirety the channel is its largest customer."

Direct Marketers / Retailers Evolve, As Well

All partners in Microsoft's product distribution channel rely on volume for margins and have consequently suffered in the past several years. As distributors evolve to serve the expanding needs of their reseller customers and Microsoft's segmentation and vertical initiatives, direct marketers, likewise, are evolving their business models and adding new value-added services. The highly efficient model of direct marketers—the direct model—has enabled players to stake a bigger claim in the software distribution market. Direct marketers use the same direct model as OEM reseller Dell in distributing software to the masses. Yet, as customers require end-to-end solutions, DMRs are attempting to pair with other partners in Microsoft's partner ecosystem to fill gaps in their product-delivery service. As corporate customers purchase through direct marketers, it has prompted Microsoft and other vendors to create agent programs to ensure that services partners and smaller resellers are compensated for influencing a software purchase.

The top three direct market resellers (DMRs) are CDW, PC Connection and Insight Express. Direct marketers are large software resellers that buy half of their goods from distributors and roughly half from Microsoft, and sell directly to customers. Their size and influence in the industry and as Microsoft partners is important to note. Consider CDW: it was number 381 on the Fortune 500 in 2003, a US$4.7 billion business based on the resale of 80,000 hardware and software products, of which Microsoft products alone accounted for nearly seven percent of the total. CDW serves the consumer, small-to-medium business and enterprise markets. It qualifies as both a retailer and a LAR. In addition, CDW has branched out into services and assorted system-builder solutions. CDW and the other mentioned firms are huge and they have succeeded as a direct or indirect result of partnering with Microsoft.

While the largest DMRs access as much as 50% of their inventory through distributors, they are often viewed, like Dell, as a direct competitor to traditional channel partners, such as solution providers, VARs and distributors. Like other software reseller channels, the DMR industry has experienced significant consolidation and changes in business models as software margins have dipped to between three and four percent, down from at least eight percent in the IT-buying boom. CDW's purchase of MicroWarehouse in autumn 2003, created a US$5 billion giant, and Insight Express's acquisition of Comark a year earlier expanded it even more so into the solution provider and distributor markets. Inasmuch as these Microsoft partners have expanded their software reselling empires, they are also experimenting with new partnering models with Microsoft's solution providers and VARs to ensure that they deliver full solutions to customers. Their doing so is viewed with suspicion by Microsoft's traditional channel partners.

Based on the perspectives of these resellers and a refined awareness of market conditions, DMRs need to bear in mind that they have two key requirements when partnering with Microsoft:

- grow, even if Microsoft falters, and bring in new customers or face de-authorization and/or loss of rebate funds; and

- Microsoft believes many customers are using pirated or copied software and it is pushing DMRs, at least, to find these customers and sign them up.

There are certain mechanics and guidelines to be observed by DMRs when partnering with Microsoft. Attendance to paperwork is an imperative; it cannot be overlooked. In terms of the overhead, one of the mentioned DMRs has a team of 10 people whose sole job is to manage day-to-day transactions and to provide an audit trail and asset-management services for customers and especially for Microsoft. The process is not automated but many think it should be. "It is a big expense for resellers, but consider it a cost of doing business with Microsoft."

Network Service Providers:
Software as a Service

The Network Service Provider (NSP) is another type of reseller that has embraced an emerging business model in the software distribution market: software as a service and application hosting. Microsoft's NSP Partners provide a variety of services to enterprise and SMB customers. The broad array of NSPs includes application hosting firms, internet service providers, mobile operators, network operators and cable operators as well as the developers and consultants affiliated with those service providers. Microsoft offers several hosted licensing models and programs for NSP-partners, including Windows-based Hosting, Hosted Exchange and Call Center Frameworks.

Until 2004, these service providers were housed separately under the Microsoft Gold Certified Partner Program for Hosting and Application Services. After 2004, Microsoft opted to fold its NSP-partners into its mainstream partner program. They were migrated to the Microsoft Advanced Infrastructure Partner (AIP) competency. AIPs in the Gold certification program provide managed application services, managed web hosting and .NET-hosted services. They operate data centers and mobile networks for Microsoft and include Attenda, Data Return, MCI, DMData, Intensive, Rackspace and KT IDC.

Another class of NSPs are Application Service Providers (ASPs), which are certified for specific Microsoft product and platform-hosted solutions including Hosted Exchange, eCommerce, Office Online, Windows Media Services and hosted business applications. These include Apptix (a case-studied firm in Chapter Five), Equant, Surebridge, USA.net and USInternetworking.

Microsoft has provided infrastructure and blueprints designed to enable those service providers to host applications and services with varying degrees of success. In 2001, for instance, Microsoft developed an automated purposing framework for service provides in the company's partner solutions center. Microsoft also has Windows Web hosting and ASP.NET hosting programs.

During the dot.com era, Application Service Providers (ASP), Internet Service Providers (ISPs) and all types of service providers emerged. ISPs prospered but the ASP market proved, at that time anyway, to be unsustainable. Microsoft's planned .NET platform based on XML web services and code-named Hailstorm was cancelled. Most service providers shut down or shifted gears and served as outsourced data centers for customers. The market for web services, likewise, was nascent.

Microsoft maintains that there will be a strong market one day for ASPs based on customer demand for outsourced applications and software-as-a-service in both the enterprise and SMB markets, and the company is relying heavily on partners to make this happen. Microsoft itself delivers software updates as a service to its customers but expects that professional hosting companies will provide value-added services for selling software by subscription or in an on-demand mode. These models also have significant application in the utility computing model espoused for the data center of the future. Partners are currently working to make the economics of the hosted applications and services model more appealing to corporate customers and consumers.

Reseller Partnering Tactics in a Volatile Market

A Microsoft reseller-partner's business is no longer just about volume, volume, volume—it is now equally about value. Such partners must adhere to several principles to remain afloat and to maintain a place in Microsoft's ecosystem. These include strengthening relationships at the customer account level; knowing the programs and taking advantage of Microsoft's evolution; leveraging Microsoft's brand in accounts; and educating their sales forces to focus on industry verticals but to be guided by Microsoft's GTMs.

The consolidation of the Microsoft reseller industry has made for fewer players. There are a number of tactics that resellers can employ to manage their businesses in this tighter marketplace, as outlined below:

- keep connected to customers, and deepen the relationship with value-added services whether these are provided by your firm or by partners;

- push licensing programs and Software Assurance because that is what Microsoft is pushing for (currently 75% of all Microsoft software is sold through licensing programs);

- focus on distinct customer segments for new sales, especially in the middle and upper mid-markets because that is where Microsoft intends to dominate;

- have the highest-educated field sales organization on Microsoft's platforms and products, and on what business problems they solve—and sell more of them;

- know the Microsoft discounting programs—the reseller must absolutely understand the programmatic elements and how to map into them to be successful in partnering with Microsoft;

- master the principal elements of success in Microsoft reselling—scalability and volume—particularly as margins have shrunk to as low as two-to-three percent, and go after new accounts and renewals;

- expand services—managed services, deployment services—and develop models for pay-per-use software;

- ensure that customers deploy the Microsoft software they licensed, and their satisfaction with them by measuring and quantifying a positive return on investment and lowered costs of ownership;

- form closer alliances with local and regional VARs and services partners to meet the above requirements, and with Microsoft Certified Learning Partners to ensure that customers use free training offered to IT administrators as part of SA;

- investigate, choose and aggressively pursue a unique reseller strategy in each market; and, finally,

- leverage all of the Microsoft resources at your disposal and work with other Microsoft partners to solidify and extend your favorable position in the market based on your pursuit of all of the above tactics that are appropriate to your firm.

In general, picking a unique strategy for each market is the key to reseller success. Keep the focus on the customer first and, second, on the supplier. In some markets, going into an account with Microsoft is clearly the best strategy since resellers have a unique opportunity to leverage Microsoft branding to sell products. However, in other markets—where your firm is well-established, for example—you ought to focus your organizational energy directly on customers and only opportunistically bring Microsoft into them.

Increasingly, resellers are teaming with VARs and other partners to deliver end-to-end solutions to customers. Resellers must also observe the rules of the partnering game, which are set by Microsoft Account ownership is Microsoft's goal in the enterprise and corporate account space. Microsoft has hundreds of named accounts in the Fortune 1000 market. In the small and middle market, reseller account ownership is the best option. This will continue to be a key differentiator and opportunity for both LARs and VARs. Educating your staff to the differences between the two sectors is a key element of your strategy, and something that is relatively easily done.

You must also know that the partnering game is as dynamic as Microsoft's culture, strategy, organization and response to global industry trends, such as acquisitions, globalization and verticalization. Account teams and licensing programs are in constant flux in the Microsoft world. Adjusting to these changes on a quarterly and annual basis, and understanding discount periods and incentive programs, are vital to your stability and success. Select customers are up for licenses and maintenance renewals each quarter; it is, therefore, important for resellers to be mindful of the ebbs and flows of business opportunities each quarter, adjusting and assigning resources accordingly. Again, the yearly push in June for year-end sales is also critical, and you must be perceived as being on-board when the all-hands-on-deck call is made on the SS Microsoft.

The incentive programs are extensive and foster success in winning quarterly and year-end sales as long as you are tied in with Microsoft, attentively and aggressively working in synch with the company. ASAP contends that one major challenge for resellers remains uncovering and exploiting available resources and promotions from Microsoft. "I have a fulltime person figuring out how to use all the Microsoft resources at our disposal." The key bit of advice for LARs—and perhaps for any reseller—is to "know your PAM, know whom you are working with. The better you know them, the more they will do for you. Be vocal. Share what you know. Participate in the pipeline and bring opportunities to them. If you do these things, they will bring opportunities to you."

So keep close to Microsoft: extend globally if you can, but always align locally. In this respect, an integrated or hybrid operating model—product sales and provision of services—might make sense, especially if you are able to complement your firm's core business model with homegrown services or partnerships with services firms in various markets. Strengthen your partnering programs and offer one-stop shopping to maximize customer convenience and satisfaction, if only because of the diversified revenue stream it enables. Resellers that offer a full range of services to their customers with Microsoft technologies and solutions as a large portion of them are in a better strategic position to be considered as the go-to partner on accounts and thus to win new accounts. Some resellers and direct marketers are taking this approach by partnering with VARs, as indicated above. This strategic approach to virtual diversification and synergy with Microsoft begins and ends by staying close to Microsoft for ever-changing marching orders.

It is very important to focus on Microsoft's established and growing penetration into market verticals. This latter point, as suggested, is increasingly important to Microsoft and, indeed, to resellers. Microsoft is going vertical and so should you. In tandem with this is the mentioned need to wrap services, whether your own or through partners, around product sales to add downstream value to customer accounts. This is, after all, a hallmark of the most successful resellers, and their core mechanism to get and to stay close to their customers, which accentuates sales success.

Of course, your strategy must be aligned with Microsoft's Go-To-Market (GTM) campaigns, especially as reflected in the licensing solutions competency for resellers introduced in 2005. That competency—the first such offering for licensing—offers two specializations: License Delivery and Software Asset Management (SAM) services. A significant by-product of reseller alignment with Microsoft's GTMs is to bring more value to customers' software purchases and the ability to calculate with precision the optimal licensing mix for each customer. This class of large account reseller and Enterprise Software Agent must also be able to measure and demonstrate for customers a lower total cost of ownership and highest return on investment relative to competitive solutions and increasingly in vertical market sectors. The Microsoft-designed Solutions Selling course, employed by many services firms, is a tool that may help your firm master these guidelines. It would also commend you to Microsoft if your firm's key representatives attended it.

In general, then, you should strive to help Microsoft perceive your firm as augmenting its success. This is in day-to-day and month-by-month interactions, but is also manifested in a certain posture of your firm relative to the Microsoft ecosystem. Networking with Microsoft and its partners—particularly services firms that specialize in desktop and server deployment, and certified learning partners—is an important strategy. Staying informed and demonstrating that you are informed about issues, pending licensing deals and renewal opportunities are good strategies, particularly as Microsoft faces a myriad of challenges in this arena. Demonstrating that you are thinking ahead and acting in anticipation of market needs that may favorably impact Microsoft's success is another step that can be taken. The more you show Microsoft that you value the partner ecosystem, realize its rewards and help Microsoft—and its partners—succeed, the more Microsoft will be inclined and energized to look after your success. And remember, sales and licensing opportunities abound in the SMB market. Consider the examples of Nortec Communications and IT Advisor Group, both of which took direct action to address Microsoft's licensing priorities—renewals and Open Value, respectively—and got ahead of the curve in an area where they had only a peripheral interest.

The Microsoft reselling business has changed dramatically in recent years. The shifts in software acquisition trends and models have caused significant consolidation of resellers and forced value-added resellers to develop alternative revenue streams, including managed services, hosting services and vertical services.

In short, the reselling industry has evolved from a pure product distribution model to one of value-added services and solutions being the core driver. The old model for Microsoft's large account resellers and smaller value-added resellers, traditionally a product-driven model, has given way to a services-led product model. That is, resellers continue to reap margins from product volumes but the bulk of revenue shifts to managed services. In its hurried move to help its customers settle into an agent model, Microsoft ensures that the LAR and VAR partner categories continue to evolve and grow.

In this new world, more emphasis is placed on value-add, rather than resale. Resellers become agents that drive the most value out of Microsoft's product purchases. So resellers can play a valuable role in instructing customers how to derive the best total cost of ownership and return on investment. Microsoft is indeed a product-centric, customer-focused and partner-driven company when it comes to resellers. Microsoft will deliver features and functions in its products to enhance the value of customer software purchases but the company remains as dependent, if not more so, on its partners to translate the more complex valuables to customers. Microsoft will continue to nurture and grow its channel, but one that is increasingly specialized in order to deliver value.

The new emphasis on value provides all resellers with opportunities to enhance the value of software delivery and helps Microsoft fend off competitive technologies. As suggested, nearly all resellers are forming pacts with other partners to achieve greater efficiencies and to deliver end-to-end solutions for customers. Such programs encourage software resellers, for example, to team with VARs, ISVs and training partners in order to ensure that customers derive maximum value from their Microsoft software purchases.

Clearly, this tightening of bonds among Microsoft's reseller partners—in part, fostered by Microsoft itself—helps them and the company deliver end-to-end solutions and drive their respective products and services to market more cost-effectively and with greater "stickiness" with customers. The mechanics of the tightening relationship among resellers, in some ways, mirror those employed by resellers to partner with Microsoft itself. At any rate, the sum is greater than the parts, and this increasing tightening of resellers in the Microsoft Partner Ecosystem may be the most important equation for them to generate growth and exploit new opportunities in Microsoft's changing economy.

Chapter 7

Extend the Opportunity Focus: Partnering with Other Microsoft Partners

During the course of any given work week, Microsoft services partners receive at least one phone call or email request from a Microsoft software partner seeking a channel relationship to expand its sales. This approach among firms in the Microsoft Partner Ecosystem has increasingly become the norm. An analogue of such partner-to-partner partnering may suffice to highlight its need and complexity.

Over coffee at a Manhattan Starbucks recently, the sales director of an ISV tossed a hackey sack—or footbag as it is called in some parts of the world—emblazoned with his firm's logo at his breakfast companion, a Microsoft services–partner sales executive. Hackey sack is an interesting game whose objective is to keep the ball in the air, using one's feet, elbows, knees or chest, but never one's arms or hands. The ball gets passed back and forth and if the ball gets dropped and hits the ground the game is lost. Analogously, the ball—a business opportunity—gets passed between players—partners—who must work in unison to keep it in play, ideally always moving the ball forward, together. When the ball gets dropped, the opportunity is lost. The hackey sack game at the Manhattan Starbucks had some high points and a really low one. The partners made their way with the hackey sack out the store and onto the sidewalks. Thanks to some clever volleying and deft moves, they kept the ball in play. Until, due to a bad move, it got knocked into the street and run over by a yellow taxi. Such are the risks-and rewards of the game. Coordination, cooperation, common vision—in short, teamsmanship—are essential traits to play and win this game.

Microsoft partners are similarly engaged with Microsoft itself, as we have seen in foregoing chapters. But they are increasingly engaging one another, as well, to move

their respective initiatives and opportunities forward together. This partner-to-partner coordination, cooperation and common vision is a natural extension of partnering with Microsoft because

- working and extending your connection points within Microsoft is a form of networking that extends your reach into the Microsoft Partner Ecosystem, its extended
sales force, a vast network that spans the globe and has all shapes and sizes of
partners; and

- it is in Microsoft's interest to refer its partners to one another so that their respective offerings—whether products or services—can complement each other in an
integrated solution that bolsters the Microsoft brand and products through their
common partnership with Microsoft itself.

Indeed, successful partnership with Microsoft will result in referrals to like-minded,
complementary partners with which a partner in good standing can explore synergies and identify, pursue and secure opportunities together.

So working and extending your connection points with other Microsoft partners
can extend the value of your partnership with Microsoft and extend your firm's
influence while broadening your opportunities for success. These are the principal
advantages of working within the Microsoft Partner Ecosystem.

As should also be clear, there are natural affinities between the various types of
Microsoft partners –ISVs, services partners, and resellers—and, though Microsoft's
core focus is on software, the company is incubating and actively promoting such
a vision of their complementarity and cooperation. The partner ecosystem is the
context in which Microsoft builds its partner community, and its extended business,
and engages partners individually and amongst themselves to realize this vision.
Microsoft intercedes on occasion to play matchmaker between various partner types
but the actual engagement between partners is theirs to pursue.

This chapter outlines the mechanisms and the benefits of engaging Microsoft
partners.

See the Benefits of Partnering from Your Customers' Perspective

Any customer—and, for that matter, Microsoft itself—would prefer one solution
from one vendor to solve a business problem and, optimally, one go-to person for its
delivery. In short, one-stop shopping. But individual firms rarely have all the capabilities—skills, resources, time—to deliver a fully integrated solution to their customers. So every firm needs to extend itself—again, in skills, resources and time—to
round out its offerings, whether they are products or services. Often, the most cost-
effective way to do this is to partner with another firm.

Rather than adjust one's business model and raise capital to seek, interview and hire dozens of other people, and train them to work productively in the firm for customers' benefit, prudent firms seek partners with complementary capabilities to engage in delivering a broader array of expert products and services to their customers.

In this scenario, who wins? Clearly, customers benefit if the offerings are indeed expertly delivered. But so do the partnering firms, which may charge a premium for the convenience of one-stop shopping and the quality of the delivered product. In addition, those firms gain from the efficiencies of partnering: they compound their sales impact by leveraging one another and reducing their individual and collective cost of sales. And this cost-of-sales reduction may get passed on to the customer, who would then benefit additionally.

Because a happy customer is likely one to refer others to a favored product or service provider, the objective of any Microsoft business is to not only to meet but exceed customer expectations and the optimal way to do this is through partnering. It is advisable to view the partnering imperative, as well as the risks and rewards, then, from your customers' perspective.

Keep Your Eyes Open: Partnering Is Promising but It Can Also Be Perilous

If that is the desired outcome, how should Microsoft partners partner among themselves? To begin, partners should explore the ecosystem to identify apparently likeminded, conveniently located and complementary firms that are also Microsoft partners with which to open discussions. As in any partnering scenario, however, the partner's own fundamentals—business model, culture, capabilities, target market, customer base, corporate strategy, particular needs—must be kept at the forefront.

Your firm's interests are predominant when sizing up prospective partners, and serve as a set of criteria for measuring them as such. Many partnering initiatives have failed because the firms involved did not conduct adequate due diligence on their respective capabilities and needs in advance of making partnering arrangements; others have failed because partners moved too hastily, failed to ask the right questions, and agreed to partner with firms that were in fact—or were inclined to—compete with them, rather than advance their hoped-for common cause. So, to start, you must investigate with your eyes wide open in the Microsoft Partner Ecosystem to identify prospective partners for their complementary capabilities and market reach based on your firm's own capabilities and needs, which serve as a measure of your prospects. Look hard at all of the aspects of the potential pairing, the pros and the cons, the rewards and the risks, because, while promising, partnering can also be perilous.

This investigation and appropriate assessment of prospective partners within the Microsoft Partner Ecosystem is the first step and often the lengthiest part of the process. Perform due diligence thoroughly on partner prospects before you make contact with the most likely candidates. And be cognizant of the fact that many of these firms—like many of the Microsoft partners interviewed for this book—share experiences similar to your firm. That is, Microsoft partners often consider other Microsoft partners essentially as cousins, who hold in common a relationship with a much larger company, their mutual benefactor. Consequently, they may assume that their interests are in common as partners and do not think twice about making contact, often indiscriminately. As indicated earlier, many of the Microsoft partners we interviewed for this book receive several calls on a weekly basis from other Microsoft partners, all seeking to partner. Services partners will call other services partners in the hope of getting subcontracting work (which is rare unless there is a prior relationship among the firms). ISVs will call services partners hoping to establish channel relationships through them on a specious win/win basis. Resellers will contact services partners hoping similarly for a value-added services relationship so that they can compete with larger players in the reseller market whose business models have diversified to the extent of implementing the hardware and software that they sell. In short, partner-to-partner contact with a view to partner-to-partner partnering is at an all-time high. Unfortunately, many Microsoft partners, as suggested, have not conducted the requisite due diligence—first on their own firms' capabilities and needs, then on their prospective partners' complementarity—so the majority of these efforts do not bear fruit. They waste time. And partnering is a time-consuming process that too rarely provides ample return on the substantial investment of time and energy.

So do not take partnering with other Microsoft partners lightly. Engage in it as you do partnering with Microsoft: seriously. In your investigation and discovery process of prospective partners, it is often sufficient to maintain of list of reputable candidates that are available for cooperative partnering and that have requisite expertise in domains you may need. Stay apprised of their developing capabilities and the extent of their complementarity, or lack thereof, with your own firm over time. There may be opportunities down the road to co-engage on a deal with these prospects in a more casual manner during which you will learn about their principal personnel and decide whether to forge a formal partnership that may bear fruit. Be aware that their superficial presence—on their website, according to their reputation—may be different from their day-to-day business practices and methods. They may appear to have complementary capabilities and a need for synergy that commends them as partners, but this could be illusory. You need to get to know your prospective partners—to understand them in the same manner as this book counsels you to understand Microsoft's culture, strategy and organization—before engaging them professionally in a formal partnership. So developing relationships with these firms is an essential next step after your due diligence is completed toward establishing a partnership. This investment in relationship development is imperative, and will likely save you time and optimize the possibilities of partnering. The alternative is to make cold calls to prospective partners, which, like cold-calling customers, often leads to wasted time and more catch-up work as a result.

In partnering with other Microsoft partners, take a cue from Microsoft itself: in 2004, the company had 38 executive titles containing the word "partner," which attests to the depth of Microsoft's commitment to partnering and its partner-driven culture. It also signifies the level of corporate commitment required for partnering itself.

The lesson: if your firm is not committed to being partner-driven, it is best not to engage in developing a partner channel or partnering relationships at all. It takes a tremendous amount of work to do so. And partnering is not simply a way to conduct business but an expression of a cultural value, a particular corporate mindset, that differentiates one firm from another. So knowing your firm's own culture and its capabilities, and assessing its partnering-readiness, is a prerequisite to partnering.

Assuming that your firm is fully conversant on its capabilities and needs, partnering-ready and able to conduct due diligence on prospective partners in the Microsoft Partner Ecosystem, we present in the sections that follow some theory and best practices for partnering. This information answers two basic questions: how does your firm find complementary partners? and how does your firm recruit the partner prospects that fit best with your firm? The answers to these questions pertain, of course, to partnering with any firm, but in this book they are focused on partnering with other Microsoft partners.

How To Find and Land Complementary Partners

You should view partnering with other Microsoft partners—and the need to do so—from the perspective of your customers' benefit. Let your customers steer your choices based on their needs. By staying close to your market—asking, listening, heeding, refining—you will position yourself for success. Do not presume to identify partner prospects in a vacuum; rather, seek customer input on their needs and how you can appease them. Ask your customers which skills and solutions they would like, or need, that your firm does not provide. It is rare that customers voluntarily provide such unsolicited information, and it never hurts to ask. Your customers will not likely answer the question with clarity. But their feedback will contain hints and indications that should point you in the right direction and provide you with a basis for beginning your investigation. If, in fact, you do not provide what they say they need. And if enough of them indicate the same or at least a similar need to warrant the investigative time required in identifying, developing relationships with and securing prospective partners. It is from your customers that you should identify the need that a partnership will address, not from blue-sky thinking about scale and synergy irrespective of market opportunity.

If your customers orient you to a need that partnering could or would address, what do you do next? Begin your investigation of prospective partners. Visit Microsoft's partnering website (partner.microsoft.com) or work with and through your Microsoft counterparts to access its range of partner databases—some are public, some are internal only (but still accessible by partners if you work your connections)—to identify and to get a feel for the reputation of prospective partners. Microsoft is a natural source of information because your firm is a Microsoft partner, which means it has some degree of interest in Microsoft's go-to-market strategy, and so you are presumably seeking a like-minded and complementary Microsoft partner.

You can also visit the website of the International Association of Microsoft Certified Partners (IAMCP) (www.iamcp.org) to find firms with competencies in the relevant areas. Seek input from other trusted Microsoft partners as to likely prospects. Attend Microsoft's worldwide partner conference and use networking tools provided by Microsoft to identify and meet with promising partner prospects. Rely on your PAM or existing Microsoft counterpart relationships to achieve the same end. Cast a broad net and refine your search as you go along. After all, finding complementary partners is a lot like finding new customers, so the typical sales funnel approach is applicable to your search.

Establish objectives, as you would in a sales process, of identifying a large number of partner prospects by a certain date. Then refine your list to a smaller number by a subsequent date based on similarly refined criteria. Put a plan in place to short-list the most promising candidates and to contact or at least generate interest among the short-listed firms within a specific timeframe that makes sense for your needs.

IAMCP

IAMCP was founded in Dallas, Texas, in 1994. Currently, there are 2,000 members with 22 chapters in the United States and 11 international chapters in the United Kingdom, Germany, Italy, Sweden, South Africa, India, Bulgaria, and Estonia. As of this writing, chapters are planned to open in Switzerland, Austria, the Netherlands, Norway and Denmark. Other IAMCP chapters are planned for Ireland, Israel, the Philippines, Brazil and throughout Asia.

IAMCP is a non-profit organization that started as an industry lobbying group for Microsoft but expanded its charter in early 2000 to refocus on peer-to-peer networking and partnering. Its mission statement is simple and effective: "To maximize business opportunities for Microsoft Certified Partners through local networking, aligning with the Microsoft Go-To-Market campaigns and connecting the traditional Microsoft Certified Partner community and Microsoft Business Solutions partners." And it is certainly right for Microsoft partners seeking to partner with other Microsoft partners: IAMCP's biggest value is in networking for specialized partners across competencies and geographical boundaries.

Reflecting Microsoft's evolving partner-ecosystem goals, IAMCP opted to invite ISVs and non-certified Microsoft partners to become members. It is also trying to foster more international participation and networking opportunities. Stockholm, Sweden-based IDE Nätverkskonsulterna's CEO Per Werngren currently serves as IAMCP president; Reginald Howatson, a manager at the former Nexxlink Technologies of Montreal, Quebec, Canada, was past president. IAMCP offers three levels of membership—member, associate and affiliate—and its chapters—international, national, regional and local—are run by elected members. The nine members on the executive board of directors consist of a president, vice president, treasurer, secretary and members-at-large, featuring a mix of US and international partners. A Microsoft representative also sits on the board of directors. IAMCP's annual budget is US$150,000, and each chapter funds its own activities through fees. Microsoft is a sponsor and provides more funding to the association than in past years yet each IAMCP chapter is self-sufficient.

The goal of the association is to provide a united partner voice to influence Microsoft partner and marketing programs, receive advance notice of Microsoft's programs and directions, mentor others to elevate their partner status, leverage Microsoft's brand through the IAMCP to help partner members differentiate their companies, gain access to best practices, broaden solution offerings through partnering and help build community relationships and develop business opportunities. Each year, an IAMCP Summit is held at Microsoft corporate headquarters at Seattle. In addition to networking, for example, the organization provides feedback to Microsoft and delivers Microsoft messaging and support programs to its members, associates and affiliates. IAMCP also sponsors seminars and speaking engagements by business specialists, such as CFOs, to educate its members about business issues and to provide tips about how to write better proposals and contracts. So IAMCP is made up of a relatively small but highly motivated cadre of partners, and it has influence with Microsoft.

Representatives from the international organization report to Microsoft corporate at Seattle while IAMCP chapters interact with their own subsidiaries, whether nationally, regionally or locally. There is a high degree of networking between IAMCP and Microsoft itself. In fact, IAMCP officials observe that Microsoft partner-focused executives are beginning to tap more into the organization to solicit feedback on technologies and programs. Indeed, both Microsoft partner executives Margo Day and Don Nelson, general manager of MBS managed partners, view IAMCP as an effective vehicle for building networks between traditional partners as well as among traditional partners and MBS partners. "IAMCP recognized the power of partnership long before we started talking about circles of trust," says Ms Day, vice president of Microsoft's US Partner Group.

So IAMCP is a fertile ground for networking in a more intimate, extended manner with other Microsoft partners with a view to keeping current with the ecosystem and identifying promising partnership candidates in the organization.

Internet Search Engines

In addition to word-of-mouth referrals or anecdotal evidence, an indirect way to find complementary prospective partners is to use Internet search engines—Google, MSN, Yahoo! and the like—to discover and probe candidates. It is probably best to pursue an investigation of the attributes and capabilities of partner prospects using search engines only after you have identified a large number of prospects from Microsoft's partner ecosystem website, conferred with your Microsoft counterparts, and whittled the list down to a manageable number. Of course, the Internet has a wealth of information on technology firms and people (have you googled for your firm, even yourself lately? Surely someone in the world has recently.). You can find a rich, diverse set of information on your prospects that will help you discern their fitness for your firm.

Again, in your interpersonal and networking discussions with others about prospective partnering candidates, do your best to assess a prospect's fitness for your firm through the lens of your customers, since their need is driving your pursuit. Cultural fit, which can be discerned from relatively objective, at least detached sources is paramount, as is a track record of results and success. Search engines, if used properly (with the right search terms), can shed a great deal of light on the attributes and fitness of those prospects for your firm and its purposes.

Short-listing Prospective Partners—Measurably

From your due diligence on partner prospects, a number of promising candidates will emerge. In addition to assessing their complementarity to your firm and their fitness for your customers, there are other obvious guidelines—or criteria—for narrowing down the list of prospects further. These guidelines are offered on the assumption that these potential partners will be leveraged to help your firm drive sales and deliver results, whether in products or services. The top three guidelines are as follows:

Alignment: Does the candidate's business model and market approach align with that of your firm? Is there sufficient evidence from all available information that the partner-candidate has a track record of success, integrity and capabilities necessary to work with your firm? Is there a cultural fit with your firm? What is the nature of the candidate's relationship with Microsoft, and other partners? Is there any indication that the partner candidate would be competitive with your firm, or that it has prior relationships with a firm that is competitive with yours?

Financial: Is your partner-candidate profitable? Does your firm offer appropriate financial incentives to the partner candidate to make partnership attractive? For example, if an ISV intends to partner with a services partner, what commissions are to be paid to the services partner to provide incentives for its sales personnel to promote the ISV's product? Are they substantial enough? Perhaps there are alternative financial incentives between firms that can benefit both parties.

Geographical: Is there a relevant geographical or vertical-market connection between the potential partnering firms that would enable their sales and delivery personnel to work together effectively? Two adages come to mind—"out of sight, out of mind" and *"el amor de lejos es amor de pendejos"* (faraway love is foolish love)—to indicate that there had better be propinquity—geographical or market proximity—among the firms that will foster their collaboration. Virtual collaboration in a partnering context is often unworkable and yields few results.

Partner Definition Matrix

In assessing prospective partners and boiling them down to a short list of partner candidates, dwell not only on their attributes but also on your specific needs, which you can categorize and measure. Partners can be

- *essential,* which demands significant time and financial investment on your part to make them integral to your firm in the development, sale and delivery of its products, services and solutions;

- *strategic,* which requires some investment and coordinated connections to your firm on both sales and marketing initiatives or, perhaps, operations, including product or service delivery; or

- *opportunistic,* which fills a gap in your product or service portfolio or go-to-market approach—such partners are occasionally useful to your firm in the development, sale and delivery of your products or services.

Depending on the type of partner that you seek from the breakdown above, it is best to stratify the relevant attributes of your partner prospects and to assign appropriate metrics to these categories. In other words, develop a workable system for sorting through and classifying partner prospects according to their utility to your firm as categorized above. Doing so helps you craft a partnering model that strategically aligns your needs and your opportunities, and will—if properly executed—enable your firm to compete on a higher level than might otherwise be the case.

Generating Interest from Other Partners

Once you have identified the most promising partner candidates, you must decide how to approach them. The best way to contact prospects, like customers, is through trusted referrals. By relying on people you know, who know the partner candidates also, you can generate advance interest in them—and learn more about them in the process—through a facilitated introduction.

As suggested, it is often beneficial to rely on your existing Microsoft relationships—the more connection points you have within Microsoft, the farther your reach into the Microsoft Partner Ecosystem—to help you identify the most promising candidates for partnership. Your Microsoft colleagues can also make the appropriate introductions and broker preliminary discussions between your firm and the candidates on your short list.

In every case, you must relay as much information about your firm as possible—full disclosure is best—and be precise and succinct about what you need to advance your cause. You are working through intermediaries and so it is important that they readily understand what you seek and communicate that on your behalf effectively with your partnering prospects. So the KISS principle—keep it simple, silly—is warranted.

In addition to your Microsoft colleagues, of course, you can take advantage of the well-established network of Microsoft partners you may know or associations such as the IAMCP, to identify, investigate, pursue and secure complementary partners.

Thereafter, the role of communicating your firm's interest and intent, assessing those of your prospects and gauging your firms' respective and collective fitness and complementarity falls to you. Take full advantage of the network—your relationships—and sustain your relationships by keeping your colleagues apprised of your progress.

How Do You Make Those Relationships Work?

Let us assume that you have identified a candidate interested in partnering with your firm and you have discussed favorable terms and an appropriate contractual basis for advancing. It is advisable to agree to a pilot test in which the sales group and, if applicable, delivery personnel of both firms work together to develop and close leads. Of course, keep close tabs on the progress of the pilot, and leverage your network to help it succeed. As this pilot phase unfolds successfully, move to shore up the partnership and be vocal with Microsoft, IAMCP and all other parties that have encouraged the pairing about the partnership's success. Sing the praises of the partnership in your respective firms.

Generally, create an atmosphere of goodwill around the partnership, in your communities, among your customers, with Microsoft and all other relevant associations about the partnership. And stoke that goodwill to generate even more favorable results. Too often, firms partner in a perfunctory manner—as if partnering for its own sake—while losing sight of the purpose and obscuring the significance of partnership, which boils down to two firms independently and collectively succeeding in a joint initiative. Such success deserves attention, especially in your Microsoft network, because the celebration of success as an impetus to generate more success is an important cultural attribute of Microsoft.

Even in an atmosphere of celebration, be realistic and objective. Regularly review the partnership and the contributions of both parties with a view to constant refinement and resolution of issues that may arise. If both sides are committed to the relationship, it is wise to hold monthly reviews initially and quarterly reviews thereafter. These discussions will highlight any issues and problems and provide a forum to resolve them without straining schedules. It will also enhance communications and encourage sustained dialogue, which is essential to partnering. It may be beneficial to involve your Microsoft contacts and account managers in your partner relationships and periodically hold checkpoint meetings to keep them apprised of your collective progress and hopefully open doors based on their insight. It may also benefit your partnership and your respective firms to gather and structure customer feedback on your partnership to assess the product and results of its founding purpose.

In general, bear in mind that the simplest approach to partnership is the best. Partnerships are about collaboration for a common purpose and a mutual benefit. Effective collaboration is not possible without communication. So, in order to attain the best possible results, partnering firms must communicate regularly and constructively. Soliciting the insight of your common partner, Microsoft, and of your customers in common, is advantageous because it will enable the partnership to deliver a progressively higher level of service and create new opportunities and revenue streams.

How Long Do You Carry Someone's Water Before You Drop It?

If you determine that the relationship is not working and that it may be irreparable, it is best to call it quits before too much damage is done. Two principles apply here: in any common-law contractual arrangement, it is the obligation of both parties to minimize damages lest they both be penalized not only by such damages but as a result of their contractual negligence. In addition, it is best to sign the terms of your divorce while you are still in love, that is, while the partnership is getting underway and goodwill abounds. It is advisable to determine its success measures and the least disruptive "out clause," or divorce, should the partnership not work. Because candor is fundamental to proper communication, which fosters collaboration, always assess—and constantly re-assess—the merits of your partnerships and work together to resolve any issues that may exist. Again, involve your Microsoft colleagues to help your firms refine your partnership.

Of course, there may be occasions when one firm is assuming more of the burden of the partnership than the other. This is to be expected. Professional—indeed, human—decency demands that both firms accept this eventuality as a reality of partnering. If, however, a pattern emerges in which one firm is consistently shirking its obligations of partnership or making half-hearted attempts, it behooves the other party—often with Microsoft's help—to address those thorny issues while advancing the cause of the partnership. But if the partnership becomes unworkable for this reason, it is best to dissolve the arrangement per prior agreement and establish provisions to minimize ill will. Often, poor or non-performance on partnership obligations boils down to unclearly stated expectations of the under-performing partner. For example, an ISV may seek partnership with a services partner, in which it sets an expectation that it will provide the services partner with qualified leads and a defined margin of the ISV's sales in exchange for the services partner's bringing that ISV into its customer accounts. From the services partner's perspective, the situation may seem too good to be true—that it can get get leads and a margin merely for providing leads? In this circumstance, however, there is insufficient term-setting and the need for a defined *quid pro quo*—"this for that"—to make the arrangement valid. The best approach is for both parties to be specific upfront and to define crisply what they each expect of the other and what they intend to give in return. In the context of this communication, set metrics for performance and monitor progress in achieving them throughout the life of the partnership.

A general rule of thumb in assessing the value of a partnership—especially within the Microsoft Partner Ecosystem—is that, if incommensurate work has flowed both ways in any given three-month period, the viability of the partnership is at least worthy of serious assessment with a view to repair or perhaps dissolution.

Common Pitfalls of Partnering with Other Microsoft Partners

In partnering with any firm but especially in partnering with Microsoft partners, there are several common pitfalls to avoid as you decide on and particularly as you engage your new partner. Below are some considerations to bear in mind:

Inefficiencies of alignment: Be aware of the driving intention and advantages of partnering with Microsoft partners: you have a large, very capable partner in common—Microsoft—that you need to leverage for your individual and collective benefit. From this perspective, there are a number of inefficiencies that result from misalignment of partnering firms with Microsoft and thus with one another. These include:

- *geographical misalignment*: If your partner claims to have a plan or presence in Atlanta, southeast Asia or Ireland, determine the precise nature and scope of this presence. It could mean that the firm has or will have a remote person in, respectively, South Carolina, Australia or London, whose purview includes the mentioned areas. Obviously, there is quite a distance between the actual location of their remote worker and the areas to be covered. This suggests that the firm is not as close to these markets as implied and that the travel time required to provide adequate coverage may limit the firm's attempts to get traction there. If your strategy is to penetrate distinct markets, it is best to ensure your partner's geographical alignment—direct coverage—in them, and to gauge the extent to which your partner can leverage Microsoft offices in these locations. It is important that the partners' respective geographical coverage areas complement one another. So ensure that your partner's geographical alignment corresponds to and extends yours, that its presence in distinct markets is sufficient to leverage Microsoft relationships, and that there are no inefficiencies obstructing timely and complete coverage of sales and delivery that would impair your traction as partners.

- *market misalignment:* If your partner-firm focuses on the financial services vertical market and your firm focuses on the insurance vertical market, there might be inefficiencies in your combining forces to boost traction together in either market; to be sure, the insurance sector shares some of the same attributes and needs of financial services firms but there is not a direct connection. In addition, since Microsoft essentially stove-pipes its vertical market groups, and its financial services and insurance groups are distinct, the collective leverage you might expect from Microsoft's vertical group could be illusory.

- *competency misalignment:* If your firm custom-develops .NET applications for front-office business processes and your partner implements .NET applications as a sideline to its primary competencies in such products as SharePoint, Exchange and SQL Server, there might not be sufficient alignment of your competencies to warrant partnership. In fact, the loose alignment of your firms' respective competencies may lead to slippage not only in communication about what to sell and how to deliver it but also in your strategic and operational inter-relationship. Your investigation of your partner must factor in the attitudes and aptitudes of its personnel and, of course, their Microsoft-centric qualifications and competencies.

- *communications misalignment:* If your partner is a "voice shop"—and as such relies on the telephone and voicemail to get its work done—and your firm, by contrast, is a "document shop"—it relies primarily on email and hardcopy memos to communicate and process workflow—there will likely be considerable slippage in your interactions. Therefore, you need to ensure up front that both of your firms communicate in and between themselves in a "natural" manner—that is, in the same or complementary way—or make adjustments to ensure alignment. Communication is the *conditione sine qua non* of collaboration; without all due collaboration, the results of your partnership will be negligible.

- *cultural misalignment:* Many firms focus on markets, strategies, operations and finances when making partnering decisions and executing arrangements, yet these are secondary in importance to cultural considerations. Consider that the first three chapters of this book—almost half of the work—is devoted to explaining what makes Microsoft tick—the historical development of its culture and the cultural expressions of its organization, strategy and operations. This focus was purposeful; the intent is to emphasize the need to appreciate what makes Microsoft tick as well as your firm's inner workings in order to form the best partnership possible. Naturally, this applies to your relationships with other partners. Your firm ought to dwell on your partner's culture first and foremost—understand and assess it—in order to forestall any complications or inefficiencies in partnering. It may seem like a great fit immediately if you sense strong synergies in executive temperament and the personalities and work styles of your respective workforce, but it is essential to analyze how your partner's business runs and whether your firms are culturally complementary.

- *Microsoft misalignment:* You need to assess your partner's historical interaction with Microsoft and its current status with the company. How long has it been a Microsoft partner and what are its competencies? What are its connections points into Microsoft, and how is it extending its Microsoft relationships? What results has the firm generated as a result of its partnership with Microsoft? What do Microsoft insiders say about the company? Which other Microsoft partners has it partnered with and what were the results of those pairings? What are its intentions with respect to Microsoft partnership? Is it growing the relationship? Is it is aligned with its local field-office and its GTMs, and where does it stand on the importance of corporate GTMs? How does the firm engage with Microsoft (purely professional one-on-one interactions or regular attendance at Microsoft events), and with what results? In addition, you must determine if your potential partner tinkers with Microsoft-competitive technologies: does it develop or sell Linux solutions, for example? If so, you must think twice about engaging in an in-depth partnership with such a firm because it could subject your firm to guilt by association if Microsoft learns of that partner's competitive posture. If you are a Microsoft-centric partner, it would not be a good cultural fit.

- *Operational disintegration:* Be cognizant that the operational integration of your respective firms is paramount, and "where the rubber meets the road" in terms of making your partnership successful. Without strict attention to how your firms will function together on a day-to-day basis, your partnership may not gain desired traction. Problems may occur in the following areas:
  - *lead-flow definition:* Both partners must define, agree upon and enforce a mechanism to ensure that sales lead generation is reliably bi-directional. Mea-

sures and operating processes can be put in place to ensure this occurs and that both partnering firms can trust their expectations of the partnership. Without lead and deal flow occurring both ways, the partnership may not survive for very long. Leverage Microsoft in this lead-flow process, as well, because an objective of your partnership should be to garner more leads from (and to) Microsoft based on the accentuated market benefit your partnership should offer relative to your firms' working independently.

- *sales process:* If your firms plan to collaborate on sales calls and closures, ensure that your sales personnel and their pre-sales technical colleagues are of one mind as to what must get done in the sales process—who does what, when, where, why and how—in order to sell your partnership's solutions. It is particularly important to review responsibilities and ensure that action items do not fall through the cracks. The sales process between and among your firms' personnel should be seamless, and factor in your Microsoft relationships.

- *delivery mechanics:* The same principles apply to your partnership's delivery of solutions not only from the perspectives of project management and technical substance but also from your collective leverage of Microsoft, as applicable, for technical contributions to the delivery, account management and marketing assistance.

- *credits and collections:* Your firms, of course, need to define processes for crediting one another and paying one another for work performed by each party in the partnership.

- *strategic flux:* You must come up with a game plan for handling potential changes in Microsoft's strategy that impact your firm, your partner's firm, or the goals of your partnership. If one firm's relationship or alignment with Microsoft changes substantially, are the grounds for the partnership itself eroded? Of course, it depends on the particulars of the case. Assume that your partner's firm is a Microsoft services partner focused on custom application development and that your partnership is intended to leverage that competency to complement your solutions delivery capabilities. Assume further that this partner lands a customer engagement with Microsoft in which its application-development capabilities are leveraged to the fullest extent possible. In fact, in the course of this customer engagement, and with a modified agreement with Microsoft, your partner develops a solution for a vertical market in which your firm focuses, and that the solution is potentially competitive with your own. Does it make sense to partner anymore? As a result of its modified agreement with Microsoft, your partner retains ownership of its custom-developed solution and decides, in turn, to become "a true ISV," bringing to market its vertical solution in shrink-wrapped fashion in a way that competes with your solution, and that it positions itself for Microsoft leverage in seizing this market. In such a scenario, which has occurred between Microsoft partners in the past, your partnership dissolves, and you have a new competitor from an erstwhile partner, which now has Microsoft backing. While such a transition from a custom application-development shop to an ISV is indeed a difficult one to make, it has, as stated, happened before. It represents not only a business model change but a shift in strategy that can be as prejudicial not only of partnerships but to the partners, as well. What recourse do you have in such a strategic shift? What course of action do you then pursue? These questions are difficult to answer, but they point to an abiding need in any partnership to keep close to your partner to understand what developments are ongoing and anticipate which ones may have a bearing, whether positively or negatively, not only on your partnership but on your firm. Communication is the bedrock of partnering collaboration, and it is both an antidote to such strategic shifts in partnership and a lever of sorts to sustain the integrity of your respective firms and their opportunities.

In general, then, when partnering with another firm, you must keep close to it but also factor in the nature and evolution of the partner's relationship with Microsoft and its engagement in the market. Perhaps you might insist on a non-compete in your agreement that establishes the partnership. Are there other safeguards you may insist upon before signing a partnership agreement?

Regardless of such contractual efforts, staying close to your partner is the key to your firm's safeguarding and advancing its strategic intent in forming the partnership. For staying close to your partner will help you recognize what is promising and what is perilous in developments as they occur, and may enable you prudently to leverage Microsoft, which is active in partnering with firms and fostering partnerships among them.

As we have discussed, Microsoft is quite active in fostering partnerships among partners in its ecosystem to ensure that all customer needs are met and to grow solution sales. For instance, Microsoft has played matchmaker of sorts and provided incentives for its reseller partners to establish formal partnerships with desktop-management software vendors to ease the process of upgrading software at customer sites, which traditionally has been a costly proposition. Microsoft has also encouraged deals between resellers and certified learning partners to ensure that customers, once upgraded, will get the necessary training on their software and thus generate maximum return on investment and lower the total cost of ownership. These two criteria are deemed most important when measuring the value of software purchases. Microsoft's activity in this regard is for the sake of goodwill—it wants and needs its partners, where realistic, to work with one another and to develop synergies that

Extend the Opportunity Focus: Partnering With Other Microsoft Partners
will help them grow their businesses and advance Microsoft's, too. And Microsoft
wants to help its customers enjoy a return on their investment and to help itself
defeat its competitors and sell more software—and Software Assurance contracts—
by leveraging its ecosystem through partner-to-partner partnerships.

There are several case studies in Chapter Five that detail how services firms
wrested opportunities away from IBM and other open-source competitors at
the brink of defeat, and how Microsoft rewarded them for those victories.
Partners can score major points with Microsoft by leveraging other partners
in the ecosystem to counter competitive threats and to deliver end-to-end
solutions to customers that would have been impossible without the pairing.
This is becoming particularly important since Microsoft lacks the internal services capabilities of IBM Global Services or Oracle. It is beneficial to consider
this latter approach more systematically in the context of new partnering models emerging in the Microsoft Partner Ecosytem and how partners benefit.

Ross-Tek Expands Its SMB Interests with Microsoft, Other Partners

Remember Ross-Tek (www.rosstek.com) from Chapter Five? It is a Microsoft Certified Partner from Cleveland, Ohio, which is focused on Windows Small Business
Server implementations in Microsoft's Great Lakes District. The firm's interaction
with Microsoft was negligible until an independent consultant connected them
together. Since then, Ross-Tek has helped Microsoft develop materials for its SMB-
certification examinations and held Microsoft-subsidized seminars in its district. In
addition, Ross-Tek has substantially improved its market traction as a result of
adding value in customer implementations with other Microsoft products. Until
recently, Ross-Tek saw little participation from Microsoft in the small business space
or in developing programs designed for SMB services companies. That has changed
significantly, Ross-Tek's CEO Frederick Johnson said. "We are seeing a new partner program starting to emerge into what Microsoft said it would be a year ago.
Now there is a true commitment to serve the SMB market and not just with products but having resources behind it, such as partner engagement managers and small
business seminars."

Microsoft has begun, for example, subsidizing partner-driven seminars as part
of its marketing services bureau for ISVs and services partners. Ross-Tek was one
of the companies that pilot-tested the seminar service and saw three immediate deals
in the days that followed. The small services company is also trying to align itself
more seamlessly with Microsoft by attempting a vertical focus with local pediatric
offices.

More significantly, Ross-Tek is aiming to expand its Microsoft technology offerings to its current customers by forming "Circles of Trust" with other Microsoft services partners, with Microsoft's backing. Johnson maintains that such circles of trust are increasing in number, although Microsoft may not be fully aware of the risks partners potentially face when joining forces with other partners. Still balancing out those risks are the many rewards that can result from partnering.

Ross-Tek planned to become a Microsoft Business Solutions partner in order to enter the CRM space but instead opted to partner with local CRM specialists. First, Ross-tek formed its own alliance with Avvenire Solutions LLC, of Broadview Heights, Ohio, in order to sell CRM and collaborative solutions to its SBS customers. Avvenire, a Microsoft Business Solutions partner and developer of SharePoint and CRM solutions, now recommends Ross-Tek to handle all of its SBS installations. Microsoft was instrumental in connecting Ross-Tek to its second MBS alliance partner, C-Biz, a much larger organization with an office in Cleveland. The recommendation took place over a shoeshine, Mr Johnson said. He met the Microsoft PAM at a shoeshine stand during a Microsoft-sponsored seminar, mentioned that he had a potential CRM installation and asked for a recommendation. The Microsoft PAM recommended C-Biz, a large, publicly traded company that provides services for Great Plains Software and CRM. Ross-tek has benefited significantly from the partnering recommendation, including access to market development funds it would not have been eligible for on its own. C-Biz received US$60,000 in marketing funds from Microsoft. "I would never get that," Mr Johnson said, pointing to such funding as one of the big benefits for small business partners forming pacts with other Microsoft partners. The two partners have engaged in a joint-marketing campaign and are targeting those funds at specific verticals so they can approach the same audience with different solutions.

Note that Ross-Tek's success with Microsoft in partnering with other Microsoft partners is relatively informal, and the result of personal interactions with Microsoft personnel at joint seminars or over a shoeshine. These instances do not represent structured measures to foster partnering. Yet what matters to Microsoft is the amount of sales activity and the growing small business customer influence of a firm such as Ross-Tek. In fact, whether partnerships develop formally or informally, all that matters to Microsoft is its partners' ability to partner to increase software sales.

Still, it is no wonder that Microsoft is trying to structure both partner performance and effective co-partnerships as a means to enhance its sales. Microsoft has historically lacked an effective means of measuring its partners' sales performance—how much in sales did each partner influence, or bring to Microsoft?—so it has always been problematic for Microsoft to determine which partner is best for which engagement based on its sales activity. Many methods and matrices have been developed and shelved to address this problem, and the latest iteration is the partner points program. Needless to say—but important to repeat—this is another structured attempt at criteria that will measure and reward partners' progress in the ecosystem. And the criteria are important both to Microsoft and its partners: customer references and certifications.

Of course, these criteria mean that your firm must demonstrate to Microsoft its fitness and progress as a Microsoft partner. Being subject to these criteria may incline you to view Microsoft as your "Big Brother," watching over your shoulder. But remember: this is Microsoft's game, and these are its rules. And there are many benefits that partners may realize as a result of this effort at structured partnering on Microsoft's part.

While there are partner program mechanisms for navigating requirements and establishing your firm's fitness and progress as a partner, what really matters—what will likely always matter most—is the set of relationships within Microsoft that you have and nurture. People, not programs, can vouch for your firm and help you succeed jointly with Microsoft and other Microsoft partners. As Microsoft's personnel see that your firm's services and solutions are focused and progressively stronger— as evidenced by certifications, customer wins, customer satisfaction and increased sales of Microsoft software—and that you are focused on replicating your success to other customers in the same and new vertical markets, you will find yourself in progressively better standing with Microsoft. As a result, Microsoft will facilitate your partnering with other Microsoft partners to achieve still-higher sales, and greater market successes will be more easily and effectively secured. Microsoft reserves its best help for its best partners.

Microsoft's best partners help the company sell progressively more of its software and benefit at the same time by the increased efficiencies and expanded resources of co-partnering. Top partners are highly attuned to the markets in which they are engaged, and especially mindful of competitive threats that not only impact their firm but Microsoft, as well. In addition to the more general threat of the open-source movement, Microsoft and its partner ecosystem is facing more pointed competition from IBM, which has expanded its Linux and open-source agenda in many vertical markets and down-market as well. IBM has tremendous resources in-house, and its global services unit is vigorously working to win Linux-driven successes from Microsoft and its partner ecosystem. Moreover, IBM has been more aggressive in growing its base of business partners for its Linux and Websphere initiatives.

In view of these developments, how do the best Microsoft partners compete? One imperative is to stay close to Microsoft and to work aggressively with the company and its related programs—such as CompHOT (CRN Online, 10 February 2005)—to protect Microsoft's base and ground encroached upon by IBM. There are several case studies in Chapter Five that detail how services firms wrested opportunities away from IBM and other competitors at the brink of the jaws of defeat, and how Microsoft rewarded them for those victories. Partners can score major points with Microsoft by leveraging other partners in Microsoft's ecosystem to counter competitive threats and deliver end-to-end solutions to customers that would have been impossible without the pairing. This has become particularly important since Microsoft lacks the internal services capabilities of IBM Global Services or Oracle. It is beneficial to consider this latter approach more systematically in the context of new partnering models emerging in the Microsoft Partner Ecosystem.

New Partnering Models Emerging in the Microsoft Partner Ecosystem

Traditionally, Microsoft's partners operated as islands unto themselves loosely interconnected by their common affiliation with Microsoft. It was a connection in name only. With the emergence of a more structured Microsoft Partner Ecosystem, though, and the pressing competitive threat of the open-source movement and large players such as IBM backing it, non-traditional models of partnering have emerged. And they have done so with Microsoft's backing not merely as a feature but as a necessary function and outgrowth of the partner ecosystem. These new modes of partnering by Microsoft partners have spawned new business models—not only within firms but among them—as Microsoft partners entertain new ways of doing business and of succeeding more fully.

The Microsoft partnering model, then is evolving to address cracks that the existence of an ecosystem has only partially addressed: end-to-end software-and-services delivery. Yet these new partnering models—and the corresponding refinements of partner business models—reflect what gave them rise: the need to protect Microsoft competencies against the onslaught of Microsoft-competitive threats. Accordingly, some of the more pervasive partnering models are characterized by greater collaboration among partners, co-optation of competitive thrusts and structured partner networks such as subcontractual aggregation and membership entities.

The effect of these models is to make any given firm seem larger and more efficient than it is and to extend its reach by staying close to Microsoft, tightening the ties between the two, and working more in unison to counter competition that might erode the grounds of their collective success. Again, these models truly reflect the spirit of the Microsoft Partner Ecosystem, which may not always have a discernible logic but definitely has an algorithm all its own. Partners that grasp the essence of the ecosystem and the importance of these partnering initiatives will increasingly reap the rewards ... together.

Simple Collaboration

In this and foregoing chapters, we have outlined the manner in which various partners—SPs, ISVs and resellers—have leveraged one another in order to seize opportunities. Most often, this collaborative work among Microsoft partners is indeed opportunity-driven, meant to plug a hole or to fill a gap in a partner's portfolio to exploit immediate prospects within a customer account. But such partnering can be more strategic, intended to extend and enhance a partner's capabilities long-term or to refine its go-to-market approach with a view to seizing, say, a bigger stake in a vertical market. To this extent, simple collaboration among partners, while often of a lower-level variety relative to other partner-to-partner collaboration mechanisms, is common.

In fact, as we have stated, it is increasingly common for ISVs, SPs and resellers in the ecosystem to contact one another for the sake of *ad hoc* collaboration on an opportunity. The large reseller CDW, for example, launched an agent model that compensates its smaller competitors and services partners for steering customers to it. Microsoft and Citrix are experimenting with similar agent models, as each seeks to find some mechanism to reward partners that influence a sale. Services partners and ISVs are forming more formal alliances in which the former are compensated for implementing the latter's software solutions in its customer accounts, or in which both provide managed services to customers in a vertical market. There is some benefit in these loose couplings of partners within the ecosystem in that both parties have common objectives and, together, share the rewards of their collaboration. In general, though, simple collaboration is just that, largely opportunity-driven, in which a drift into strategic partnering is possible.

Co-Optation: Collaborate Against the Competition

What we have often seen lacking among Microsoft partners is an awareness of how competition threatens not only Microsoft but its partner ecosystem, as well. Competitive threats include, of course, open-source solutions being promulgated and pushed into various vertical markets—financial services, insurance, manufacturing—and market segments—especially the small- and mid-sized business (SMB) market. In addition, competitive threats abound from the likes of IBM and Oracle—the former driving Linux and competitive solutions, the latter driving competitive database platforms and workflow solutions—into markets in which Microsoft and its partners may or may not have substantial traction.

We have seen some Microsoft partners beat competitive initiatives and players in market opportunities, and be hailed by Microsoft as exceptional partners. Yet we have also seen that many are essentially single-partner, single-opportunity victories—one small partner beats a Linux adversary in an account—often with the same methods (ROI analyses) and flair (lower your TCO) employed first by competitors. Such victories are noteworthy indeed—Microsoft lauds them—and may prove an opportunity for Microsoft partners to join forces in co-opting the best of what Microsoft's competitors are using to win market share in order to defeat them at their own game. Such partnership can be opportunistic and provide a means into a desirable customer engagement—but they can also be strategic—the joining of forces in a more formal manner to defeat competitors in, say, financial services accounts in a certain geography.

This sort of co-optation among Microsoft partners exceeds the demands of simple collaboration and strengthens Microsoft with an additional defense against what the partners hold dear in common—their partnership with Microsoft, their commitment to build customer successes on that basis and thus to extend their firms' influences—by focusing constructively on their core competencies and pushing back, offensively, against a competitive threat. It is clearly in Microsoft's interests to foster such co-optation among its partners yet it has rarely done so. The spoils of the war yet to be waged belong to the partners who can innovate by creating and executing such alliances for the mentioned strategic objectives: push back the open-source threat, beat IBM and Oracle, among others, at their own game.

Partner Channel Builder and Circles of Trust

Along these lines—but not crossing over the line to qualify as a co-optation strategy—Microsoft is encouraging the creation of partner-to-partner networks, both formally and informally, to ensure that

- its .NET platform gains market traction,

- Windows client and server continue growing faster than their competitors, and

- customers realize the full benefit of their software investments.

Microsoft believes that the IT services industry must be able to deliver predictable and reliable planning, installation, implementation, consulting, licensing, support and training services that yield maximum ROI and incur minimal TCO for customers, or the entire technology industry will languish.

In the past, vendors—including Microsoft—focused primarily on sales quotas while the actual deployment of purchased software was left up to its partners and customers. While the Y2K technology ramp up and the dot.com boom realized many profits for software and hardware companies, the overselling and oversupply of under-deployed and unused IT assets at customer sites was one factor that led to a sharp decline in technology spending from 2001 onward. Microsoft, like other IT vendors hit hard by the downturn, tuned in to the reality that the sale is only the first step of the solution and that they must deliver ROI with their products to ensure customer satisfaction and their own continued growth. This has become a key tenet in Microsoft's renewed emphasis on its partners and its restructuring of the partner program.

Ad hoc business partnering has been a mainstay of the IT services industry since its inception. Technology, of course, is far more complex than most other products on the market. Large systems integration partners, such as Accenture, Avanade, Capgemini and HP have, for many years, operated well-established services companies that serve all the needs of enterprise customers. Partners in the SMB space are now offering many managed services to meet the increasing needs of this customer segment. But there are virtually no partners in the SMB space that offer full end-to-end services for customers and few that have a well-rounded portfolio of vertical practices.

Consequently, Microsoft is fostering the creation of partner networks that can quickly, nimbly assemble to meet the spectrum of customer needs in specific vertical industries and specific customer segments. These virtual partnerships, dubbed alternately partner micro-ecosystems and "circles of trust," can be *ad hoc* or more formally established business partnerships. It is critical for Microsoft to seed these partner ecosystems since it lacks an internal services arm.

Yet the company is addressing the need virtually with its "Partner Channel Builder" solution, which launched in January 2005. Partner Channel Builder is a web portal and a series of networking events held worldwide. With respect to the web portal, any Microsoft partner can access it but only Certified and Gold partners can post information to it. The portal provides partners a searchable database of partner-posted partner profiles, solution profiles and opportunity profiles. It is thus an Internet-accessible clearinghouse of information by and for partners that fosters their awareness, communication and collaboration on partnering sales and execution. This formal mechanism is intended to help partners in a self-service manner to build partnerships among themselves and to facilitate the often-difficult reality that one-half of all engagements involve more than one partner. Because it is a global solution—like the ecosystem itself—partners can plumb the depths of Microsoft's worldwide partner ecosystem and help one another. With respect to Partner Channel Builder events, up to 60 are planned in 2005, and they, too, will be worldwide. With speakers and networking opportunities (a la Rio events at the worldwide partner conference), these are excellent opportunties for partners to get to know one another and to extend their reach into the ecosystem. Partners are encouraged to learn more about—and to use—this new solution (partner.microsoft.com/channelbuilder).

Since the debut of its .NET web services platform in 2001, Microsoft has envisioned and tried to harvest both *ad hoc* and formal partner ecosystems to create a "network effect" around .NET. While both the next-generation web services platform and partnering model have been slow to take root, Microsoft is harnessing more resources to help these virtual ecosystems form and flourish.

Some of the major changes in Microsoft's partner program reflect this goal. For example, Microsoft is advocating a specialist—rather than a generalist—approach by requiring partners to be certified in select competencies and to earn points. In this way, the company is playing a role, albeit limited, to ensure that customers and partners align to deliver and receive comprehensive technology services.

Getting "circles of trust" to flourish is no easy task. It can take years for a formal partner network to form and operate efficiently. As indicated above, one Microsoft certified partner has engaged in three different partner micro-ecosystems. The benefits are there but so are the risks, said Ross-Tek's CEO Frederick Johnson. "It is increasing. But it really comes down to trust. There is a big disconnect here and I do not think Microsoft understands that it comes down to a trust factor. I have to know when I call my circle-of-trust partner that it will take care of my customer as if it were its own. So we really have got to have that down-to-earth conversation when we sign NDAs."

Microsoft is trying to help partners forge ties and form virtual service companies. One approach to this is to make informal introductions during hosted "Rio" networking sessions at partner conferences. Microsoft has also created and enhanced its Windows Resource Directory website that lists partners by many criteria, including competency, geography and size. Microsoft also plays the role of matchmaker as customer opportunities arise. For example, one former Microsoft ISV executive introduced Irish ISV Meridio to many US-based services partners at past partner conferences. Those introductions have led to many positive engagements for the ISV. This informal approach is true to Microsoft's culture—it is relationship-driven—but it has distinct limitations for partners.

Microsoft partner executives are treading the circle-of-trust waters cautiously. They want to encourage partner-to-partner engagements but they do not want to cross the line into dangerous territory. "We have seen over the last few years how difficult it has been for the partner to be the total end-to-end solution provider and focus on their core competencies. There is an opportunity for us to foster these circles of trust and we should play a role in helping partners discover one another. But we do not want to get involved in the contractual commitments or the business models they are developing," commented Microsoft's Margo Day.

Ms Day's explanation of Microsoft's position makes sense both for Microsoft and its partners. Yet circles of trust are developing with Microsoft's help in a manner that may, in time, evolve strategically to push back Microsoft's competition while entertaining a constructive approach to gaining market share for Microsoft and its partner community. At this stage, circles of trust are innovative and focused on segmented opportunities, a fine start to what could become the norm in the Microsoft Partner Ecosystem.

One Circle of Trust: SoftChoice, InterLink Group, New Horizons

In addition to the circle of trust engaged in by Ross-Tek (see the case study earlier in this chapter), Microsoft points to one example of a circle of trust formed between three of its partners that delivers a full solution to customers that results in true ROI and TCO gains. In this model, which involved a licensing specialist, a services partner and a training company, the customer gets full end-to-end services. SoftChoice, an Enterprise Software Agent (ESA) or licensing-services specialist, helps customers plan for the selection, acquisition and management of various Microsoft technologies as well as servers, desktops, notebooks and Pocket PCs. Following that process, the second member of the virtual services company, services specialist Interlink Group of Colorado (see its case study in Chapter Five), steps in to deploy, optimize and manage the customer's software, recommend a storage strategy and offer ongoing security services including patch management. Then comes the third link in the chain, New Horizons, a top training partner, to fulfill the last mile of the value chain: helping customers get the most benefit from their software investments by providing expert training on how to implement, use and manage their Windows environment with Active Directory and Group Policy.

This particular circle of trust, which is illustrated in Microsoft's marketing materials for partners, is a model scenario that conceptually delivers the intended benefits of Microsoft's ecosystem: customer and partner satisfaction and a virtual team of Microsoft's corporate, field and partners working in concert to deliver a full full-fledged solution.

Aggregate Contractor Model

Another emerging partner-to-partner micro-ecosystem is the so-called aggregate contractor model in which one firm owns and manages customer relationships and acts as a broker for other partner firms. This model has the advantage of low overhead for participating firms, but it also entails the risk that contractors could go around or bypass the aggregator and undercut the aggregator's business. As in all models, such partnerships require a high level of trust between the contractors and subcontractors, and their customers. There is one compelling example of this aggregate contractor model, Coast Solutions Group, which is based in Irvine, California.

Coast Solutions Group

Founded in 2002, and presently boasting more than 85 members and 13 full-time employees, Coast Solutions Group (CSG) is a collaborative services network. It began when some executives at regional VAR Coast Technologies of Southern California came up with a novel concept that would unite many independent services partners together into a profitable network. A year later, spinoff CSG opened its doors as a value-added distributor of technology services. The network does not sell products.

The business plan was simple: CSG would serve as the project contractor while its network of services partners would deliver pure technology services. CSG views itself as more than a technology staffing service because it provides "soup-to-nuts" business services, including sales and demand generation, solution development, project management, contract negotiations, billing and end-to-end support services, for its aggregated firms. Because CSG does not have to hire full-time IT staff to perform technical services, it can price its services competitively. And with fewer overhead business costs, its network of services partners can also slash prices on their services. CSG has a margin-sharing formula that splits profit fairly with each participating services company. It also has a formal partner program. So far, the concept has worked well.

It is not a dedicated Microsoft shop but roughly 80% of its business is Microsoft-related. For example, of 42 projects ongoing in mid-2004, more than 80% had Microsoft technologies involved, including many Active Directory and NT migrations, Exchange work and SharePoint projects. Almost all of its enterprise solution providers have Microsoft skills. By 2005, CSG has built up a network of more than 80 services partners and generated US$1 million in profit and more than US$5 million in partner delivered services. More than 15 of its firms are Microsoft Gold Certified Partners and another 30 are Microsoft Certified partners. In 2005, Coast Solutions Group launched a new affiliate program that entitles smaller VARs, manufacturers and distributors to access CSG services and sell them to their respective customers. This enables smaller partners to provide full end-to-end services for their customers and retain account control.

CSG drives Microsoft business but executives still have not formed a relationship or alliance directly with Microsoft. Paul Freeman, CSG's president, observes that Microsoft does not know how to deal with companies such as CSG because its key value proposition is vendor-independence and multi-platform support, and its business model is so different. "We have had communications with Microsoft partner management folks regionally and at the corporate level and they do not know what to do with us. Under the current partner engagement model they cannot figure out where to plug us into their partner network. We do not sell products and we do not have Microsoft certified services personnel on staff. We feel that we are not competing with Microsoft to build a network—in fact, we are helping Microsoft by providing assistance to Microsoft partners in scoping and delivering Microsoft–based solutions that they may not be qualified or certified to deliver themselves," Mr Freeman noted. At some point, CSG will have to define its relationship with Microsoft in order to continue growing its program around Microsoft-related business." The same situation likely applies to any other aggregate-contractor models.

Membership Organizational Model

Another emerging network-for-success approach among Microsoft partners is the membership organizational model. Its fundamentals are as follows:

- *shared methodology:* a common vision of solutions delivery to a market that can be shared among several partners joined in a partnering membership organization;

- *shared resources in an extended geography:* by recruiting partners to become members in an extended geography, the organization can include competitors in its ranks, and channel the shared expertise, products and services of its members within distinct sections of the geography that permits competitors to co-exist within the organization and actually profit from their competitors' successes elsewhere;

- *regular board meetings:* the membership organization's governance is an essential component of its success and so, too, is the regular meeting of its representative board of directors;

- *dynamic leadership:* the membership organization's leaders are recruited from member-firms with provisions for its continuity and also its regular refreshing so as to reduce the ongoing burden of the organization's administration on the part of certain executives and to encourage innovative thinking and collaboration among member-executives, who thus gain a greater stake in the organization's success.

Perhaps the best example of this type of organization is Interdyn, an alliance of many organizations to create a services firm focused on the Great Plains/MBS segment. Interdyn currently spans North America and several countries, with 500 employees and US$75 million in annual revenues. According to Alan Kahn of Interdyn AKA, the organizational structure evolved through a dynamic partnership of its members. Taking advantage of the local, field-level focus of Microsoft, the organization's only strategic vendor, Interdyn has achieved for itself and its members national name recognition.

The net result of this membership-organizational model pays off in several ways, primarily in its ability to have named reference customers and industry recognition as a national services vendor for Great Plains.

Ironically, one of the challenges of marketing the organization is its message to Microsoft. Should Interdyn deliver its message locally or nationally to Microsoft? After much debate, Interdyn decided that a combination of local and national marketing initiatives vis-à-vis Microsoft would be best for its members. Each member has Interdyn as the first name of its company and then the local brand as the second, as in Interdyn AKA, where AKA is the name of Mr Kahn's firm. So when a client says it is a reference for Interdyn, this is applicable for the entire group. Likewise, Microsoft recognizes Interdyn. However, all of these names are doing-business-as (DBA) denominations to the local company so, locally, the brand name and the company's marketing message can be delivered as a local brand.

Aside from marketing, what are some of the challenges of the membership-organizational model? Since each entity is independently owned, a strategic change in direction on the part of one of the members can create a vacuum in that particular market. Acquisitions are common in the IT industry and, if a member-firm gets acquired, it can cause a problem for the organization as a whole since it relies on a national marketing model. Occasionally, major holes in competencies caused by outgoing member-firms need to be filled quickly in order for all of the members to sustain the benefits of national name recognition. In this circumstance, replacement members may be recruited.

Guidelines and rules of interaction have been established in order to achieve a requisite degree of trust in the membership organization among its constituent firms. Yet there is also substantial flexibility to enable firms to work with one another, especially at the deal level, which can be negotiated in good faith among participating member-firms. If any issues that arise around a deal are not resolved satisfactorily for a member, the member must yield to the benefit of the organization and interact with the other members on a quarterly basis. So member firms do not want to let each other down and, in fact, will work together for the benefit of the membership organization itself. Trust among members evolves, consequently, especially for long-standing members but also for new members, who are integrated gradually into the membership organization.

Microsoft's verticalization within the Great Plains/MBS segment has also proved to be an occasional challenge for member firms. If Microsoft penetrates the lumber-manufacturing industry in North Carolina, and Interdyn's primary lumber-manufacturing specialist for Axapta is in Colorado, for example, the organization faces pressure to extend itself to meet a need that Microsoft has created. While there are challenges, in this case stretching members beyond their territory, there is no doubt that the opportunities for growth are outstanding owing to the membership organization's riding Microsoft's coat-tails geographically and vertically.

There are other challenges and constraints—and opportunities—of a membership organization. But the opportunities would seem to outweigh the constraints on firms that can accept a confederal approach to doing business together. Within Microsoft's verticalization and extension under MBS and other auspices, membership-organizational models, for the right firms, may assume far greater prominence and promise of returns in the Microsoft Partner Ecosystem. But their growth and success, of course, depends on the commitments that individual firms make to such organizations in the same way that their growth and success depend on their ability to work with Microsoft to advance their causes.

Your Partnering Potential, Your Destination

In this book, we have used a battleship, sports and games as metaphors to highlight some of the unique dynamics of partnering with Microsoft.

In one aspect, we liken Microsoft's partners to a flotilla of small craft sailing in the wake of the SS Microsoft, suggesting the potential perils, and treasures, of sailing alongside a powerful battleship. The crew of the SS Microsoft maintains its chartered course at high speed, crushing anything that dares to cross its bow and jeopardizing all those that sail aft of it, risking its crew and threatening destruction, while also energizing the smaller craft sailing properly amidships. Of course, while this comparison is instructive, it is neither universally applicable nor comprehensive in scope. Microsoft's nimbleness cannot be captured in a simple nautical allusion. There is often more collaborative steering in play between Microsoft and its partners than the image conveys. The currents and winds that buoy and bellow the battleship bestow a chaotic symmetry of market forces, and the influence of other players and Microsoft's partners in the market. But, at the end of the day, partnering with Microsoft is more than this simile can convey.

We have commented, as well, that partnering with Microsoft is akin to playing a fast-moving team sport such as football (or soccer or as it is called in the United States), in which partners are subject to rules of play set by Microsoft. The game has objectives and a scoring system, and all players, anyone who can keep up the pace, are welcome to play. And Microsoft itself is fully engaged as a referee, and a player, too. If the game were poker, Microsoft would have all its cards on the table and all its cards up its sleeve, too, according to the comparison. So this comparison breaks down because it suggests a certain all-powerful capriciousness on Microsoft's part that is absent from the reality of partnering with the company. While helpful as a metaphor, it, too, is imperfect. Partners have far more input in the rules of play than this scenario suggests.

Finally, as depicted on the cover, we suggest that partnering with Microsoft is analogous to playing chess against an obscure opponent, whose pieces come into focus only as the game proceeds. In the same way, this book is intended to bring into focus for partners the culture, strategy, organization and partnering commitment of Microsoft within a broad yet relevant context, and also to demystify partnering with the company through the insight of successful partners who engage with Microsoft day-to-day. This demystification of the company brings into focus its core pillars and field of play. Of course, Microsoft has goals and objectives that could never be reduced to a simple chess game and, from a cynic's perspective, Microsoft owns the board, the pieces and, by analogy, dominates all play. But this analogy, too, is imperfect. We have learned that while Microsoft competes in some cases with partners, to bestow an adversarial identity to Microsoft, thus painting the benefactor as opponent, is plainly false. When partners win, Microsoft wins.

So, at the end of the day—and at the end of this book—what is the appropriate metaphor that conveys the depth and breadth, and essential nature, of the Microsoft partnering experience? We will give it a final try, from the familiar vantage point of a business professional.

Partnering with Microsoft can be thought of, in some ways, as traversing an international airport. It generally exists in the limits of a municipal district, yet is set apart from the city, in a world unto its own. Traveling there requires energy and expense, and then additional efforts to park and walk to the terminal—you essentially make your own way, getting to where you want to go in the airport. Once you have arrived, you find all provisions for living—restaurants, hotels, food, shops and supplies—readily available in a complex that is large enough to accommodate many thousands of people and to have its own postal codes. You meet people from all over the world rushing through and criss-crossing the many walkways in the facility. There are also airport personnel, whose primary mission is to maintain order in the facility and on its grounds, to ensure the safe and timely arrival and departure of flights, and to assist travelers in getting where they want to go. The culture of the place is different from other mass transit facilities; the airport's atmosphere and operations are on a far grander scale than, say, a bus terminal, a train station or a subway.

While in the facility, you compete with other travelers for resources including support for personal and professional needs, and vie for the attention of airport and airline personnel to answer questions that help you move forward. Airport personnel screen who can, or cannot, enter privileged areas. All people in secure areas—the terminals—have in common their authentication to be there as ticketed passengers. And all of them have been cleared by the airline to fly to some other city, although their eventual destination is their choice. Inside the terminals are gates that lead passengers, many like you, to nearly every destination on earth; indeed, the world is literally a few steps away.

Partnering with Microsoft is much like navigating an international airport. Most importantly, you must leverage its personnel to determine where you want to go and direct you how to get there. But getting there requires some first steps—understanding the culture, the rules of the facility, the ways of getting things done—before you can gain access to the terminal. The various gates with departures and arrivals signify paths and competencies that Microsoft's partners decide is where they want to go, and with whom. But they are within the airport—in the Microsoft Partner Ecosystem—and thus subject to its culture and its peculiar ways of getting things done. Within that milieu, partners—and customers—have only one key question that they need to answer, as was once cleverly concocted by Microsoft's marketing machine: "Where Do You Want To Go Today?"

Of course, the answer depends on many things—your resources, your available time, your fitness for the trip, your credentials—as reflected by Microsoft's subsequent marketing campaign, which appropriately suggests a more fundamental proposition: "Your Potential. Our Passion."

While it is true that Microsoft's product marketing message is focused on its customers, you should realize by now that partners are an essential ingredient to the success of Microsoft along with its products and its customers. We hope that this book has convinced you of that verity, at least. And another one: partners should feel at liberty to work with Microsoft—and other partners—to determine and round out their potential, and count on Microsoft's passion to help them advance their businesses and reach their goals.

Microsoft's marketing message—like this book, we hope—offers partners a great deal of excitement and anticipation about the business opportunities ahead of them while also orienting partners to potential pitfalls. It places the responsibility for—and the realization of dreams—on the shoulders of customers, and partners, just as reaching an exotic destination relies to a great extent on the navigational skills of the single passenger.

Going to the airport is a means to an end, not an end in itself. So, too, is participating in Microsoft's partner program, working the ecosystem. There are many roads to choose from, and many ways to get lost. Your success in partnering with Microsoft is up to you. But it is good to know that you have substantial support and backing from Microsoft, if you choose to engage the company, its vast resources and its partner network as we have explained in this book.

Ultimately, your success as a Microsoft partner depends on how much you give to the business of mastering its products, satisfying its customers, forging and extending Microsoft relationships, and extending your network into the Microsoft ecosystem. Where you go today depends on your vision, your prudence and your energy in partnering with Microsoft.

Index